"*The George W. Bush Legacy* is edited and written by the top presidential and congressional scholars in political science. It sets the 'gold standard' for an assessment of George W. Bush. All of the major perspectives about the way President Bush was reelected and the way he led during an unpopular war and divided party government are presented in this one volume. It blends theory and empirical observation in a way that makes this book perfect for university students, the general public, and even President Bush. Yes, President Bush should read it. He will learn a great deal about his leadership and legacy, and so will the general reader."

—James A. Thurber, *American University*

"This early assessment of the George W. Bush presidency by leading American politics experts sets a high standard for future work on the subject. Summing up without dumbing down, the volume is nuanced and nonpartisan, scholarly but accessible. Agree or not with its main themes and theses, it will inform and challenge both supporters and critics of the Bush 43 White House."

—John J. DiIulio Jr., *University of Pennsylvania, and former director, White House Office of Faith-Based and Community Initiatives*

"When a sports team takes the field to start a new year after a record-setting performance, hardly any observers predict that they'll repeat the winning season. Well, Campbell and Rockman are back, and the prospects look good. They've retooled the lineup, matching the seasoned experience of the senior editors with the energy of a new coeditor, Andrew Rudalevige. And they've kept the great strength from their earlier volumes—a consistent focus on the big questions behind the headlines—embedding the analysis of Bush's actions in thoughtful models of the constitutional balance among the branches of government; the influence of public opinion and interest groups; and the impact of an ideological policymaking system on foreign policy, the judiciary, and the military. Throughout, the writing manages to be at once vigorous, authoritative, and thought provoking. This collection should be required reading for ill-informed talk show pundits, and it will surely strengthen the capacity of students and ordinary citizens to exercise their responsibility to hold the government accountable."

—M. Stephen Weatherford, *University of California, Santa Barbara*

"This volume does far more than recount the details of the presidency of George W. Bush. Essays by prominent scholars also offer thoughtful, systematic, and provocative analyses of the administration's driving values and key initiatives and of the challenges and constraints it confronted. They highlight as well the problems and possibilities that Bush 43 will bequeath to his successors. Telling historical comparisons and careful political science analysis weave throughout and inform the discussion. Students and presidency scholars alike will learn from this stimulating collection."

—Karen Hult, *Virginia Polytechnic Institute and State University*

"This volume provides a comprehensive and timely appraisal of the Bush 43 administration. It systematically examines the governing style and policy choices of President George W. Bush across a wide range of topics, both foreign and domestic. *The George W. Bush Legacy* will be essential reading for anyone who seeks to understand the administration's political leadership as well as its decisions about the economy, Supreme Court nominations, the war in Iraq, and other key issues in American politics in the early twenty-first century. The thoughtful chapters written by noted scholars of the presidency will be informative for students and faculty alike."

—Meena Bose, *Hofstra University*

"This book does something rare and valuable: it explains current American politics and teaches political science, and does so in a way interesting to professors as much as to students. Well-written, complete, and filled with unobtrusive but skilled political science, this book will delight and benefit faculty and students alike. My students, professionals with a wide range of political and policy interest and knowledge, all benefit—the ones with advanced understanding of the issues and work in politics react to the high intellectual level, while the ones with less background in politics and political science see that both headlines and other course readings make sense in the various chapters."

—Scott Greer, *University of Michigan*

"The Bush presidency has been a historic one, for better or for worse. If you want to understand and evaluate the legacy of George W. Bush, these senior scholars provide the guideposts with excellent scholarship and incisive writing."

—James P. Pfiffner, *George Mason University*

The George W. Bush Legacy

edited by

Colin Campbell
University of British Columbia

Bert A. Rockman
Purdue University

Andrew Rudalevige
Dickinson College

CQ PRESS

A Division of Congressional Quarterly Inc.
ocn 145431787
Washington, D.C.

CQ Press
1255 22nd Street, NW, Suite 400
Washington, DC 20037

Phone: 202-729-1900; toll-free, 1-866-4CQ-PRESS (1-866-427-7737)

Web: www.cqpress.com

Cover photo: AP/Wide World Photos
Cover design: Diane Buric Design and Illustration

♾ The paper used in this publication exceeds the requirements of the American National Standard for Information Sciences—Permanence of Paper for Printed Library Materials, ANSI Z39.48-1992.

Printed and bound in the United States of America

11 10 09 08 07   1 2 3 4 5

LIBRARY OF CONGRESS CATALOGING-IN-PUBLICATION DATA

The George W. Bush legacy / edited by Colin Campbell, Bert A. Rockman, Andrew Rudalevige.
    p. cm.
  Includes bibliographical references.
  ISBN 978-0-87289-346-7 (alk. paper)
  1. Bush, George W. (George Walker), 1946—Political and social views. 2. Bush, George W. (George Walker), 1946—Influence. 3. United States—Politics and government—2001–
4. United States—Foreign relations—2001– 5. United States—Social policy. 6. Political leadership—United States—Case studies. I. Campbell, Colin. II. Rockman, Bert A. III. Rudalevige, Andrew. IV. Title.

  E903.3.G46 2008
  973.931092—dc22

                                                        2007025852

To Prudence

Contents

The next president, taking office in a new century thus far no less conflict riven than the previous one, will inherit both grand rhetorical commitments and a vastly enlarged American military presence around the world, while finding the United States isolated in world opinion. He or she will face grand commitments at home, too—especially in the entitlements due an aging population—while also facing immense budget and trade deficits. A question by which an administration is fairly judged is whether it leaves the resources to meet the demands it stimulated. By this standard the George W. Bush legacy is problematic.

In the polarized, partisan, and competitive world of American politics in 2004, the prospects for gaining cooperation across party lines were dim, and the center was shrinking. The conservative Republican base proved crucial to President Bush's electoral victory in both 2000 and 2004. It seems eminently reasonable for the president and his advisers to have concluded that they should build their governing constituency from those who provided the votes for the 2000 electoral win, namely, his party's base.

The Bush presidency significantly strengthened the ability of the White House to control and distribute information and promote presidential poli-

*and politicization that ensured responsiveness to the president's policy
preferences—but excluded analyses and alternatives that the president
needed to be able to calculate those preferences in an informed way in the
first place.*

BARBARA SINCLAIR

*George W. Bush had ambitious legislative goals and was aggressive in
dictating them, taking full advantage of the political capital that accrued
to him through the tight bonds of party loyalty and the shock of external
events. That winner-take-all style won impressive short-term legislative
victories but may have undermined the chances for long-term change,
especially after the 2006 midterm elections returned Democrats to the
majority in Congress.*

DAVID A. YALOF

*A close assessment of the Bush judicial nominees reveals that they varied
in their degree of social conservatism when nominated. The unifying
thread in the administration's selection process has been its overriding
concern that judges be deferential to claims of expansive executive
authority.*

RAYMOND TANTER AND STEPHEN KERSTING

*President Bush's involvement in foreign policy has varied from active
leadership, in the formation of the Bush doctrine, to passivity. That passive approach is partly responsible for failure in Iraq and an uncertain
stance toward Iran. As Iraq continues to slide into chaos, George W.
Bush's legacy in foreign policy suffers as well.*

COLIN CAMPBELL

*The administration's advisory system proved to be a breeding ground for
unrestrained ideological entrepreneurship—a result both of President
Bush's seeming detachment from open discussion about the crucial
issues he faced and of the surfeit in the administration generally of doctrinaires. In consequence little effort went to ensuring that policy initiatives*

would receive intense collegial scrutiny, and very little structure was in place to do so. The kind of war in Iraq that resulted had negative conse-quences for another important administration initiative, the transforma-tion of the military.

Contextual forces empowered, then undermined, the Bush administra-tion's forays in the domestic arena. During the first term, consequential changes were achieved in education, Medicare, and tax policy, but the political capital the president claimed for his second term proved hard to bank. Overall the narrative arc of the Bush domestic presidency is a tale of two cities: New York and New Orleans.

Though proclaiming broad national purposes, the Bush administration was strikingly consistent in its approach to organized interests, using its power to aid friends, mobilize allies, and shut out opponents from the fruits of policy outcomes. Even as political circumstances changed, for better and worse, the administration used interest group relations to strengthen its governing coalition rather than as a means of outreach or inclusiveness. The results suggest that muscular parties and an energized group system need not be at odds with each other.

The power of presidential assertion will likely come under attack when people take a president's vision to be only a mirage and a president's convictions to be mere willfulness. But critical attack is one thing; the power to alter a president's behavior is another. Bush has managed to demonstrate that a president need not be shackled by thin electoral mar-gins, by bare majorities in Congress, or by modest or even low levels of popular approval.

Tables and Figures

Preface

George W. Bush entered office through controversial means—the famous chad-hanging, suspenseful, and ultimately judicially decided election of 2000. At the sunset of his two-term administration, he will leave office as one of the most controversial presidents in modern history. His presidency has been one of *consequence*. And consequential presidencies are likely to be controversial. For the first time since the 1920s, a Republican president had a Republican majority in both chambers of Congress for most of his time in office. That majority was slim, but it was cohesive. Though it tallied some major legislative accomplishments, and helped shepherd controversial nominations to the courts and the executive, that majority's most notable legacy may be that it was able to shield the president from investigations, while not challenging ambitious presidential assertions of unilateral authority or the actions grounded in those assertions. The authors of the chapters that follow point to the impacts of this presidency.

But if the George W. Bush administration has left big footprints, how durable will they be? The sands of time tend to erase many of the outcomes that we think will be long lasting when they occur. From our current perspective, we cannot be certain. None of us has the power to look that far into the future. Nevertheless, a presidency of consequence—however controversial the consequences may be—is apt to leave much for its successors to deal with or build upon. The durability of Bush's legacy remains to be seen, but he will have left a long to-do list for his successor.

Bush's presidency came at a time in American history when our parties have been unusually cohesive internally and sharply divided from each another. Bush came into office claiming to be a healer but found that path unlikely to provide political payoff. As a result, he has been labeled a highly divisive president, one who has governed from a narrow base despite having had threadbare majorities electorally and in Congress during most of his time in office. There is no doubt that Bush has done little to ease our era of "bad feeling." Indeed, there is every reason to believe that his presidency has contributed to the intensity and depth of the partisan division that exists in the United States. But how much of this was uniquely Bush's contribution, and how much has derived from the vast gulf of differences between congressional politicians of the two parties, the party activists, and even the rank and file of party identifiers? Close to sixty years ago, a committee commissioned by the American Political Science Association decried the lack of cohesion and responsibility in our then ideologically identifiable, but less cohesive, parties. Their hopes for a more coherent party system have come true, and consequently, George W. Bush is both a product of, and a contributor to, the current divisions.

Yet another aspect of the George W. Bush presidency that has been emphasized has been the so-called Bush bubble—implying that the president has seemed to be shielded from critiques of current or contemplated policy. Bush has repeatedly emphasized the decisional elements of his presidency, his willingness to stand steadfast at high noon when others have packed and left town. He has emphasized that he has limited tolerance for self-doubt and that once he has decided, he will stand firm in his choices. The Bush presidency has illuminated the two faces of leadership: we want leaders to have convictions and to be firm in upholding their choices, but we also want them to respond to adverse consequences and make adjustments. We want them to be sure of themselves but also wise and judicious. We want leaders to be strong but not to distance themselves too greatly from the median voter. It seems as though George W. Bush is more sure of who he is than we may want him to be. Unlike his father, George H. W. Bush, "W" has lots of vision; unlike his father, however, he may come up short on prudence. It is not easy to combine vision with prudence, or vice versa. The absence of vision can harm a president; the absence of prudence can harm the country. A president probably does need to argue with himself or herself, after all.

This is the fifth book in a series dating back to the presidency of George H. W. Bush; when we began, we did not know that we would have to refer to him using all of his initials. It is the second published by CQ Press, which has done its usual superb job of putting all of the production pieces together, in a timely way and with due concern for what the editors and authors want to accomplish. We are particularly grateful to Charisse Kiino, who oversaw the book from concept to finished product. She both listened to us and advised us in ways that should set an example for any president. Nancy Geltman did a wonderful job yet again of copyediting, consigning many of our most cherished but unnecessary phrases and sentences to the cutting room floor. Talia Greenberg responded patiently to our insistence on wanting to tweak things just a little more at the page proof stage. Allie McKay, Erin Snow, and Chris O'Brien helped get the book into production, get it known, and get it marketed, respectively. Our thanks to you all.

The late Ed Artinian inspired this series at the now-defunct Chatham House Press. Ed has been gone for a decade, but his legacy lives on in this book.

Any book series that goes on long enough also experiences some changing of the guard. Careful readers will note a number of new contributors to this volume. We are most grateful to them—and to past contributors as well—for their thoughtful and creative grappling with assessing presidencies and their possible legacies without the benefit of history. On the editorial side, Andy Rudalevige has joined this series as a coeditor for the first time. He is the face of a newer and younger, highly sophisticated generation of presidency scholars. Colin Campbell has been a founding coeditor of this series. His contributions to scholarship on the presidency and executive politics in the United States, the United Kingdom, Canada, and Australia are legendary. He has labored heroically under trying circumstances to see through his contributions to this book. He is our deeply valued friend and colleague. Perhaps like the famous baseball pitcher Roger Clemens, who retires annually only to come back and do wonders for his current team, Colin might still fire a few high hard ones for future editions.

CHAPTER 1

Introduction
Legacies and Leadership in Context

Colin Campbell, Bert A. Rockman, and Andrew Rudalevige

THE 2008 PRESIDENTIAL CAMPAIGN was in full swing some twenty-one months before election day. By early 2007 the field already included nearly twenty candidates, with another half-dozen important political figures still potential entrants. Press reports breathlessly trumpeted the maneuverings of Hillary Clinton and Barack Obama, Mitt Romney and John McCain, Rudy Giuliani and John Edwards, and even noncandidates (to date) such as Newt Gingrich, Al Gore, and Fred Thompson.

The formerly "invisible" primary season, in which potential nominees vied for money, staff, and organization below the media radar well in advance of actual voter decisions, had become so visible that the current occupant of the White House, President George W. Bush, seemed to be struggling for attention.[1] With Bush's public approval ratings hovering around 30 percent and Democrats newly in control of both chambers of Congress, it was popular to declare the Bush administration essentially complete, at best limping along as the lamest of lame ducks. "A lot of Americans consider this presidency over," concluded CNN commentator Bill Schneider. *New York Times* columnist Thomas Friedman opined that the 2006 midterm elections had "fired" the president, and "we're now just watching him clean out his desk."[2]

In response the president suggested the futility of "trying to write the history of this administration even before it's over," when two years—a full quarter—of his term had yet to unfold. "I'm going to sprint to the finish," he promised, "and we're going to get a lot done." Certainly, the conventional wisdom might be overstated; no one could know what unanticipated events at home or abroad might do to rework the interbranch dynamics. Nor should any president's ability to shape the political arena proactively be underestimated.

Nonetheless the early months of 2007 did mark an appropriate time to assess the legacy of the George W. Bush administration, at least in a preliminary way. In fact, an inevitable result of the early start of the 2008 presidential election campaign—the first in eighty years with no sitting president or vice president in the running[4]—was to provoke just such assessments. Would candidates praise the Bush record or disavow it? Would they seek to articulate his policies or repudiate them? Would members of Congress, their own eyes already on 2009, continue to add to the substantial body of legislation passed since 2001—or start to reverse it?

And President Bush himself was increasingly looking toward history. The global battle against terror was "the calling of our time," he said in a December 20, 2006, press conference, "the beginning stages of an ideological struggle . . . that's going to last a while." Bush had even adopted a preferred model for historians to use in assessing his presidency, that of Harry S. Truman. Though Truman's foreign policy choices and administrative missteps led to contemporary popular disdain (and approval ratings in the mid-20 percent range), over time he had attracted admiration for his iconic integrity and willingness to stick with tough choices. The implication was that Bush's controversial policies in Iraq and elsewhere could only be assessed in the long term and would receive better reviews decades hence. Others, however, laid down less-flattering analogies—perhaps most commonly to Lyndon B. Johnson, whose ambitions for a Great Society to rival Franklin D. Roosevelt's New Deal were drowned in the quagmire of the Vietnam War. Another nominee was Woodrow Wilson, whose similarly sweeping moral internationalism was finally undermined by domestic ambivalence.[5]

Assessing Legacy and Leadership

Such past parallels are irresistible and often useful. They provide a shorthand for trying to categorize one presidency in the sweep of American history: A president occupies a place in "political time," as well as on the calendar, and thus has a sort of peer group scattered irregularly across the decades. But an analogy is not itself a legacy, for history aggregates even as it "rhymes."[6] The framework for Bush's leadership was different than that for Truman's, or Johnson's, or even that of his own father—whose "mistakes," especially the 1990 tax increase and 1991 pullback from Baghdad, the younger Bush has sought constantly to avoid. After all, their past actions shaped his choices, and in any case new events constantly shape the incentives and constraints of the policy arena.

Bill Clinton supposedly mused with his political advisers that no one could be a great president without holding office during a war or other great crisis.[7] And a cursory review does suggest that the American presidents who consistently rise to the top of historians' rankings—Washington, Lincoln, Franklin Roosevelt—are those who held office during deeply perilous times. "Reconstructive" presidents, as

Stephen Skowronek has termed them, require almost by definition a dilapidated or endangered polity—in other contexts there is no need for reconstruction. If Shakespeare were writing in the American setting, he might find that most leaders, to attain greatness, must have it "thrust upon 'em." Perhaps more broadly we might think of "the leadership question" as the effective mobilization of support to meet the challenges that presidents governing in perilous times face. But even more important than solving a given challenge is the ability of the president to inspire popular confidence in the helmsman (or helmswoman). Equally vital is a president's ability to use crises to create new agendas and new long-term coalitions—a goal of George W. Bush's. In this regard, FDR did not really solve the Great Depression (the war helped to do that). Instead, he cushioned its shocks by investing in a social insurance state and by empowering labor unions to organize. In so doing, he also altered the political landscape by fashioning a new political coalition that under-girded the domination of the Democratic Party for at least a generation.[8]

Yet presidents, at least the successful ones, make their own circumstances as well. We should consider, then, the question, How much discretion—how many degrees of freedom—did George W. Bush have in setting his own course? How much of what he leaves behind, will be of the man, and how much of the times?

The chapters in this book answer those questions in different ways and by considering different arenas of policy and politics. However, it is worth noting here the broadest outlines of George W. Bush's years in office in terms of two contexts that shaped his presidency and, in turn, were shaped by his actions. These might be thought of as the situational and the institutional. The first suggests the historical setting bequeathed to a president, with the opportunities and constraints it conferred. What mandates were conferred by election or externality? What "policy windows" were open, or closed?[9] The second context is the president's place in the web of interlinking organizations that both empowers American government and constrains individual actors within it. In each context, President Bush took bold actions that won short-term successes but that may incur great long-term costs.

Situations

George W. Bush took office in 2001 after an election in which he won the presidency despite losing the popular vote, the first candidate to do so since 1888.[10] The Electoral College victory came after a month-long delay, as the state of Florida tabulated and retabulated its votes, a process stopped abruptly by the Supreme Court's landmark 5–4 decision in *Bush v. Gore*. Bush took office, then, with the legitimacy of his win in question and with very narrow congressional majorities: ten seats in the House and a fifty-fifty Senate organized by the Republicans only after January 20, when Vice President Dick Cheney was inaugurated and took up his constitutional post as president of that body. The chances for large-scale policy change were seemingly constrained by this "perfect tie."[11]

Nonetheless President Bush moved ahead with little hesitation, choosing to ignore the divisiveness and to behave as though he had a clear mandate for the policies he had propounded during the campaign. That they were part of a platform of "compassionate conservatism" did not, in general, make those proposals less conservative. And though one Democrat (Norman Mineta) was named to the new cabinet, suggestions that Bush try to lead "from the middle out" were generally sidelined. The strategy worked: the public was eager for closure and questions of legitimacy quickly faded as the president acted as president. Moreover, despite the narrowness of the margins, Bush was the first Republican president to have a congressional majority in both chambers of Congress since Dwight Eisenhower nearly five decades before. The members of that majority were suitably ready to follow the president's lead.

Education and taxes were Bush's clear priorities, in terms of time and capital. Both programs were ambitious and important: the No Child Left Behind Act (NCLB) was the largest restructuring of the federal role in education since the original Elementary and Secondary Education Act of 1965; the 2001 tax cuts, estimated at $1.35 trillion, were the largest since 1981. Both passed.

In May 2001, however, Sen. Jim Jeffords of Vermont—peeved by the treatment of his own legislative priorities by the White House—left the Republican Party, giving Democrats control of the Senate. His shift did not affect NCLB or the tax bill, but as the end of the summer recess approached, gridlock impended. The prospects for the rest of the president's legislative agenda were unclear.

As it turned out, of course, a new agenda arrived shortly after Labor Day. Whether or not the brutal terrorist attacks of September 11, 2001, "changed everything," as many mused at the time, they certainly changed both American politics and the president's worldview. During the 2000 campaign, then-governor Bush discounted "nation-building" and argued for humility in foreign policy. "I'm not sure the role of the United States," he argued during one debate that year, "is to go around the world and say 'this is the way it's got to be.'" The administration consciously disengaged from the long-standing Israeli-Palestinian dispute and set aside even the Clinton team's nominal commitment to the Kyoto treaty effort to address global climate change.

But after September 11 the president concluded that "you can't talk your way to a solution to a problem," and by 2002, the *National Security Strategy of the United States* presented unilateral, preemptive action as an overt part of the nation's defense posture, suggesting that the nation had an obligation to act on threats even before they were fully formed. The president won enthusiastic (at the time) congressional approval of expansive authorizations to use force against the perpetrators of the attacks—most immediately, the Taliban theocracy of Afghanistan, which harbored Osama bin Laden and his followers, and then against Saddam Hussein's dictatorial regime in Iraq, which purportedly combined the "world's worst weapons" with malign intent as to their dissemination and use.[12] Afghanistan and later Iraq presented military challenges and massive nation-building exercises. In his second inaugural address, Bush further upped the ante. He declared that, since human freedom and peace were inseparable, it was the "policy of the United States to seek and support the growth of democratic movements and institutions in every nation and culture, with the ultimate goal of ending tyranny in our world."[13]

The war on terror had important implications at home, most of them, at the outset, positive for the president. Prior to the September 11 attacks, Bush's approval ratings had been in the low 50 percent range, reflecting the lingering even split of 2000; soon they brushed 90 percent instead. After a powerful, informal address at the rubble of the World Trade Center, delivered by bullhorn, and an equally powerful formal address to the nation on September 20, 2001, even the most liberal members of Congress moved into his corner. "Right now," said Maxine Waters, D-Calif., "the president of the United States has support for almost anything he wants to do."[14]

As troops mobilized and an anthrax scare gripped the home front, the president wanted to do a lot. An array of initiatives dealing with "homeland security"—a term that itself will be a legacy of this era—were passed, some of them drawn from congressional proposals. For example, airport security was federalized and placed in the hands of the new Transportation Security Administration. In 2002 the new Department of Homeland Security (DHS) brought together 170,000 employees previously compartmentalized in twenty-plus executive branch bureaus, the largest government reorganization since the National Security Act after World War II.[15] More traditional law enforcement powers were augmented by the USA Patriot Act, passed with little debate in October 2001 and renewed with few changes in early 2006. The Patriot Act created a host of new federal crimes and extended government search and surveillance powers.

The public seemed to back these changes. Despite sluggish economic growth, the 2002 congressional elections bucked the historical tendency toward losses for the ruling party at the presidential midterm. Voters returned Republicans to the majority in the Senate and slightly boosted their numbers in the House. Despite the fact that most presidential involvement in past midterm elections had been ineffective, Bush campaigned vigorously, making ninety appearances on behalf of House, Senate, and gubernatorial candidates. He battered Democrats who opposed his security measures, even painting them as unpatriotic. A front-page headline in the *New York Times* blared, "Shift of Power to White House Reshapes Political Landscape"; or as a Brookings Institution analysis observed, "George W. Bush played for high stakes in the 2002 midterm elections and won. . . . President Bush shaped the outcome of the 2002 elections, and now his decisions on foreign and domestic policy will determine what Congress does."[16] Although Senate Democrats were able to use that chamber's permissive rules of debate to dilute some Republican proposals, additional tax cuts, fast-track trade authority, a massive Medicare restructuring, and other GOP initiatives passed, including long-sought legislation banning so-called partial-birth abortion. The proposals and, as various authors describe in this book, the strategies used to achieve their passage were divisive; 90 percent approval gave way to renewed polarization. But in 2004, President Bush was reelected, defeating Sen. John F. Kerry, D-Mass., by a narrow margin. Immediately afterward he declared, "I earned capital in the campaign, political capital, and now I intend to spend it."[17]

Yet the history of enervated second terms—from Franklin Roosevelt's Court packing, to Watergate, to Iran-contra, to Bill Clinton's travails with the independent counsel—suggested that short-term euphoria could not mask the changed situational context.[18] To be sure, the president had won the election, and his party still controlled Congress. He remained in the "bully pulpit," ready to build on his dexterous use of the presidency's agenda-setting power. Some early legislative victories (e.g., on bankruptcy and tort reform) followed. But it was not clear that the support engendered by September 11 would translate to support for the large, complex, and potentially divisive domestic initiatives that Bush had advocated in the 2004 campaign, such as Social Security reform, expansion of NCLB, and revamping the tax code. And whereas Bush did not have to face the voters again, his legislative allies did. Thus when events impinged, the president's bank account of political capital was less flush than he had estimated. Iraq elections in January 2005 inspired hope and lifted spirits there and abroad, but delays in forming a government in Iraq, continued investigations into prisoner abuse, and regular, deadly insurgent attacks on both American soldiers and Iraqi civilians soon dampened hopes for peace and democracy there. At home, later that summer, Hurricane Katrina ravaged the Gulf Coast, putting much of New Orleans and parts of Mississippi underwater. The administration's reaction was widely derided, not least by the televised crowds of refugees languishing in fetid shelters. Two weeks after the storm hit, the president gave a dramatic speech from the center of New Orleans, promising to activate "one of the largest reconstruction efforts the world has ever seen," but follow-through was slow and halting.[19] Thus, an event that might have shown the power of the federal government to mobilize resources and aid floundering communities— as indeed the Bush administration did effectively in late 2004, after the horrific tsunami that killed more than 200,000 people in South Asia—wound up showing the opposite.

After an additional stumble or two (for example, the nomination of White House counsel Harriet Miers to the Supreme Court) Bush was able to regain the initiative. Still, as the situation in Iraq continued to stagnate into 2006—by the end of October more than 2,800 U.S. troops and thousands more Iraqis had died in the conflict, with tens of thousands wounded—public and legislative support for the war and the president himself continued to decline. As the 2006 elections approached, only a third of Americans approved of the way the president was handling the war, and barely 40 percent felt it had been worth fighting in the first place. At the polls, two-thirds said that the war was "extremely" or "very" important to their vote.[20] This malaise, combined with well-publicized cases of corruption by (mostly) Republican members of Congress, swept Democratic majorities back into Congress in November. Democrats netted thirty seats in the House, making Nancy Pelosi, D-Calif., the first female Speaker of the House, and six seats in the Senate, including gains in "red" states such as Montana and Virginia. Once again, the governance context had been transformed.

President Bush argued that his Oval Office "microphone" was louder than ever and promised a newly bipartisan approach. He refused, however, to accept the recommendations of the centrist Baker-Hamilton Commission report regarding the Middle East. Instead insisting, "I believe we're going to win," he announced in December a "surge" of more than 20,000 additional American troops into Iraq, with the aim of pacifying sectarian strife in Baghdad.

But this time the new context did not favor such unconstrained presidential leadership. In the American constitutional structure, ambition (as Madison said long ago) is supposed to counteract ambition; but whereas President Bush was nothing if not ambitious, until 2007 Congress rarely pushed back. The comment of Majority Whip Roy Blunt, R-Mo., was typical: "The truth is that in time of war . . . there is not a whole lot for Members of Congress to do."[21] Even as late as 2006, Congress followed up the Supreme Court's scolding in the *Hamdan* case—which overturned the president's system of military tribunals for "enemy combatants"—by largely formalizing that system, truncating detainees' ability to bring their cases to the civilian courts and expanding the executive branch's authority to designate individuals (including American citizens) as enemy combatants in the first place.

That seemed likely to change in the 110th Congress. By early March 2007, new Democratic committee chairs had already convened hearings on issues ranging from the proposed "surge" in Iraq (the House and Senate would soon pass budget bills tying continued funding for the war to a schedule for troop withdrawals), to the Presidential Records Act, to the dismissal of a number of U.S. attorneys seemingly on partisan grounds. Presidential freedom of movement, on Capitol Hill at least, had been greatly constricted.

Institutions

September 11 renewed two related national debates—the first over the balance between civil liberties and national security, and the second over the balance among the branches of government.

Because of revelations that promising leads into the 9/11 attacks had been short-circuited by lack of cooperation between the FBI and CIA, the Patriot Act, for example, sought to tear down "the wall" between domestic investigations and foreign intelligence and rework the 1978 Foreign Intelligence Surveillance Act (FISA). But it did not change the requirement that government agencies seek a warrant from a special court to impose long-term wiretaps on intelligence targets. In October 2001, however, President Bush effectively overrode FISA by executive order in directing the National Security Agency (NSA) to track communications between Americans within the United States and individuals abroad thought to be connected to terrorism. The president argued that such a policy was both necessary ("We are at war . . . [and] this information has helped prevent attacks and save American lives") and legal under a broad reading of Congress's Authorization for the Use of Military Force (AUMF), passed in September 2001, and even more decisively, the president's inherent constitutional authority to gather battlefield intelligence as commander in chief.[22]

In early 2007 the attorney general announced that the FISA court had approved the president's surveillance program. Questions remained about the nature of that approval. Still, the earlier assertion that other branches had no authority over the program is worth examining inasmuch as it is consistent with a developing set of wider claims about executive authority. Those claims, fleshing out what President Bush has called his "obligation to make sure that the Presidency remains robust" and his "duty to protect the executive branch from legislative encroachment," may prove an important part of the Bush legacy to future presidents.[23]

What had Bush inherited in that regard? During the 2000 election campaign, he spoke frequently of the diminution of presidential authority, not just the president's moral stature but Article II's "executive power" itself. Vice President Cheney, who began his political life as a staffer in the Nixon White House, put the aim bluntly: "For the thirty-five years that I've been in this town, there's been a constant, steady erosion of the prerogatives and the powers of the president of the United States, and I don't want to be a part of that." He cited the War Powers Resolution and Congressional Budget Act as examples.[24]

But whereas Congress had indeed sought to regain institutional ground against the "imperial presidency" of the Vietnam/Watergate era, most of that turf had been retaken by successive chief executives, even before September 11, 2001. The War Powers Resolution and Intelligence Oversight Act had rarely, if ever, been effective checks on presidential use of overt force or covert action, nor had Congress been able to abide by the deadlines and discipline of the Congressional Budget Act. (Indeed, Congress granted the president the line-item veto in the mid-1990s, but it was overturned by the Supreme Court.) Furthermore, presidents had continued to expand their use of unilateral administrative tools, from executive orders to regulatory review, and revived the use of "executive privilege," in various guises, to withhold information from interbranch interlocutors.[25]

The George W. Bush administration built on that revival of presidential prerogative to seek additional space for presidential endeavor free from interference by other institutional actors. At the heart of the question is the doctrine of the "unitary executive," developed most fully prior to the second Bush's presidency by Ronald Reagan's Office of Legal Counsel (OLC). In one sense, the doctrine simply states that all of the executive powers vested in the president by Article II of the Constitution must be exercised by the president. As Samuel Alito, a veteran of the Reagan OLC who would be appointed to the Supreme Court by George W. Bush, put it in 2000, "The president has not just some executive powers, but the executive power—the whole thing."[26] That formulation leaves open the questions of what the executive power encompasses and who gets to make that determination. The Bush administration has been far more aggressive than its predecessors in arguing for expansive powers within Article II's vaguely defined "executive power" and concurrently for the notion that the executive would draw the boundaries between the branches. Thus the proposition is not only that executive power is the indivisible purview of the president, but also that the scope of that power is defined by the president, potentially preempting congressional involvement. If, for example, FISA could not be read to allow the president to authorize warrantless wiretapping, then the statute itself would be unconstitutional.[27]

In the same way, the administration warned off efforts to set limits on its ability to manage the detention of suspects imprisoned as part of the wider war on terror. It claimed it could, for instance, designate "enemy combatants," even U.S. citizens, and place them outside the reach of the civilian court system, to be tried by military tribunals also established by presidential order. "In order to respect the President's inherent constitutional authority to manage a military campaign," concluded one working group of administration attorneys, prohibitions against torture, "as well as any other potentially applicable statute must be construed as inapplicable to interrogations undertaken pursuant to [the president's] Commander-in-Chief authority."[28] When Congress pushed the point, clarifying that torture was illegal in all cases, President Bush appended a signing statement to the statute: The administration would enforce the law, he informed Congress, "in a manner consistent with the constitutional authority of the President to oversee the unitary executive branch and as Commander in Chief." Such signing statements have become frequent vehicles for qualifying the implementation of new statutes, and George W. Bush has used them more often than all other presidents combined.[29]

Signing statements and other forms of executive order may be deployed to manage not only the external boundaries but also the internal actions of the executive branch. As Jeffrey Rosen has observed, "the initial purpose of the unitary executive theory was to strike a blow at the heart of the regulatory state."[30] If executive power could not be divided without being lost, the congressional creation of independent regulatory agencies partially insulated from presidential reach was basically illegitimate. In its widest form, that argument has not prevailed, but the Bush administration continued to work around its edges by incrementally extending White House influence over agency outputs. In 2001 the president launched the President's Management Agenda, which rated agencies and programs on a variety of fronts ranging from financial and personnel management to general effectiveness and aimed to link an agency's performance with its funding, in part via the expansive use of outside contractors. This was of a piece with an aggressive "administrative presidency" that included close vetting of appointees across the executive branch to ensure their loyalty to presidential preferences and a large role for those political appointees, as well as the Office of Management and Budget, in policy development and implementation.[31]

This strategy had benefits, especially given the difficulties that any legislative body faces in taking collective action. Indeed, even in 2007 the newly ascendant majority party found it hard to coalesce around a single opposition strategy. "Senate Democrats Vow to Confront Bush on Iraq," read one typical headline, before adding the kicker: "but Are Still Working Out the Details."[32] But over time such unilateralism incurred clear costs, in part because members of Congress grew resentful of being sidelined from their own constitutional duties; in part because the promises of policy effectiveness implied by strict executive control were not always kept; and in part because when they were not, the president had little residual support based in shared ownership of the endeavor. When operations soured in Iraq or the Gulf Coast, few were eager to stand by the president's side.

Assessments

George W. Bush, then, reacted well to some of the conditions "thrust upon him" and less well to other situations. The administration's hallmark inflexibility was related to those outcomes. The president prided himself on taking a clear stand and sticking to it, refusing to "negotiate against himself," whatever circumstances arose. This consistency—or stubbornness, as critics preferred—won plaudits for clarity. But its success depended on events' (or other political actors') adapting to the policy, rather than adapting policy to the circumstances.

The point highlights a key aspect of governance: the need to build coalitions. There is risk in reaching out to build a broad alliance behind a policy. Most obviously, it is an effort that can easily fail—and that gives one's less-congruent partners veto power over moving forward. There is risk as well, however, in seeking to govern with bare majority support. Such a "minimum winning coalition" is a fragile reed on which to build lasting policy change.

President Bush spoke, early and late in his term, of working across party lines. In his first speech after *Bush v. Gore* was decided in late 2000, he spoke from the chamber of the Texas House of Representatives, reminding the public of his success in building bipartisan coalitions as governor. In his 2007 State of the Union address, he took a similar tack: "Our citizens don't much care which side of the aisle we sit on," he told assembled legislators, "as long as we're willing to cross that aisle when there is work to be done."[33]

In between, however, the administration's rhetoric grew increasingly binary. This tone, unlike the war on terror itself, was clearly a matter of choice, even if it was driven by a sincere conviction that the president had made the correct choices in implementing that war.[34] Those who dissented from the administration's policies were deemed unpatriotic—told that their position "aids terrorists" and that vigorous debate, by undercutting the war effort, "erode[d] unity" and even verged on treason. As late as February 2007, Vice President Cheney said that the House Democratic leadership supported "a policy of defeat" that "would validate the al Qaeda strategy."[35] Democrats, naturally, resisted this characterization.

President Bush's contribution to the big picture of American coalition politics and its electoral map in 2008 and beyond hinges to a considerable degree on the outcome of this tactic. Bush's legendary political adviser, Karl Rove, often said that he hoped to forge a new Republican dominance after a long period of electoral stalemate, as William McKinley did in 1896. After the 2004 election, President Bush was at last a "majority president" and "the leader, as well as one of the builders, of the nation's new majority party." But that description seemed far less apt after the 2006 midterm elections, though many argued that those election results owed more to GOP officeholders' failing to live up to core Republican principles than to any defect in the principles themselves.[36] The 2008 election will help resolve whether there has been realignment or perhaps simply dealignment, in which voters have become more independent of (or disaffected from) partisan allegiance.

It should be noted also in this regard that the Bush administration, which meets with virtually unparalleled hostility from Democrats, also has encountered opposition from the more libertarian wing of the Republican Party, which has been critical in some instances of what some of its advocates see as the free-spending, big government ways of the administration and its incursions into privacy, as well as its bellicosity internationally.[37]

In all these areas, then—foreign, domestic, administrative, electoral—the Bush presidency leaves important, if at this point inconclusive, legacies. The Bush administration has rarely lacked boldness in pushing its policies and what it believes to be its prerogatives. But whether boldness translates into durability is another matter. How, then, can we assess these developments? How much will they matter to future presidents and to the polity in general?

The Plan of the Book

The authors of the following chapters seek to answer those questions. They trace the governing incentives and constraints set by public opinion and electoral realities; the interaction of the Bush White House with Congress, the judiciary, and the rest of the executive branch; and the policies and politics that resulted. They provide a wide range of approach and ideology. No reader will agree with everything here, nor do we. But for all their divergent assumptions, the authors converge on several critical features of the Bush administration that will influence its successors and American politics for years to come. They trace the "vision thing," derided by George H. W. Bush but crucial to the makeup of his eldest son, who with insistent surety was willing to follow his vision, acting unilaterally where it was possible, demanding loyal support from allies and bulldozing opposition where it was not. When these tactics worked, they served to level the gridlock of American incrementalism and promote important policy change. When they did not, they led to bitter impasse. Bush's methods either reflected or caused (or both) bitter polarization among policy elites and perhaps, ironically, created a 2008 presidential election campaign safe for a "uniter, not a divider."

The Governing Context

That partisan polarization is a focal point of several chapters in the book's first section. Gary Jacobson examines public divisions through the prism of a crucial case study, the Iraq war. He finds that the actions of the Bush administration prompted historic divisions between Democrats and Republicans in the electorate, with independents tipping the balance—for the president in 2002 and 2004 but against him in 2006. Morris Fiorina likewise argues that this rocky political terrain was not determinative and that Bush's actions cemented polarization. Elites were red or blue, but real people were (and are) purple. Fiorina suggests that Bush's choice to divide, not unite, had consequences for politics and polity.

Yet there is healthy debate over the causes and consequences of polarization. James E. Campbell argues that President Bush's appeals to the Republican base on "values" were smart politics, and necessary if he was to succeed in office: "The constellation of political factors presented to him in his 2004 election indicated greater potential support for a conservative Republican president than for a moderate Republican president." Playing to the base, not the middle, combined with outreach to just enough centrist voters impressed either with the compassionate side of "compassionate conservatism" or with Bush's tough stance on national security, allowed the president to win reelection in 2004.

Lawrence Jacobs and Robert Shapiro examine public opinion more widely, demonstrating a gap between public opinion and administration policy in some areas but not others. Jacobs and Shapiro find that Bush actually did not govern exclusively from his party's base—at least not in a fashion completely dismissive of public opinion. Generally, however, as Bush's party became more dominant in Congress after the 2002 elections, until the 2006 elections, his policies became less congruent with public opinion than they had been earlier.

Institutions of Governance

In her discussion of George W. Bush's interactions with those Congresses, Barbara Sinclair observes that the president's legislative strategy sometimes built bipartisan alliances, as with the No Child Left Behind Act and the use-of-force resolutions. More often, though, Bush relied on the tight discipline of loyal, narrow majorities, especially in the House of Representatives, which could hold the line against compromise. And that approach had significant successes, from the passage of multiple tax cuts to Medicare and energy legislation. When asked why his first veto was so long in coming—it was issued in his sixty-sixth month in office, the longest period without a veto since Thomas Jefferson's administration two hundred years prior—the president asked, in turn, "How could you veto . . . if the Congress has done what you've asked them to do?"[38]

The strategy worked so long as Republicans in Congress saw the president's program as achieving their own goals. But GOP leaders relied less on deliberation than on dictate, providing little opportunity for minority input and tending to demonize those who opposed administration policy preferences. As Sinclair reminds us, living by the sword has well-known drawbacks when the point of the blade is reversed. The 2006 elections might have done just that.

On the other hand, as already mentioned, before 2007 both parties were generally supine before the unilateral strategies that Bush pursued to broaden his control over a wide swath of policymaking. The president was perfectly comfortable using such authority. The Framers of the Constitution, as Joel Aberbach notes in his chapter, feared that human nature was predictably selfish and believed that forging the public good from competing notions of self-interest required linking that ambition to the interests of the "separated institutions sharing power" that human beings would occupy.[39] The checks and balances of the constitutional structure would correct for human defects by taking advantage of them, protecting civil liberties from government intrusion.

Aberbach argues that that balance was largely lost in the Bush administration. From signing statements to politicization, he richly details the "unitary executive" theory in practice. Andrew Rudalevige relatedly examines executive decision making in the Bush administration. He traces the structure of the White House staff and the information flows it promoted—and prevented—especially with regard to Iraq. President Bush called himself "the decider," but his decisions did not always draw on the detail or nuance central to complex choices. The White House was organized around a president who placed great stock in his first principles rather than in engaged discussion.

In discussing the interaction of the White House with the courts, David Yalof adds that Bush, like Reagan before him, spent a fair amount of time deciding on a judicial strategy. The administration vetted judicial nominees carefully, in part to cement a conservative social agenda. But Yalof concludes that "the unifying thread in the administration's selection of judges has been its overriding concern that judges be deferential to claims of expansive executive branch authority." Given their lifetime tenure on the bench, those appointees could prove a genuinely long-term bequest to future presidents.

Outputs and Outcomes

The final chapters consider what policies and politics the intersection of situations and institutions generated. Foreign policy, of course, will be a crucial element of the Bush legacy. Raymond Tanter and Stephen Kersting take a broad view in assessing the administration's grand strategy, how it has sought to "use military, political, economic, and ideological means to promote its national interests." They describe the shift in that strategy over time, aimed at preventing potential attacks on the United States. The chapter carefully details the evolution of administration rhetoric on national security issues, how that rhetoric has mirrored (and shaped) events and also addressed perceived new threats such as Iran. They note the disengagement of the president when it came to seeing through the implementation of his preferred policies and that, to some degree, those policies were being sculpted by others to whom Bush gave latitude.

Colin Campbell's subsequent chapter stresses that last point as well, with particular regard to the ramifications for a next-generation transformation of the Pentagon. Bush's disengagement from policy debate and review meant that long-range reform goals at the Pentagon were sacrificed to the policy agendas of a set of neoconservative, high-level civilian officials under former secretary of defense Donald Rumsfeld. In Campbell's view, failures to seriously review policy options resulted in the overstretching of the U.S. military in Iraq and inability to focus on important, longer-run reforms dealing with overall military organization and command.

Although some deference may be extended to most presidents in international relations—at least until they get themselves into trouble or act high-handedly—Christopher Foreman notes that "presidential assets in national security politics do not pervade the political system." In domestic affairs, the president also had an ambitious agenda. Some of it, as we have said, was achieved, including broad expansions of Medicare and the federal role in elementary and secondary education; dramatic, repeated tax cuts; and government reorganization. At the same time, presidential proposals intended to rein in the cost of long-term entitlement programs, rationalize the immigration system, or wean the country from foreign oil made little progress, and as large structural deficits replaced the brief period of "surplus politics" of the late 1990s, those issues became even more difficult to address.

Mark Peterson then discusses how the administration approached its interaction with interests, organized and not. Peterson examines what he calls a "government of chums": the administration's efforts to make institutional connections to friendly interest groups and discourage those less sympathetic to presidential preferences. The chapter comes full circle from the original discussion of polarization in providing telling detail concerning the way in which administrations seek to strengthen their base and expand it or, conversely, how they write off parts of the electorate.

Finally, Bert Rockman's concluding chapter asks, What precisely is a president's legacy? What are the conditions promoting an enduring legacy, and specifically, what are George Bush's legacies? Some of these legacies are of his administration's making. Others are largely the result of unforeseen events. How will they constrain choices—of presidents and polity—in the future?

Presidents, Precedents, and Legacies

George W. Bush's time in office will thus leave a significant policy legacy, in terms both of what changed and of what did not. His choices produced landmark shifts in some policy arenas and stalemate in others; they will both empower and constrain his successors. The next president taking office, in a new century thus far no less conflict riven than the last, will inherit both grand rhetorical commitments and a vastly enlarged American military presence around the world, while finding the United States isolated in world opinion. He or she will find grand commitments at home, too, especially in terms of the entitlements due an aging population—while facing immense budget and trade deficits. A question by which an administration may fairly be judged is whether it left the resources available to meet the demands it stimulated.

The chapters in this book suggest, unfortunately, that the answer in the present case may be no. One theme that emerges is that of the short term versus the long. President Bush himself recognized this in his use of the Truman metaphor: in this telling, immediate costs will produce long-run gains. Yet history may find the reverse a closer fit. President Bush's tactics enabled him to impose his preferences on governmental outcomes; they made him, without doubt, a powerful president. Yet his very successes may cause long-term damage to his place in history.

Despite the quick overthrow of the Taliban, for example, administration efforts to date have failed to decapitate al Qaeda, which after a series of setbacks in the immediate U.S. response to 9/11 has begun to reconstitute both in and near

Afghanistan and on a global scale.[40] In Iraq, as reporter Thomas Ricks has commented, "90 percent of the effort" was expended on "10 percent of the problem," the fall of Baghdad,[41] while the resources needed to achieve the revolutionary imposition of democracy there were not provided or even thought necessary. The president successfully seized control of "enemy combatants"—but Guantanamo and Abu Ghraib became lamentable symbols of a gap between America's ideals and its endeavors. Consider, on a much smaller scale, the nomination of John Bolton to be U.S. ambassador to the United Nations in 2005: Bush made an aggressive, provocative (arguably needlessly so) choice, and the battle over confirmation was tough, narrow, and loudly divisive, capped off by executive unilateralism. It succeeded in seating Ambassador Bolton in New York, but he could not win confirmation to continue when that recess appointment ended.

More broadly, tactical victories thusly achieved rarely contribute to the conversion of their gains into a lasting electoral coalition and policy regime. As one observer suggested rather ruefully, "It is already clear that Bush's legacy will not be the policies he has championed," whether miscalculated or worthwhile. Instead, "his legacy will be the momentum of the backlash against them." This possibility seems particularly pertinent to an era that has revisited the notion of the "imperial presidency," considering its close analogy to the histories of national empires' overstretch and collapse.[42]

Our deliberative, divided system likes to be sure only after being slow; President Bush, by contrast, has been sure from the start. Indeed, he told the *Washington Post*'s Bob Woodward that one thing he had discovered about the presidency is that "the vision thing matters."[43] So it does. Yet in any number of cases there has been a large gap between the clarity of the stakes laid out in presidential rhetoric and the administrative effort devoted to achieving them. If five years after September 11 "the safety of America depends on the outcome of the battle in the streets of Baghdad," and if "we are fighting to maintain the way of life enjoyed by free nations," why have so few been asked to make that fight?[44] Why a presidential "management agenda"—and so little focus on results or implementation?

That assessment may prove overly pessimistic. There remains room for possibility—not least the chance that regional efforts to stabilize Iraq, or contain Iran, or new energy in dealing with the Israeli-Palestinian impasse will bear fruit. At home the president said that a Democratic Congress could work with him to pass legislation dealing with immigration and education, among other priorities. But both international cooperation and bipartisanship have been made less likely by the administration's reputation for scorning such approaches. "Either you're for us, or you're against us," the president proclaimed in October 2001, an attitude that carried over from the war on terror to matters of legislative or administrative support.[45] Debates in spring 2007 over scheduling troop withdrawals reinvigorated such rhetoric. Once again, developments suggest that repeated reliance on a minimum winning coalition, at least one emotionally sustained by strategic divisiveness, may ultimately undermine wider substantive goals.

If so, a key Bush legacy—one that is bitterly ironic in view of the many like assessments of the Clinton presidency before him—may center on missed opportunity. After the attacks of September 11, the country was as united as it had ever been in the post-Vietnam era. For the first time since the 1960s, a majority of respondents said they trusted government to do the right thing. Grand change was possible—even craved. The president put it this way: "I believe we've been called by history to lead the world. I believe this great, strong, compassionate country has been given a unique moment." He added: "I'm not going to miss the moment."[46]

Unfortunately, he may have, though we cannot yet be sure. What we have learned is that "the vision thing" that was so problematic for George H. W. Bush was abundant in George W. Bush. One problem is that the younger Bush's vision was not widely shared. Another is that W's father, although perhaps short on vision, was not reputed to be short on competence in governing—a failing, though debatable, of the younger Bush's presidency. Comparing the two Bush presidencies, one is reminded of a popular television program of the 1950s called *Father Knows Best.* It's nice to have vision—American voters have often rewarded it.[47] But it is essential to have competence.

Notes

1. Emmett H. Buell Jr., "The Invisible Primary," in *In Pursuit of the White House: How We Choose Our Presidential Nominees,* ed. William G. Mayer (Chatham, N.J.: Chatham House, 1996). Other prominent candidates included governors Michael Huckabee, R-Ark., and Bill Richardson, D-N.M., and senators Joseph Biden, D-Del., Sam Brownback, R-Kan., and Christopher Dodd, D-Conn.

2. See, e.g., the Gallup and Associated Press/IPSOS polls released the first week of February 2007. In each, 32 percent of those surveyed approved of the president's performance in office. Schneider and Friedman quoted in Howard Kurtz, "The Press, Turning up Its Nose at Lame Duck," *Washington Post,* February 5, 2007, C1.

3. "Press Conference by the President," Office of the White House Press Secretary, December 20, 2006; Ron Brownstein, "Bush Suffers Waning Influence," *Los Angeles Times,* October 27, 2005.

4. Since 1928, when Herbert Hoover defeated Al Smith; 1952 provides a partial exception, since the elderly vice president, Alben Barkley, was a putative candidate but made no impact on the race.

5. Holly Bailey, Richard Wolffe, and Evan Thomas, "Bush's Truman Show," *Newsweek,* February 12, 2007, 25–29. The Truman revival is often associated with David McCullough's treatment in *Truman* (New York: Simon and Schuster, 1992).

6. Stephen Skowronek, *The Politics Presidents Make* (Cambridge: Harvard University Press, 1994). Mark Twain once observed that "the past does not repeat itself, but it rhymes." See Ferenc M. Szasz, "Quotes about History," History News Network, http://hnn.us/articles/1328.html (accessed February 26, 2007).

7. Quoted in Dick Morris, *Behind the Oval Office* (New York: Random House, 1997), 307–308.

8. Skowronek, *The Politics Presidents Make*; William Shakespeare, *Twelfth Night*, act II, scene 5; Bert A. Rockman, *The Leadership Question: The Presidency and the American System* (New York: Praeger, 1984).

9. John Kingdon, *Agendas, Alternatives, and Public Policies*, 2nd ed. (New York: Harper-Collins, 1995), esp. chaps. 7–8.

10. For detailed treatment of the first years of the Bush administration, see Colin Campbell and Bert A. Rockman, eds., *The George W. Bush Presidency: First Appraisals* (Washington, D.C.: CQ Press, 2003).

11. James W. Ceaser and Andrew E. Busch, *The Perfect Tie: The True Story of the 2000 Presidential Election* (Lanham, Md. Rowman and Littlefield, 2001).

12. See, inter alia, "President Presses Congress for Action on Defense Appropriations Bill," Office of the White House Press Secretary, September 27, 2002.

13. Debate at Wake Forest University, October 11, 2000; quoted in Bob Woodward, *Bush at War* (New York: Simon and Schuster, 2002), 341 and, on nation-building, 192–193; *National Security Strategy of the United States of America*, November 2002; "President Sworn into Second Term," Office of the White House Press Secretary, January 20, 2005.

14. Quoted in Carolyn Lochhead and Carla Marinucci, " 'Freedom and Fear Are at War': Message to Americans, Warning to Taliban," *San Francisco Chronicle*, September 21, 2001, A1.

15. See P.L. 107-71 and P.L. 107-296.

16. E. J. Dionne and Thomas Mann, "After the Midterms," Policy Brief 115, Brookings Institution, February 2003, www.brookings.edu/comm/policybriefs/pb115.htm (accessed February 28, 2007); Adam Nagourney, "Shift of Power to White House Reshapes Political Landscape," *New York Times*, December 22, 2002, A1.

17. "President's Press Conference," Office of the White House Press Secretary, November 4, 2004.

18. See the essays in Robert Maranto, Douglas M. Brattebo, and Tom Lansford, ed., *The Second Term of George W. Bush: Prospects and Perils* (New York: Palgrave Macmillan, 2006).

19. John Maggs, "Katrina, from the Rose Garden," *National Journal*, January 14, 2006; Michael Fletcher, "On Visit to Gulf Coast, Bush Hears Frustrations," *Washington Post*, March 2, 2007.

20. See the *Washington Post*/ABC News polls of October 8 and 22, 2006; CNN's national exit poll of November 7, 2006, available at www.cnn.com/ELECTION/2006/pages/results/states/US/H/00/epolls.0.html (accessed March 2, 2007).

21. Carl Hulse and David Firestone, "On the Hill, Budget Business as Usual," *New York Times*, March 23, 2003; see also Andrew Rudalevige, *The New Imperial Presidency: Renewing Presidential Power after Watergate* (Ann Arbor: University of Michigan Press, 2005), chap. 1.

22. "President Visits National Security Agency," Office of the White House Press Secretary, January 25, 2006.

23. Jerry Seper and Stephen Dinan, "FISA Court Will Monitor Domestic Wiretapping," *Washington Times,* January 18, 2007; "President Bush Holds Press Conference," Office of the White House Press Secretary, March 13, 2002.

24. Quoted in Rudalevige, *New Imperial Presidency,* 211.

25. Arthur M. Schlesinger Jr., *The Imperial Presidency* (Boston: Houghton Mifflin, 1973); Richard Nathan, *The Administrative Presidency* (New York: Wiley, 1983); Rudalevige, *New Imperial Presidency,* chaps. 5–6.

26. Jess Bravin, "Judge Alito's View of the Presidency: Expansive Powers," *Wall Street Journal,* January 5, 2006, A1; and see Justice Antonin Scalia's dissent in *Morrison v. Olson* (1988).

27. U.S. Department of Justice, "Legal Authorities Supporting the Activities of the National Security Agency Described by the President," January 19, 2006, 35.

28. "Working Group Report on Detainee Interrogations in the Global War on Terrorism: Assessment of Legal, Historical, Policy, and Operational Considerations," U.S. Department of Defense, April 4, 2003, 21 and Section III generally. This and other useful documents are reprinted in *The Torture Memos,* ed. Karen Greenberg and Joshua Dratel (New York: Cambridge University Press, 2005).

29. "President's Statement on Signing of H.R. 2863," Office of the White House Press Secretary, December 30, 2005; Christopher S. Kelley, "The Significance of the Presidential Signing Statement" in *Executing the Constitution: Putting the President Back into the Constitution,* ed. Christopher S. Kelley (Albany: SUNY Press, 2006).

30. Jeffrey Rosen, "Power of One," *New Republic,* July 24, 2006.

31. Amy Goldstein and Sarah Cohen, "Bush Forces a Shift in Regulatory Thrust," *Washington Post,* August 15, 2004, A1; James P. Pfiffner, "The First MBA President: George W. Bush as Public Administrator," *Public Administration Review,* January/February 2007, 6–20; Jonathan D. Breul, "Three Bush Administration Management Reform Initiatives," *Public Administration Review,* January/February 2007, 21–26.

32. Carl Hulse and Jeff Zeleny, "Senate Democrats Vow to Confront Bush on Iraq but Are Still Working Out the Details," *New York Times,* March 2, 2007.

33. "President Bush Delivers State of the Union Address," Office of the White House Press Secretary, January 23, 2007.

34. As the president put it relatively early, "Either you believe in freedom, and want to—and worry about the human condition—or you don't." Thus, opponents of his policies deserved to be marginalized. Quoted in Woodward, *Bush at War,* 340.

35. See quotes in Rudalevige, *New Imperial Presidency,* 245, 256; "Interview with the Vice President by Jonathan Karl, ABC News," Office of the White House Press Secretary, February 21, 2007.

36. Michael Nelson, "George W. Bush: Majority President," in *The Elections of 2004,* ed. Michael Nelson (Washington, D.C.: CQ Press, 2005), 2; James Traub, "The Submerging Republican Majority," *New York Times Magazine,* June 18, 2006, 30; George F. Will, "A Loss's Silver Lining," *Washington Post,* November 9, 2006, A29, which in syndication was titled "Republicans Lost, Conservatism Won."

37. Michael D. Tanner, *Leviathan on the Right: How Big-Government Conservatism Brought Down the Republican Revolution* (Washington, D.C.: Cato Institute, 2007); Bruce Fein, "Restrain This White House," *Washington Monthly* 38 (October 1, 2006): 38.

38. "Press Conference of the President," Office of the White House Press Secretary, November 2004.

39. Richard E. Neustadt, *Presidential Power and the Modern Presidents* (New York: Free Press, 1990), 29.

40. See, e.g., Mark Mazzetti and David Rohde, "The Reach of War: Terror Officials See al Qaeda Chiefs Regaining Power," *New York Times,* February 19, 2007; David Sanger and Mark Mazzetti, "Bush to Warn Pakistan to Act on Terror," *New York Times,* February 26, 2007.

41. Thomas E. Ricks, lecture at Dickinson College, Carlisle, Pennsylvania, February 26, 2007; and see his *Fiasco: The American Military Adventure in Iraq* (New York: Penguin, 2006), 127–130.

42. Clive Crook, "Don't Think I'm Defending Bush, But . . . ," *National Journal,* February 3, 2007, 18; for a similar but more systematic take, see Richard M. Pious, *The American Presidency* (New York: Basic Books, 1979). On empires, see Paul Kennedy, *The Rise and Fall of the Great Powers* (New York: Vintage, 1989).

43. Quoted in Woodward, *Bush at War,* 341. Recall that George H. W. Bush derided the "vision thing."

44. "President's Address to the Nation," Office of the White House Press Secretary, September 11, 2006.

45. "President Unveils Back-to-Work Plan," Office of the White House Press Secretary, October 4, 2001.

46. "Presidential Q&A with Pool Reporters," Office of the White House Press Secretary, March 1, 2002.

47. It is worth recalling the irony that George H. W. Bush's 1988 opponent, Massachusetts governor Michael S. Dukakis, was derided for arguing that competence was more important than ideology.

CHAPTER 2

Presidential Politics in a Polarized Nation

The Reelection of George W. Bush

James E. Campbell

IN A REPRESENTATIVE DEMOCRACY there is and should be a continuity of politics between elections and governing.[1] Success in governing in a representative democracy, no less than success in winning elections, depends on assembling greater political support than the opposition. From a very practical political standpoint, those who supported the president and the reasons why they supported him in the campaign provide the basis for both the president's electoral victory and his governing constituency. Elections affect governing, in other words, not only by deciding who governs but by influencing how they govern. There is every reason for a president to expect to receive most of his support while serving in office from the same quarters as in his election. This chapter explores the electoral context for governing and how that context may have affected the way that President George W. Bush approached the second term of his presidency.

Who Evaluates What

Presidential candidates and sitting presidents receive political support from many sectors of the public and for many reasons. Presidential constituencies are routinely characterized by virtually every demographic, economic, and geographic characteristic and a great many of their combinations (e.g., soccer moms, NASCAR dads).[2] There is also a lengthy list of reasons for supporting or opposing presidential candidates and presidents. Perceived personal strengths or deficiencies, from intelligence to trustworthiness, and a long menu of issues understood in a variety of ways provide rationales for evaluating a president or a presidential candidate. Some of the reasons are sensible, substantive, and grounded in reliable information; others are superficial, irrelevant, and based on distorted perceptions—but what is important is that voters find them of use in evaluating candidates and presidents.

Stepping back from the many constituent groups and boiling down the lengthy list of reasons undergirding their assessments, there are essentially two broad constituencies involved in assessing presidential candidates and presidents and two broad considerations on which they base their evaluations. The two general constituencies are the president's base and the center, and the two general considerations involve values and presidential performance.[3]

The Base and the Center

Presidents, whether as candidates or in office, assemble their election and governing coalitions from citizens who are either in the partisan base or in the moderate, swing vote.[4] Presidents are pushed outward to their base and pulled inward to the political center for support.[5] Just as political parties are composed of a more ideological wing and a more moderate wing, every successful candidacy must pull together a coalition of those predisposed toward the candidate and those who are "up for grabs." Democratic Party presidential hopeful Howard Dean sarcastically stated the distinction at the outset of the 2004 nomination season when he declared that his candidacy represented "the Democratic wing of the Democratic Party," implying that moderate Democrats were not really Democrats. Decades earlier, conservative Republicans similarly derided members of the more conciliatory or centrist wing of their party as "me too Republicans."

Presidents and presidential candidates may have different levels of strength among base and swing voters. Some appeal more strongly to their base. Others have a greater ability to reach out for support from centrists. Whether a president's strength lies more in ties to the base or appeals beyond the base, in the competitive world of presidential politics, success depends on doing well with both groups. Neither constituency can be neglected. Centrist voters have a real option to vote for the opposing party, and voters in the base may decide to sit out an election if they feel neglected. As a result, presidential appeals, whether directed to the base or to the center, are matters of emphasis. Roger H. Davidson succinctly states the essential campaign puzzle as devising a message to "motivate your 'base' without alienating undecided potential voters."[6]

Values and Performance

The two broad constituencies each use two fundamental criteria to evaluate presidential candidates and presidents. Presidential candidates and presidents are evaluated by some combination of what the public thinks of their *values* and their *performance*—what candidates think should be done and what incumbents have done. Perhaps the most prominent reference to the values-performance dimensions of evaluation in American politics came in the 1988 nomination acceptance speech by Democratic presidential candidate Michael Dukakis when he told his party's convention that "this election isn't about ideology. It's about competence."[7] That was wishful thinking. All elections are about both.

In recent years, "values" in politics have often been construed quite narrowly as "moral values" or "traditional family values." This is only the tip of the values iceberg, however. More broadly, "values" refers to the general principles or gut instincts that guide people to take certain positions on issues—what the candidates and voters care about, their priorities. These are often summarized as political ideologies. Though there are some differences among conservatives about what values they prize, conservatives are generally more inclined than liberals to value individual liberties (including property rights) and take a stricter view of what is in the public sphere and appropriate for government intervention (e.g., national defense, preservation of social order, protection of innocent life). Similarly, although there are different views about their core principles, liberals tend to place a greater emphasis on equality and take a more expansive view of the scope of government action. The candidates' positions on everything from abortion and gay marriage to tax cuts and defense policy are influenced by their ideological values, and their decisions, as well as their personality traits, can be interpreted by voters as reflecting those values.[8]

In addition to values, presidents can be evaluated on the effectiveness of their performance in office—how well they handle the economy, defend the nation, provide for needed services, or maintain law and order ("domestic tranquility" in the Framers' language). Performance evaluations boil down to the simple matter of stability or change—whether the in-party has performed well enough to justify maintaining the status quo, or whether its performance fell far enough short of expectations that change is in order.

The values-performance distinction generalizes the more limited, prospective-retrospective distinction that has long been applied to economic policy.[9] In essence, citizens rate presidents and presidential candidates more favorably to the extent that they share the same views about what government ought to be doing (pursuing the correct ends, that is, values) and regard the president or candidate as successfully administering the office (effectively executing the means, that is, performance).

Appeals by presidential candidates based on values or on performance have different characteristics. Values-based appeals tend to be based on long-term or stable considerations. Neither voters nor candidates change their values easily, and candidates who appear to change their stated values are regarded with a good deal of skepticism by the public. That being the case, values are also likely to be a greater consideration for a candidate's base—those with more durable commitments. The downside of values-based appeals is that they are often in conflict with other values.

For instance, an appeal favoring more limited government may be at odds with an appeal favoring more expansive and aggressive government policies to protect the environment or reduce poverty levels. In contrast to values, performance considerations tend to be short term (though the parties develop reputations for effectiveness in particular areas). They are also universal in their appeal. For example, everyone appreciates peace and prosperity. Although centrists may be won over by appeals to moderate and temperate values, the very moderation of their values in a partisan world means that they may be more prone to evaluate candidates and presidents on performance or likely performance grounds. The downside of performance appeals is that they are more difficult for the candidate or president to control. All presidents would like to preside over a peaceful, secure, prosperous, and crime-free nation with a just, efficient, and compassionate government, but no administration achieves all of these goals, and whether by their own doing or through confronting particularly difficult circumstances, some fall shorter than others.

Values considerations differ from performance considerations in one very important respect: a voter's values may also affect perceptions of presidential performance. There is usually (but not always) some ambiguity in a candidate's record. Given some room for varying interpretations of the record, a voter's values may substantially affect his or her perceptions of a president's performance. Values, which are embedded in ideology and partisanship, may be set aside for short periods apart from elections—as in the immediate aftermath of the terrorist attacks of 9/11—but they are likely to reemerge to affect performance perceptions when campaigns remind them of value differences.

Every president is engaged in steering between appeals to the base and to the center in assembling and maintaining a majority coalition. George W. Bush's 2000 campaign message of "compassionate conservatism" exemplifies the twin appeals—the compassion aspect of the message is meant to persuade centrists that the message is not too harsh, and the conservatism aspect is meant to reassure the base that the message does not depart from basic principles.

Though presidents seek support from both the center and their base, the amount of emphasis is not necessarily equal. Whether a president in an election depends more heavily on support from his ideological and values-sensitive base or from a performance-sensitive center may signal which constituency and which appeal he will emphasize in governing—whether he governs more to please his base or to satisfy moderates. The strategies pursued in elections, of course, may not be identical to those pursued in governing. Most presidents would like to expand support among both groups, and a strong performance in office (a booming economy and a secure, peaceful nation) allows a president to gain ground in both constituencies. However, issues, circumstances, and the limits of agendas often require presidents to choose between emphasizing the interests of their base or the interests of potential swing-vote centrists. It is only reasonable to assume that presidents will be influenced by what happened in the election when they make such governing decisions.

Whether presidents govern for their base or for the center can be either praised or disparaged depending on one's political views. If a president steers policy toward pleasing his base, he may be portrayed positively, as exhibiting the courage of his convictions or displaying principled leadership. Alternatively, governing for the base may be derided as polarizing and divisive. By the same token, a president steering policy toward the center may be regarded positively as unifying, acting as a responsive and conciliatory leader, or negatively, as being unprincipled, governing by polls, and acting as a demagogue. The fact is that there is no one right way to govern. No one size fits all. There are benefits and costs to both approaches, and no president appeals exclusively to one side of the constituency spectrum. We need to understand better the electoral conditions that steer a president toward a more base-oriented approach or toward a more centrist-oriented approach to governing.

I therefore turn to the electoral influences that may have shaped the way President George W. Bush in his second term has steered a course between pleasing his base and appealing to centrists. President Bush's approach to governing undoubtedly reflected to a significant degree his own thoughts about presidential leadership and what he thought was the right policy, regardless of the politics. But presidents are political animals, and the political context in which they operate must also have some impact on how they choose to govern. What were the pressures and incentives evident in the 2004 election that would turn this presidency toward governing to please his conservative base, and what might have turned the president toward more centrist policy positions?

The analysis finds that President Bush was reelected substantially because of his appeal to the values of his conservative base rather than an appreciation by moderate voters of achievements during his first term. The political message of both his election in 2000 and his reelection in 2004 was that he would receive greater political support from his conservative base than from political moderates. Perhaps moderates could be won over, but the evidence from the election was that that would not be easy and might not be possible. President Bush's reelection depended more heavily on support from his base and less on support from centrist voters than the election of any other recent president. Whether he desired to govern as a principled leader of the right or a conciliatory leader of the center, the constellation of political factors presented to him in his 2004 election indicated greater potential support for a conservative Republican president than for a moderate Republican president. When his unusual political strengths in his base are combined with the removal of the electoral incentive for a second term administration, and with Republican majorities in both the House and the Senate, the alignment of political forces, opportunities, and incentives was clearly such that the greater prospects for political success were in governing to please the base rather than a more bipartisan approach in an attempt to please those in the political center.

Electoral Forces

Leading into the 2004 election a number of important conditions were in place that affected the extent to which President Bush would seek votes from his base or the center and whether he would emphasize values or performance in his campaign's message. Compared with other recent presidencies, the electorate that would decide whether President Bush would receive a second term was substantially polarized in their political perspectives, highly partisan, very much aligned in their ideological and partisan allegiances, and evenly divided. These conditions would affect where and how the president could most safely secure the votes necessary for reelection and may have influenced how he would decide to govern once reelected.

A More Polarized Nation

Perhaps the most important characteristic of American electoral politics in 2004 was that the electorate was highly polarized. Although there has been some dispute about the extent to which the public has become more polarized in recent years (as evidenced in Morris Fiorina's contribution to this volume), the evidence of electoral polarization is compelling.[10] Figure 2.1 presents the percentages of reported voters in the American National Election Study (NES) who were moderates, conservatives, and liberals. Both self-described moderates and respondents who said that they did not know how to classify themselves ideologically are counted as moderates. This is a generous count, since some of the "don't knows" may have ideological leanings that they simply do not know how to label, but the fact that they are unaware of an applicable ideological label may be interpreted as a sign of its being unimportant to them. Conservatives include those who declared themselves slightly conservative, conservative, or extremely conservative. Liberals also include the equivalent three degrees of commitment to the liberal label. The data series begins in 1972, the first year that NES asked the ideological question.

The figure indicates that the American electorate is quite polarized and has become more so in recent elections. About half of all voters were moderates in the 1970s and 1980s. Their numbers declined in the late 1980s and 1990s. Since 1990, moderates have been a minority of voters in every election, regularly falling below 45 percent of the electorate. The minority status of moderates in recent years is also evident in General Social Survey data, as well as the Gallup data that Fiorina examines in his chapter in this volume.[11] The number of conservatives among voters has rivaled and on occasion exceeded the number of moderates (including "don't knows") in these last six national elections. There is also some evidence that the

FIGURE 2.1   The Political Ideologies of Voters, 1972–2004

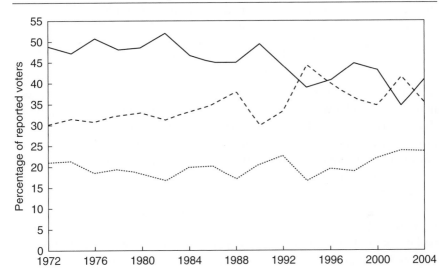

Source: Calculated from variable VCF0803 in the NES Cumulative Data File dataset. Weight variable VCF0009A was used.

Note: The percentages are of those reporting that they voted. Those who claimed that they did not know how to classify themselves are grouped with the moderates. Conservatives include those classifying themselves as slightly conservative, conservative, or extremely conservative. Liberals include those classifying themselves as slightly liberal, liberal, or extremely liberal.

number of liberals has increased slightly in the last few elections. Since the size of a potential constituency should bear some relation to its influence, American politics in recent years should have diminished the political weight of moderates and increased the political heft of conservatives for a Republican president.

It is also clear from Figure 2.1 that the electorate's polarization predates President Bush's first term. Some analysts, most prominently Gary Jacobson and George Edwards, have asserted that Bush caused, or was the major contributor to, polarization—that he was a "divider, not a uniter."[12] However, the increase in polarization that is evidenced in the decline in the percentage of moderates in the electorate began in the late 1980s and accelerated during the Clinton administration. An OLS trend regression with a counter variable (the year minus 1972) and a dummy variable for the Bush 2002 and 2004 elections indicates that polarization in 2002 and 2004 was no more severe during George W. Bush's presidency than would have been expected given the long-term trend. In short, there was division during the Bush years, but there is no evidence that he was any more the divider than preceding presidents had been. The fact that the public is divided in their ideological perspectives and divided in their evaluations of President Bush does not mean that he is divisive—only that he is the focus of and the product of a divided public. The trend toward greater division simply continued to grow during Bush's term as it had for more than a decade before his election. He was undoubtedly the prime subject of political polarization in the nation, and there is always the possibility that a different president in different circumstances might have turned back the tide of polarization.

Was the nation more polarized as a result of the Bush presidency? It probably was. In appealing to his base on a number of issues, and in his handling of a number of issues (most notably Iraq), President Bush unquestionably triggered a good deal of animus from those inclined to oppose him. This may have contributed to the intensity of polarization. However, the nation had been growing more polarized for some time. President Bush as well as his predecessors may have contributed to increased polarization, but the general trend suggests that polarization has deeper roots. Whatever its cause, polarization was a fact of political life in 2004—a fact that would shape that election, President Bush's second term, and American politics for years to come.

A Highly Partisan Electorate

The electorate that George W. Bush faced in 2004 was also highly partisan.[13] Nearly 40 percent of voters in the 2004 election indicated a strong identification with either the Democratic or the Republican Party. Though this was the highest percentage of strong party identifiers among voters in any election since 1964, and was nearly as high as has ever been measured, partisanship in the electorate has been growing stronger since the mid-1980s.

Figure 2.2 plots the percentage of strong party identifiers, either Democrat or Republican, among reported voters since 1952. The figure displays the decline and subsequent rise of partisanship in the electorate. As measured by the proportion of strong party identifiers among voters, strongly held partisan attachments were prevalent in the 1950s and early 1960s, ebbed during the dealignment period of the late 1960s and 1970s, and were restored in the 1980s. In elections since 1988, partisanship has been about as strong among voters as it was in its heyday of the 1950s and early 1960s. The 2004 electorate was not appreciably more partisan than electorates had been in the preceding four elections, but it was substantially more partisan than the ones that had elected Richard Nixon, Jimmy Carter, and Ronald Reagan.

FIGURE 2.2   Strong Party Identifiers as a Percentage of Voters, 1952–2004

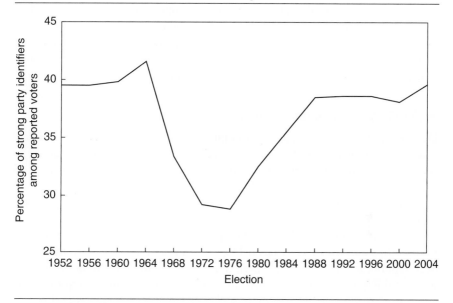

Source: Calculated from variables VCF0310 (party indentification) and VCF0705 (presidential vote) in the NES Cumulative Data File dataset. The data have been reweighted to the known actual vote division. See James E. Campbell, *The American Campaign: U.S. Presidential Campaigns and the National Vote* (College Station: Texas A&M University Press, 2000), appendix A.

A More Aligned Electorate

Not only were voters in 2004 ideologically divided and highly partisan, but their ideological predispositions had become much more tightly aligned with their party identification than they had been historically.[14] Voters in the 1950s and 1960s were often thought of as largely nonideological, in part because the parties were not so clearly ideological. There were significant numbers of liberal Republicans and conservative Democrats. That is no longer the case. The average correlation between ideological predisposition and party identification in the eleven national elections from 1972 to 1992 was .44. The mean ideology-party correlation in the six national elections since 1994 is .59. The increased correspondence of ideological disposition and party identification undoubtedly contributed to the increase in the number of voters claiming a strong identification with either the Democrats or the Republicans.

With fewer conservative Democrats and liberal Republicans (reflected in the stronger correlations), those with ideological leanings are less likely to be cross-pressured. Voters ideologically disposed to a candidate are more likely than before to vote for that candidate and are thus more attractive targets for candidate appeals. In 1972, a highly ideological election for the time, about 80 percent of self-described liberals and conservatives voted for the ideologically compatible party's candidate.[15] In 2004, not only were there more liberals and more conservatives, but they were more inclined to vote accordingly. About 89 percent of liberals and conservatives voted for the ideologically compatible party's candidate.

Highly Competitive National Politics

Despite the fact that conservatives outnumber liberals, and votes now quite closely correspond to ideological dispositions, American politics nationally is unusually competitive. Party identification is near parity. Among voters in 2004, once the NES data are corrected to the actual division of the national vote, 46.6 percent described themselves as Democrats, 48.0 percent were Republicans, and the remaining 5.4 percent were independents.

From 1952 to 1980, the Democrats enjoyed a double-digit lead in party identification. In some years Democrats held an advantage of more than twenty points over Republicans. Those days are over. Since 1984 Democrats have normally outnumbered Republicans by a few percentage points. In 2004 among reported voters, and correcting the data to mesh with the actual presidential vote division, Republicans for the first time slightly outnumbered Democrats.[16]

The nearly even division of partisans has been reflected at the polls. The controversial presidential election of 2000 between George W. Bush and Al Gore ranks among the closest elections in all of U.S. history. A shift of fewer than three hundred votes in Florida, out of more than one hundred million votes cast nationally, would have changed the election's outcome. As it stood, President Bush became the first president in over a century to be elected without a popular-vote plurality. Congressional politics has been almost as competitive. Republicans won a bare-bones majority in the House in 1994, and except for a brief time following the decision of Vermont's Senator Jim Jeffords to abandon his Republican Party affiliation in 2001 to become an independent, they held a slim majority in the Senate. Both majorities were dramatically reversed in the 2006 midterm elections. However, like the Republican majorities they replaced, the new Democratic majorities in both the House and the Senate are quite narrow. Democrats hold their majorities by just sixteen (of 435) seats in the House and one seat in the Senate.

Although President Bush was reelected in 2004 with a majority of the popular vote, the first presidential majority vote since his father's in 1988, it was still a very close election.[17] It was the narrowest victory of an incumbent president since the Civil War (though Cleveland's losing reelection bid in 1888 was closer), and a shift of fewer than 60,000 votes out of more than 122 million cast could have reversed the outcome. In short, the 2004 election was fully in keeping with the highly competitive division of American national politics.

Conceivably this intense national political competition could have two differ-ent consequences for approaching electoral and governing constituencies. On the one hand, even though their numbers have declined in the polarized electorate, the importance of moderate swing voters might increase with the political parties near parity. If the nation is split, with 45 percent strongly disposed to the Democrats and 45 percent strongly disposed to the Republicans, the split of the remaining 10 per-cent determines the election outcome. Certainly President Bush was called upon by many to recognize the narrowness of his victory and the divisions in the nation and to govern in a bipartisan or centrist mode. On the other hand, highly com-petitive political parties may cause polarized positions on each side to become even more adamant and less accepting of compromise. Those on either side of the polit-ical divide may demonize the opposition when there is some real possibility of that opposition winning the election. Bipartisanship requires cooperation from both sides (even if they are just slightly to one side or the other). If neither side trusts the other, governing to the center may be desirable but unrealistic.

The Base and the Center in Perspective

What were the consequences of these electoral forces for President Bush's success in attracting support from the base and from moderate, swing voters? It is possible to gain some historical perspective on this question by examining the contributions to win-ning presidential candidates' popular votes from those firmly in the candidate's base and from moderate, swing voters. There are, of course, many voters in between the hard-core base and those squarely in the political center, but the relative contribution of each to the president's victory may reveal whom he was appealing to and who he might feel would provide the most support for his policy agenda once elected.[18]

The percentages of the vote for the winning presidential candidate provided by the president's base and by moderate, swing voters in the nine presidential elections since 1972 are plotted in Figure 2.3. The analysis begins with the 1972 election, since that is the first in which the NES asked respondents to declare their ideological disposition. Voters in the president's base are defined as those identifying with the president's party who also are ideologically disposed to that party (conservative Republicans and liberal Democrats) and voted for their party's winning presiden-tial candidate.[19] Moderate, swing voters are self-described moderates or voters who say they do not know how to describe their ideological disposition and voted for the winning presidential candidate.

Figure 2.3 shows just how fundamentally different the electoral circumstances were for President George W. Bush than for any of his recent predecessors. President Bush depended much more on votes from his base than from centrists. The president with the closest configuration of support from the base was George H. W. Bush, but even he depended far less on his base than did his son. Of the nine presidential

FIGURE 2.3   The President's Base and Moderate Vote as a Percentage of the President's Popular Vote, 1972–2004

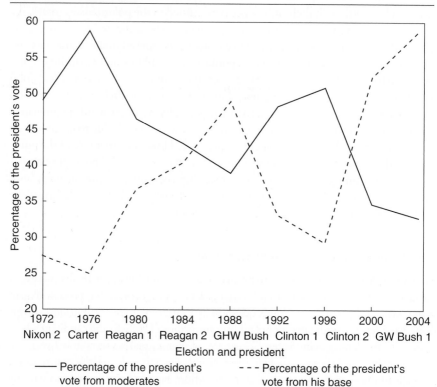

Source: Calculated from variables VCF0310 (party identification), VCF0803 (ideology), and VCF0705 (presidential vote) in the NES Cumulative Data File dataset. Weight variable VCF0009A was used. The base vote consists of party identifiers claiming an ideological perspective consistent with the president's party (e.g., liberal Democrats for a Democratic president, conservative Republicans for a Republican president). Partisan leaners and slightly liberals or slightly conservatives are counted as partisans having an ideological preference. The moderate vote consists of self-declared ideological moderates and those who did not know how to classify their ideology. Both votes are percentages of all reported voters for the president.

constituencies examined in Figure 2.3, every president other than the Bushes received a larger share of their votes from moderate and nonideological voters than they received from their partisan-ideological base. Presidents Nixon, Carter, and Clinton received about half or more than half of their votes from the ranks of the moderates and nonideologicals. Even President Reagan, generally thought of as one of the most conservative presidents of the twentieth century, depended more on moderates than on his base for his election in 1980. In his 1984 reelection President Reagan drew about evenly from both centrists and his conservative Republican base. Prior to George W. Bush's election in 2000, only George H. W. Bush had depended more on his base than on centrist votes for his election. The difference for George H. W. Bush was about ten percentage points (49 percent from the base and 39 percent from moderates).

Compared to every recent president, George W. Bush drew a much greater portion of his electoral support from his base than from the swing-vote center. He is the only president in recent history to have drawn a majority of his vote from his base, and he did so in both of his elections. In the 2000 election, Bush received 52 percent of his vote from conservative Republicans and 35 percent from moderates. His 2004 vote drew even more heavily on the base, with 59 percent of the Bush vote from his base and only a third from centrists. Of all votes cast for major-party candidates in 2004, more than 30 percent were those of conservative Republicans casting their votes for President Bush.

There are two sides to the unusual character of the Bush vote. While he did unusually well in his base, he performed unusually poorly among centrists. According to NES data, Bush lost the moderate vote to Gore in the 2000 election by 38 percent to 62 percent and to Kerry in 2004 by 40 percent to 60 percent.[20] Every other president in the series except George H. W. Bush in 1988 (who narrowly lost the moderate vote to Dukakis 46 percent to 54 percent) won a plurality of the votes cast by moderates. In short, unlike any of the seven other presidential victories since 1972, George W. Bush's elections were strongly grounded in support from his base and drew only weakly on support from centrists.

Bush's base in the 2004 election had a number of defining sociodemographic characteristics, but it was large enough that there was more diversity within it than journalistic stereotypes suggested. The typical voter in Bush's base was an upper-income, college-educated, middle-aged, churchgoing, married, white male home owner. Although these were the characteristics of the typical voter in President Bush's base, according to NES data his base vote also included a large number of women (45 percent of his base vote), modest-to-middle-income voters (37 percent), and people who do not attend weekly religious services (52 percent). The idea that the conservative base is dominated by the religious right considerably overstates that aspect of the base. The defining characteristic of voters in President Bush's base was not common demographics or religious commitment but ideological perspective.

Values and Performance in the 2004 Campaign

As one might expect, given the unusually strong support he received from his conservative Republican base, President Bush's election depended more heavily on evaluations based on values than on performance. With conservatives outnumbering liberals in the very polarized electorate, more voters saw their perspectives on politics reflected in President Bush than saw them in his opponent, Senator Kerry. With mixed assessments on his administration's performance in its first term, the president's representation of conservative Republican values tilted the election in his favor.

The Comparative Advantage on Values

George W. Bush held a clear advantage with the voters over his Democratic rivals in both 2000 and 2004 when it came to values. Figure 2.4 displays the percentages

FIGURE 2.4 Percentages of Poll Respondents Saying That the Presidential Candidates Share Their Values, Sept.–Oct. 2004

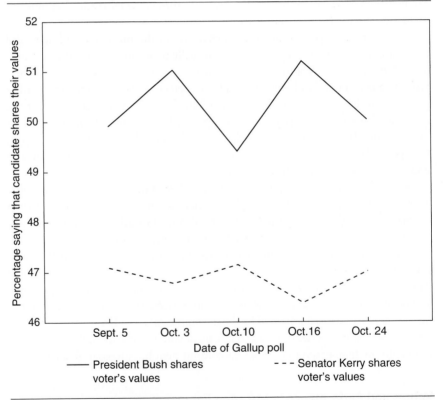

Source: The data are from Gallup. The question to respondents was, "Next, thinking about the following characteristics and qualities, please say whether you think each one applies more to John Kerry or more to George W. Bush. How about—Shares your values?" "Both equally" volunteered responses were added to each candidate's totals.

of respondents in five Gallup polls, from early September through late October of the 2004 campaign, who said that Bush or Kerry shared their values. Those who said that they thought both candidates shared their values are counted for both. These data demonstrate consistently that more of the public regarded President Bush as sharing their values. The differences are not large, ranging from about two to about five points, but they consistently favor President Bush. A Gallup poll in late October 2000 indicated that Bush had a six-to-seven-point lead over Vice President Al Gore on the "shares your values" question.

Other evidence corroborates President Bush's greater appeal to voters in representing their values.[21] In two surveys conducted in early September and mid-October, the Gallup Organization asked potential voters whether each candidate's political views were too conservative, too liberal, or about right. In both surveys, more respondents found Senator Kerry's positions too liberal than assessed President Bush's positions as too conservative. Whereas 40 percent said that Bush was too conservative, about 48 percent (47.9 in September and 47.4 in October) said that Kerry was too liberal.

Further corroboration can be found in the 2004 exit poll results. Although considerations of values infuse many different issues in the campaign, from tax policies to the war in Iraq, 22 percent of voters in the exit polls indicated directly that "moral values" were the most important issue for them in the campaign. More respondents mentioned "moral values" as the most important problem than mentioned the economy (20 percent), terrorism (19 percent), or Iraq (15 percent).[22] Of those that explicitly mentioned "moral" values as the key issue—a subset of all values considerations in the election—80 percent said that they voted for President Bush. In short, combined with the "shares your values" responses and the "too liberal or too conservative" responses, there is solid evidence that considerations of the values that the candidates stood for were important to reelecting President Bush.

Mixed Grades on Performance

On performance grounds the 2004 electorate gave President Bush decidedly mixed reviews for his first term. When asked in mid-October by Gallup which candidate would better handle particular issues, respondents gave Bush higher marks than Kerry on terrorism, the situation in Iraq, and taxes and gave Bush lower marks than Kerry on the economy, health care, the budget deficit, and Social Security.[23] Though the economy was more robust than it had been when President Clinton sought reelection in 1996, many Americans were uneasy about it: The Democrats successfully claimed a lack of job creation, and NES data indicate that only 44 percent of voters approved of the president's handling of the economy. Opinions about the war in Iraq were fairly evenly divided. Though a Gallup poll in late August showed President Bush favored over Senator Kerry by 49 percent to 43 percent in handling the situation in

Iraq, only 44 percent of voters in the NES approved of the president's handling of the issue. Offsetting some of these lower marks were the high marks the public gave President Bush for his administration's handling of the war on terrorism. Bush held about a twenty-point advantage over Kerry on the terrorism issue, and Gallup polls in September and October found that between 57 percent and 62 percent of Americans approved of the president's handling of the terrorism problem.

The mixed reviews for the president's first term are best summarized in his overall approval ratings—the percentage of the public indicating that they approved of the way he was handling his job as president. In the months leading into the 2004 campaign, President Bush's approval ratings were between "electable" and "unelectable." Since 1948, seven presidents had approval ratings of over 50 percent in the Gallup poll in July of the election year. The president, or the candidate of the president's party, went on to win the election in all seven cases. In the same period, six presidents had approval ratings in July that stood at 45 percent or lower. Five of those six presidents, or the candidate of the president's party, lost their elections. Only Harry Truman managed to beat the odds and win his 1948 election with a sub–45 percent approval rating. In July 2004, President Bush's approval rating in the Gallup poll was 47 percent. His approval rating in the final preelection Gallup poll was 48 percent. These performance evaluations were not an obstacle to reelection, but they were not much of a help, either.

President George W. Bush's performance evaluations may have been mixed because that was how voters objectively judged his performance, but there is also evidence suggesting that Bush received middling performance ratings because the values of his raters in the public were spilling into their performance perceptions. As both Jeffrey Jones and Gary Jacobson have observed, there has been an unusually large partisan gap in President Bush's job evaluations.[24] Republicans have tended to rate him unusually positively, and Democrats unusually negatively. This suggests that a significant portion of what ostensibly are performance evaluations are, in fact, indirect evaluations of the president's values.

Causes of the Values Appeals to the Base

Two explanations seem plausible for why George W. Bush stands apart from other recent presidents in his unusually large amount of support from his base and his unusually small amount of support from moderates. First, the long-term changes in American politics noted above may account for the unusual mix of base and center support. With the increased level of polarization, and particularly with the increase in the number of conservative voters in the electorate, the potential for support from the conservative Republican base grew at the same time that the potential for support from a smaller number of voters in the political center declined. The growth in Republican numbers and the greater alignment of ideological and partisan dispositions also strengthened the potential of the base to supply votes, and the highly competitive nature of recent politics may also have heightened party loyalties.

Second, the political contexts and candidate strategies of both the 2000 and 2004 elections may have contributed to the unusual division of support between the base and center. In the 2000 election, the public generally gave high ratings to the performance of President Clinton and the in-party Democrats. Despite widespread distaste for his personal conduct, President Clinton's approval rating in the Gallup poll in late October 2000 stood at 57 percent, and better than 60 percent of respondents in an early October Gallup poll indicated that they were satisfied with the way things were going in the country. With clear majorities of the nation giving the Democratic administration high marks for performance, the only viable strategy for Republicans and the Bush campaign was to run on values that resonated with their base. Luckily for Republicans, Democratic candidate Al Gore also decided to run a values-based, prospective campaign, rather than a more bipartisan, retrospective campaign on past performance.[25] Whether this was an attempt by Vice President Gore to emerge from Clinton's shadow or to distance himself from the scandals surrounding President Clinton, the campaign was fought on territory favorable to the Republicans.

The context and candidate strategies of 2004 also may have steered Bush toward appeals to the base. Unlike 2000, performance evaluations seem to have been neutral between the two parties. The president could benefit by running on the record so long as debate focused on security and terrorism; beyond that, the record either cut both ways or was a drag on the ticket. On the other hand, when it came to questions of values, the president had a clear lead over his Democratic Party rival, and those values-based votes were generally from the conservative Republican base.

From Elections to Governing

When George W. Bush accepted the Republican Party's presidential nomination in 2000, he pledged to be a "uniter, not a divider." Six years and two presidential election victories later, critics turned his phrase inside-out to claim that he has been a "divider, not a uniter." They claim that he has governed to satisfy his base and not centrist Americans. It is beyond the scope of this chapter to evaluate that claim, but it should be noted that, as has every president, George W. Bush has pursued some policies to the liking of his base and some to the liking of centrists. One can easily assemble a reasonably long list of differences between the Bush record and his base. On the list would be his immigration/guest worker initiative, the failure to press for significant cuts in domestic spending programs, the prescription drug benefit plan for Medicare, the No Child Left Behind program that more deeply involved the federal government in education, the failure to press the faith-based initiative more strongly, and the proposal for progressive indexing of Social Security benefits. These are not policies and actions designed to appeal to his conservative base. Moreover, as the first Republican president to preside over a unified party government since Dwight Eisenhower in the early 1950s, Bush may be regarded as a "divider" by those unaccustomed to and frustrated by this political configuration. Whether fully justified or not, analysts commonly concur with the late Wilson Carey McWilliams's conclusion that President George W. Bush "pursued an ideological and partisan agenda."[26]

To the extent that the critics are correct in claiming that President Bush has governed as a partisan—and there are good reasons to suspect that those conclusions have been overstated—were the conditions of his elections pulling him toward that course? Or did Bush pursue that mode of leadership despite the electoral message? Did the fact that he received an unusually large share of his vote from his conservative Republican base and an unusually small share of his vote from moderates, and won his reelection largely on an appeal to values, rather than approval of his administration's performance, affect how President Bush governed in his second term?

From the perspective advocated by many of his critics, President Bush's narrow reelection victory and the strong vote from his base argued that he should reach out to the political center to govern in a bipartisan way. According to this view, with his base secure, his victory narrow, and the nation polarized, Bush lacked a mandate for change and should have geared his appeals to bridge political differences. "Many expected him," as James P. Pfiffner wrote regarding Bush's first term, "to take a conciliatory approach to Democrats in Congress and seek out moderates of both parties to forge an agenda in the middle of the spectrum."[27] According to this perspective, if President Bush had run for reelection more as a centrist and pursued a more moderate political agenda, he would have been reelected by a larger margin in 2004 and would have been a more popular president during his second term.

Contrary to that perspective is an argument for governing with particular sensitivity to the base. Although no successful candidate or president can neglect the political center, President George W. Bush has had less reason than any modern president to govern from the center. First, there are the institutional reasons: President Bush is a second term president and will not stand for election again—there is no personal moderating impulse to bend to swing voters in anticipation of another tight reelection campaign. Then there is the fact that Republicans controlled both houses of Congress until 2007—again dampening the moderating impulse to draw support across party lines. Beyond these institutional reasons is political reality. There is hard evidence from both the 2000 and the 2004 elections that President Bush could assemble considerable support from his base and has had much less success in dealing with moderates. In neither of his elections did he receive more than 40 percent of the moderate vote. In the polarized, partisan, and competitive world of American politics in 2004, the prospects of gaining cooperation across party lines were dim, and the center was shrinking. The conservative Republican base proved crucial to the electoral victories of both 2000 and 2004.

Critics could claim that President Bush's weak showing with moderates is a result of his being immoderate. A hard conservative agenda is not going to pull in moderate support. However, as noted above, President Bush has advocated some proposals that are more moderate than his base would support (the No Child Left Behind education initiative, the Medicare prescription drug benefit, no significant cuts in domestic programs, and sparing use of the veto), but these have won him precious little goodwill among moderates. Despite appeals to moderates through "compassionate conservatism," relatively few moderates were won over in either 2000 or 2004.[28] As they say, "It takes two to tango," and many moderates were not inclined to support the president regardless of what overtures he made to them.

There is also a very personal reason for President George W. Bush to be wary of the centrist strategy. President Bush's father, the only other president in modern times to have received more votes from his base than from the center, made the politically fatal mistake of compromising with "centrist" Democrats on the budget and agreeing to a tax increase that violated his "Read my lips; no new taxes" campaign pledge to the nation (and his base). That won him high praise from some moderates and the media but also made him a one-term president. Despite his centrist compromise on his tax policy, President George H. W. Bush attracted only 37 percent of the two-party vote of moderates in 1992.

As appealing as the govern-to-the-center argument is, President George W. Bush has twice been elected by attracting substantial support from conservative Republicans. Nearly 60 percent of his votes in 2004 were from conservative Republicans, and only about a third were from moderates. His critics suggest that there is great room for growth in support from moderates. This is true, but a majority of moderates have exhibited an unwillingness to support President Bush in two elections, even when he reached out to them through both policy overtures and adoption of the "compassionate conservatism" theme. It seems eminently reasonable for the president and his advisers to conclude that they should build their governing constituency from those that provided the votes for the 2004 electoral plurality, and that is largely the base. As the old saying goes, "You should dance with the one that brought you."

Postscript: A Base-Based Presidency in a Divided Government

With the results of the midterm elections of 2006, the final two years of the Bush presidency will be conducted in a very different context than the prior six. As the 2006 midterm approached, the public had become increasingly impatient and dissatisfied with the conduct of the war in Iraq, and their frustration precipitated a slide of the president's approval ratings. President Bush had been reelected in November 2004 with approval ratings hovering around 50 percent. Two years later, on the eve of the midterm, his approval ratings had dropped into the high–30 percent range. His support dropped among Democrats (from the teens to single digits) and among

Republicans (from the low 90s to the low 80s), but especially among the perfor-mance-sensitive independents (from the mid-40s to the high 20s).

The dissatisfaction provided the foundation for Democratic Party victories in the 2006 midterm elections. Voters replaced Republican majorities with Demo-cratic majorities in both the House and the Senate. Although midterm elections have often produced divided governments (in eight of the ten midterms since 1970), Democrats had not held a majority in both congressional chambers since 1994. President Bush, who governed through most of his two terms with Republi-can majorities in Congress, now faced a Congress held by the opposition.

How would a second term president who had depended on support from his base function when his base no longer controlled Congress? As we have discussed, there are many reasons why George W. Bush may tilt to his base more than to the center. Most of them are still intact. He is a second term president and is constitu-tionally prohibited from seeking reelection. He also has received and continues to receive much greater support from his base than from the center, and one would expect governing support to come from the same sources that provided electoral support. He no longer, however, is dealing with a hospitable Congress, and that may make a difference.

On the one hand, as David Mayhew has observed more generally, neither the president nor Congress desires a do-nothing or obstructionist legacy.[29] Though nei-ther is prone to bipartisanship, President Bush and the Democrats in Congress might work together in the few areas where collaboration is most feasible. In the same way that the Republican Congress of the 1990s worked with Democratic Pres-ident Clinton on the North American Free Trade Agreement, it is quite possible that the current Democratic Congress will come to terms with President Bush on the issue of immigration reform.

On the other hand, beyond the immigration issue, both short- and long-term politics portend intense partisan conflict. The president has made a firm commit-ment in the Iraq war, and Democrats, generally supportive of his position at the start of the war, have largely gravitated to more aggressive opposition as it has dragged on and as the 2008 presidential nomination race has begun to heat up. This short-term difference is reinforced by long-term party polarization. The parties have basic dif-ferences in values that are not going to go away anytime soon and cannot be readily compromised. The Republican minority in the Senate is large enough to block unacceptably liberal initiatives by the Democrats, and the veto pen is at the ready, to be used if necessary. The stage is set for policy gridlock.

Notes

1. The connection between election campaigns and governing has been termed "the perma-nent campaign." See Norman J. Ornstein and Thomas E. Mann, eds., *The Permanent Cam-*

paign and Its Future (Washington, D.C.: AEI and Brookings, 2001). Some have concluded that this is antideliberative and "antithetical to governing." See George C. Edwards, *Governing by Campaigning: The Politics of the Bush Presidency* (New York: Pearson Longman, 2007), 285. However, both political reality and democratic principles argue for the linkage of campaigns and governing. The political reality of involving the public in governing debates, at least defensively, was brought home to conservatives in the 1980s when liberal interest groups successfully campaigned to block the nomination of Judge Robert Bork to the U.S. Supreme Court. Liberals relearned the lesson a few years later when conservatives successfully campaigned against President Clinton's proposed health care program. Both cases are examples of what E. E. Schattschneider termed "expanding the scope of the conflict." See E. E. Schattschneider, *The Semisovereign People: A Realist's View of Democracy in America* (Hinsdale, Ill.: Dryden, 1960).

2. See, for example, Richard J. Powell and Mark D. Brewer, "Constituencies and the Consequences of the Presidential Vote," in *A Defining Moment: The Presidential Election of 2004*, ed. William Crotty (Armonk, N.Y.: M. E. Sharpe, 2005), 20–45; Paul R. Abramson, John H. Aldrich, and David W. Rohde, *Change and Continuity in the 2004 Elections* (Washington, D.C.: CQ Press, 2006), chap. 5.

3. The base versus center or swing voter distinction applies to the potential source of votes for nonpresidential as well as presidential candidates and in all electoral systems. Essentially, candidates draw support from those who are predisposed to support them and some who are not. Though base and centrist voters are referred to as belonging in distinct constituency groups, in reality voters are spread across a spectrum from those firmly committed to the candidate to those with more ambivalent attachments. That is, the base-versus-center distinction is really one of degree and not dichotomous types. By the same token, many issues and assessments of the candidates' characteristics are not purely value driven or performance driven, but some blend of the two. For instance, a voter may evaluate a candidate's economic position partially on performance and partially on his or her preference for certain types of economic policies (for example, cutting taxes).

4. There are a variety of definitions and measurements of "swing voters." One variable in the definition is how far in advance of the election the voter is uncertain about how he or she will vote. In this chapter I consider ideological centrists or those unaware of their ideological bent to be swing voters in a very broad sense, though many such votes are probably quite committed as the general election campaign gets under way. For interesting alternative views of swing voters see William G. Mayer, "The Swing Voter in American Presidential Elections"; and Daron Shaw, "Swing Voting in U.S. Presidential Elections," both papers presented at the Swing Voting Conference, Northeastern University, Boston, June 10, 2006.

5. The classic study examining the convergence (centrist strategy) or divergence (base strategy) of presidential appeals is Benjamin I. Page, *Choices and Echoes in Presidential Elections: Rational Man and Electoral Democracy* (Chicago, Ill.: University of Chicago Press, 1978).

6. Roger H. Davidson, "Presidential Campaigning and Presidential Governance: The Case of 2004," in *Understanding the Presidency*, 4th ed., ed. James P. Pfiffner and Roger H. Davidson (New York: Pearson Longman, 2007), 140.

7. Michael Dukakis, "1988 Nomination Acceptance Speech," Democratic National Convention, Atlanta, Georgia, July 21, 1988.

8. Perceptions of a candidate's personality strengths and weaknesses also bear on what voters think about the candidate's values and performance (or likely performance). Certain values can be read into a candidate seen as being particularly compassionate or trustworthy. Performance or likely performance evaluations can be extracted from perceptions of a candidate's intelligence or steadfastness.

9. See, e.g., Morris P. Fiorina, *Retrospective Voting in American National Elections* (New Haven: Yale University Press, 1981). The values-performance distinction might also be considered a generalization of the position issue versus valence issue distinction. Position issues involve conflict over the proper ends or goals of the policy (e.g., abortion), whereas valence issues involve conflict over who would better handle, resolve, or execute the means of achieving a generally accepted policy goal (e.g., economic growth, national defense).

10. Those concluding that polarization is minimal and has not changed much in recent years include Morris P. Fiorina, Samuel J. Abrams, and Jeremy C. Pope, *Culture War? The Myth of a Polarized America*, 2nd ed. (New York: Pearson Longman, 2004); and Paul DiMaggio, John Evans, and Bethany Bryson, "Have American Social Attitudes Become More Polarized?" *American Journal of Sociology* 102, no. 3 (1996): 690–755.

11. Counting both self-professed moderates and those who claim not to know their ideological leanings, only 41 percent of respondents in the General Social Survey since 1994 can be classified as moderates. Ironically, the Gallup opinion data that Morris Fiorina examines in his contribution to this volume (his Figure 5.2) corroborate the finding that moderates in the 1990s and 2000s were a minority, not a majority, of the public and an even smaller minority of those who bothered to vote.

12. See Gary C. Jacobson, *A Divider, Not a Uniter* (New York: Pearson Longman, 2007), 13, as well as his contribution to this volume; and Edwards, *Governing by Campaigning*, 26, 282.

13. See Marc J. Hetherington, "Resurgent Mass Partisanship: The Role of Elite Polarization," *American Political Science Review* 95 (September 2001): 619–631; Larry Bartels, "Partisanship and Voting Behavior, 1952–1996," *American Journal of Political Science* 44 (January 2000): 35–50; and James E. Campbell, *The American Campaign: U.S. Presidential Campaigns and the National Vote* (College Station, Texas: Texas A&M University Press, 2000).

14. Alan I. Abramowitz and Kyle L. Saunders, "Ideological Realignment in the U.S. Electorate," *Journal of Politics* 60 (August 1998): 634–652.

15. Of major-party voters in the 1972 election, 31 percent of self-described liberals voted for the Republican incumbent, Richard Nixon, rather than his Democratic Party opponent, George McGovern, and 13 percent of self-described conservatives voted for McGovern rather than Nixon.

16. Correcting the NES data to bring them into line with the actual presidential vote division, 48.0 percent of voters were Republicans, 46.6 percent were Democrats, and 5.4 percent were independents. Without the correction, 46.9 percent were Republicans, 47.7 percent were Democrats, and 5.4 percent were independents. Among all respondents (not just reported voters), regardless of whether the data are corrected, Democrats still slightly outnumbered Republicans, though the differences were much smaller than they had been.

17. In 1988, George H. W. Bush won 53.4 percent of the total national popular vote for president. Bill Clinton was elected with vote pluralities in 1992 and 1996 but fell short of receiving majorities. In 1992, Clinton received 43.0 percent of the vote to President

George H. W. Bush's 37.4 percent and independent candidate H. Ross Perot's 18.9 percent. In 2000, George W. Bush won the electoral vote majority with 47.9 percent of the popular vote to Al Gore's 48.4 percent, with Ralph Nader and other minor candidates combining for 3.7 percent of the popular vote.

18. As "base" and "centrist" voters have been defined here, a large majority of the votes for the winning presidential candidate can be classified as from either the base or center, rather than from the gray area between them. The base and centrist groups have constituted between 77 percent and 91 percent of all voters for winning presidential candidates since 1972. In his contribution to this volume, Morris Fiorina indicates that he regards my definition of the base as "extremely generous." I do not believe that to be the case, since one must be both a partisan of the president's party and indicate ideological agreement with that party to be considered in the base. Moreover, what is important to the analysis is that the criteria are applied equally to all presidential constituencies since Nixon's, and in four of the nine presidential victories examined only a third or less of a president's election constituency can be characterized as coming from his base (see Figure 2.3).

19. Respondents who said that they "leaned" toward the Democratic or Republican Party are classified as partisans rather than independents. As Bruce Keith and his colleagues concluded, these "independent leaners" in nearly every important respect are like other partisans and unlike independents who do not indicate a leaning. See Bruce E. Keith, David B. Magleby, Candice J. Nelson, Elizabeth Orr, Mark C. Westlye, and Raymond E. Wolfinger, *The Myth of the Independent Voter* (Berkeley: University of California Press, 1992).

20. This might appear to be a case contradicting the "median voter" thesis, that elections turn on the vote of the median-positioned voter. However, it does not necessarily contradict that thesis. President Bush's election and reelection required support from centrists, and there is variation among the political views of those who fall in the "moderate" voter category. The median voter in the 2004 election was probably a moderate with conservative leanings. See, Anthony Downs, *An Economic Theory of Democracy* (New York: Harper and Row, 1957).

21. James E. Campbell, "Why Bush Won the Presidential Election of 2004: Incumbency, Ideology, Terrorism, and Turnout," *Political Science Quarterly* 120, no. 2: 219–241.

22. The exit poll results were accessed at www.cnn.com/ELECTION/2004/pages/results/states/US/P/00/epolls.0.html.

23. Patricia Conley, "The Presidential Race of 2004: Strategy, Outcome, and Mandate," in *A Defining Moment: The Presidential Election of 2004*, ed. William Crotty (Armonk, N.Y.: M. E. Sharpe, 2005), 108–135; also see, Helmut Norpoth and Andrew H. Sidman, "Mission Accomplished: The Wartime Election of 2004," *Political Behavior* 29, forthcoming.

24. Jeffrey M. Jones, "Views of Bush Reach New Heights of Polarization," accessed from the Web site of the Gallup Organization at http://www.gallup.com/, October 21, 2004; and Jacobson, *A Divider, Not a Uniter,* 4.

25. James E. Campbell, "The 2000 Presidential Election of George W. Bush: The Difficult Birth of a Presidency," in *Transformed by Crisis: The Presidency of George W. Bush and American Politics*, ed. Jon Kraus, Kevin J. McMahon, and David Rankin (New York: Palgrave MacMillan, 2004), 9–28.

26. Wilson Carey McWilliams, "The Meaning of the Election: Ownership and Citizenship in American Life," in *The Elections of 2004,* ed. Michael Nelson (Washington, D.C.: CQ Press, 2005), 187.

27. James P. Pfiffner, "Partisan Polarization, Politics, and the Presidency: Structural Sources of Conflict," in *Rivals for Power,* 3rd ed., ed. James A. Thurber (Lanham, Md.: Rowman and Littlefield, 2006), 33.

28. Morris Fiorina chalks up President Bush's 2000 victory, despite forecasting models that predicted that Al Gore would win at least 52.8 percent of the two-party vote, to the moderation of Bush's appeal in that election. Efforts to claim some middle ground in policy territory often ceded to Democrats may have helped President Bush a bit in 2000. However, despite his centrist appeals, he received only 38 percent of the moderate vote. Whatever appeal his centrist message had apparently did not sway many moderates his way. A more important reason for Al Gore's receiving a smaller vote than predicted in 2000 was Gore's decision to emphasize the values divide over performance appraisals. See James E. Campbell, "The Curious and Close Presidential Campaign of 2000," in *America's Choice 2000,* ed. William Crotty (Boulder: Westview Press, 2001), 115–137.

29. David R. Mayhew, *Divided We Govern,* 2nd ed. (New Haven: Yale University Press, 2005).

CHAPTER 3

Bush's Democratic Ambivalence

Responsiveness and Policy Promotion
in Republican Government

Lawrence R. Jacobs and Robert Y. Shapiro

THE FRAMERS OF THE United States Constitution feared a president who routinely appealed to the mass public. They denigrated leaders who sought out public acclaim and wielded it as a political weapon to aid themselves as dangerous "demagogues."

American political development has defied the warning of the Constitution's Framers, as twentieth-century presidents steadily developed a direct and highly personal connection with the mass public. Presidents use their bond with Americans to augment their power and break out of the stranglehold of constitutional and political constraints. George W. Bush significantly strengthened the president's public face—improving White House processes for controlling and distributing information to bolster the president.

The actual representativeness of the "public presidency" is a critical question. Presidents bill themselves as the voice of "the people" and the nation, who fight off rapacious, narrow interests, but how closely do they actually follow the public's policy preferences?

The Bush presidency poses a complicated and ambiguous legacy with respect to representativeness. The president was responsive to some of the public's wishes, and the spread of democracy was a clarion call for his foreign policy. Indeed, Bush's second inaugural address projected soaring idealism about democracy and the world: "It is the policy of the United States to seek and support the growth of democratic movements and institutions in every nation and culture, with the ultimate goal of ending tyranny in our world."

Bush's democratic proclamations also extended to the domestic front. In his campaigns for election and for his policies he embraced the rhetoric of democracy and the tools of grassroots organization. The Bush team mobilized an army of supportive volunteers and mastered "micro-targeting" to focus grassroots muscle on undecided or "lazy" but supportive voters.[1] The campaign continued after election day. President Bush's team improved White House strategies and tactics for promoting his policies, traveling the country to pressure legislators who resisted his policy proposals.[2]

The sights and sounds of populism coincided with responsiveness to public opinion on certain issues. Although the Bush White House has been portrayed as unrelentingly conservative and ideological, electoral goals—winning elections for the president and other Republicans—motivated the White House to respond to the general public and to older voters, who turn out at high rates. The drive to please centrist voters is most clearly demonstrated by the president's insistence—even in the face of resistance by congressional Republicans—on reversing decades of conservative, small-government orthodoxy to expand Medicare to include a drug benefit and to enlarge the federal government's involvement in secondary education.

Bush's responsiveness to the policy preferences of majorities of Americans on some issues coincided, however, with significant policy decisions that lacked public support or that contradicted public opinion. These gaps in popular representativeness resulted from ideological and policy objectives of President Bush and his supporters and allies. Bush, GOP partisans, contributors, and others on the political right strongly supported policy goals that ranged from lower taxes and conservative social policies to aggressive and unilateral use of U.S. military forces. Conservative policy goals formed the backbone of Bush's electoral and governing coalition. Bush used those goals to rally social conservatives and Republican stalwarts into a core group of supporters who backed his run for the 2000 Republican Party nomination and mostly stood by him after he was inaugurated. To hold those core supporters, Bush supported such policies as restricting federal funds for stem cell research and privatizing Social Security, even though they lacked the support of a majority of Americans.

In short, Bush's first six years in office left an ambiguous legacy of democratic responsiveness. His presidency both responded to broad public opinion and engaged in determined promotion of policy goals that lacked majority support but were intensely supported by Republicans and social conservatives. This duality is one of the defining features of President Bush's domestic legacy. In this chapter we evaluate the balancing of these two elements in Bush's presidency. We examine the mix of electoral and policy goals in terms of the policy decisions of both the president and Congress because of three extraordinary conditions during the Bush presidency: the Republican majorities (or near-majorities) in Congress, the unity in the voting of Republican legislators, and the close programmatic and strategic collaboration between GOP leaders in Congress and the White House.

Specifically we study the relationship between majority opinion and the decisions of Bush and Congress: Were the policy decisions of the president and Congress congruent with majority public opinion, or not? What strategies did they pursue to respond to public opinion or to shirk responsiveness in favor of promoting conservative policy goals? The answers to these questions provide insight into Bush's democratic ambivalence.

The Politics of Democratic Responsiveness

In the textbook accounts of American government, the "voice of the people" and the decisions of government merge, especially on salient issues that enjoy strong and sustained public support.

Three electoral mechanisms have been posited as links between "the people" and "the government." First, candidates and parties running in competitive, two-party elections are expected to converge toward the midpoint of public opinion (or "centrist opinion") to secure a majority of voters.[3] In current American politics, each political party can count on about a third of the electorate as loyal supporters; the challenge is to win over the middle third or so, who are "undecided." The battle for centrist opinion motivates candidates and parties to converge toward the midpoint of public opinion.

Second, elected government officials committed to a successful career in politics are expected to anticipate the reactions of voters in the next election and adjust their current positions to reflect strong and consistent public sentiments. In other words, officeholders respond to public opinion to avoid future punishment. Giving government officials a reason to "run scared" is healthy for democratic responsiveness.

The third mechanism—direct accountability—is the removal at election time of officials who are unresponsive to the public's strong views. There are many barriers to voters' casting their ballots based on policy issues, including incomplete or inaccurate information about the candidates' positions; concerns about economic conditions and threats to national security at home that fuel retrospective voting based on performance; and the guiding force of party identification. Nonetheless, highly salient policy choices moving forward, that rivet national attention and preoccupy campaigns, can influence voters. For instance, strong public opposition to the Iraq war led voters—especially independents—to vote against Republican incumbents and in favor of Democratic congressional candidates in the 2006 elections.

A distinguished body of research has found a strong (though not uniform) relationship between public opinion and policy. After World War II, a critical set of research studies by a diverse group of scholars, who became known as "the pluralists," reported that government policymaking was generally open and responsive. A series of case studies on the electoral process and on the interaction of organized pressure groups found that most Americans and interests were able to express their preferences and that strongly held views generally influenced government policy.[4]

Early quantitative research on the views of Americans and their congressional representatives confirmed a notable (though far from complete) correlation of opinion and policy.[5] The relations between the votes of members of Congress and the preferences of each legislator's constituents were especially strong on salient issues and on social policies. Later, careful comparisons of changes in public opinion and changes in public policy discovered a consistent and noteworthy relationship.[6] A more sophisticated study of the connection between broad liberal and conservative trends in public opinion and government decision making found a very strong connection, including evidence regarding the relative efficacy of electoral mechanisms and different policymaking institutions.[7]

Research studies that find a high correlation of public opinion and government policy find some support in the behavior of the Bush White House. Especially in its first term, future electoral considerations were evident in the Bush presidency's drive to expand Medicare to include a drug benefit. According to a leading Republican strategist, the White House calculated that passing the Medicare drug benefit (and the No Child Left Behind education reform) would be "another core Democratic issue that will be in the Bush column come Election Day."[8] A Republican pollster projected that "having a Republican president deliver on the largest expansion of Medicare in two generations is an enormous advantage going into the 2004 election."[9] The White House focus on appealing to the centrist voter was shared by Republican legislators (especially those vulnerable in reelection races). In addition to appealing to general public opinion, the White House and GOP allies believed that the Medicare drug benefit would be a "historic" moment in "show[ing that] our party understands the needs and concerns of seniors and is responding to them."[10] Aides to the Republican congressional leadership similarly concluded that it "will give us credibility with seniors."[11]

Although the Bush White House and congressional Republicans rarely disagreed in public, electoral concerns did occasionally split them. One visible case was Congress's passage in 2006 of legislation to allow (limited) federal research on the medical use of stem cells over the opposition of social conservatives and President Bush, who vetoed the bill. "As elections get closer," a political commentator observed, "Republicans in close districts will have to vote against the president's policies when their constituents are strongly opposed."[12]

Policy Crusades and Strategic Populism

The textbook assumption that the voice of the people and American government policy converge is wrong, however, when it comes to a significant and perhaps growing number of government decisions. The political system's incentive structure has fundamentally changed in ways that have recalibrated the balance of electoral and policy goals. Whereas many previous officeholders primarily focused on electoral objectives, they now perceive strong benefits from pursuing (with little compromise) programmatic policy goals and using various political tactics to avoid electoral punishment.

The immediate and seemingly certain political benefits of policy pursuits have resulted from a series of structural changes in the American political system over the past three decades. Following reforms in the early 1970s of the way both the Democratic and Republican Parties select their presidential nominees, power shifted from party leaders, who were principally concerned with electoral goals (winning elections), to activists within the parties who were driven by philosophical commitments and support for single issues. For presidents and members of Congress, party activists are the first hurdle to building a winning electoral and governing coalition and winning their party's nomination. They also play a critical role in recruiting candidates who share their policy goals and are driven by philosophy rather than pragmatism. Policy-driven campaign contributors have become more important to each party, as have interest groups with intense and narrow agendas, which have proliferated in Washington.

Moreover, political leaders now have much greater capacity and confidence to engage in "strategic populism"—the use of new technology to appeal to the mass public and to attempt to change the minds of Americans who oppose, or are undecided regarding, the leadership's policy goals. After settling on their desired policy, political leaders turn to sophisticated public opinion research to "craft" the presentation of their policy decisions in words, symbols, and arguments that will resonate with Americans and *appear* popular. Strategic populism does not tailor policies to the public's actual preferences but rather seeks to change public opinion. The advance of public opinion research and the potential it appears to offer to move public thinking in the period between elections have boosted the confidence of party leaders, and especially the White House, that they can both pursue their policy goals and prevail in elections.[13] The result is that political leaders focus on the benefits from championing their policy goals and discount the potential electoral costs.

Devotion to conservative policy goals is a theme of the Bush presidency. Following the 2000 election, the president's chief political adviser, Karl Rove, concluded that the Republican campaign had "failed to marshal support of the base as well as we should have." Rove precisely identified the shortfall: four million white evangelicals, who are among the GOP's strongest supporters, did not turn out to vote. This gap in voting was "bad for conservatives [and] bad for Republicans." With Bush in the White House, Rove promised that the administration and Republicans would "spend a lot of time and energy on [rallying these conservative voters]" by concentrating on social issues and taking other steps.[14] The pursuit of conservative policy goals was expected, then, to activate and turn out conservative voters on behalf of Republican candidates in midterm elections and in the president's reelection campaign.

Republican Government: President Bush's Coordination with the GOP Congress

President Bush, in close collaboration with Republican congressional leaders, pursued a mix of policies that were supported by his conservative base and ones that were favored by the general public and critical voting blocs such as seniors. Cases such as the stem cell legislation that split the White House and Congress were rare during President Bush's first six years in office, as congressional Republicans were consistently strong supporters of the president. *CQ Weekly's* analyses of the percentage of wins for the president in roll call votes on which he took a clear position show that Bush won from 78 percent to 88 percent of the time. Only the Kennedy and Johnson administrations enjoyed similarly consistent success.

The strong and consistent agreement of the White House and Congress approached the kind of coordinated "Republican Government" that James Madison's system of separation of powers was supposed to have precluded. In parliamentary systems, the executive and legislative branches are fused because they share institutional interests: legislative revolt against the policy program of the prime minister and cabinet can lead to the collapse of the government and early elections. Beginning in 2001, Republican Government was based on shared policy interests. Describing the close relations between the White House and congressional Republicans, the Speaker's press secretary explained that it resulted from being "philosophically . . . very close." According to a GOP congressional leader, "Most of the time there's no need to have a fight" because of the "similarities of the policy approaches on Capitol Hill and in the White House."[15]

The White House and congressional leaders carefully controlled the legislative agenda to focus on proposals that they both supported. "We are not going to play unless we play to win," explained the spokesman for House Speaker Dennis Hastert.[16] Part of the shared concern was to minimize the exposure of members to politically dangerous votes that lacked strong public support. As one GOP Senate aide explained, GOP leaders did not "desire to expose members . . . to some controversial and contentious votes."[17]

The White House closely coordinated the president's policy proposals. One effect was that Bush was remarkably restrained in how many and which proposals he championed. The Bush White House, *CQ Weekly* discovered, issued far fewer "statements of administration policy" that signaled Bush's positions to the GOP-dominated Congress than did his predecessor, Bill Clinton.[18]

To achieve both policy and electoral goals, the White House and congressional Republican leaders worked closely to pursue four tactics in the legislative process. First, they coordinated their "talking points" to publicly project a similar message, which was crafted to resonate with Americans even as they pursued policies that the public might not favor. For instance, majorities of Americans supported restricting "frivolous" class action lawsuits, though the public has also long favored steps to deter harmful actions by businesses. Congress and President Bush enacted legislation to restrict class action lawsuits, even though legal liability does serve to focus business on consumer safety.

Second, congressional leaders used huge "omnibus" bills to push through policies that the White House and conservatives supported. The effect was to bury policy decisions that were not popular with the public and obscure the responsibility of Republican members for those decisions. This strategy by congressional leaders was supported and facilitated by the White House.

In 2003 and 2004, for instance, separate bills to reduce social services put Republicans from moderate districts at odds with the views of many of their constituents. They bolted the party to side with Democrats on key appropriation bills and undermined GOP congressional leaders and the White House. The leadership reversed those defeats in a year-end omnibus spending bill. "The omnibus appropriations bill," *CQ Weekly* explained, "has become the GOP leadership's tool of choice: . . . By wrapping popular spending into one 'must-pass' package, leaders force rank-and-file members to accept provisions that they might otherwise oppose."[19] A *New York Times* editorial criticized omnibus bills for their political purpose—the "full contents and damages will not be known for weeks, even by the lawmakers who vote for approval. . . . [T]he real political goal," the *Times* observed, is to push through "an incongruous mix of resurrected controversies, hometown pork and hot-button proposals."[20] Omnibus legislation, a 2003 *Washington Post* op-ed reasoned, allows members to "make unpopular legal changes behind closed doors" that would "never make it through the ordinary lawmaking process."[21] Longtime Washington watcher Norman Ornstein observed that "leaders [can] get their way without scrutiny or challenge" by "folding legislation into a small number of huge omnibus bills, bringing them up with little notice and less debate, structuring the votes around restrictive rules that limit or forbid amendments, and demanding party fealty on the votes that take place by labeling them 'procedural.'"[22]

When legislation could not be collapsed into an omnibus bill, GOP leaders could make their decisions appear ambiguous. Phrasing of bills that obscured their meaning, the use of procedural votes to decide substantive issues indirectly, and other tactics helped to blur the link between a member's vote and a potentially unpopular policy decision.

Third, the White House and congressional Republicans appeared to "play-act" through coordinated actions that counteracted each other and allowed Republicans both to be responsive to the general public and to cater to their social conservative base. For instance, the GOP used its control of the lawmaking branches to respond to majority public opinion, through congressional approval of (limited) federal research into the use of embryonic stem cells in medical treatment, and also to accommodate the intense demands of their base, through Bush's veto. Put simply,

Republicans capitalized on America's separation of powers to have it both ways politically.

The fourth strategy was to seize on nonsalient issues to pursue policy goals. On matters on which there was little or no visible, high-level debate and public polling, the White House and GOP leaders enjoyed wide discretion to act without a pressing threat of punishment. Although students of American politics are frustrated by the lack of publicly available polling data, it is not a problem for politicians; indeed, it creates an opportunity.

Republican Government and Public Opinion

The Key Votes of Republican Government and Popular Representation

We investigated the extent and nature of the connection between Republican Government and public opinion by comparing polling data with congressional action on key legislative and presidential initiatives. To track legislative activity, we used the Congressional Quarterly annual listings of key votes in Congress. These are votes on presidential priorities and controversial bills that could have a great impact on the country.[23] We studied key votes from 2001 to 2006, a period of Republican control of the White House, the House, and part of the time, the Senate. (After the Republicans gained a 50–50 tie in the Senate in the 2000 elections—which Vice President Richard Cheney broke in the GOP's favor—GOP senator Jim Jeffords, Vt., left the Republican Party to become an independent. That gave the Democrats a majority, but they were forced to work closely with the Republicans given their narrow hold on the majority and the GOP's control of the House and the White House. The GOP took a majority in the 2004 elections.)

We tracked public opinion using responses to survey questions that were specifically on the subject of each key vote or were related to the general policy issue of the key vote.[24] We examined CQ's key votes and majority opinion to investigate directly our core question: How often have the policies of Republican Government agreed, and how often have they disagreed, with public opinion? We incorporated the observations of officials from Congress and the Bush administration to help explain their motivations for facilitating or thwarting opinion-policy congruence.

Our analysis is divided into two sections. The first measures whether a key vote was *congruent* or *not congruent* with public opinion on the specific vote or on the policy. The limitation of this approach is that it does not consider policies that the public strongly supported but that were not placed on the policy agenda by Republican leaders. On the other hand, the approach has the advantage of providing a direct and readily measurable count of individual cases of presidential and legislative agreement or disagreement with what most Americans prefer. The alternative strategy of collecting polling data and then searching for whether and how policy changed would be useful, but it faces a host of challenges—the arduous task of unpacking and separating all the elements of omnibus legislation, the need to sample from many thousands of questions found in the available survey data—and it rests on a heroic assumption that government has the capacity to handle over a short period of time a large rush of policy proposals in a system with multiple veto points.

The second section examines key votes on which the policy choices or the nature of public opinion were not clear. We consider three possible reasons for the lack of clarity: (1) The public may not have formed views because the legislation and policy were not salient—a situation characterized by an absence of publicly available public opinion data. Because the public's attitudes are neither particularly intense nor well formed on nonsalient issues, they are "permissive," which is to say, they grant the White House and members of Congress significant discretion and latitude to pursue policy goals.

The other two explanations for finding no clear relationship between a key vote and public opinion stem from legislative strategy to obscure clear, traceable, cause-and-effect impacts of legislative decisions.[25] (2) GOP leaders tried to obscure legislative actions by relying on procedural votes and on long and complicated legislative steps. The effect was to make legislative actions ambiguous to voters, indeed hard to decipher without careful scrutiny—a cognitively taxing process that few voters invest in.

Yet another difficulty is (3) the use of omnibus legislative packages to fold many distinct policies together with the explicit aim of burying controversial or unpopular policies in a conglomerate of many parts. This deliberately diminishes the ability of voters to single out a particular decision and to hold an officeholder accountable for it.

We compare key votes and public opinion survey results from 2001 to 2006 to sort policies into five categories: (1) congruent with public opinion; (2) not congruent with public opinion; (3) no polling data; (4) unclear because the policy is folded into omnibus bills; and (5) too ambiguous to code with respect to public support or opposition. We also draw on journalistic accounts and the accounts of influential participants to understand the intentions and strategies of the White House and Republican congressional leaders.

Responsiveness, Evasiveness, and Obstruction

Although Republican leaders were intent on achieving both policy and electoral goals, the political importance of conservatives to their coalition and the party's attentiveness to them generated criticisms that the White House and GOP legislators were out of touch with the preferences of the majority of Americans. The *St. Louis Dispatch* editorial page proclaimed the president "out of touch" on a range of policies from Hurricane Katrina to the Iraq war and declared that he is not merely "living in a bubble" but is actually "living in a sensory deprivation chamber."[26] Paul Krugman declared in his *New York Times* column that Bush's optimistic economic appraisals were "out of touch" and "disconnect[ed from] . . . the growing squeeze on many working Americans."[27] The *Seattle Times* editorial page concluded that Bush's distance from most voters on such issues as embryonic stem cell research "shows . . . how far he is willing to go to appease religious conservatives and . . . how out of touch he is with the needs and hopes of millions of Americans."[28]

These sweeping conclusions that Bush and congressional Republican leaders had defied what a majority of Americans preferred ignore the strong incentives we have discussed for the GOP leadership to respond to majority opinion. Missed in the black-and-white descriptions of defiance are the policies Republican Government enacted that did respond to public opinion. They also overlook the overall behavior of Republican Government. Again, the president's veto of the stem cell research legislation was incongruent with public opinion, but its passage by Congress aligned with what a majority of Americans preferred.

The reality may be more mixed than either the caricature of an all-responsive government (as the textbook model suggests) or a government that caters only to social conservatives and party activists (as charged by critics of Bush and Republican Government). The question is how to decipher the mix of responsiveness and unresponsiveness to majority public opinion. Moreover, if Republican Government is able to pursue policy goals that are disconnected from public opinion, it is important to understand how it attempts to truncate or circumvent the threat of electoral punishment. As Republican setbacks in the 2006 elections suggest, the electoral check on unresponsiveness can be potent.

Congruence is more prevalent than noncongruence. The presumption of Bush critics that Republican Government was fully disconnected from public opinion appears mistaken according to our evidence. Table 3.1 shows that Republican Government was far more congruent with public opinion on key votes than not. There were 74 congruent cases and only 19 that were not congruent. In 80 percent of the cases in which public opinion data were available, Republican Government policies were congruent. This suggests responsiveness to what Americans prefer and

TABLE 3.1   Key Votes and Public Opinion, 2001–2006

	2001	*2002*	*2003*	*2004*	*2005*	*2006*	*Total*
Congruent	15	12	9	10	12	16	74 (80%)
Not congruent	3	1	2	3	4	6	19 (20%)

Source: Compiled by the authors using Congressional Quarterly's annual key votes analyses and data from the iPOLL data archive of the Roper Center for Public Opinion Research.

undermines the sweeping conclusions of Bush's critics who equate his "base strategy" with general unresponsiveness.

The 2003 expansion of Medicare to cover prescription drugs and the tax cuts in Bush's first term generally aligned with public opinion. A large portion of the president's and congressional Republicans' measures for fighting the war on terrorism also enjoyed public support. Overall, the scope and number of presidential proposals and congressional votes that are in agreement with public opinion is actually quite significant. Table 3.2 presents a selected list. Although some of the divergences

TABLE 3.2   Selected Presidential Proposals and Congressional Votes That Public Opinion Supports, 2002–2006

- Alito nomination and confirmation
- Enactment and reauthorization of the Patriot Act
- Passage of legislation to overhaul class action lawsuits
- Passage of bills to increase spending on defense and to fund wars in Afghanistan and Iraq
- Roberts nomination and confirmation
- Passage of reductions in family and corporate taxes
- Passage of legislation to protect the fetus
- Passage of bills to fund highway and other transportation projects
- Passage of legislation to overhaul U.S. intelligence
- Authorization to launch Iraq war
- Passage of authorizations for war in Iraq
- Passage of legislation to establish "Do Not Call" Registry
- Passage in the House of legislation to reauthorize Head Start
- Passage in the Senate of legislation to reverse the Federal Communications Commission decision to allow businesses to own a greater proportion of local media markets
- Passage of "partial birth" abortion ban
- Passage of Medicare reform including new prescription drug benefit
- Passage of legislation to overhaul accounting industry and strengthen corporate governance
- Passage of legislation to overhaul campaign finance system (McCain-Feingold)
- Passage of Help Americans Vote Act of 2002
- Passage of bill to aid farmers
- Establishment of Homeland Security Department
- Passage of authorization for the president to use force to fight terrorism after 9/11 attacks
- Ashcroft nomination and confirmation
- Passage of legislation to allow expedited congressional vote on trade agreements

Source: Compiled by the authors using Congressional Quarterly's annual key votes analyses and data from the iPOLL data archive of the Roper Center for Public Opinion Research.

from public opinion are quite visible, on balance President Bush and congressional Republicans enacted a number of publicly supported bills.

The public support for the policies of Republican Government may surprise or disappoint some critics. But the reality is that most Americans are conservative on some social and civil liberties issues, especially after the September 11, 2001, terrorist attacks. Bush and the Republican Congress focused on policies for which they had, or could get, public support. The public did not favor partial-birth abortions, for example, and there is a long tradition of Americans' deferring to the government to conduct intelligence and other activities to protect them. There are some cases—such as the overhaul of class action lawsuits—that have been successfully framed by Republicans and their allies to win public support, even though Americans might have more mixed reactions to the effects of the policy change (e.g., reduced incentives for businesses to protect consumers).

Even though Republican leaders of the executive and legislative branches were, in general, jointly responsive to public opinion, there were some divisions. For instance, the House and Senate sided with public opinion in passing bans on torture, despite opposition from the White House and especially Vice President Cheney.

Some divisions and legislative rules, however, allowed Republicans to address both their policy and electoral goals. Congressional passage of legislation allowing stem cell research responded to public opinion, while Bush's veto followed the views of GOP activists. The push of congressional Republicans and the White House for a ban on same-sex marriage pleased the intense views of social conservatives; the failure to overcome a filibuster in the Senate was consistent with public opinion. Even though the outcome fit with majority opinion, the high-profile defeat on gay marriage (and other social issues), *CQ Weekly* observed, "ended up turning into political victories in the eyes of some conservatives . . . [and] allowing Bush to energize social conservatives upset by court rulings in favor of gay marriage."[29]

There were also striking cases of noncongruence. The gap between Republican Government activity and public opinion was evident on trade, for instance. Bush proposed and Congress passed the Central America Free Trade Agreement in 2005, even though a majority of Americans did not support it at a time of rising anxiety over globalization and the threat of free trade to employment.

Dodging public scrutiny. Republican Government's responsiveness to public opinion is, however, a good deal more complicated than measuring congruence and noncongruence alone. Although there were far more cases of congruence than noncongruence, there were also a number of instances in which policy action and public opinion were not clear. These cases deserve attention because they may reveal instances where Republican leaders evaded public scrutiny or may have been unresponsive to majority opinion (we refer to these as "permissive cases").

Two themes emerge from the additional data in Table 3.3. First, when one adds the cases in which neither policy content nor public opinion is clear, the number

TABLE 3.3   Cases When Key Votes and Public Opinion Are Not Congruent, 2001–2006

	2001	2002	2003	2004	2005	2006	Total
Congruent	15	12	9	10	12	16	74 (56%)
Unclear and not congruent[a]	6	7	13	9	12	12	59 (44%)

Source: Compiled by the authors using Congressional Quarterly's annual key votes analyses and data from the iPOLL data archive of the Roper Center for Public Opinion Research.

[a]Includes key votes where there are no public opinion data and the content of legislative bills is unclear.

of Republican Government policies that were congruent with public opinion is not as great as it initially seemed. In comparison to the 74 congruent cases, 59 policies were noncongruent or unclear. Put another way, congruent cases were still a majority of Republican Government policies, but the proportion fell from fully 80 percent to a not-overwhelming 56 percent.

The second theme is that there appears to be a shift away from congruence. From 2001 to 2006, Republican Government policies change from being largely congruent with public opinion to more evenly split, especially after 2002. After Bush's first two years in office, there are similar numbers of cases that are congruent and cases that we classify as permissive, 47 versus 46.

The prevalence of noncongruent and permissive policies from 2003 to 2006 fits with a major political change in Congress that reduced the electoral constraint on Republican leaders. In 2001, after Jeffords's departure from the GOP gave the Democrats a majority, Congress acted in mostly congruent ways—fifteen legislative actions were congruent and only three stood against public opinion. Even when we look at the cases more broadly, congruence remained dominant: Compared to the fifteen cases of opinion-policy agreement, legislative actions that were not congruent or were unclear in terms of policy content and public opinion totaled six. But starting in 2003, when the Republicans regained a majority in both chambers, the number of congruent legislative actions was close to the number of actions that were either contrary to public opinion or about which there was not clear evidence to judge public attitudes. From 2003 through 2006 when the Republicans enjoyed majorities in the House and Senate, there was a notable increase in legislative actions that were neither congruent nor clear with respect to policy content and public opinion.

A critical question, then, is what explains the vagueness and its connection to the strategy of the White House and congressional GOP leaders. Is this a coincidence?

TABLE 3.4   Reasons That Public Opinion or Policy Content Were Not Clear on Key
Votes, 2001–2006

	2001	2002	2003	2004	2005	2006
No polling data	1	5	7	6	8	6
Ambiguous	2		1			
Omnibus legislation		1	3			
Total unclear and not congruent cases	3	6	11	6	8	6

Source: Compiled by the authors using Congressional Quarterly's annual key votes analyses and data from the iPOLL data archive of the Roper Center for Public Opinion Research.

Or could it reflect strategic decisions by Republican Government leaders to diminish the risks of electoral punishment as they pursued their policy goals?

Table 3.4 identifies three reasons for permissive cases. First, legislative leaders used omnibus bills to bury controversial items on which Americans were divided or which they opposed. As we suggested earlier, officials in Congress and associated with the White House used omnibus bills to pressure members to approve unpopular policies that were favored by the GOP base. (The apparent peaking of omnibus bills is an artifact of our coding: omnibus bills from other years were coded under different categories, such as the lack of polling data.)

Second, the content of some policies that Republican leaders promoted was ambiguous. This category could also have been expanded; our count of ambiguous legislation was artificially depressed, in part, because the cases were sometimes coded as lacking polling data. News reports suggested—as we indicated above—that Republican leaders structured votes to avoid clear up and down votes on controversial policies.

Third, a prominent and growing element of Republican leaders' key votes is that they occurred on nonsalient issues. For most years from 2001 to 2006, about a fifth to a third of key votes lacked polling data (meaning that the issues were not sufficiently salient to have been included in publicly available national polls). Lack of polling data is a strong indicator that Americans are not attentive to an issue. The White House and GOP congressional leaders thus enjoyed substantial latitude on these issues to pursue policy goals for social conservatives and other core Republican supporters. Table 3.5 shows a selected list of key votes of this kind that range widely from issues of intense concern to social conservatives to matters of great interest to the GOP's business allies.

Some policies that were difficult for the general public to follow were of intense interest to social conservatives. For instance, the GOP's religious supporters enthusiastically supported socially conservative judges such as Miguel Estrada, whom Bush nominated to the U.S. Court of Appeals for the District of Columbia.

TABLE 3.5   Selected Presidential Proposals and Congressional Votes on Which the Policy Content and Public Opinion Were Not Clear, 2001–2006

- Passage of legislation that made it more difficult to declare bankruptcy
- Passage of legislation to overhaul corporate taxes, resulting in an overall reduction and more business-friendly rules on overtime
- Passage of energy legislation that, in part, lowered taxes for energy companies
- Passage of reauthorization of Voting Rights Act that, in part, excluded bilingual voting assistance
- Promotion of Estrada nomination, which was ultimately blocked by filibuster
- Passage of forest management legislation that opened more land to logging
- Passage of legislation to insure businesses against terrorist attacks
- Passage of legislation that disapproved the Ergonomics Rule, which had been opposed by business

Source: Compiled by the authors using Congressional Quarterly's annual key votes analyses and data from the iPOLL data archive of the Roper Center for Public Opinion Research.

Although the general public was apparently not familiar with Estrada, Bush's promotion of him energized social conservatives (and perhaps Latinos). Other Republican Government policies that eluded public notice and were too convoluted to follow intelligently were fervently supported by the GOP's business allies. To take but one example, Bush and congressional Republicans persistently pressed for legislation that made declaring bankruptcy harder for individuals. After Democrats had blocked it, the GOP capitalized on Bush's reelection and the wider congressional majorities to enact it in 2005.

On these policies, Republican Government moved in a "twilight zone" of democratic representation. We cannot say that the public opposed them and that therefore Republican Government fails a strong test of democratic responsiveness. But Americans also did not evidently have clear and strong views in favor of them. The political result is that Republican leaders enjoyed wide latitude to pursue policy goals that they and their supporters favored.

Omnibus legislation, ambiguous policy content, and the pursuit of policies unfamiliar to ordinary Americans offer strategic opportunities for leaders seeking the political benefits of particular policy goals and looking to diminish the risks of electoral punishment. Journalistic accounts consistently explained these ploys as means for dodging damaging criticism that would resonate with the public.

Bush's Democratic Ambivalence

Although President Bush aggressively promoted democracy abroad, he was an ambivalent practitioner at home in terms of responding to public opinion when making policy with his Republican allies in Congress. The attacks on Bush as out of touch with Americans and unresponsive to public opinion are too sweeping. At least half of the key votes in Congress (many of which the president promoted) were congruent with majority opinion.

The president and GOP congressional leaders did, however, defy public opinion or pursue policies that were unclear or lacked detectable public support in many cases. The overall effect was to allow them to diminish the risk of electoral punishment while pursuing conservative policy goals that they and their backers supported.

The ultimate checks on political leaders who shirk democratic responsiveness are competitive elections. The 2006 elections punished Republicans, who lost their majorities in Congress. Many Republicans lost, however, because of the public backlash against the extraordinarily salient and unpopular war in Iraq. Without the war, Republicans would almost certainly have held their Senate majority and might have sustained their control over the House. The sobering reality is that the strategies Republicans (and Democrats) have developed for diminishing electoral punishment as they pursue policy goals may now be so effective that it requires a generational firestorm to unseat them.

Notes

We would like to acknowledge the superb research assistance of Melanie Burns and James Kim. We are also grateful for the research setting and assistance provided to Shapiro as a 2006–2007 visiting scholar at the Russell Sage Foundation. The public opinion data used in our research were obtained from the iPOLL database of the Roper Center for Public Opinion Research. All responsibility for analysis and interpretation is the authors'.

1. Tom Hamburger and Peter Wallsten, *One Party Country: The Republican Plan for Dominance in the Twenty-first Century* (New York: Wiley, 2006).
2. George C. Edwards III, *Governing by Campaigning* (New York: Pearson and Longman, 2007).
3. Anthony Downs, *An Economic Theory of Democracy* (New York: Harper and Row, 1957).
4. Robert Dahl, *A Preface to Democratic Theory* (Chicago: University of Chicago Press, 1956); Charles Lindblom, "The Science of Muddling Through," *Public Administration Review* 19 (1959): 79–88; David Truman, *The Governmental Process* (New York: Knopf, 1951).
5. Warren E. Miller and Donald E. Stokes, "Constituency Influence in Congress" *American Political Science Review* 57 (March 1963): 45–56.
6. Benjamin I. Page and Robert Y. Shapiro, "Effects of Public Opinion on Policy," *American Political Science Review* 77 (March 1983): 175–190.
7. Robert S. Erikson, Michael B. MacKuen, and James A. Stimson, *The Macro Polity* (Cambridge: Cambridge University Press, 2002).
8. David Broder and Ceci Connolly, "Bush Poised to Claim Victory; but Bill's Effects Are Hard to Gauge," *Washington Post,* November 25, 2003, A4.

9. Elisabeth Bumiller, "A Final Push in Congress," *New York Times,* November 23, 2003.

10. Broder and Connolly, "Bush Poised to Claim Victory."

11. Mike Allen, "Bid to Change Social Security Is Back," *Washington Post,* November 21, 2003.

12. Isaiah Poole, "Presidential Support: Two Steps Up, One Step Down," *CQ Weekly,* January 9, 2006, 80.

13. Lawrence R. Jacobs and Robert Y. Shapiro, *Politicians Don't Pander: Political Manipulation and the Loss of Democratic Responsiveness* (Chicago: University of Chicago Press, 2000).

14. Richard Berke, "Aide Says Bush Will Do More to Marshal Religious Base," *New York Times,* December 11, 2001, A22.

15. Joseph Schatz, "Presidential Support Vote Study: With a Deft and Light Touch, Bush Finds Ways to Win," *CQ Weekly,* December 11, 2004, 2900.

16. Poole, "Presidential Support."

17. Schatz, "Presidential Support Vote Study."

18. Poole, "Presidential Support."

19. Schatz, "Presidential Support Vote Study."

20. *New York Times,* "The Incredible Bloated Money Bill," editorial, November 21, 2003, 30.

21. Anne Applebaum, "No Bottom to This Barrel," *Washington Post,* February 12, 2003, A29.

22. Norman Ornstein, "Part-Time Congress," *Washington Post,* March 7, 2006, A17.

23. Our count of "key votes" is lower than CQ's total for several reasons related to our effort to compare them with public opinion. On key votes where the House and Senate took separate actions, we merged them and treated them as one case. For instance, the separate House and Senate handling of tax legislation was coded as one case. This minimized situations where procedural votes and various floor votes inflated the *N*.

24. These data were obtained from the iPOLL database of the Roper Center for Public Opinion Research through keyword searches matching the contents of the legislation with the available survey data during the year of the legislation and the prior year. Using a method similar to Monroe's, we compared majority opinion (excluding "don't know" and "no opinion" responses in the calculation of majority opinion) with the final disposition of the legislation [Alan D. Monroe, "Consistency between Public Preferences and National Policy Decisions," *American Politics Quarterly* 7 (January 1979): 3–19]. We drew on CQ's key votes to study the Bush presidency because they offer a relatively clear, scoreable, and generally reliable proxy for the policy positions of Republican Government. We compared the key votes with opinion to draw inferences about the degree and nature of representativeness regarding majority opinion. Case studies and careful scrutiny of individual cases make it possible to carefully evaluate the Bush presidency's responsiveness.

25. R. Douglas Arnold, *The Logic of Congressional Action* (New Haven: Yale University Press, 1990).

26. *St. Louis Post-Dispatch* (Missouri), "War: What a Bummer," editorial, January 18, 2007, B8.

27. Paul Krugman, "The Big Disconnect," *New York Times,* September 1, 2006, 17.

28. *Seattle Times,* "The Backward Veto," editorial, July 21, 2006, B6.

29. Schatz, "Presidential Support Vote Study."

CHAPTER 4

George W. Bush, Polarization, and the War in Iraq

Gary C. Jacobson

AS A CANDIDATE for president in 2000, George W. Bush aspired to be "a uniter, not a divider." He has instead become the most divisive president in modern history. Although it was by no means the only polarizing action of his administration,[1] Bush's decision to use military force to effect "regime change" in Iraq and its consequences are the primary reasons. From the beginning, the American public's opinions of the war and the president responsible for it have been tightly linked. Bush's standing with the public has been a prisoner of events in Iraq, even as partisan attitudes toward the president have powerfully influenced popular assessments of the war, its rationale, and its consequences. These interactions have contributed to the widest partisan division among ordinary Americans regarding any war or any president since the advent of scientific survey research on such questions more than sixty years ago. In this chapter, I examine these linkages for insights into the evolution of public opinion on the president, the war, and prospects for continued public support for the president and the venture, as the war's costs in lives and money continue to mount with—as of the beginning of Bush's last two years in office—no end yet in sight.

At first, Operation Iraqi Freedom, launched on March 20, 2003, appeared to be a swift and stunning success, politically as well as militarily. The British took Basra on April 7, Baghdad fell to American forces on April 9, and the Kurds took control of Kirkuk on April 11. The most fearsome consequences envisioned before the invasion—burning oil fields, chemical or biological weapons used against U.S. forces, Iraqi attacks on Israel, uprisings in other Middle Eastern countries, terrorist operations in the United States, bloody urban house-to-house combat, thousands of American casualties, massive destruction of Iraqi cities, widespread civilian deaths, millions of refugees—had not materialized. Bush celebrated the victory on May 1 by landing on the aircraft carrier *Abraham Lincoln* in full flight regalia to greet sailors returning from the Middle East. A huge sign reading "Mission Accomplished" served as the backdrop for a speech televised nationally from the carrier's deck, in which Bush declared that "the major combat operations have ended. In the Battle of Iraq, the United States and our allies have prevailed."[2]

The American public generally shared Bush's euphoria and rallied behind both the president and the war. As Figure 4.1 shows, support for the action, measured by a variety of differently worded questions (hence the noisiness of these data),[3] rose sharply after hostilities began. So, too, did approval of the president's job performance (Figure 4.2); only the record-setting rally following Bush's vigorous response to the terrorist attacks on New York and Washington, D.C., of September 11, 2001, gave the president more impressive approval ratings than he received in April 2003.

The euphoria did not last. Although the Battle of Iraq may have been won, the war was not over. Unanticipated troubles appeared immediately, with the complete collapse of law and order, widespread and destructive looting, incidents of summary vengeance, and the beginnings of an insurgency that gradually metastasized into sectarian violence verging on civil war. Secretary of State Colin Powell's "Pottery Barn" analogy—You break it, you own it—became all too apt: The United States found itself engaged in a frustrating effort to build a reasonably democratic regime, that could govern effectively while respecting the rights of its citizens, out

FIGURE 4.1   Popular Support for the Iraq War (All Question Wordings)

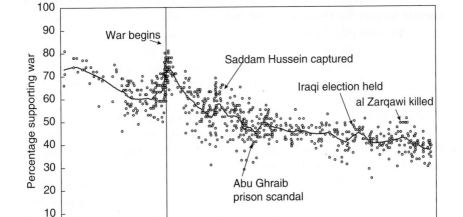

Source: Compiled by the author from 706 national surveys conducted by twenty polling organizations and reported at www.pollingreport.com (various dates). See endnote 3.

FIGURE 4.2   Approval of George W. Bush Job Performance, 2001–2007

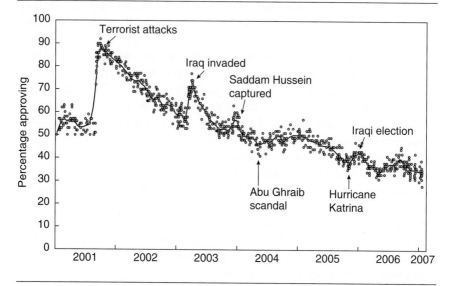

Source: Compiled by the author from 802 national polls by eleven major media polling organizations, reported at www.pollingreport.com.

of the most unpromising tribal, sectarian, and institutional fragments. Over time, popular support for the war eroded, but the decline was irregular, sometimes reversed temporarily by positive developments (Saddam Hussein's capture in December 2003, the transfer of sovereignty to the Iraq government at the end of June 2004, legislative elections in December 2005, and the death of terrorist leader Abu Musab al-Zarqawi in June 2006), sometimes accelerated by bad news—for example, the Abu Ghraib prison scandal.

Although responsive to specific events in Iraq, popular support for the war followed a clear downward trajectory over the forty-seven months from March 2003 through January 2007. John E. Mueller, examining trends in opinion regarding the wars in Korea and Vietnam, had concluded that public support for such engagements declined as a logarithmic function of cumulative casualties: *"Every time American casualties increased by a factor of 10, support for the war dropped by about 15 percentage points."*[4] Mueller detected a similar pattern for the Iraq war, but with a steeper rate of decline.[5] His observation is confirmed by the first equation in Table 4.1, which applies the model that Mueller used for Korea and Vietnam to opinion data on the Iraq war (measuring war support with three questions comparable to those Mueller used for the previous wars).[6] Support for the Iraq war drops with log of cumulative U.S. deaths and at a steeper rate than it did for either the Korean or the Vietnam war.

TABLE 4.1   Casualties, Time, and Support for the War in Iraq

	Coefficient	Standard error	Coefficient	Standard error
Log_{10} of cumulative U.S deaths	−19.51*	.55		
Log_{10} of months since war began			−21.42*	.59
Constant	108.45*	1.66	76.44*	.76
Adjusted R^2	.776		.782	
Number of cases	366		366	

*$p < .001.$

As American casualties have increased by a factor of 10, support has fallen by nearly twenty percentage points. The equation predicts that as total casualties grew, from 65 in March 2003 to 3,112 in December 2006, support for the war would drop from 76 percent to 41 percent; the actual monthly averages went from 73 percent to 39 percent supporting the war over this period.

Although the fit is excellent and the regression coefficient on casualties is estimated very precisely ($t = −35.59$), the second equation in Table 4.1 suggests that some skepticism about direct causality is warranted. When the count of months since the war began is substituted for casualties, the relationship is slightly stronger; as the number of months since the onset of war increases by a factor of 10, support is estimated to fall by nearly twenty-one percentage points. The statistical problem here is that the number of U.S. casualties has been sufficiently consistent from month to month to make the correlation between elapsed time and cumulative deaths nearly perfect ($r = .998$), so the effects of these two variables cannot be distinguished. The data are thus consistent with gradual disillusionment with the war (but at a declining rate over time) for any reason, and additional reasons are not hard to find.

The most obvious alternative explanation for a decline in support for the Iraq war lies in the particulars of the war itself (although as Mueller points out, the same particulars may also explain why the public's tolerance of casualties has been lower for Iraq than for Vietnam or Korea). First, far more clearly than previous conflicts, the Iraq war was discretionary and preventive. The war's proximate provocation was the terrorist attacks of September 11, 2001, but its public justification was preemption rather than retaliation. Although Saddam Hussein was widely suspected of complicity in September 11, proof was lacking. The Bush administration's primary argument for using force to depose Saddam's regime was thus that he was defying the United Nations by producing and hiding weapons of mass destruction (WMD), including possibly nuclear weapons, posing an intolerable and growing threat to the

United States and its allies. The evidence was equivocal, however, and both the need for war and the urgency of taking action remained open to question (the UN Security Council and major European allies, including France and Germany, were not convinced).

Second, the war's original pretexts grew increasingly threadbare over the months following the invasion, as the searches for Iraq's caches of WMD and for evidence of Saddam's links to terrorists targeting the United States continued to come up empty. As the war's central premises were gradually proved faulty and were publicly, if reluctantly and with considerable hedging and backsliding, acknowledged to be so by the war's promoters, including Bush himself, it is unsurprising that public support for the venture declined, especially as lawless chaos and violence, both directed at American troops and among rival Iraqi sects, showed no sign of diminishing. In this context, disillusionment about the cause for which American soldiers were dying, rather than the deaths themselves, would be the primary explanation for declining support for the war.

In an exchange with Mueller, debating the determinants of popular backing for the Iraq war, Christopher Gelpi reiterated his rival thesis that Americans are "defeat-phobic" rather than "casualty-phobic": "Public support for a military operation will erode sharply in the face of mounting casualties when the public believes the war is failing but will remain robust when the public believes the war is succeeding."[7] The rises in support for the war following positive developments are consistent with this claim, although Mueller's model accommodates them as well. But if Gelpi is right, then aggregate support for the war should vary over time with the public's perception of the war's progress; in particular, decline in support for the war should reflect a decline in optimism about its ultimate success. The data in Figure 4.3 cast some doubt on that relationship. Between April 2004 and January 2007, aggregate support for the war measured by the three questions used in Table 4.1 fell about thirteen percentage points, from 52 percent to 39 percent. Yet public confidence in the war's success, variously measured, tended to rise rather than fall until the last quarter of 2006, when it finally showed signs of eroding. Thus trends in popular belief in an ultimate U.S. victory do a poor job of explaining trends in support for the war. Mueller's thesis is also challenged by some of the survey data. Even though it has declined, support for the war has not fallen quite as steeply as, and remains far more widespread than, belief that "there has been an acceptable . . . number of U.S. military casualties in Iraq" (Figure 4.4).[8]

The trends depicted in Figure 4.4 lend credence to Mueller's observation that, "given the evaporation of the main reasons for going to war and the unexpectedly high level of American casualties, support for the war in Iraq is, if anything, higher than one might expect."[9] But if Gelpi's view is correct, then support for the war should not have fallen at all until late fall 2006. Such notable gaps between expectation and observation suggest that the evolution of public attitudes toward the Iraq

FIGURE 4.3   Expectations of U.S. Success in Iraq

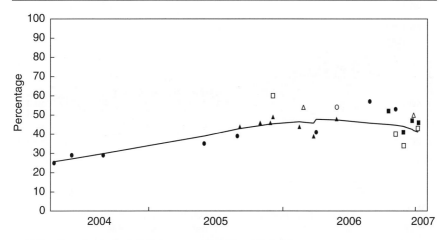

• U.S. will probably or definitely accomplish its goals in Iraq
○ Very/somewhat likely that America's involvement in Iraq will eventually be successful
▲ U.S. will definitely or probably win the war in Iraq
△ U.S. certain or likely to win the war in Iraq
■ U.S. very or somewhat likely to succeed in Iraq
□ U.S. will win in Iraq

Source: Gaullup, ABC News/*Washington Post*, CBS News/*New York Times*, Pew Research Center for the People and the Press, CNN, and NBC/*Wall Street Journal* polls, reported at www.pollingreport.com/iraq.htm (accessed January 23, 2007).

war has been more complex than can be captured by these data alone. Among the sources of complexity, two stand out as worthy of further examination: the extraordinary differences by party in popular reactions to the war, and the crucial distinction between retrospective support for the war—which is what the war support questions actually measure—and support for staying the course in Iraq regardless of whether the war was a good idea in the first place.

Party Differences in Support for the Iraq War

A unique and striking feature of the Iraq war is the degree to which it has divided Americans along party lines. Figure 4.5, which displays the data points and Lowess-smoothed trends in support for the war, disaggregated by party, reveals that partisan assessments of the war have diverged from the beginning. The gap between Republicans and Democrats grows steadily wider leading up to the war and continues to expand afterward, with only a brief narrowing during the first month or

FIGURE 4.4   Acceptance of Casualties and Support for the Iraq War

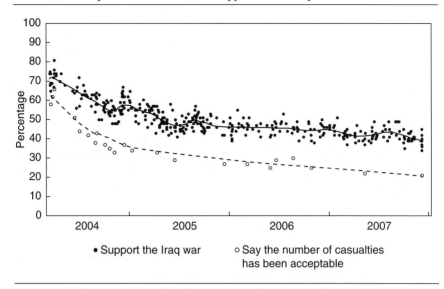

Source: Compiled by the author from ABC News/*Washington Post*, Associated Press/IPSOS, CBS News/*New York Times*, Gallup, *Los Angeles Times*, NBC/*Wall Street Journal*, *Newsweek*, Pew Research Center for the People and the Press, and *Time* polls.

FIGURE 4.5   Party Identification and Support for the Iraq War (All Question Wordings)

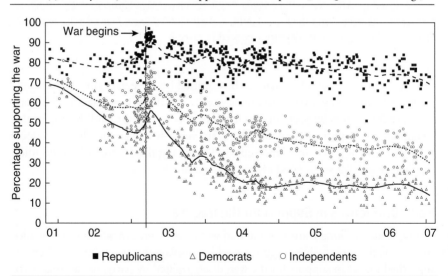

Source: Compiled by the author from ABC News/*Washington Post*, CBS News/*New York Times*, Gallup, *Los Angeles Times*, NBC News/*Wall Street Journal*, *Newsweek*/Pew Research Center for the People and the Press, Quinnipiac, *Time*, and Zogby surveys.

so of the conflict. It levels out to an average of about sixty-two percentage points from July 2004 through the end of 2005 before narrowing to about fifty-six points during 2006.

These data stand in sharp contrast with comparable data from previous engagements in Korea, Vietnam, the Persian Gulf, Kosovo, and Afghanistan. For none of those is the partisan gap anywhere nearly as wide as it is for the Iraq war. Ironically, the divide is narrowest in the most controversial of these engagements, Vietnam, averaging only five percentage points. The Vietnam War certainly divided Americans, but the divisions were much greater within than between the parties, and support for the war declined at about the same pace for partisans in all categories (Figure 4.6). Party differences over involvement in Korea, Kosovo, and Afghanistan averaged eleven to twelve points. George H. W. Bush's Gulf War produced the widest partisan gap in this set, and it is also the only one for which the data suggest increasing divergence over time. Still, the party difference averaged only twenty-one points and peaked at twenty-nine points months after the fighting had concluded.[10] Clearly, partisan differences on the Iraq war are in a class by themselves, three to ten times as large as for any comparable engagement.[11]

A glance at the data in Figure 4.5 makes it clear that the relationship between support for the war and both casualties and time must differ sharply by party, as the equa-

FIGURE 4.6   Partisanship and Trends in Support for the Vietnam War (U.S. Did Not Make a Mistake in Sending Troops to Fight in Vietnam)

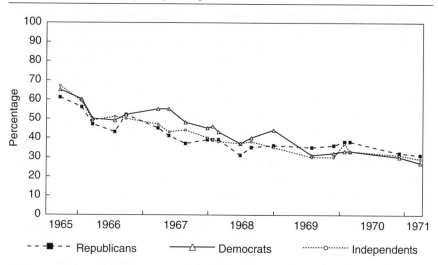

Source: John E. Mueller, *War, Presidents, and Public Opinion* (New York: Wiley, 1973), 271.

TABLE 4.2   Casualties, Time, and Support for the War in Iraq, by Party Identification

	Republicans		Independents		Democrats	
	Coefficient	S.E.	Coefficient	S.E.	Coefficient	S.E.
U.S deaths (Log_{10})	−9.89*	.72	−22.16*	.90	−24.09*	1.03
Constant	110.74*	2.17	113.17*	2.72	98.24*	3.11
Adjusted R^2	.401		.688		.661	
Number of cases	282		278		282	
Months since war began						
(Log_{10})	−10.95*	.79	−24.51*	1.00	−26.97*	1.09
Constant	94.64*	1.01	77.08*	1.29	59.41*	1.40
Adjusted R^2	.407		.683		.686	
Number of cases	282		278		282	

*$p < .001$.

tions in Table 4.2 confirm. Measured in terms of time or casualties, support for the war drops about two-and-one-half times more steeply among Democrats than among Republicans, with independents closer to Democrats in this regard. Moreover, these variables account for much less of the variance in Republicans' support for the war (observe the adjusted R-squares)—there being, of course, much less variance to account for. Note that once again time explains as much of the variance as casualties.

What is the explanation for the uniquely partisan responses to the Iraq war? The most obvious place to look is in the distinctive features of the war itself, and they are, as we shall see, clearly a major part of the story. But they are by no means the whole story; no less important are distinctive features of the Bush presidency, which provoked sharp partisan divisions even before Iraq was invaded. Figure 4.7 displays the trends in Bush's job approval ratings among Democrats, Republicans, and independents from his first inauguration in 2001 through January 2007. Largely, though not entirely, because of his controversial route to the White House through Florida and the Supreme Court, Bush took office with the widest partisan difference in approval recorded for any newly elected president.[12] After September 11, he received the highest ratings from the opposing party (and from independents) of any president ever. The subsequent downward trends in approval among Democrats and independents were reversed temporarily by the rally events already noted, but the overall pattern is one of increasing disaffection, to the point where by 2006 Bush was receiving the lowest ratings from the opposing party's identifiers ever recorded for any president. In a May 2006 Gallup poll, only 4 percent of Democrats said they approved of his performance, a figure seven points lower than Richard Nixon's worst, just before he resigned in disgrace in 1974. No previous president had ever received single-digit ratings from the opposition in

FIGURE 4.7   Approval of George W. Bush Job Performance, 2001–2007, By Party Identification

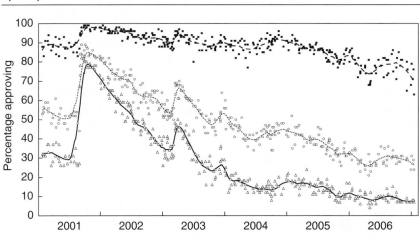

Source: Compiled by the author from 332 CBS News/*New York Times* and Gallup polls.

any Gallup poll. Bush's ratings among Democrats were in single digits in twenty of the thirty-two Gallup surveys taken between January 2006 and January 2007.

Meanwhile, Republicans continued to approve of Bush's performance by overwhelming margins. Indeed, Bush has so far received the highest approval ratings among his own partisans of any president since the question has been asked. Even after its 2006 decline, Bush's average level of approval among Republicans in the Gallup polls taken through January 2007—89.5 percent—exceeds the next-highest, that of Dwight D. Eisenhower (87.6 percent), by a statistically significant margin ($p = .002$). These high ratings combined with the historically low approval ratings given by Democrats produce the most polarized evaluations of a president ever recorded. Before Bush, going back to Eisenhower, the partisan difference in approval ratings had never exceeded 70 percentage points in any Gallup poll and never averaged more than 66 points for any quarter. In the 111 Gallup polls taken between January 2004 and January 2007, the gap exceeded 70 points 78 percent of the time, averaged 73 points, and reached as high as 83 points in a couple of polls taken near the 2004 election.[13] The average partisan difference in approval of Bush during the last quarter of 2004, 79 points, exceeded by 13 points the greatest quarterly difference recorded for the second-most-polarizing president, Bill Clinton.[14]

Notice also that Bush's approval ratings among independents have tended to stay closer to those of Democrats than to those of Republicans; the ratings of

Democrats and independents have also varied together more closely ($r = .94$ for the series, compared to $r = .81$ between independents and Republicans). These differences underline the most consequential revelation in these data: the degree to which ordinary Republicans have continued to support the president despite mounting problems in Iraq (not to mention diverse domestic setbacks such as the handling of Hurricane Katrina, the whiffs of scandal—for example, news stories about convicted lobbyist Jack Abramoff's White House connections—the Dubai Ports affair, spikes in gasoline prices, etc.). Lyndon Johnson's approval ratings among Democrats dropped by twenty-eight points (from an average of 85 percent to 57 percent) between 1965 and 1968 as the Vietnam War dragged on; Harry Truman's dropped by twenty-seven points during his full term as the Korean War took its toll (from an average of 74 percent in 1949 to 47 percent in 1952).[15] In contrast, Bush's support within his own party started higher, has fallen less, and thus remains at a substantially higher level (averaging 76 percent, October 2006 though January 2007) than that of either of those other wartime presidents. Whether Republican support for Bush will remain at this level, decline further, or rebound will depend on reactions to, and more important, the effectiveness of, the president's "new way forward"— 21,500 more troops, tactical changes on the ground, better performance from the Iraq government—announced in January 2007 (I will have more to say about popular reaction to this change in policy at the conclusion of this chapter).

Why did Republicans remain so supportive of Bush and his war for so long, while Democrats (and, to a considerable degree, independents) soured so completely on both? The most parsimonious explanation is that partisan biases have interacted strongly with the peculiarities of the war to produce starkly divergent responses to virtually every question concerning its wisdom, effects, and prospects. The case for the war was built more on rhetoric than on evidence, and the need for immediate action was by no means obvious; since the invasion, the extent of progress and the wider consequences of the war have remained debatable as well. Ambiguity and uncertainty give prior attitudes full sway. Positively disposed toward the president from the start, but especially after September 11, an overwhelming majority of Republicans resolved any doubts they might have had prior to the war in his favor and accepted his word that action was imperative.[16] Democrats were of no mind to resolve ambiguity in Bush's favor—rather the opposite, given their doubts about the legitimacy of his election, opposition to most of his domestic agenda, and annoyance with the administration's political tactics[17]—so their support depended crucially on belief in Saddam's complicity in September 11 and the threat his WMD posed to American lives and interests. Lacking a partisan anchor, independents' support for the war was also quite sensitive to those beliefs.[18]

After Baghdad fell and neither WMD nor an al Qaeda connection could be found, most Republicans either continued to believe they existed (implicitly invoking defense secretary Donald Rumsfeld's maxim that "the absence of evidence is not evidence of absence")[19] or accepted the substitute justifications offered by the administration after the fact, whereas Democrats, and to a lesser degree independents, with no inclination to miss the message or adopt new reasons for backing the war, grew increasingly disillusioned with it. They also increasingly disapproved of a president they came to believe had deliberately misled the nation into the war.

Evidence supporting this explanation can be found in the responses to a wide range of survey questions on aspects of the Iraq war. Figures 4.8 and 4.9 display the divergent partisan responses to questions about the war's main premises—that Saddam possessed WMD and that he was in league with al Qaeda and probably complicit in the attacks of September 11. Although Republicans were more likely than Democrats to believe these allegations from the beginning, differences prior to the war were small by later standards, on the order of ten to fifteen percentage points. Before the war, a large majority Americans, regardless of party, believed that Saddam was hiding WMD, and about half thought he was personally involved in September 11. After the war began, as time passed and the search for WMD and an al Qaeda connection continued to turn up nothing of substance, Democrats abandoned those beliefs to a much greater extent than did Republicans. In February 2003, 79 percent of Democrats thought Saddam possessed WMD; within about fifteen months that figure had fallen to 33 percent, and it has subsequently remained near that level.

FIGURE 4.8   Responses to the Survey Question, Does (Did) Iraq Possess Weapons of Mass Destruction?

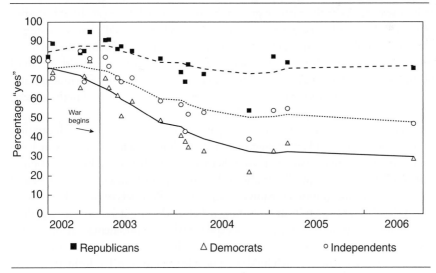

Source: Compiled by the author from CBS News/*New York Times,* ABC News/ *Washington Post, Newsweek,* and Harris polls.

FIGURE 4.9   Responses to the Survey Question, Was Saddam Hussein Personally Involved in September 11?

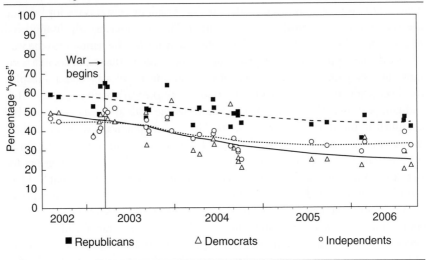

Source: Compiled by the author from CBS News/*New York Times* and Gallup, *Newsweek,* and *Time* polls.

Among Republicans, belief in Saddam's WMD peaked at 95 percent just before the war and did not fall below 69 percent over the next two years. It actually increased a bit thereafter, with the partisan gap on this question stabilizing at about forty-five points.[20] Belief in Saddam's involvement in September 11 also declined less steeply among Republicans than among Democrats or independents. In three national surveys taken around the fifth anniversary of September 11, in 2006, more than a third of the public, including 45 percent of Republicans and 24 percent of Democrats, still said they believed that Saddam Hussein had been personally involved in the attacks, figures virtually unchanged from a year earlier.[21]

The simplest explanation for these patterns is that Americans of all political persuasions tended to have strong prior beliefs about Saddam Hussein's malevolence that led them to assume his complicity in September 11 and his possession of illicit WMD, while Republicans also had a strong prior faith in the president and thus in the administration's version of Iraq realities. Both sets of priors kept subsequent revelations from fully undermining beliefs in the original *casus belli,* and their compound effect among Republicans explains why the president's partisans were especially slow to acknowledge new, discordant information. The classical theory of cognitive dissonance, which holds that people tend to absorb information selectively so as to keep perceptions and cognitions from contradicting firmly held prior beliefs, effectively accounts for these patterns.[22]

The widespread resistance to revelations challenging the administration's case for war also suggests that for many Americans, and certainly most Republicans, support for the war came first and the specifics of the factual case for it were of decidedly secondary importance. If they were forced to recognize that the war's original premises were faulty, they would be willing, as loyal followers of President Bush, to accept the others he proffered. Thus, for example, most Republicans continued to accept the Bush administration's contention that Iraq posed a threat that could not be contained but required immediate action; the proportion taking this view exceeded 80 percent just after the war began and has not fallen below 60 percent since. Forty-six percent of Democrats shared that opinion at the start of the war, but by October 2004, just 12 percent continued to do so. Belief in the need for immediate action also lost ground among independents, falling from over 50 percent to less than 30 percent.[23]

Similarly, most Republicans continued to accept Bush's main fallback rationale for fighting the war in Iraq—that regardless of mistaken assumptions about Saddam's WMD or complicity in September 11, Iraq was central to the war on terrorism—whereas Democrats became increasingly doubtful. Not coincidentally, the war's connection to the terrorist attacks of September 11 became the subject of a pivotal dispute during the 2004 presidential campaign. The Democratic candidate, John Kerry, argued that the Iraq invasion had unwisely taken resources from the pursuit of Osama bin Laden and other al Qaeda terrorists who had actually attacked the United States, as Iraq had not. When Bush reiterated, during their first debate, that "Iraq is central to the war on terror," Kerry came back with "Iraq was not even close to the center of the war on terror before the president invaded it."[24] Figure 4.10 shows that a large, if slowly eroding, majority of Republicans has continued to accept Bush's argument that the Iraq war is part of the war on terrorism, whereas the share of Democrats taking that position had fallen to an average of about 30 percent by the 2004 election and has remained at about that level since.

Finally, Republicans were also far more likely to continue to believe that the Iraq war was helping in the war on terrorism and thereby contributing to the long-term security of the United States (Figure 4.11), while that has become a distinctly minority view among Democrats and independents. Again, ambiguity—who really knows what the war's long-run consequences for terrorism will be?—makes it easy for partisans to go with their biases and has helped the president to maintain at least his own party's backing for the war.

It is now possible to see why support for the war in Iraq is higher, in Mueller's view, than cumulative U.S. casualties seem to warrant. Mueller attributes the discrepancy "to the fact that many people still connect the effort there to the 'war' on terrorism, an enterprise that continues to enjoy huge support."[25] He is right, with the proviso that a large majority of those people are Republicans who accept Bush's repeated assertion that, as he put it in a September 2006 address to the nation, "the

FIGURE 4.10 Responses to the Survey Question, Is the War in Iraq Part of the War on Terrorism?

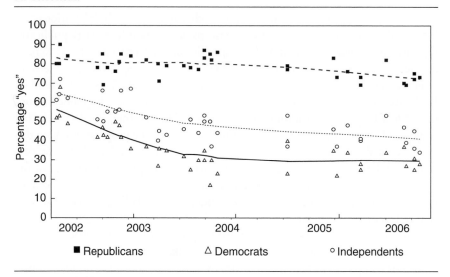

Source: Compiled by the author from CBS News/*New York Times* and Gallup, *Newsweek,* and *Time* polls.

FIGURE 4.11 · Poll Respondents' Views on the Effect of the Iraq War on Terrorism and U.S. Security, by Party

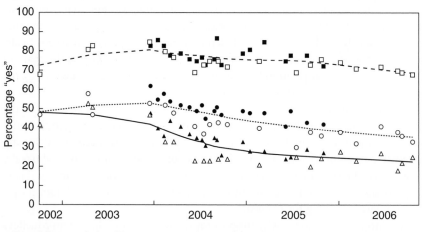

Source: Compiled by the author from ABC News/*Washington Post*, CBS News/*New York Times*, *Time*, and Pew Research Center for the People and the Press polls.

safety of America depends on the outcome of the battle in the streets of Baghdad."[26] The president's partisans have largely stuck with him despite the evaporation of his original case for war and despite the war's violent and expensive aftermath. Nothing comparable happened during the Korean and Vietnam Wars.

Retrospective versus Prospective Support for the War

In this and previous research on the subject, most of the survey questions used to measure the American public's support for wars have been retrospective: Was going to war a mistake? Was it worth the cost? Was it the right thing to do? Most of the data points in Figures 4.1 and 4.4 and all of the numbers used for the analyses in Tables 4.1 and 4.2 are based on questions of this sort. There is, however, another crucial question: Having gone to war, what should the United States do next? The question is particularly acute for the Iraq war. Even if the United States should never have gone into Iraq in the first place, might it not compound the damage to leave before the Iraqis have established a government capable of imposing order and preventing their country from becoming exactly what the war's proponents claimed it had become under Saddam Hussein: a prime staging ground for anti-American Islamic terrorism? The difficulty that Democratic leaders have found in moving beyond criticism of the original decision to articulating an alternative strategy for dealing with its consequences illustrates this quandary.

The quandary has had two important consequences for the president. To his benefit, it has kept the pressure to withdraw troops from rising in step with the public's increasingly negative retrospective assessment of the war. To his cost, it has probably made some Democrats and not a few independents even angrier with him than they would otherwise be, bitter that his misguided decision has left the nation with no option but to stay in Iraq at great cost for fear of compounding the disaster.

Figures 4.12 and 4.13 illustrate the first point. Figure 4.12 displays the distribution of responses to questions regarding whether the United States should stay or leave Iraq and under what circumstances. The questions represented by the black markers (smoothed by the black line) posed the options as staying until the situation has stabilized, or withdrawing troops "as soon as possible" or "immediately." Questions giving the alternatives of withdrawing some or all troops in the near future or doing so on a timetable are represented by the white markers (smoothed by the dashed line). Support for staying is typically higher when the alternative is leaving immediately rather than gradually. By either measure, support for staying has ebbed, but very gradually, and it remains higher than support for having gone to war in the first place.

The difference between retrospective support for having invaded Iraq and support for staying there until the situation has stabilized is especially pronounced for

FIGURE 4.12   Support for Keeping U.S. Troops in Iraq

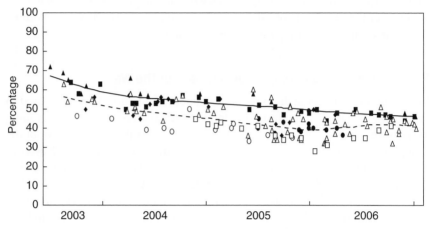

◆ Stay as long as it takes to make Iraq a stable democracy, or withdraw troops as soon as possible

■ Keep U.S. troops in Iraq until situation has stabilized, or bring troops home as soon as possible

▲ Keep troops until civil order restored despite US casualties, or withdraw forces even if civil order not restored

● U.S. should not set timetable for withdrawal

○ Keep troops in Iraq until there is a stable government, or bring most troops home next year

△ Send more troops/same as now or withdraw some/all troops

□ Maintain troop level to secure peace and stability, or reduce number of troops

◇ Stay as long as it takes, or set timetable for withdrawal

Source: Compiled by the author from ABC News/*Washington Post*, CBS News/*New York Times*, Pew Research Center for the People and the Press, IPSOS, Harris, Gallup, CNN, and NBC News/*Wall Street Journal* polls, reported at www.pollingreport.com/iraq.htm (accessed 2005–2007).

Democrats and independents (Figure 4.13). Since the beginning of Bush's second term in January 2005, support for seeing the war through (measured by questions with black markers in Figure 4.12) has, among Democrats, run about twelve points higher than support for having started it in the first place (averaging 32 percent compared to 20 percent). Over the same period, independents were also typically more supportive of staying the course (average 46 percent) than of the initial decision to invade (39 percent). Only Republicans remain more supportive of the war in retrospect (78 percent) than for continuing the effort (73 percent). That many Americans who came to believe the war was a mistake nonetheless continued to oppose a precipitous withdrawal helped to limit the domestic political pressure on Bush to begin withdrawing American troops.

FIGURE 4.13   Support for Keeping U.S. Troops in Iraq, by Party

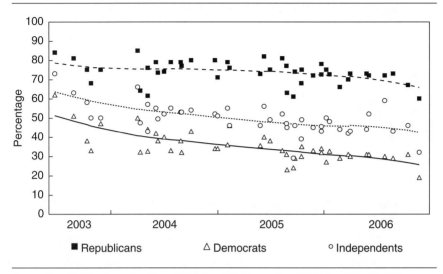

■ Republicans   △ Democrats   ○ Independents

Source: Compiled by the author from ABC News/*Washington Post,* CBS News/*New York Times,* and Pew Research Center for the People and the Press polls.

The War and the President

The difficulty of formulating an alternative to Bush's strategy for coping with the violent aftermath of the Iraq invasion may have helped keep popular support for continuing the U.S. effort from collapsing, but it did not make people who thought the war had been a mistake any more favorable to the president who got us into it. Thus, for example, in the January 2006 Gallup poll Bush's approval rating among those who said the war had been a mistake stood at 9 percent, regardless of whether the respondents preferred to stay the course or set a timetable for withdrawal. Indeed, people who thought the war had been a mistake, but that the country now had little choice but to bear the heavy costs of trying to redeem it, might be especially angry with the person chiefly responsible. Most of those people were of course Democrats, and their animus toward the president was fed by, and probably contributed to, the growing belief that he not only had made the wrong decision in attacking Iraq but had deliberately deceived the country into following his lead (Figure 4.14). At the start of the war about half of Democrats had been skeptical about the administration's candor in making the case for it; by 2006, more than 80 percent had concluded that the administration had misled the public intentionally. A majority of independents have also come to believe that the administration deliberately misled them. Republicans, meanwhile, continue by overwhelming majorities to believe that the administration offered its justifications for the war in good faith.

FIGURE 4.14   Responses to the Survey Question, Did the Bush Administration Intentionally Mislead the Public in Making the Case for the Iraq War?

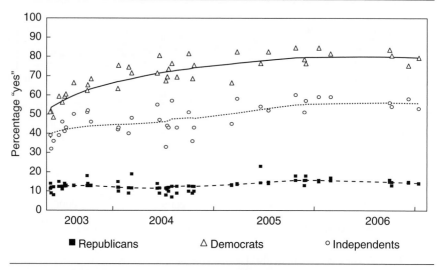

■ Republicans   △ Democrats   ○ Independents

Source: Compiled by the author from ABC News/*Washington Post*, CBS News/*New York Times*, Gallup, *Los Angeles Times*, NBC News/*Wall Street Journal*, *Newsweek*, and *Time* surveys.

In this light, it is no surprise that the Iraq war has become the primary nexus of people's evaluations of the president. A Pew center study found that Bush's handling of Iraq and foreign policy has the highest correlations with his overall approval of any of the twelve issue domains probed.[27] The consistency of people's opinions of the war and of the president's job performance is also higher than it was for the other presidents similarly beset by increasingly unpopular wars (Table 4.3). Evalu-

TABLE 4.3   The Consistency of Opinions on Wars and Presidents

President	Dates	Average	Range	Number of surveys
H. S. Truman	August 1950–August 1951	59.6%	54.4%–64.7%	7
L. B. Johnson	January 1965–October 1967	64.3%	59.2%–68.8%	9
G. W. Bush	March 2003–December 2006	83.2%	74.1%–90.6%	110

Source: Compiled by the author from ABC News/*Washington Post,* CBS News/*New York Times,* Gallup, and Pew Research Center for the People and the Press surveys.

Note: Consistent opinions are those that support the war and approve of the president's job performance, or oppose the war and disapprove of the president's job performance.

FIGURE 4.15 Support for the Iraq War and Approval of George W. Bush's Job Performance

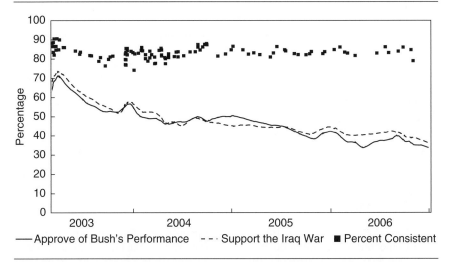

Source: Compiled by the author from ABC News/*Washington Post*, CBS News/*New York Times*, Gallup, *Los Angeles Times*, NBC News/*Wall Street Journal*, *Newsweek*, and *Time* surveys.

ations of Truman and Johnson were related to opinions about the Korean and Vietnam wars, but nowhere near as closely as opinions on Bush and Iraq.[28]

The relationship between approval of George W. Bush's performance and support for the war has remained robust as both have declined over time. Figure 4.15 shows how the Lowess-smoothed trends in approval of Bush and support for the war have moved in concert since the war began and that the relationship between the two has continued to be very strong.[29] These patterns are generally replicated when respondents are separated by party identification, but with an interesting twist indicating that the war is not the only thing that matters to partisans (Figure 4.16). Republicans have, until very recently, been more supportive of the president than the war, but Democrats have consistently been more supportive of the war than of the president.

Losing Faith

By midsummer 2006, a consensus was emerging among senior government officials that the Bush administration's current approach to Iraq was not working. During a July 14, 2006, briefing of congressional staffers on the war, the army chief of staff, General Peter J. Schoomaker, was asked, "Is the U.S. winning?" After reportedly mulling over the question for more than ten seconds he replied, "I think I would answer that by telling you I don't think we're losing," and he went on to say, "I think

FIGURE 4.16   Approval of George W. Bush's Performance and Support for the Iraq War, by Party

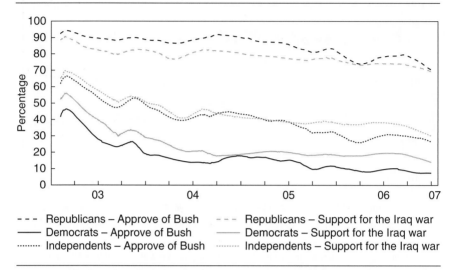

Source: Compiled by the author from ABC News/*Washington Post*, CBS News/*New York Times*, Gallup, *Los Angeles Times*, NBC News/*Wall Street Journal*, *Newsweek*, Pew Research Center for the People and the Press, and *Time* surveys.

that we're closer to the beginning than to the end of all this."[30] Schoomaker's sobering assessment matched the news coming out of Iraq as well as the confidential National Intelligence Estimate's assessment that "insurgents and terrorists retain the resources and capabilities to sustain and even increase current level of violence through the next year [2007]."[31] For political reasons, Bush and other administration officials continued to insist until after the 2006 elections that the United States was winning, but in December both the departing and incoming secretaries of defense, Donald Rumsfeld and Robert Gates, conceded that victory was nowhere in sight.[32]

The growing sense that victory, even if possible, was not on the horizon, was shared by the public. During 2006 belief that the United States was currently winning fell, while belief that the insurgents were winning or that neither side was winning rose (Figure 4.17). By the beginning of 2007, nearly two-thirds saw the war as, at best, a standoff, and partisan differences on the question, although still evident, had become uncharacteristically small. In surveys taken during December 2006 and January 2007, on average, only 35 percent of Republicans thought the United States was winning, compared with 5 percent of Democrats and 8 percent of independents; 53 percent of Republicans and 69 percent of both Democrats and independents called it a stalemate. Similarly, opinions on how the war was going grew increasingly pessimistic after midsummer 2006 (Figure 4.18), with Republicans

FIGURE 4.17   Who Is Winning the War in Iraq?

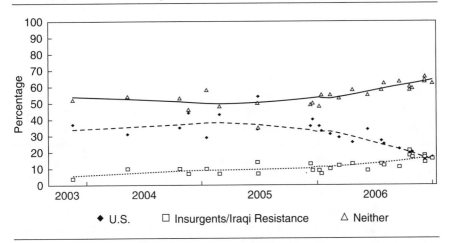

Source: Compiled by the author from CBS News/*New York Times, Los Angeles Times,* Gallup, and CNN polls.

FIGURE 4.18   Evaluations of How Well the War in Iraq Is Going, by Party

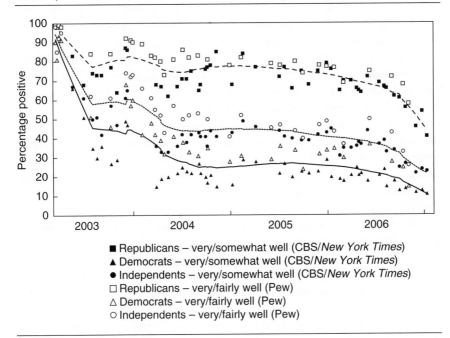

Source: Compiled by the author from ABC News/*Washington Post,* CBS News/*New York Times, Time,* and Pew Research Center for the People and the Press polls.

showing the largest drop-off in optimism after Republican leaders stopped insisting that the war was being won.

The 2006 Elections

Public disillusionment with the war was expressed in no uncertain terms in the 2006 midterm elections, which cost the Republicans control of both houses of Congress. The Democrats succeeded in making them a national referendum on the war and the president (as well as corruption in the Republican Congress), and the electorate's judgment was clearly negative on both.[33] As in other recent elections, partisans were quite loyal to their congressional candidates. But whereas in 2002 and 2004 Republicans were a few points more loyal than were Democrats, the opposite was true in 2006. Moreover, according to the exit polls, the partisan composition of the electorate was slightly more favorable to the Democrats in 2006 than it had been in 2004. The largest single contribution to the Democrats' gains, according to these data, came from independents.[34] Voters classifying themselves as independents had favored Republican candidates in 2002 and had given the Democrats a modest edge in 2004; in 2006, they broke decisively for the Democrats. Calculations based on 2004 and 2006 exit poll data indicate that nearly half the total vote swing to Democratic House candidates between these elections was supplied by independent voters, although they make up only about a quarter of the electorate.[35]

A compelling explanation for the Democrats' advantage among independent voters in 2006 is provided by the data in Figures 4.5, 4.7, 4.10, 4.11, 4.13, 4.14, and 4.18, which show that by 2006, the distribution of independents' opinions on Bush and the Iraq war had become much more similar to that of Democrats than of Republicans. For example, in surveys taken during the month before the election, Bush's average approval rating among independents, 29 percent, was fifty points below his average rating among Republicans (79 percent) and only twenty points above his rating among Democrats (9 percent). Similarly, independents' average level of support for the Iraq war during this period, at 36 percent, was more than twice as far below that of Republicans (73 percent) as it was above that of Democrats (19 percent).

The relationship between these opinions and how voters cast their ballots in 2006 is illustrated in Figure 4.19. Views on Bush and the Iraq war affected the House votes of people in all three partisan categories but made a much larger difference for independents than for either Democrats or Republicans. Thus the predominantly negative opinions on Bush and the war among independent voters produced a decisive Democratic advantage in this segment of the electorate. Overall, 86 percent of the respondents in this survey voted for House candidates in a way that matched their views on the Iraq war—they voted for Democrats if they thought it was a mistake and for Republicans if they thought it was not. The same

FIGURE 4.19   Relationship between Opinions on George W. Bush and the Iraq War, and Respondents' Preferences for House Candidates, 2006

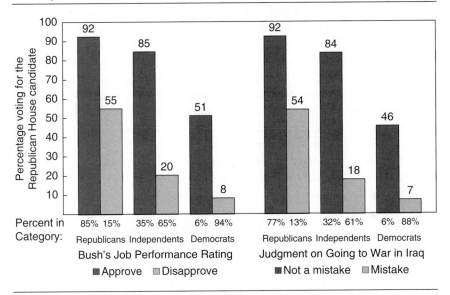

Source: Cooperative Congressional Election Study, 2006.

proportion cast votes consistent with their evaluations of Bush's job performance. Because the public leaned against both the president (only 41 percent approving in this survey) and the war (59 percent calling it a mistake), Democratic candidates benefited. A comparable but even stronger pattern appeared among Senate voters in this survey, with 89 percent of reported vote decisions consistent with either opinions on the Iraq war or opinions on President Bush.[36]

The Iraq Study Group Report

The electorate's negative verdict on the war rendered the strategy of simply staying the course in Iraq politically untenable and underlined the urgency of developing more promising ways to manage the invasion's chaotic and violent aftermath. The most negative assessment of progress in Iraq and the starkest challenge to the president's strategy came from the Iraq Study Group, a bipartisan body of ten eminent national leaders charged by Congress in March 2006 with exploring alternative ways of achieving an acceptable outcome in Iraq. The commission was jointly headed by a Republican, James Baker, secretary of state in the senior Bush's administration and George W. Bush's point man in the Florida recount battle, and a Democrat, Lee Hamilton, a former congressman, who had cochaired the September 11 Commission.

To keep its deliberations free of campaign politics, it withheld its report until after the 2006 elections. Delivered in December, the study group's report described the situation in Iraq as "grave and deteriorating" and judged the administration's approach as failing and having little hope of ever succeeding.[37] It recommended seventy-nine specific changes, the most important of which was to initiate a comprehensive "diplomatic offensive" to bring all of Iraq's neighbors, including Syria and Iran, the UN Security Council, and the European Union, into a process for stabilizing Iraq and addressing broader Middle Eastern issues, particularly the Israel-Palestine conflict. It also recommended shifting the role of U.S. troops from combat to training Iraqi forces with the goal of gradual disengagement, although it did not call for setting a firm timetable for withdrawal of U.S. forces. And it proposed that the United States threaten to withhold military, economic, and diplomatic support if necessary to induce the Iraqi government to improve its poor performance. The report's authors made an impassioned plea for the president and Congress to forge a bipartisan consensus on a way forward, warning that "U.S. foreign policy is doomed to failure—as is any course of action in Iraq—if it is not supported by a broad consensus."[38]

Bush's initial reaction to the report was noncommittal; he welcomed "some really very interesting proposals" but declined to respond in detail until three internal reports he had ordered from the Pentagon, State Department, and National Security Council, reviewing the options in Iraq, had been completed.[39] Nonetheless, Bush clearly maintained aspirations for the war that the Iraq Study Group had, by omission, implicitly abandoned: military victory on the ground and a peaceful, democratic Iraq. In a joint press conference with British prime minister Tony Blair the day after the report was submitted, the president declared, "We will stand firm again in this first war of the twenty-first century. We will defeat the extremists and the radicals. We will help a young democracy prevail in Iraq."[40] For good measure, he later added cautionary references to nuclear blackmail and September 11. Bush made it clear that he was not prepared to change objectives or to adopt any policy that was inconsistent with his past vows to persevere until victory as he defined it was achieved. As he had declared Iraq the main front in the war on terrorism, it was psychologically and politically impossible for Bush to disengage short of something that could be portrayed as victory, for doing so would be to concede failure in his presidency's defining mission.

A New Way Forward?

Thus in a nationally televised speech on January 10, 2007, the president rejected the main thrust of the Iraq Study Group's recommendations, telling the nation that he would continue to pursue victory in Iraq by adding 21,500 American troops to the 132,000 already there and assigning most of them to help clear and hold Baghdad neighborhoods. In line with one component of the study group's recommendations, Bush promised to pressure the Iraq government to attack all sources of sectarian violence, including Shiite militias, but he would not engage in the diplomatic outreach to Iran and Syria that the report had advocated. In deciding to pursue victory through escalation, Bush implicitly abandoned any attempt to find common ground with the war's critics, effectively rejecting the call to pursue a bipartisan national consensus on Iraq.

To a large majority of congressional Democrats, now joined by several prominent Republicans, the proposed "way forward" was simply more of the same, with the same dim prospects of success. Most Americans were also skeptical. The initial public response to the president's proposed "surge" in troop levels reiterated the stark partisan divisions that had become the norm for opinions on the Iraq war, with the difference that ordinary Republicans were no longer as united in supporting the president as Democrats were in opposing him. In eight national polls taken in January in the two weeks following Bush's address, an average of 64 percent of Republicans, 11 percent of Democrats, 32 percent of independents, and 33 percent of Americans overall supported his plan to send more troops.[41] Popular support for the troop increase was limited in good part because Bush had yet to persuade most Americans that it would help. Not surprisingly, surveys generally found that the proportion who thought the move would help matched the proportion who supported it and replicated the familiar partisan divisions. For example, in the *Los Angeles Times/Bloomberg* Poll taken January 13–16, 2007, 67 percent of Republicans, but only 14 percent of Democrats, 30 percent of independents, and 34 percent overall, agreed that the proposed troop increase "will now allow the U.S. and Iraqi forces to defeat the insurgency and win the war in Iraq."[42]

Overall survey data offer little evidence that Bush's January 2007 speech or proclaimed new strategy for Iraq altered in any way the long-term trends in public attitudes toward the president or the war. Popular opinions on the war and its consequences, as measured by the survey questions examined in this chapter, were distributed similarly in the weeks before and after the January 10 speech. That may have been the best Bush could hope for at this point in his presidency. Even if Mueller's theory is right, and public support for the war were to continue to decline with increasing casualties at the same rate as it did over the first forty-seven months of war, or if support were simply to erode over time at the rate observed through the beginning of 2007, the projected consequences for public support of the war turn out to be quite modest. As Figure 4.20 illustrates, according to the equations in Tables 4.1 and 4.2, if support for the war were to continue to diminish in the same way that it has since 2003, it would be only 3.6 points lower among all respondents in December 2008 than it was in December 2006. Among Democrats, it would be 4.4 points lower, among independents, 4.0 points lower, but among Republicans, only 1.8 points lower. This last result would be good news for the president because

FIGURE 4.20 Cumulative U.S. Casualties and Projected Support for the Iraq War

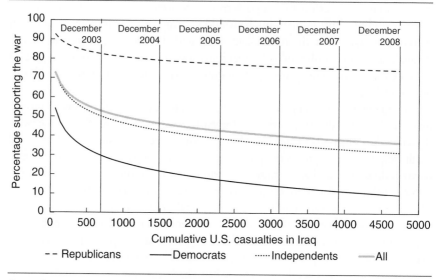

Source: Cooperative Congressional Election Study, 2006.

as long as he holds onto a solid majority of Republicans, his position with the American public is unlikely to deteriorate much further, at least insofar as it is shaped by the Iraq war. The bad news is that he has already lost the good opinion of more than 90 percent of ordinary Democrats and more than two-thirds of independents (Figure 4.7) and is very unlikely to get it back as long as the Iraq war dominates the national agenda.

This projection assumes no major change, positive or negative, in the Iraq situation. Neither can be counted out, but significant deterioration is easier to imagine than significant improvement during Bush's remaining time in office. The strategy of sending more troops to fight insurgents in Baghdad is likely to increase the American casualty rate, and unless it produces visible progress within a relatively short time, Bush runs a very real risk of losing his remaining cushion of support among ordinary Republicans. Partisan differences in assessments of the president and the war would then finally diminish, but obviously not for reasons that Bush would want to see. Regardless of what else he may try to accomplish in his final two years in office, it is a virtual certainty that Bush's standing with the public will continue to be dominated by events in Iraq over which he has only limited control. Colin Powell's warning to Bush before he invaded Iraq that *"this will become the first term"*[43] proved prescient but overoptimistic; the invasion and its aftermath have become the second term as well.

Notes

1. Gary C. Jacobson, *A Divider Not a Uniter: George W. Bush and the American People* (New York: Pearson Longman, 2007), 69–78.

2. Text of speech accessed July 15, 2006, at www.cbsnews.com/stories/2003/05/01/iraq/main551946.shtml.

3. For more detail on the questions, see Jacobson, *A Divider,* 265–269. Questions asking whether the United States did the right thing in becoming involved in Iraq, whether the war was a mistake, and whether, all things considered, it was worth the cost generate higher support; when the question mentions U.S. casualties, support is lower. Jacobson, *A Divider,* 129. These and other data points shown in this chapter are summarized by Lowess smoothing.

4. John E. Mueller, *War, Presidents, and Public Opinion* (New York: John Wiley, 1973), 60; emphasis is in the original.

5. John E. Mueller, "The Iraq Syndrome," *Foreign Affairs,* November/December 2005; accessed June 20, 2006, at http://fullaccess.foreignaffairs.org/20051101faessay84605/john-mueller/the-iraq-syndrome.html?mode=print.

6. Jacobson, *A Divider,* 129. The questions ask whether the war was a mistake, whether the United States did the right thing in going to war, and whether the war was worth fighting. U.S. casualties are from monthly data accessed January 15, 2007, at www.globalsecurity.org/military/ops/iraq_casualties.htm.

7. Christopher Gelpi and John Mueller, "The Cost of War," *Foreign Affairs,* January/February 2006, http://fullaccess.foreignaffairs.org/arp/to_fullaccess?u=%2F20060101faresponse85114%2Fchristopher%2Dgelpi%2Djohn%2Dmueller%2Fthe%2Dcost%2Dof%2Dwar%2Ehtml (accessed June 20, 2006). See also Christopher Gelpi, Peter D. Feaver, and Jason Reifler, "Success Matters: Casualty Sensitivity and the War in Iraq," *International Security* 30, no. 3 (Winter 2006): 7–46.

8. The casualty question is from ABC News/*Washington Post* polls: "Again thinking about the goals versus the costs of the war, so far in your opinion has there been an acceptable or unacceptable number of U.S. military casualties in Iraq?" War support is measured by the three questions noted in note 3 above.

9. Mueller, "The Iraq Syndrome."

10. As would be expected, the party of the president determines whether support for military action is higher among Republicans or Democrats; it is true for every survey regarding the Iraq war and in 97 percent of the surveys taken regarding the other five wars. For more detailed comparisons see Jacobson, *A Divider,* 134–138.

11. Ibid.

12. Ibid., 66.

13. Evaluations of Bush's performance in different policy domains were also highly polarized along party lines during this period; see ibid., 10–13.

14. Ibid., 6–7.

15. Author's analysis based on Gallup poll data acquired from the Roper Center for Public Opinion Research at www.ropercenter.uconn.edu.

16. This was especially true for the white, born-again or evangelical Christians in the party, who were virtually unanimous in approving of Bush's performance during the year following 9/11. See Jacobson, *A Divider,* 93–94.

17. Ibid., 65, 71–79.

18. Ibid., 115–116, 144.

19. "Rumsfeld Says Iraqis Growing More Confident about Country's Future," *Defense Department Report,* August 5, 2003, www.globalsecurity.org/wmd/library/news/iraq/2003/02/iraq-030805-usia03.htm (accessed July 8, 2005).

20. Republicans also were much more likely to believe that the Iraq war was justified even if WMD were never found, and this view become more predominant after the war began; see Jacobson, *A Divider,* 143.

21. CBS News/*New York Times* polls, August 17–24 and September 15–19, 2006; *Time* poll, August 22–24, 2006; CNN poll, August 30–September 2, 2006; at http://pollingreport.com/terror.htm (accessed September 27, 2006).

22. Leon Festinger, *A Theory of Cognitive Dissonance* (Stanford: Stanford University Press, 1957).

23. Jacobson, *A Divider,* 146.

24. "Transcript: The First Presidential Debate," September 20, 2004, www.washingtonpost.com/wp-srv/politics/debatereferee/debate_0930.html#c (accessed August 5, 2005).

25. Mueller, "The Iraq Syndrome," 2.

26. "President's Address to the Nation," transcript of speech delivered September 9, 2006, www.whitehouse.gov/news/releases/2006/09/20060911-3.html (accessed October 10, 2006).

27. Michael Dimock, "The Iraq-Vietnam Difference," Pew Research Center for the People and the Press report, May 16, 2006, http://people-press.org/commentary/display.php3?AnalysisID=134 (accessed May 30, 2006).

28. Bush's father's short, militarily successful engagement in the Persian Gulf sparked a rally in support for the war and the president that found few dissenters while it was in progress, generating a consistency level of about 88 percent in surveys taken January–March 1991. After that time the level of consistency declined to an average of 74 percent; overall consistency averaged 81 percent.

29. War support is measured by the three questions mentioned in note 3; presidential approval is from Figure 4.2.

30. Peter Spiegel, "Is U.S. Winning: Army Chief at a Loss," *Los Angeles Times,* July 15, 2006, A11.

31. Bob Woodward, "Secret Report Disputes White House Optimism," *Washington Post,* October 1, 2006, A1.

32. Michael R. Gordon and David S. Cloud, "Rumsfeld Memo Proposes 'Major Adjustment' in Iraq," *New York Times,* December 3, 2006, A1.

33. Gary C. Jacobson, "Referendum: The 2006 Midterm Congressional Elections," *Political Science Quarterly* 122 (Spring 2007): 1–24.

34. Independents who lean toward one of the parties—and who are usually as loyal as weak partisans—have to be treated as independents in this analysis because these surveys do not consistently distinguish partisan leaners from pure independents.

35. Jacobson, "Referendum," 12.

36. These analyses are from the 2006 Cooperative Congressional Election Study, conducted for a consortium of academic researchers by Polimetrix, based on a large sample (36,501) constructed from a much larger set of online respondents.

37. Paul Richter, "Iraq Policy 'No Longer Viable,' " *Los Angeles Times,* December 7, 2006, A12.

38. " 'There Is No Magic Formula,' " *Los Angeles Times,* December 7, 2006, A13.

39. " 'An Opportunity to Come Together,' " *Los Angeles Times,* December 6, 2006, A13.

40. "President Bush Meets with British Prime Minister Tony Blair," White House transcript, December 7, 2006, www.whitehouse.gov/news/releases/2006/12/20061207-1.html (accessed December 8, 2006).

41. CBS News/*New York Times* Poll, January 10, 2007; ABC News/*Washington Post* Poll, January 10, 2007; Pew Research Center for the People and the Press Poll, January 10–15, 2007; Fox News Poll, January 16–17, 2007; *Los Angeles Times*/Bloomberg Poll, January 13–16, 2007; Diageo/Hotline Poll, January 11–14, 2007; *Newsweek* Poll, January 17–18, 2007; CBS News/*New York Times* Poll, January 18–21, 2007. The partisan distribution of responses is quite consistent across these polls: among Republicans it ranged from 56 percent to 73 percent supporting the additional troops; among Democrats, from 7 percent to 14 percent supported the move.

42. *Los Angeles Times*/Bloomberg Poll, January 13–16, 2007, accessed January 18, 2007, at http://www.latimes.com/media/acrobat/2007-01/27427417.pdf.

43. Bob Woodward, *Plan of Attack* (New York: Simon and Schuster, 2004), 150; emphasis in the original.

CHAPTER 5

A Divider, Not a Uniter—
Did It Have to Be?

Morris P. Fiorina

There is a religious war going on in this country, a cultural war as critical to the kind of nation we shall be as the cold war itself, for this war is for the soul of America.

> —*Pat Buchanan at the 1992 Republican Convention*

In the wee small hours of November 3, 2004, a new country appeared on the map of the modern world: the DSA, the Divided States of America. . . . not since the Civil War has the fault lines between its two halves been so glaringly clear. . . . It is time we called those two Americas something other than Republican and Democrat, for their mutual alienation and unforgiving contempt is closer to Sunni and Shia, or (in Indian terms) Muslim and Hindu. How about, then, Godly America and Worldly America?[1]

> —*Simon Schama, after the 2004 presidential election*

DURING THE LONG DECADE between pundit Pat Buchanan's declaration of cultural war and professor Simon Schama's angry election postmortem, the conclusion that America had split down the middle culturally and politically became widely accepted. The once-United States had separated into red (Republican) states and blue (Democratic) states. In contrast to Americans in earlier eras who cast their votes on the basis of economic and foreign policy issues, Americans now voted on the basis of religion and moral values. The "vital center" had vanished, as political moderates departed from the scene, ceding the field to staunch liberals and conservatives. Swing voters similarly had vanished, leaving elections to be determined by straight-ticket-voting, die-hard partisans. As Republican strategist Matthew Dowd commented, "You've got 80 percent to 90 percent of the country that look at each other like they are on separate planets."[2]

To some observers these developments threatened the very stability of the country. In a 2003 column in the *Washington Post*, E. J. Dionne Jr. observed, "The red states get redder, the blue states get bluer, and the political map of the United States takes on the coloration of the Civil War. . . . Up in heaven, Abe Lincoln must be shaking his head in astonishment. The country he sought to keep united is pulling apart politically, and largely along the same lines that defined Honest Abe's election victory in 1860."[3] And in a 2006 segment on ABC's *20/20* pundit George Stephanopoulos similarly claimed that the country was more divided than at any time since the Civil War.[4]

Fortunately, Abraham Lincoln can rest easy. An examination of the facts provides little support for the prevailing image of America as a polarized nation riven by a culture war. Yes, our national elections are close, but the narrow vote margins do not reflect deep divisions in political beliefs and positions. Although Americans today split almost evenly in elections, we do so not because we belong to bitterly opposed camps, but because most of us seek to strike a balance between conflicting interests and values, while our parties and candidates too often offer all-or-nothing choices, which most of us reject. Contrary to Professor Schama's division of the country, most Americans want godly *and* worldly.

Certainly it is true that our politicians in Washington and in many state capitals are more polarized than they have been for several generations. And there are numerous distressing examples of polarized politics in city councils and other governmental bodies. Campaign workers and contributors are polarized. Radio talk shows spew vituperation over the airwaves, and bloggers send their screeds over the ether. But most such Americans, who are active in politics or who actively follow politics, fail to appreciate how unrepresentative they are. Most Americans are busy earning their livings, raising their families, and otherwise going about their daily lives. They are not as focused on politics, not as informed about politics, not as intense in their political views, and they are certainly not as polarized as those who purport to represent them.

Although I agree with Gary Jacobson (this volume) that George W. Bush has governed as a divider, not a uniter, I do not think he had to do so. Nor do I think that Bush had to rely more heavily for support on his party base than any president in the preceding half-century, as James Campbell argues (this volume). President Bush's governing style and electoral strategy were in large part deliberate choices, not inescapable responses to a polarized country. In this chapter I expand on these claims and examine how a distorted picture of American politics has become so widespread.

How Polarized Are Americans?

Let us first consider the division of the country into red and blue states, a colorful but highly misleading metaphor that has captivated many in the news media. Pundits often compare sociological characteristics of red and blues states, contrasting the proportions of gun owners, born-again Christians, and the like. Such contrasts are indeed striking, but also deceiving, because their relationships with political choices are far from perfect. All gun owners did not vote for Bush in 2004; in fact, upwards of 35 percent of gun owners voted for John Kerry. Nor did all born-again Christians vote for Bush in 2004; close to one-third voted for Kerry. Similarly, differences in sociological characteristics generally do not translate into comparable differences in political affiliation. In the 2004 elections self-identified Democrats made up the same proportion of voters in the red states as in the blue states— 32 percent in each. In both red and blue states self-identified independents were more common than partisans. Similarly, avowed conservatives were barely more common in the red states than in the blue states—22 percent in the former compared with 18 percent in the latter. Majorities in both categories of states preferred the "middle-of-the-road" or "slightly liberal" and "slightly conservative" labels.5 Figure 5.1 compares the distributions of political ideology in red and blue states in 2004. Evidently, the differences are on the margins.

FIGURE 5.1   Ideological Self-Placement of All Respondents Living in Red and Blue States: Both Red and Blue State Residents Are Basically Centrists

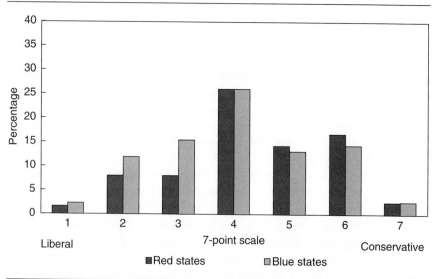

Source: 2004 National Election Study.

The general picture does not change when we focus on specific public policy issues rather than on general orientations such as partisanship and ideology. On the whole, public opinion surveys that contrast the policy preferences of red state and blue state residents show that they do not differ nearly as much as is commonly presumed.[6] Although the size of the majorities varies, rarely are red state and blue state majorities on opposite sides of an issue, even on so-called hot button issues. In 2004, for example, a narrow majority of red state residents joined a larger majority of blue state residents who favored making gun regulations stricter. Solid majorities of blue state residents shared red state residents' support for the death penalty and their opposition to gay marriage. Differences on economic issues such as taxes, Social Security, and health care were even smaller. Political differences? Yes. Cultural chasms? No. The differences between red and blue areas within California and within Texas probably are as big as the difference between blue California and red Texas.

Have Americans Become More Polarized?

Even if the American public is not as polarized as many commentators have assumed, is it now more polarized than in some past golden era when harmony reigned? Again, there is little evidence that polarization has increased. In his contribution to this volume, James Campbell notes (see his Figure 2.1) that since the 1980s there has been a small, but statistically significant decline in the percentage of voters placing themselves in the exact center (position 4) of the National Election Study seven-point, liberal-conservative scale depicted in Figure 2.1

But the more frequent Gallup surveys that ask about political ideology report that the number of self-identified moderates *increased* between the 1970s and the 2000s. In fact, as Figure 5.2 shows, according to Gallup a higher percentage of Americans in the 2000s considered themselves moderates than did in the 1970s, before all the talk about polarization began. And for all the exultation (on the right) and hand-wringing (on the left) about the country's becoming more conservative, self-identified conservatives make up about the same proportion of the electorate today as they did in the 1970s. The extremes have not engulfed the middle.

Of course, the American public could have polarized on a few specific issues without showing any change in general ideological outlook. But there is little evidence of such issue-specific polarization, either. After exhaustive analyses of a large and disparate set of surveys of American public opinion, DiMaggio, Evans, and Bryson concluded that rather than increased polarization during the three decades from 1972 to 2002, the more common finding was *decreased* polarization.[7] Old and young Americans; affluent and poor Americans; black, white, and brown Americans; well-educated and poorly-educated Americans; Catholic, Protestant, and Jewish Americans; northern, midwestern, southern, and western Americans—all were becoming more similar in their political attitudes rather than more distinct.

FIGURE 5.2   Gallup Liberal-Conservative Self-Identification, by Decade, 1970–2000: Americans Today Are No Less Moderate than a Generation Ago

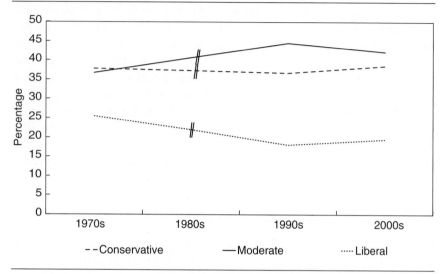

Source: Gallup poll, conservative and liberal self-identification combined responses from "Very conservative" and "Conservative" and "Very liberal" and "Liberal," respectively. Moderates include "Don't know" responses.

Similarly, in addition to ideology the National Election Study asked Americans about six public policy issues in every presidential campaign between 1984 and 2004. Five questions offered seven-point scales analogous to the ideology scale mentioned above, and the sixth was an abortion question with four categories. Table 5.1 reports the percentage point changes over the twenty-year period (the rows do not sum to zero because of rounding). Ignoring sampling error, declining response rates, and other complicating factors in surveys, and treating these numbers as exact, we see very little evidence of polarization; rather, the picture is more complex. Two scales—the liberal-conservative scale that Campbell analyzes, and the responsibility of government for jobs and standard of living—show a very slight polarization pattern: between 1984 and 2004 there was a single-digit decline in the number of people placing themselves in the exact center of the scale and a marginal increase in the numbers placing themselves on the left and right. (On the ideology scale the number of self-identified moderates was actually three percentage points higher in 2004 than in 1984, but the number of people who declined to classify themselves at all was ten percentage points lower in 2004 than in 1984. Campbell classified these people as moderates, and I do so here as well.)

TABLE 5.1   Percentage Point Changes in Policy Views, 1984–2004

	Extremely liberal —————————————→ *Extremely conservative*						
Polarization							
Jobs/SoL	2	1	0	−2(−7)	0	1	3
Liberal-conservative	0	2	3	3(−7)	−1	3	1
Left shift							
Health insurance	6	2	3	0(−9)[a]	0	−2	−2
Spending/services	5	4	5	−3(−5)	−3	−3	−2
Right shift							
Aid to blacks	0	−2	−5	−5(−7)	−1	6	8
Defense spending	−5	−4	−3	−5(−4)	8	4	2
No change							
Abortion	1		−1			3	−1

Source: Pietro S. Nivola and David W. Brady, eds., *Red and Blue Nation? Characteristics and Causes of America's Polarized Politics* (Washington, D.C.: Brookings, 2007).

[a]Numbers in parentheses are changes when "Don't know" responses are treated as moderates.

Four other scales do not show increasing polarization. On each scale the number of respondents in the exact middle declined by single digits, but on the responsibility of government versus the private sector for health insurance, and the trade-off between public spending and public services there was also a decline in the number of conservatives—public opinion shifted leftward, increasing its support for active government. Conversely, on defense spending and aid to African Americans there was a decline in the number of liberals—public opinion shifted rightward to favor more defense spending and less aid to African-Americans. (As was the case with the liberal-conservative scale, all of the decline in moderates on the health insurance scale and most of the decline on the jobs scale reflected a decline in the number of respondents who did not classify themselves at all, rather than a decline in self-placed moderates.) On the four-point abortion item, the middle is ambiguous, but there was essentially no change.

In sum, analyses based on available data from a range of academic and commercial databases indicate that the issue positions of the American population have changed little over the past two decades and fail to reveal any pattern of systematic polarization.

Has Religion Displaced Economics as the Basis of American Voting?

The conventional interpretation of the 2004 election held that voters concerned about "moral values" (the phrase came from a single, poorly worded exit poll question) decided the outcome.[8] The media interpreted the term "moral values" to mean abortion and gay marriage, but in fact, various studies have found that voter positions on gay marriage and abortion had little or nothing to do with the outcome; the election hinged primarily on concerns about homeland security and leadership.[9] If one wished to credit a single group with reelecting President Bush—always an iffy proposition in a close election—it would not be evangelical Christians, who made up about the same proportion of the electorate in 2004 as in 2000 and who voted for Bush at only a little higher rate than in 2000.[10] Rather the group to credit or blame would be American women, who were particularly sensitive to the terrorist threat. Their four-to-five-percentage-point swing to Bush between 2000 and 2004 accounted for virtually all of his 2.4 percent popular vote margin.

Nevertheless, as numerous commentators have pointed out, religion (in the sense of religious commitment, not denomination) has become more closely associated with partisanship and presidential voting in recent decades.[11] More precisely, as Figure 5.3 shows, in the 1992 election the correlation between religiosity and how people voted in the presidential election dramatically increased; it then fell back somewhat in each of the three succeeding elections. Today, an American who attends church weekly is much less likely to vote Democratic than an American who thinks of Sunday as a day to get a few more hours of sleep.

To some extent, the increased relationship of religiosity to partisanship and voting surely reflects the religious revival that occurred in the United States (and around the world) in the late twentieth century.[12] But it may have as much or more to do with how the parties and their candidates have changed the political agenda. Why should religiosity have correlated with how people voted in the 1950s and 1960s, when both parties' candidates projected images as god-fearing, churchgoing heterosexual males, with loving, supportive wives and respectful, well-behaved children? (Not that this was always the reality, but the media didn't report the seamy side of personal life in those days.) Why would churchgoers have been much less likely to vote Democratic in 1976 and 1980, when the Democrats nominated a born-again Sunday school teacher (Jimmy Carter), and in 1984, when the Democrats nominated the son of a Methodist minister (Walter Mondale)? But in 1992 Democrats nominated a gay-friendly marijuana user and adulterer, suddenly signaling a difference with Republicans where traditional morality was concerned. Similarly, in 1980 and 1984 the Republicans nominated a divorced Hollywood actor who took a somewhat casual attitude toward religion, but in 2000 and 2004 they nominated a reformed lush who had been saved by God's grace.

The simple fact is that we do not know whether tens of millions of Americans suddenly decided in 1992 that religion and morality were of greater relevance to politics than they thought previously, or whether they only reacted to candidates whose personae and strategies put issues on the agenda that tapped into religion and morality in a way that economic and foreign policy issues did not. Even if Americans in the 1950s and 1960s were every bit as pious as Americans today, issues such

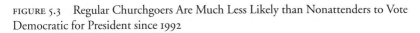

FIGURE 5.3   Regular Churchgoers Are Much Less Likely than Nonattenders to Vote Democratic for President since 1992

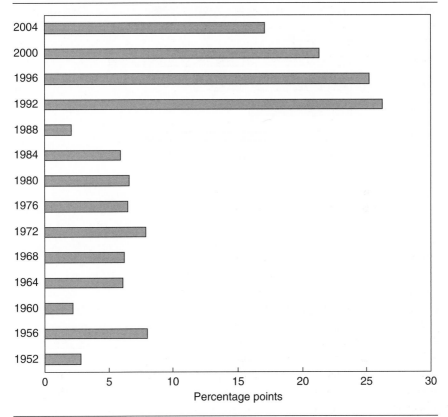

Source: Calculated from the National Election Studies.

Note: The length of the bars represents the percentage point difference in Democratic presidential vote between respondents who report attending church weekly or more often, compared to those who attend only on ceremonial occasions (weddings, funerals) or not at all. Includes white voters only.

as the minimum wage, Medicare, civil rights, and the war in Vietnam would not have divided them along church attendance lines the way that issues such as abortion, gay marriage, stem cell research, and other cultural issues do so today.

Furthermore, far from disappearing, economic considerations loomed large in the 2004 voting. As Figure 5.4 shows, contrary to the claims of various political commentators, the difference in presidential voting between high-income and low-income Americans was the third-largest in a half-century.[13] We will have more to say about economics and voting below.

FIGURE 5.4   The Income Divide in Presidential Voting Is Greater than a Generation Ago

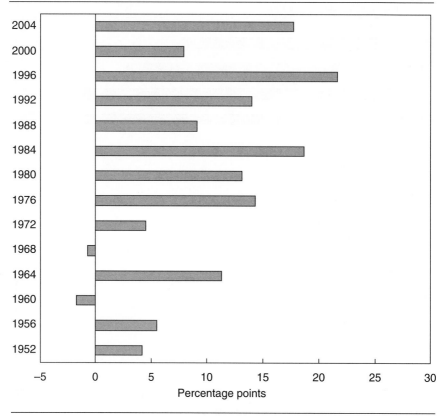

Source: Calculated from the National Election Studies.
Note: The length of the bars represents the percentage point difference in Democratic presidential vote between respondents living in the poorest third of households compared to those living in the wealthiest third of households.

Why Do So Many People Think That the Country Has Polarized?

Given the aforementioned facts, why do a large number of well-informed people persist in thinking that the country is deeply divided? A variety of misconceptions underlie the distorted picture of American politics.

A major reason is that party sorting has been mistaken for popular polarization. Consider the hypothetical opinion distributions in Figure 5.5. The top panel shows a centrist distribution: Most voters are congregated in the middle, with fewer and fewer present as we move toward the liberal and conservative extremes. Here public opinion is not polarized. In contrast, the bottom panel shows a bimodal distribu-

FIGURE 5.5   Two Very Different Close Election Scenarios

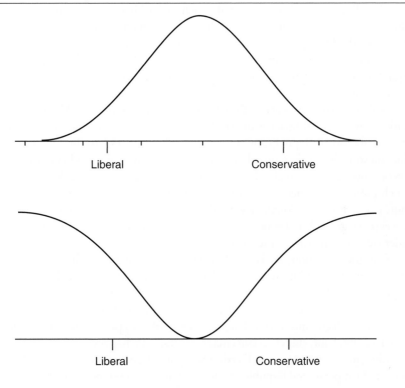

tion. Most voters congregate on the liberal and conservative extremes, and their numbers diminish as we move toward the middle. Here public opinion is polarized. As we have discussed above, public opinion in the United States tends to look more like the top distribution than the bottom distribution, and there is little indication that opinion is changing to resemble the bottom distribution more closely.

What has happened, however, is that party affiliations have become more closely correlated with ideology. A generation ago, partisans were more ideologically heterogeneous than they are today. According to the National Election Studies, in 1972, 11 percent of self-identified Republicans placed themselves left of center on the liberal-conservative scale, whereas in 2004 only 4 percent did. Over the same period self-identified Democrats who placed themselves right of center on the scale declined from 26 percent to 12 percent. Thus, today's parties are more distinct than those of a generation ago. Although the aggregate distribution of the ideological positions and issue stances Americans hold remains essentially centrist and has changed little over the years, Democrats and Republicans have sorted themselves out. The Republican Party has shed much of its liberal wing, especially in the Northeast. The Democratic Party has shed much of its conservative wing, especially in the South. The result is that an average Republican and an average Democrat differ more from each other than they did a generation ago. (Such comparisons, of course, ignore the 35 percent or so of Americans who classify themselves as political independents.)

Still, it is easy to exaggerate the extent of party differences. As Matthew Levendusky shows, the country is still very far from a situation in which all Democrats are liberals and all Republicans conservatives. The parties have become more distinct on some issues than on others, and on some issues one or other of the parties has become more internally divided rather than united.[14] In particular, contrary to much political commentary, not only are Democratic and Republican partisans more distinct on traditional, New Deal, social welfare issues than on racial and the newer social and cultural issues, but they have become increasingly distinct on those older issues during the past few decades.

Consider abortion, an issue often viewed as a defining difference between Democrats and Republicans today. Gallup data (Figure 5.6) indicate that only about 30 percent of self-identified Democrats believe that abortion should be "legal under all circumstances," and only about 30 percent of Republicans believe abortion should be "illegal in all circumstances." Large pluralities of both parties prefer the middling option of "legal only under certain circumstances."[15] Perhaps even more surprisingly, according to the 2004 National Election Study significant minorities of self-classified "strong" Democrats and Republicans deviated from the clear position of their party's leaders and activists. Twenty-three percent of Americans who classified themselves as strong Republicans said that abortion should *always* be legal as a matter of personal choice—the position of the national Democratic Party—compared with 22 percent who said that it should *never* be legal—their own party's position. And only 54 percent of strong Democrats said abortion should always be legal as a matter of personal choice—their party's position—compared with 43 percent of strong Democrats who chose the pro-life positions that abortion should never be legal or should be legal only in cases of rape or incest or when the woman's life is in danger.

That such findings seem surprising points to a second reason for the exaggerated picture of American polarization. The prevailing picture largely reflects an unrepresentative political class that the news media portray as representative. Officeholders and their entourages, interest group leaders, political "infotainers," and issue activists—people in these roles constitute a political class that is the public face of politics in America. In contrast to the larger public, this political class is deeply interested and informed (although their information typically is biased). Research shows that their beliefs *are* polarized and have become more so in recent years.

FIGURE 5.6   When Should Abortion Be Legal? Partisans Are Not Very Different

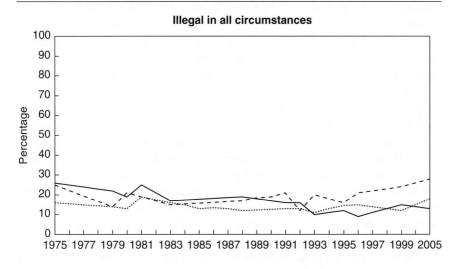

Illegal in all circumstances

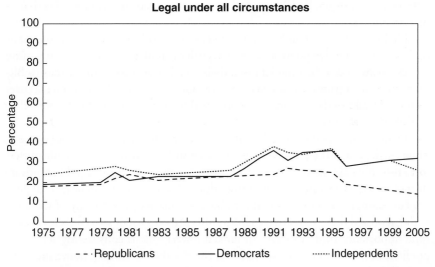

Legal under all circumstances

- - ·Republicans ——Democrats ······Independents

Source: Gallup Organization.

Although it numbers in the millions, the political class is nevertheless a small and unrepresentative slice of an American public that now numbers more than 200 million eligible voters. They are the exception, not the norm. In an earlier exchange, James Q. Wilson expressed skepticism about my skepticism about American polarization, commenting that anyone who believed that "must not listen to talk radio, read liberal or conservative blogs, or pay any attention to poll data showing a vastly increased gap between the two parties on key public issues."[16] Wilson's third point refers to party sorting, which I have just addressed, but as for talk radio and blogs, he is correct. I do not listen to the former or read the latter, and neither should he (except for entertainment). Talk radio and blogs are extremely unrepresentative communications outlets, and anyone who infers from them anything about the preferences of the American people will go seriously astray. Polls report that about 16 million Americans tune in at least once a week to Rush Limbaugh, the reigning king of the radio talk show scene. Even if every one of them was a devoted "dittohead," which is doubtful, that would be about 8 percent of the country's eligible voters. Bloggers are even less representative. An estimated eight million Americans visit political blogs each day, but even if that number represented eight million different eligible voters, which is certainly not the case, and even if every political blog evidenced a staunch liberal or conservative point of view, which is also not the case, that would still amount to only 4 percent of the country's eligible voters. Rather than listening to more radio talk shows and reading more blogs, political commentators should spend more days wandering the aisles of grocery stores, Wal-Marts, and auto parts stores to get acquainted with normal Americans.

Media coverage is doubly distorting because in addition to its focus on a seriously unrepresentative political class, news values emphasize conflict. Polarization makes a better story than moderation, division a better story than consensus. Bitter disagreement trumps reasoned discussion. Given a choice, the news media cover conflict. Small wonder that many Americans think they are more divided than they actually are.

In addition to being more centrist, more conflicted, and—for some people—more clueless than the political class, research shows that the larger public differs from the political class in two other important ways. First, the issues that motivate the political class are often different from those of most concern to the general public. For example, despite all the furor about gay marriage, one study of the 2004 voting reported that gay marriage ranked fifteenth on a list of sixteen issues in electoral importance (only tort reform ranked lower).[17] Polls consistently show that public concern focuses on broad national issues—the war in Iraq, homeland security, education, health care, and the like. Hot-button issues that get a lot of press often fall low on lists of public concerns. Table 5.2 reports the results of a Pew poll conducted a few months before the 2006 elections that asked registered voters to rank the electoral importance of nineteen issues. Note that abortion and gay marriage came in dead last. Flag burning, which had occupied the attention of the U.S. Senate a few weeks earlier, was fourteenth. In sum, the political class deflects the political agenda away from the broad concerns of the public and toward issues that primarily concern small and unrepresentative minorities.

TABLE 5.2   Issues That Registered Voters Rated "Very Important," June 2006

Issue	Percentage
Education	82
Economy	80
Health care	79
Social Security	75
Situation in Iraq	74
Terrorism	74
Taxes	68
Job situation	66
Energy policy	64
Immigration	58
Budget deficit	56
Environment	52
Minimum wage	52
Flag burning	49
Government surveillance	44
Inheritance tax	44
Global warming	44
Abortion	43
Gay marriage	34

Source: The Pew Research Center for the People and the Press poll, June 2006.

Second, members of the political class frequently behave in a manner that would be unacceptable in most other spheres of American life. Too often they are loud, disrespectful, vituperative—in a word, uncivil. Most Americans raise their children not to behave like that. Diana Mutz and Byron Reeves have shown experimentally that Americans react more negatively to uncivil argument than to the substance of the disagreement.[18] In sum, not only does the political class take more extreme positions than those preferred by normal Americans, but they have different priorities and act in ways that normal Americans disapprove.

Finally, it is absolutely essential to distinguish between voters' political positions on the one hand and their political choices and evaluations on the other. At the time of the 2004 election Democrats overwhelmingly disapproved of Bush and voted for Kerry, and Republicans overwhelmingly approved of Bush and voted for him. Similarly, as Jacobson describes in his essay in this volume, the partisan divide in presidential approval ratings is historically unprecedented. Some commentators erroneously interpret such statistics as strong evidence that Americans are polarized, but people's evaluations of their public officials can be polarized even when their positions are not (and vice versa). The reason is that votes and candidate evaluations depend not only on a voter's position, but also on where the candidates stand and what they have done.

Again, consider Figure 5.5, which depicts two electorates distributed on a left-right scale. In the top panel the electorate is centrist, with most voters located between the liberal and conservative poles, but if both the Democratic and Republican candidates take extreme positions because of, say, the need to win closed primaries, an ideologue will be elected, and an observer who focuses only on the outcome might conclude (erroneously) that the electorate is polarized. In the bottom panel the electorate is polarized, with most voters clustered at the extremes and relatively few in the moderate center. But if both candidates compete for the voters in the center by taking moderate positions, a moderate will be elected, and an observer who focuses only on the choice might (erroneously) conclude that the district has a moderate electorate. Voters can only choose between the alternatives that are offered. As we have discussed, the survey evidence indicates that voters' positions are not particularly polarized, and so if their voting has become more polarized it must be the alternatives that have changed. Whether people approve of the president depends not only on what they would like him to do, but also on what he already has done. Whether you love him or loathe him, the simple fact is that President Bush is a divider, not a uniter.

Exhibit A is, of course, the war in Iraq, the eight-hundred-pound gorilla of the Bush second term. A recent study of the Iraq war issue in the 2004 voting nicely illustrates the distinction between people's positions and their evaluations.[19] Philip Klinkner contrasted the views of Democrats and Republicans on U.S. foreign policy *goals* (e.g., to advance human rights, to combat terrorism) and found that although partisans' views were significantly different in a statistical sense, the differences were not large. Contrasting the views of partisans on the *means* that the United States uses to carry out foreign policy (e.g., military power or diplomacy), Klinkner again found differences that were statistically different but not substantively large. The same was true for partisan attitudes on national defense *issues,* such as the importance of a strong military, and partisan attitudes on *values,* such as patriotism and national pride. But when it comes to partisan attitudes toward George Bush, Klinkner found the same huge partisan divide that Jacobson has so well described.[20] The list of contributors to the partisan gulf is long: unfounded assertions of a relationship between al Qaeda and Saddam Hussein, failure to find Iraqi weapons of mass destruction, a war that has not turned out to be a "cakewalk" and a mission that is far from "accomplished," characterizations of Democrats as unpatriotic if not disloyal, assertions of a unitary presidency and the right to ignore statutory and constitutional limits in conducting the war on terror. In these ways and others Bush polarized evaluations of his presidency, even if Democrats' and Republicans' underlying *positions* are not nearly as divided as their *evaluations* of the administration and its actions.

But how deep and how permanent is this partisan divide? From a purely academic standpoint it would be very interesting if one or both parties nominated an "atypical" candidate for president in 2008. If the Republicans were to nominate John McCain—who takes positions unpopular within the party on such matters as campaign finance reform, climate change, and some of the Bush tax cuts—or even Rudy Giuliani—whose positions on social issues are closer to liberal Democrats' than to those of social conservatives in the Republican party—and if the Democrats were to nominate Barack Obama, I predict that we would see a weakening of the relationship between party affiliations and presidential votes. Swing voters would suddenly reemerge, and voting across party lines would increase. Something such as I envision occurred in California in the 2003 recall election and the 2006 midterm elections. California today is one of the bluest of the blue states, and Republican candidates for national and statewide offices have performed miserably there since 1992. But when offered a more moderate Republican choice, many Democrats who would not have considered voting for Republican Bush in 2004 were willing to vote for Republican Arnold Schwarzenegger in 2003 and 2006.[21] Again, how Americans vote depends on the choices they are offered, not just on their own positions.

Could President Bush Have Been a Uniter?

In chapter 2, James Campbell argues that President Bush's governing style grew out of the electoral conditions surrounding his election. To a historically unusual degree Bush owed his election to voters whom Campbell classifies as belonging to the Republican base, rather than to moderate, swing voters.[22] With little hope of any payoff from reaching out, Bush chose to "dance with the ones that brung him." Campbell's position certainly is defensible, but I offer an alternative account of what might have been.

The latter years of the Clinton administration were marked by severe partisan conflict. Both strong Republicans and Democrats were embittered by the impeachment imbroglio, the Republicans because they failed (and lost seats in the 1998 elections, which added injury to insult), and the Democrats because Republicans had tried to impeach the president in the first place. Characteristically, the American people were somewhere in the middle, with two-thirds supporting censure to show their disapproval of Clinton's behavior but opposing impeachment. That Bush lost the popular vote and nevertheless became president further antagonized those already not inclined to support him. Under such conditions it might be reasonable to conclude that there was little to be gained by fishing for votes in the middle.

But might the president and his political advisers have drawn the wrong lessons from the 2000 election? After all, most political science forecasting models predicted that Bush should have decisively *lost* the 2000 election—seven forecasting models predicted a Gore victory with between 53 percent and 60 percent of the popular vote.[23] That Bush came so close to winning the popular vote, while running as the head of a party recently slapped down by the electorate and against an incumbent vice president in a time of peace and prosperity, perhaps should have been viewed as evidence of the appeal of compassionate conservatism and an indication of its potential to draw support from a broader segment of the electorate.[24]

Even if that were not so, the aftermath of 9/11 offered another opportunity for Bush to unite the country. To be sure, no president could have sustained the record-high approval ratings recorded in fall 2001, but after the widely supported and generally successful invasion of Afghanistan, suppose the president had followed a different course. Rather than adopt the role of "war president," what if he had chosen instead to position himself as a national unity president? Suppose he had announced that the campaign to stamp out terrorism and root out its causes would be a difficult, lengthy, and costly task that would require sacrifice. Further tax cuts would be impossible since the money would be needed to fund the war on terror. Suppose he had said that the United States could no longer allow its economic health and security to be dependent on unstable and/or dictatorial Middle Eastern regimes and proposed a major initiative to develop greater energy independence by supporting alternative fuels. Suppose he had said that Americans could no longer afford to fight each other over moral questions about which people of good faith strenuously disagreed; the states and civil society would have to deal with those. And above all, suppose he had admitted that the main reasons the American public would support a war in Iraq—Saddam's complicity in 9/11 and his possession of weapons of mass destruction—rested on evidence too weak to launch a war and chosen instead to continue to work through diplomatic channels. Given these suppositions, I think that President Bush could have been reelected in 2004 with a margin comparable to Bill Clinton's in 1996, and Karl Rove's dream of a durable Republican majority reminiscent of McKinley's would not be the fantasy that it has become.

Of course, had George Bush followed this alternative path, he would most certainly have lost some support in his base. But given the state of public opinion, I believe he could have drawn from more moderate voters support closer to that drawn by earlier Republican presidents and sufficient to guarantee an easy reelection. Perhaps Bush himself was unwilling to act in this fashion, but I do not believe that he was the prisoner of conditions and events and incapable of acting in any way other than the way that he did.

The Next Eight Years

Political historians tell us that American political development is irregular: One does not have to be a believer in critical realignment theory to recognize that long periods of relative stability are interrupted by periods of rapid change in political issues and voting alignments. The 1930s saw the collapse of a dominant Republican coalition under the pressures of economic distress, and the 1960s saw the disruption of the New Deal coalition, as race and a costly war split the Democratic Party and as social and economic changes brought new issues and patterns of thinking into politics. Republicans again became the dominant presidential party, but then Bill Clinton and Ross Perot broke the Republican lock on the presidency.

Electoral change is hard to foresee. In November 1990 few people imagined that George H. W. Bush would be defeated by a little-known Democratic bench player. But my sense today is that we may be approaching another point at which change is imminent. A new generation has matured, one for whom the old battles of the 1960s seem no more relevant than the Great Depression did to my generation. Partisans may be polarized, but 35 percent to 40 percent of the country declines to state a party affiliation.[25] The cold war is over, and we are struggling to formulate national security policies for a new era. Many Americans are uncertain about aggressive Bush administration policies but simultaneously uncertain that Democrats are tough enough to meet contemporary threats. Many Americans realize that significant fiscal challenges lie ahead, as baby boomers age and make major demands on Social Security and especially Medicare, but both parties treat such impending problems as fodder for political campaigns rather than national problems to be solved. The same is true of health care. Democrats substitute interest group alliances and ideology for evidence in social policy, while Republicans substitute interest group alliances and religion for science in health and environmental policy. The political system seems disconnected from the country.

Under such conditions, pressure builds and eruptions occur. Parties fissure between old guard and maverick factions, and wild cards like George Wallace and Ross Perot come out of nowhere, surprising the political establishment and upsetting old equilibriums. Perhaps we are building toward such a flash point. Certainly the 2006 elections showed signs of disruption. Although detailed analyses remain in the future, and the war in Iraq is undoubtedly a large part of the explanation for the election outcomes, preliminary evidence indicates that moderates and independents thought to be safely wrapped up by the Republicans went the other way. Swing voters had not disappeared; they just had seen little reason to change their behavior in the three preceding elections.

But if I am correct that the country as a whole is far less divided and politically stable than is often assumed, then everything depends on the candidates. As we approach the 2008 elections, uncertainty reigns. If, in the end, the presidential contest pits a traditional Democrat like Hillary Clinton or Joe Biden against a Bush-like Republican such as Mike Huckabee or Sam Brownback, the appearance of polarization likely will persist. But the two leading Republican candidates in 2007 are John McCain and Rudy Giuliani, who are very different from George W. Bush.

McCain appears to polarize Republicans more than he polarizes the country, and the nomination of either would likely disrupt recent voting patterns. And one can only imagine the potential disruption of an Obama-Giuliani contest. Ironically, the electoral legacy of the Bush administration might be the end of the voting alignments that elected and reelected him.

Notes

1. Simon Schama, "Onward Christian Soldiers," *Guardian,* November 5, 2004, http://www. guardian.co.uk/uselections2004/story/0,13918,1344144,00.html (accessed August 23, 2006).
2. Matthew Dowd, Bush reelection strategist. Dowd was explaining why Bush had not tried to expand his electoral base. Quoted in Ron Brownstein, "Bush Falls to Pre-9/11 Approval Rating," *Los Angeles Times,* October 3, 2003, A1.
3. E. J. Dionne Jr., "One Nation Deeply Divided," *Washington Post,* November 7, 2003, A31.
4. http://abcnews.go.com/2020/story?id=2140483&page=1 (accessed July 5, 2006).
5. Morris P. Fiorina, Samuel Abrams, and Jeremy Pope, *Culture War? The Myth of a Polarized America* (New York: Pearson Longman, 2006), 47.
6. Ibid., chap. 3.
7. Paul DiMaggio, John Evans, and Bethany Bryson, "Have Americans' Social Attitudes Become More Polarized?" *American Journal of Sociology* 102 (1996): 690–775; John Evans, "Have Americans' Attitudes Become More Polarized? An Update," *Social Science Quarterly* 84 (2003): 71–90.
8. On the problems with the exit poll survey item see Fiorina, Abrams, and Pope, *Culture War?* 146–149.
9. Alan Abramowitz, "Terrorism, Gay Marriage, and Incumbency: Explaining the Republican Victory in the 2004 Presidential Election," *The Forum* 2 (2004); Barry Burden, "An Alternative Account of the 2004 Presidential Election," *The Forum* 2 (2004); D. Sunshine Hillygus and Todd Shields, "Moral Issues and Voter Decision Making in the 2004 Presidential Election," *PS: Political Science and Politics* 38 (2005): 2001–2008.
10. Various sources report somewhat different figures because of the lack of comparable survey questions between 2000 and 2004. For example, Pew reports a ten percentage point increase in evangelical support for Bush in 2004 over 2000, but the 2000 figure is an estimate from a preelection poll because the 2000 exit polls did not include a variable to identify evangelicals; http://people-press.org/commentary/display.php3?AnalysisID=103.
11. Michael Barone, *Almanac of American Politics* (Washington, D.C.: National Journal, 2002), 27–28; Geoffrey Layman, *Religious and Cultural Conflict in American Party Politics* (New York: Columbia, 2001), chap. 5.
12. Peter Berger, ed., *The Desecularization of the World* (Washington, D.C.: Ethics and Public Policy Center, 1999).
13. The relationship between income and presidential vote in 2004 has spawned a lively controversy. For the claim that moral issues have replaced economic issues among many lower-income voters see Robert Frank, *What's the Matter with Kansas?* (New York: Metropolitan Books, 2004); cf. Larry Bartels, "What's the Matter with What's the Matter with

Kansas?" *Quarterly Journal of Political Science* (in press); Andrew Gelman, Boris Shor, Joseph Bafumi, David Park, "Rich State, Poor State, Red State, Blue State: What's the Matter with Connecticut?" unpublished manuscript.

14. Matthew Levendusky, "Sorting: Explaining Change in the U.S. Electorate" (PhD diss., Stanford University, 2006).

15. Fiorina, Abrams, and Pope, *Culture War?* 89–91.

16. James Q. Wilson, letter to the editor, *Commentary,* May 2006, 6.

17. Hillygus and Shields, "Moral Issues and Voter Decision Making."

18. Diana Mutz and Byron Reeves, "The New Videomalaise: Effects of Televised Incivility on Political Trust," *American Political Science Review* 99 (2005): 1.

19. Philip Klinkner, "Mr. Bush's War: Foreign Policy in the 2004 Election," *Presidential Studies Quarterly* 36(2006): 281–296.

20. Gary Jacobson, *A Divider, Not a Uniter* (New York: Longman, 2007).

21. California is by no means unusual. After the 2004 elections twenty-two states had governors of the party other than the one that won the 2004 presidential vote.

22. Campbell's definition of the "base" (strong and weak partisans plus independent leaners who do not place themselves in the exact center of the ideological scale) is extremely generous.

23. For explanations of and excuses for the 2000 performance of forecasting models, see recaps in *PS: Political Science and Politics,* March 2001, and in the May 2001 issue of *American Politics Research.*

24. Interestingly, Edsall reports that Karl Rove was content with the compassionate conservative strategy but was persuaded by pollster Matthew Dowd to adopt a "feed the base" strategy because swing voters had disappeared. Ironically, Dowd later became Arnold Schwarzenegger's chief campaign strategist. The Schwarzenegger phenomenon is nothing if not a creation of swing voters. Thomas Edsall, *Building Red America* (New York: Basic Books, 2006), 50–52.

25. This is the proportion of Americans who answer "independent" when asked the standard NES party identification question: "Generally speaking, do you consider yourself a Democrat, a Republican, or an Independent?" I do not have the space to debate the common practice in which independents who lean toward a party are classified as partisans. Rather, I agree with Warren Miller that it was a mistake for the authors of *The American Voter* to differentiate degrees of partisanship and independence because the latter are so subject to short-term influences. Moreover, someone who declines to classify themselves as a partisan is announcing a kind of separation from party, even if they generally vote for a particular party because they agree with its values or positions more than they do with the other party. See Miller, "Party Identification, Realignment, and Party Voting: Back to the Basics," *American Political Science Review* 85 (1991): 557–568; cf. Angus Campbell, Philip Converse, Warren Miller, and Donald Stokes, *The American Voter* (New York: Wiley, 1960).

CHAPTER 6

Supplying the Defect of Better Motives?

The Bush II Administration and
the Constitutional System

Joel D. Aberbach

BACK IN 1788, THE AUTHOR of *Federalist* 51 grappled with the problem of maintaining the separation of powers that is at the heart of the American constitutional system. To secure against the "gradual concentration" of power in the same "department of government," it was thought necessary to give to "each department the necessary constitutional means and personal motives to resist encroachment of the others." No. 51 then holds, in one of the most oft-cited statements in the *Federalist Papers:*

> In framing a government which is to be administered by men over men, the great difficulty lies in this: you must first enable the government to control itself. A dependence on the people is, no doubt, the primary control on the government; but experience has taught mankind the necessity of auxiliary precautions.
>
> This policy of supplying, by opposite and rival interests, the defect of better motives, might be traced through the whole system of human affairs, private as well as public.[1]

Of all the issues that the administration of George W. Bush has raised, none is as central as its relationship to the constitutional order in the United States. The odds are that long after the problems caused by its huge budget deficits and its disastrous war in Iraq have been resolved, students and practitioners in American government will still be debating (and living with) the effects of its conceptions of executive power. Of the many controversial aspects of the administration, its notions and actions with respect to the role and powers of the presidency may be the most fundamentally important and controversial legacy it leaves behind. Some may embrace the package of doctrines and techniques that the Bush II administration has employed. Others will reject it all outright. And most will probably fall somewhere in between. But few are likely to escape its impact.

Presidential Power

Presidential power and the efforts of presidents to expand their powers are staple subjects of the literature on the American presidency. Some scholars stress the limits on presidential power. They typically see presidents as constrained by the separation of powers system (or the system of "separated institutions sharing powers," as Richard Neustadt famously phrased it) and obligated by the structure of the system to bargain with others, since their opportunities to command effectively are few and far between. To quote Neustadt again, the president's power is "the power to persuade." Presidents are important, but so are others who, in the American constitutional system, have been given their own means and motives to resist and to act. Presidents are advised to teach realism to the people to avoid the disappointments that may follow promises that cannot be fulfilled.[2]

Other scholars, while not necessarily denying the intent of the Framers, have a different take on the presidency. They also see a president who is hemmed in by the design of the American system, with its multiple centers of power, but one who reacts in a variety of ways aimed at avoiding the bargaining and compromises that are the hallmark of Neustadt's version of the presidency. Whether because presidents simply crave power or because of the expectations of the public that presidents act decisively to solve problems, or both, presidents in this version of the office do what they can to govern on their own. They politicize the executive branch to the maximum extent possible in order to overcome the influence of the "permanent government" (career civil servants). And they centralize decision making as much as possible in the White House, seeking to turn cabinet members and the departments into instruments for carrying out White House directives and subjugating or ignoring Congress when it will not follow the president's lead.

Scholars who work in this latter tradition, or who examine its validity and utility, focus on the many tools presidents have used to enhance their power. Books with titles like *Power without Persuasion: The Politics of Direct Presidential Action; With the Stroke of a Pen: Executive Orders and Presidential Power;* and *By Order of the President: The Use and Abuse of Executive Direct Action* have proliferated over the last few years, a testament to the increasing assertiveness of many presidents as well as to the influence of this approach to conducting and understanding the presidency.[3] There is lively debate about the legitimacy of many techniques presidents have used, but little or none about the fact of their use.

Presidential power has grown by fits and starts since the beginning of the Republic itself. In the late 1960s and early 1970s it reached a crescendo of assertiveness in the administration of Richard Nixon. Nixon's "administrative presidency" strategy was a bold and bald attempt to assert presidential control of the government using administrative techniques. Frustrated with politics as usual, Nixon aimed "to *take over* the bureaucracy and *take on* the Congress, to concentrate on administrative steps and correspondingly to downgrade legislation as the principal route for bringing about domestic change."[4] His scheme was to appoint administration loyalists (rather than notables with their own bases of power or independent-minded policy experts) to key positions in the departments and agencies, to refuse to spend moneys appropriated by Congress for programs he did not favor (impoundment), to have regulations written that would make the implementation of laws fit his policy agenda regardless of the actual statutory text, and to use reorganizations to weaken the power of established bureaus and interest groups so as to facilitate policy changes.

The administrative presidency strategy was brought low by the Watergate scandal and Nixon's eventual resignation from office, but it did not disappear from the radar of presidential politics. After an interval during the Ford and Carter administrations, the strategy burst onto the scene again in the administration of Ronald Reagan. Reagan pursued Nixon's plans in a more hospitable environment (the Senate, for example, was in Republican hands for much of the Reagan period) until the Iran-Contra scandal forced him to tread more lightly and to seek greater accommodation with his opponents. And whereas Reagan's successor, George H. W. Bush (Bush I), was not nearly as forceful about presidential power, he was demonstrably more assertive than Ford and Carter.[5] The same can be said of Bill Clinton.

In the tenure of George W. Bush (Bush II), the administrative presidency has been brought back with a vengeance; indeed, it has reached heights probably thought unattainable by Bush's most assertive predecessors. As Andrew Rudalevige observed in *The New Imperial Presidency,*

> [H]as the governmental balance of power shifted back to the president to an extent comparable to the Vietnam/Watergate era?
>
> The short answer is "yes.". . .
>
> [P]residents have regained freedom of unilateral action in a variety of areas, from executive privilege to war powers to covert operations to campaign spending. There are meaningful parallels between the justificatory language of the Nixon administration and that of our most recent presidents. . . .
>
> Read as simple sequence, the events detailed in this book present a set of linear trends: the rise of presidential power to the 1960s, the overstretch of the presidency past "Savior" to "Satan," the resurgence of other political actors through the 1970s, the countersurge of presidential initiative starting in the 1980s and accelerating into overdrive after September 11, 2001.[6]

One can argue about how linear the trend since Nixon may be or whether it was September 11 that gave the impetus for the George W. Bush administration's drive toward unilateral power. Indeed, I think the evidence is that although September 11 gave the Bush administration an opportunity to do things it might have found more difficult to do before the tragedy of that day, it was more a facilitator of its basic design than a cause. But the clear fact is that Bush has pushed the envelope to the point that one can ask whether his administration has effectively transformed the system that the authors of the *Federalist Papers* (most certainly of *Federalist* 51) thought they were bequeathing to future generations of Americans.

The balance of this chapter will be taken up in discussing the Bush administration's efforts to assert presidential authority, with particular emphasis on authority within the executive branch and in relation to Congress. I will also give brief attention to the administration's management reform program.

My major theme is that the history of the Bush administration should be seen as a concerted attack on the original model of the American political system, which was meant to produce a system of checks and balances, consultation, and bargaining that would protect against rash decisions and the ambitions and arbitrariness of rulers. The administration has been relentless in claiming and exercising presidential power with respect to Congress, the rest of the executive branch, and indeed, the world at large. It has also, parenthetically, been relentless in appointing federal judges who endorse its view of executive power, an effort, not fully successful so far, to ensure that its views will prevail when tested in the courts.[7]

After a brief review of the Bush administration's pattern of behavior, described in greater detail in earlier essays I have written on its uses of presidential power,[8] I will focus on doctrines and actions that epitomize its underlying approach to executive authority. This chapter will close with a discussion of the implications of the Bush administration for American democracy.

Administering the Government: "I'm the Decider"

George W. Bush took office in January 2001 following a closely contested election that was decided by the Supreme Court. Bush had lost the popular vote and, many believed, also the vote in Florida that was eventually awarded to him through the Court's decision. Some expected the new president to play the role of conciliator and bargainer, if for no other reason than the nature of the 2000 election and the obvious fragility of his popular support. Bush, however, was relatively undeterred by what had transpired and set out to govern with the vigor and authority of a clear winner. It was soon apparent that he was not going to be a Neustadt-style president. Bush's rather inelegant comment, in spring 2006, about his determination to retain Donald Rumsfeld as secretary of defense in the face of heavy criticism, aptly summarized his approach to governing, one adopted from the beginning and applied in numerous areas beyond personnel decisions: "I'm the decider and I decide what's best."9

Bush's advisers drew heavily on the approach used by the Reagan transition of 1980 in staffing the administration. The appointment of senior White House staff was the highest priority, so as to give "clear direction" to cabinet officers. Subcabinet appointments were made "collaboratively," according to a key White House operative, but with a big role for the members of the White House personnel staff who were to ensure that appointees had the "desired qualities for each position."10 Bush pushed, successfully in most cases, for the confirmation of administration loyalists but used recess appointments—appointments when the Senate is in recess— to put several of his most controversial appointees into office. (A prominent example was the appointment of John Bolton as ambassador to the United Nations.) Civil servants were to do as they were told and to avoid troubling the administration with information or data that might counter its policy preferences. The administration was not shy about asserting executive privilege and, in the particularly noteworthy case of the energy task force convened by Vice President Dick Cheney, was successful in refusing to disclose information to the General Accounting Office on the task force's composition, criteria for selection, and cost, in essence asserting the right to withhold information from Congress even without invoking executive privilege. "Executive orders, rule changes, and managerial realignment" were used to establish controversial programs such as the Faith-Based Initiative—attacked by opponents as a constitutionally questionable violation of the separation of church and state— that were not politically palatable enough to receive approval from the Republican-dominated Congress.11 And indeed, despite its firm control of Congress on most matters, the administration made "particularly aggressive" use of rule-making to shape policy in a variety of areas.12

One could choose many other areas to write about in painting a picture of the Bush administration's approach to presidential power and to the role of the executive branch, but I will focus here on three that epitomize both the strong role the administration has claimed and exercised and the significance for the U.S. system of government of the administration's behavior.

Signing Statements

On April 30, 2006, a story by Charlie Savage, a reporter for the *Boston Globe,* reported that George W. Bush "has quietly claimed the authority to disobey more than 750 [provisions of] laws enacted since he took office, asserting that he has the power to set aside any statute passed by Congress when it conflicts with his interpretation of the Constitution."13 Using statistics compiled by Professor Christopher Kelley, of Miami University of Ohio, Savage compared the 750 figure—a figure that neared 1,150 by the start of the 110th Congress in January 2007[14]—to the 232 provisions of law challenged or interpreted by George H. W. Bush during his four years in office and the 140 objected to by Bill Clinton in his eight years as president. The conclusion drawn was that Bush, who to that point had not vetoed a single bill, had abandoned the constitutionally prescribed veto in favor of a far more questionable method: the "signing statement."

In a signing statement the president, after signing a bill into law, issues an announcement of how he interprets the law, in many cases going so far as stating that he will not, or does not have to, carry out provisions of the law that he believes contravene his authority. An American Bar Association (ABA) report on the subject of signing statements quoted Savage at length:

> Legal scholars say the scope and aggression of Bush's assertions that he can bypass the laws represent a concerted effort to expand his power at the expense of Congress, upsetting the balance between the branches of government. The Constitution is clear in assigning to Congress the power to write the laws and to the president a duty "to take care that the laws be faithfully executed." Bush, however, has repeatedly declared that he does not need to "execute" a law he believes is unconstitutional.[15]

The ABA report also drew on the work of Phillip J. Cooper, whose research on presidential signing statements has become a standard in the field. Cooper holds that the use of signing statements has attained a special significance in the administration of George W. Bush. While presidential signing statements go back at least to the administration of James Monroe, it was in the administration of President Ronald Reagan that "the use of signing statements escalated both quantitatively and qualitatively."[16] Cooper argues that "the [George W.] Bush administration has effectively expanded the scope and character of the signing statement, not only to address the specific provisions of legislation that the White House wishes to nullify but also to reposition and strengthen the powers of the presidency relative to the Congress."[17]

In brief, Edwin Meese, President Ronald Reagan's attorney general, pioneered the use of signing statements as "a significant and commonly used instrument of executive direct action,"[18] and Reagan's successors have continued to use them. However, as the ABA report points out, the Clinton administration's internal documents cautioned that "if the President believes that the Court would sustain a particular provision as constitutional, the President should execute the statute notwithstanding his own beliefs about the constitutional issue."[19] Further,

> Whereas President Clinton on occasion asked for memoranda from the Office of Legal Counsel on his authority to challenge or reject controversial provisions in bills presented to him, it is reported that in the Bush II

administration all bills are routed through Vice President Cheney's office to be searched for perceived threats to the "unitary executive"—the theory that the President has the sole power to control the execution of powers delegated to him in the Constitution and encapsulated in his Commander in Chief powers and in his constitutional mandate to see that "the laws are faithfully executed."[20]

As I mentioned above, then, the George W. Bush administration is unique both in the extent to which it has used signing statements and in the dogged way it has applied a highly controversial notion of executive power—one in which the boundaries on presidential power are set and enforced by presidents themselves—in its statements. The administration argues that the president has exclusive administrative power and that he can nullify provisions of the law that contravene that interpretation. This claim is made over and over again in what has become boilerplate wording in the extraordinarily large number of signing statements the Bush White House has issued.

For example, President Bush signed a Department of Justice Appropriations Authorization Act on November 2, 2002. The signing statement took up two single-spaced pages and challenged a whole series of provisions. Two examples should suffice:

> Section 11015 of the Act purports to give U.S. Attorneys in certain circumstances "exclusive authority" to select an annuity broker for structured settlement purposes. The executive branch shall construe this section in a manner consistent with the President's constitutional authority to supervise the unitary executive branch.
>
> Section 402 of the Act adds sections 2002 and 2004 to the Omnibus Crime Control and Safe Streets Act of 1968, which purport to give "final authority" to a subordinate of the Attorney General over certain grants, cooperative agreements, and contracts awarded by the subordinate's office and to allow the Attorney General to act on behalf of the President to give the subordinate a role representing the U.S. Government at the United Nations and other international fora. The executive branch shall construe sections 2002 and 2004 in a manner consistent with the President's constitutional authorities to supervise the unitary executive branch and to conduct the Nation's foreign affairs and, subject to those authorities, with the Secretary of State's authority pursuant to 22 U.S.C. section 2672.[21]

I use these examples because they seem like such small potatoes, yet the statements have big implications as they accumulate. Notice that each of the sections mention that the act passed by Congress "purports" to do something. What that means is that the administration doesn't necessarily intend to pay any attention to what the act says, but intends rather to do what it thinks appropriate in line with its interpretation of executive power and supremacy. The Constitution of the United States may say in Article I, Section 7, clause 2 (the Presentment Clause) that the president must accept or reject a bill in its entirety, but the language above is effectively a presidential line-item veto.[22] A strong argument can be made that these signing statements represent a powerful amendment to the Constitution in favor of the executive, made all the more powerful, and indeed remarkable, because no process of amendment has taken place.

Were signing statements used mainly to quibble about small issues or even used somewhat ambiguously to muddy larger issues, they would be important but probably go little noticed by most and remain as Phillip Cooper describes them: "audacious claims to power hidden in plain sight."[23] However, one of Bush's signing statements was so shocking politically that it cast the entire practice into public light. That signing statement accompanied a bill containing an amendment by Sen. John McCain of Arizona that outlawed—or so its sponsors thought—the torturing of detainees. Bush had threatened to veto the bill if the McCain provision was included, but the bill passed with a veto-proof majority.

What Bush then did was sign the bill (in late December 2005), praise it in the presence of Senator McCain, and then quietly issue a signing statement that, as Charlie Savage of the *Boston Globe* wrote, "reserved the right to bypass the law under his powers as commander in chief. . . . declaring that he will view the interrogation limits in the context of his broader powers to protect national security. This means Bush believes he can waive the restrictions . . . White House and legal specialists said."[24]

An administration official quoted in the story said that Bush intended to follow the law and not have the United States use "cruel, unusual, and degrading treatment" of prisoners unless that conflicted, in the administration's view, with his "obligation to defend and protect the country as the commander in chief." Andrew Golove, a New York University professor of law interviewed for the story, had a less kind interpretation of the signing statement:

> The signing statement is saying "I will only comply with this law when I want to, and if something arises in the war on terrorism where I think it's important to torture or engage in cruel, inhuman, or degrading conduct, I have the authority to do so and nothing in this law is going to stop me."[25]

The struggle over the scope of executive power is an old one, and practical matters always have the potential to intrude on the niceties of clear doctrine. But the general principle stated by the ABA report is one that the Bush administration has challenged frontally: "Article II, Section 1, vests the 'Executive Power' in the President. But at least since 1688, the executive power as conceived in Great Britain and America excluded a power to dispense with or suspend execution of the laws for any reason."[26] The Bush administration has not been apologetic about its views and actions and, while not always shouting its doctrine from the rooftops, has, to its credit, been willing to state its perspective on presidential powers rather clearly. But in doing so, it has pushed beyond its predecessors, and, to quote from the conclusion of the ABA report, "the use, frequency and nature of the President's signing statements . . . [represent] a serious assault on the constitutional system of checks and balances."[27]

Military Commissions

As in many areas connected to the war on terror, the administration's decisions to use military commissions to try terror suspects held at Guantanamo Bay and to argue that Congress could be excluded from such decisions have both been highly controversial. As a *New York Times* report said succinctly, "At issue was whether the president could unilaterally establish military commissions with rights different from those allowed at a court-martial to try detainees for war crimes."[28]

The Supreme Court, in its June 2006 decision in *Hamdan v. Rumsfeld,* "ruled that the commissions, which were outlined by Bush in a military order on November 13, 2004, were neither authorized by federal law nor required by military necessity, and ran afoul of the Geneva Conventions."[29] The vote was five to three, with Chief Justice Roberts not participating because he had been part of the appeals court panel that had previously upheld the commissions.

Reports indicated that "the executive order establishing military commissions was issued without consultations with then-secretary of state Colin L. Powell or then-national security adviser Condoleezza Rice after a concerted push by [Vice President] Cheney's legal adviser, David S. Addington, now his chief of staff."[30] And it also became clear that the administration, as in other cases I will mention later in the chapter, dismissed the opinions of career experts in the area, in this case those in the military justice system:

> "We argued this would come back to haunt us and it would taint the military justice system," said retired Rear Admiral Donald Guter, the Navy's top uniformed lawyer when "military commission" trials for Guantanamo Bay detainees were first proposed in 2001. "We were warning that you would have to be careful to provide basic protections.". . .
> Senior administration officials told Guter and other JAGs [members of the military's Judge Advocate General's corps] that the urgency to extract intelligence meant that the traditional military justice could not be used.[31]

But there was more to the story than mere disregard of expert opinion. While administration officials argued to the JAGs that normal procedures needed to be dispensed with to extract intelligence for the war on terror, Admiral Guter said there was "another motive":

> This was seen as an opportunity, a vehicle to restore presidential power and authority. It was a very convenient vehicle. It was perfect. Fear tends to drive power to authority and to the executive branch.[32]

The military commissions, in other words, can be seen as part of a self-conscious and concerted effort to enhance executive power and to help bring to fruition a goal long sought by Vice President Cheney—restoration of the immense conception of presidential power that prevailed in the Nixon White House and that was diminished through reforms enacted in reaction to the Nixon administration's abuses.[33] (I will discuss the Military Commission Act of 2006 in the section below on Congress's remarkably weak responses to Bush's assertiveness.)

Domestic Spying

In December 2005, after the *New York Times* published an account of a clandestine National Security Agency wiretapping program that included warrantless taps on phone calls when one of the parties is in the United States, President Bush criticized the leak as harmful to the country because it threatened a program "necessary to win this war [on terror] and to protect the American people."[34] The problem, however, was that the Foreign Intelligence Surveillance Act (FISA) of 1978, one of the framework statutes passed in the 1970s to regulate executive behavior,[35] "requires counterterrorism officials to obtain court orders to eavesdrop on people inside the United States"[36] and the government had not done that. As the *Times* argued,

> If Mr. Bush had wanted to conduct the wiretapping within the law, he could have quite easily done so, using the Foreign Intelligence Surveillance Act. That law, written after the Watergate scandal and the eavesdropping abuses of the Vietnam era, created a special court to approve applications for domestic surveillance. The court operates in secret and has rarely denied the authorities' requests. Even in the post-9/11 era, it should have met the administration's needs. And if there was a problem, Congress had shown itself ready and willing to amend the law.[37]

The administration, however, argued that its legal authority to conduct the warrantless wiretapping is based in the president's inherent power in his constitutional role as commander in chief and on authority implicit in the congressional resolution authorizing the use of military force that was passed in the wake of the 9/11 terrorist attacks, and that it therefore did not need to follow the FISA requirements. The attorney general, Alberto Gonzales, also "labeled as 'myth' the idea that the program 'is an invasion of privacy and an unlawful eavesdropping tool.' The program, he said, 'does not invade anyone's privacy unless you are talking to the enemy in this time of war.' "[38]

One problem with the administration's argument is that Sen. Thomas Daschle, D-S.D., who was Senate majority leader at the time of the 9/11 resolution, asserts that the administration asked for, and was denied, the words "in the United States" in the resolution authorizing the use of force. Daschle wrote:

> Literally minutes before the Senate cast its vote, the administration sought to add the words "in the United States and" after "appropriate force" in the agreed-upon text. This last-minute change would have given the president broad authority to exercise expansive powers not just overseas—where we all understood he wanted authority to act—but right here in the United States, potentially against American citizens. I could see no justification for Congress to accede to this extraordinary request for additional authority. I refused.[39]

Another problem is more basic and is the same one that has arisen throughout the Bush administration: To what extent is the president bound by laws duly passed by Congress and enacted (signed by the president, passed over his veto, or become law without his signature)? As an open letter signed by many scholars of law and former government officials put it pointedly:

> Just as the President is bound by the statutory prohibition on torture, he is bound by the statutory dictates of FISA. . . .
>
> If the administration felt that FISA was insufficient, the proper course was to seek legislative amendment, as it did with other aspects of FISA in the Patriot Act, and as Congress expressly contemplated when it enacted the wartime wiretap provision in FISA. One of the crucial features of a constitutional democracy is that it is always open to the President—or anyone else—to seek to change the law. But it is also beyond dispute that, in such a democracy, the President cannot simply violate criminal laws behind closed doors because he deems them obsolete or impracticable.[40]

Muzzling Expertise

The Bush administration has been marked by deep commitment to policy views and approaches to administrative power that make it unwilling to give much credence to the views of others. There is, of course, no general principle that the views of the administration are wrong and those of other people (including experts) are correct, but one reason to have a civil (and military) service of experts—and the United

States has one—is that it can provide a wealth of information and interpretation that can be valuable in the decision process.[41]

The history of the Bush administration is littered with instances of expertise ignored, both domestically and in foreign and military policy. Sometimes these choices have had obviously dire consequences—the decision to invade Iraq with a relatively small force, for example—and sometimes what might generously be described as debatable consequences.

Perhaps the most famous case is the administration's disparagement as "wildly off the mark" of the warnings of former army chief of staff General Eric Shinseki that the United States would need several hundred thousand troops to secure postwar Iraq.[42] The consequences of ignoring Shinseki's assessment were, as we now know, grave. Kori Schake, a former director for defense strategy on the National Security Council staff (2002–2005), was quoted as follows in a 2007 *New York Times* article that analyzed both the treatment of Shinseki and his "vindication" by a strategy change the administration eventually embraced:

> It sent a very clear signal to the military leadership about how that kind of military judgment was going to be valued. So it served to silence critics just at the point in time when, internal to the process, you most wanted critical judgment.[43]

A statement to Congress in late 2006 by retiring General John P. Abizaid, who was completing his service as commander of Central Command in the Middle East, bluntly summarizes the current assessment of General Shinseki's advice: "General Shinseki was right that a greater international force contribution, U.S. force contribution and Iraqi force contribution should have been available immediately after major combat operations."[44]

Another prominent case is the dispute over global warming. The leading dissident on the issue within the government, Dr. James E. Hansen, a climate expert and director of the NASA Goddard Institute, accused the administration of "picking and choosing information according to the answer that they want to get."[45] The administration attempted to control Hansen's public utterances until it was embarrassed by the revelation that the young political appointee who had the task of doing so turned out to have a falsified resume, giving Hansen celebrity status and the chance to preface a review he wrote for the *New York Review of Books* by saying that the opinions expressed therein should be read "as personal views under the protection of the First Amendment of the United States Constitution."[46]

Andrew Revkin summarized the core of the disagreements and the general nature of the process as follows:

> Several dozen interviews with administration officials and with scientists in and out of government, along with a variety of documents, show that the core

of the clash is over instances in which scientists say that objective and relevant information is ignored or distorted in service of pre-established policy goals. Scientists were essentially locked out of important internal White House debates; candidates for advisory panels were asked about their politics as well as their scientific work; and the White House exerted broad control over how scientific findings were to be presented in public reports or news releases.[47]

Other examples are reluctance by the Environmental Protection Agency to undertake mercury reduction studies because of an administration "fear that the results would justify deeper and faster reductions than it favored";[48] a reported effort by John Bolton when he was undersecretary of state for arms control and international security to remove an official working closely with then-secretary of state Colin Powell from his duties in the nonproliferation bureau of the State Department "in what U.S. officials described as a third attempt by Bolton to purge career officials he perceived as impeding his policy goals";[49] and a particularly infamous case in which the Medicare program's chief actuary was illegally threatened that he would be fired if he revealed his estimates of the cost of the administration's drug benefit proposal.[50]

All in all, the Bush II administration's record appears to be one of expertise wasted. In the case of Iraq, the unwillingness to take account of the views of those who clearly knew more than the administration and many of its political appointees almost certainly cost thousands their lives and most likely led to even greater misery than the population of that unfortunate country had already been suffering.

A Broken Congress?

The American constitutional order rests institutionally on a set of separated "departments of government," as *Federalist* 51 called them, which are meant to check one another. With the Bush administration flexing its institutional muscles aggressively, where has Congress been?

A recent book on Congress by Thomas Mann and Norman Ornstein gives a succinct response in its title: *The Broken Branch*.[51] The book portrays a situation in which too many legislators have ceased to have the institutional identity (institutional patriotism)[52] that the system's logic assumes would push them to defend the interests of their chamber and of Congress as a whole when threatened by the executive. Congress has failed to do adequate oversight. It tolerates executive secrecy where it should not. ("The passivity and indifference of Congress and its leaders to their independent and assertive role fit perfectly with the Bush administration's assertive and protective attitude toward executive power and its aversion to sharing information with Congress and the public.")[53] And its leaders (particularly its

Republican leaders when there was unified government, with a Republican president and a Republican Congress) have been complicit—using leadership tools and the effects of greatly increased partisan polarization—in allowing the institution to become subordinate to the president.[54]

One can argue about the details of the Mann and Ornstein indictment, but there is little doubt that the general thrust of their critique is correct and that the Bush administration has generally faced a Congress that, in their unkind but accurate description, has been "supine." [55] Three examples, articulated to the cases examined above, should provide sufficient evidence that Mann and Ornstein have an extremely strong case.

First, in 2002 Congress passed a bill (discussed in the section above on signing statements as the Justice Appropriations Authorization Act of 2002) "which required the Attorney General to submit a detailed report of any instance in which he or any Justice Department official 'establishes or implements a formal or informal policy to refrain . . . from enforcing, applying, or administering any provision of any Federal statute . . . on the grounds that such provision is unconstitutional.' "[56] The president signed the bill and then issued a signing statement that contained the now standard boilerplate language about construing bills "in a manner consistent with the constitutional authorities of the President to supervise the unitary executive branch and to withhold information the disclosure of which could impair foreign relations, the national security, the deliberative processes of the Executive, or the performance of the Executive's constitutional duties."[57] As the ABA report on presidential signing statements indicates, the statement then instructed the agencies "not to comply with a congressional directive requiring them to report instances in which they have been ordered not to comply, . . . [a truly] absurd result . . . that underscores the reason we [the authors of the ABA report] so strongly oppose such use of signing statements as 'contrary to the rule of law and our constitutional system of separation of powers.' "[58] The case may have had an "absurd result" in constitutional terms, but to the best of my knowledge, Congress did not challenge it effectively, if at all.

Second, the Supreme Court's 2006 decision in *Hamdan v. Rumsfeld,* overturning the military commissions set up by the Bush administration, provided Congress with an outstanding opportunity to assert its authority as a coequal branch of government. Bush had acted on his own, bypassing Congress (maintaining that he did not need congressional authorization), declaring parts of the Geneva Convention inoperative ("quaint," in the words of the attorney general), and placing extraordinary limits on rights traditionally accorded to defendants.

Legislation was now imperative. Congress did pass a law, with opposition from some, particularly Democrats (though not all of them), but the result was described as follows by the *Washington Post:* "Republicans in both chambers, forgetting that Congress is supposed to be an independent branch, snapped to attention when the president told them what to do."[59] What the bill did, in the words of an analysis by

Scott Shane and Adam Liptak, was "give the president more power over terrorism suspects than he had before the Supreme Court decision . . . in *Hamdan v. Rumsfeld*":

> Rather than reining in the formidable presidential powers Mr. Bush and Vice President Cheney have asserted since Sept. 11, 2001, the law gives some of those powers a solid statutory foundation. In effect, it allows the president to identify enemies, imprison them indefinitely and interrogate them—albeit with a ban on the harshest treatment—beyond the reach of the full court reviews traditionally afforded criminal defendants and ordinary prisoners. . . .
>
> In very specific ways, the bill is a rejoinder to the *Hamdan* ruling, in which several justices said the absence of Congressional authorization was a central flaw in the administration's approach. The new bill solves that problem, legal experts said.[60]

Whether or not the bill actually solves the problem is not yet clear since there are bound to be legal challenges.[61] One thing was clear, however: one of the key voters for the bill did not believe that it was constitutional. Sen. Arlen Specter, R-Pa., chairman of the Judiciary Committee,

> voted for the bill after telling reporters earlier that he would oppose it because it is "patently unconstitutional on its face." He cited its denial of the habeas corpus right to military detainees. . . . Specter said he decided to support the bill because it has several good items, "and the court will clean it up" by striking the habeas corpus provisions.[62]

The net result to date (December 2006) is a constitutionally questionable statute that enhanced executive power, voted for by at least some in Congress who apparently had grave doubts about its constitutionality.[63]

Finally, when it comes to the NSA wiretapping program, there has been much noise, but little effective action, from Congress. There was, however, a controversial federal district court ruling, appealed by the administration, that the program is illegal. (The judge in that case wrote: "There are no hereditary kings in America and no powers not created by the Constitution.")[64] That case, plus others in the works (and a perceived opportunity for the Bush administration to put Democratic members of Congress at a disadvantage in the then-approaching fall elections if they appeared to be defending al Qaeda), prompted the administration to seek legal authority for the program beyond its claim of inherent presidential authority as commander in chief and authority under the 9/11, use-of-force resolution. Complex negotiations yielded proposals "to bring the program before a secret intelligence court to test its constitutionality" and a "proposal that would require warrants for eavesdropping on communications coming out of, but not into, the United States, and would put the whole issue on a fast track to the Supreme Court."[65]

However, there has been no resolution, only great controversy about notions such as using a court (called the Court of Review) for legal rulings, due to the fact that this court "has rendered only one opinion in its thirty-year history, and that opinion included its view that the president has inherent constitutional authority to eavesdrop without warrants as part of the U.S. effort against terrorism."[66]

A *New York Times* editorial summarized the effort to get a bill through in the waning days of 2006:

> The bill Mr. Bush wants was drafted by Vice President Dick Cheney's lawyers and by Senator Arlen Specter, the outgoing Republican chairman of the Judiciary Committee. Mr. Specter presented it as a compromise that would regulate the president's ability to spy on Americans' phone calls and e-mail without a court order. It really was a cave-in to Mr. Bush's effort to expand his power beyond limits that have existed for nearly 30 years. . . .
>
> There are plenty of responsible lawmakers in both parties who are sympathetic to the idea that the executive branch needed more flexibility to pursue terrorists after 9/11. It has been obvious all along that if the president feels current law is too restrictive, he should explain its shortcomings to members of Congress and ask them to amend it. The Republican majority was never going to insist on that, but the new Democratic leadership might.
>
> The White House refuses to explain itself because this has never been about catching terrorists. It is about overturning the crucial limits placed on executive authority after Watergate and Vietnam. Mr. Cheney and a few other hard-liners have been trying to turn back the clock and have succeeded in some truly scary ways, including the military commissions act they pushed through Congress before the elections. It is vital that they not be allowed to do any more harm.[67]

The bottom line, for this essay, of all these examples is that Congress has done little to protect its institutional position during the Bush years. What the Democratic Congress elected in 2006 will do remains to be seen.[68] But for the first six years of the Bush administration, at least, describing Congress as "the broken branch" seems more than justified. That would have been a problem for the American political system at any time, but in the face of a particularly assertive president, it threatened the very underpinnings of the system itself.

A Brief Note on Bush as Public Administrator

The Bush administration has continued the management reform program of Bill Clinton and Al Gore—called "reinventing government" in the Clinton-Gore administration, and aimed at producing a lean state that does what needs to be done efficiently and effectively—with some politically significant changes in emphasis.

The formal management agenda of the Bush II administration, issued through the Office of Management and Budget in 2001, has five main initiatives: strategic management of human capital; competitive sourcing; improved financial performance; expanded electronic government; and budget and performance integration.[69] The changes in emphasis mainly involve elimination of President Clinton's Labor-Management Partnership Councils, the use of outsourcing targets, development of the Program Assessment Rating Tool (PART) to assess and improve program performance, and a concerted effort to change the government's personnel system.

In brief, the changes in emphasis have brought significant conflict. Both the Department of Defense and the new Department of Homeland Security have been given the right to change personnel rules, but their efforts to do so have met strong challenges from civil service employee unions. (Elimination of the Labor-Management Partnership Councils cannot have helped here.) Outsourcing targets have met fierce resistance, with the administration's case damaged considerably by the many controversies that have accompanied the work of contractors in Iraq. Controversy was strong enough to prompt the administration to put out a fact sheet—"The Facts about the President's Management Agenda"—that attempted to defend the administration against numerous charges: that its personnel reforms were aimed at reducing spending; that it wanted to "gut employee rights"; that it was aiming to implement its personnel reforms before the changes at Defense and Homeland Security could be evaluated; that its competitive sourcing rules were stacked against federal workers and that competitive sourcing was not producing any savings; and that PART program assessments were neither transparent nor effective and "just a way for the government to terminate programs it doesn't like."[70]

Whether these charges are valid or not is beyond the scope of what I can assess here, but there is little doubt that the contracting fiascoes in Iraq have undermined considerably the administration's claims about the efficiency of outsourcing to private suppliers and service providers and that, ironically, the "first MBA president" has left a decidedly mixed legacy as a manager. He will be forever tarnished by the mismanagement of the response to Hurricane Katrina, and as James Pfiffner notes in an essay subtitled "The Public Administration Legacy of George W. Bush," although his management style, marked by "secrecy, speed, and top-down control . . . led to considerable political success, it ultimately led to administrative failures that undercut the longer term success of President Bush's policies."[71] Pfiffner argues that "ignoring the professionals" ultimately cost the administration dearly, a perspective developed earlier in this essay as well. I doubt that holders of MBA degrees have uniformly been taught to ignore experts, or to charge ahead without giving serious consideration to all feasible and available options or without consulting others or attending to their needs, but the first MBA president has not done much to enhance the public repute of that degree, at least when it comes to administrative skills.

Supplying the Defect of Better Motives?

In its own way, the Bush administration may offer unwitting proof of the value of the system that the Founders devised, one in which actors are forced to take account of the views of others and reach accommodation before acting. Yet the administration's success in doing what it wanted without serious opposition from "the broken branch" must also lead to questions about whether the Founders' system is itself fundamentally broken. Bush's administration has been a model of what Rudalevige calls "the *new* imperial presidency," and the results have not—in my view and with the 2006 election results in hand, the view of the majority of his countrymen— been good. Under Bush the U.S. government has eavesdropped on its citizens without benefit of warrants, when it could have used an already existing system or gotten new authority within the law; it has devised a plan to try accused terrorists that opens the career military to dishonor and greater chance of mistreatment should its members be captured by an opponent; it has implemented policies, such as the faith-based initiative, that not only were without congressional approval but threatened to upset delicate balances in a highly pluralist society; it has run up huge budget deficits that likely threaten the economic health of future generations; it has asserted over and over again in its signing statements that the president has the right to disregard provisions of laws he has signed because of the power of the "unitary executive" or powers that inhere in his position, doctrines that are highly controversial to say the least; and it has generally used the presidency to attain whatever the president and his close associates might want without much concern for constitutional or legal niceties or for the views of others.

What is most disconcerting about this from the perspective of the long-term health of the American political system is that, for the most part, Congress allowed Bush free rein during the first six years of his administration. When pressed, and sometimes without great pressure, it usually gave him the legislation he wanted and rarely challenged his assertions about the powers of his office. At least some of this is due to a factor that *Federalist* 51 did not envision: disciplined political parties in Congress, with the majority supporting the president. It is not my intention to argue against disciplined political parties, but the American separation of powers system, in an important respect, faces a severe handicap when a disciplined party controls both the presidency and the Congress. In that situation, the majority in Congress has little incentive to protect its institutional position by opposing the president, even when he threatens Congress's power and prerogatives. The courts have acted as something of a check so far, but there is no guarantee that they will continue to do so, especially given the judicial appointees chosen by the Bush administration. The system, then, does not necessarily supply "the defect of better motives," and when it does not, the president is free to do much that at a minimum should be carefully examined and, if necessary, should be checked by others. A parliamentary system at least leaves the majority the option (not always exercised) of removing by a vote of no confidence a prime minister who has made extraordinarily poor decisions or otherwise performed poorly; the American system requires impeachment and conviction, harder and even more divisive acts.

The *New York Times,* in an excellent editorial in July 2006, described what it called "the cost of executive arrogance" for the war on terror, but the message goes beyond that:

> The president's constant efforts to assert his power to act without consent or consultation has warped the war on terror. The unity and sense of national purpose that followed 9/11 is gone, replaced by suspicion and divisiveness that never needed to emerge. The president had no need to go it alone—everyone wanted to go with him. Both parties in Congress were eager to show they were tough on terrorism. But the obsession with presidential prerogatives created fights where no fights needed to occur and made huge messes out of programs that could have functioned more efficiently within the rules.[72]

In the end, this is not a partisan issue, for someday the Democrats will have unified control, and even that somewhat-less-disciplined party might countenance a government of the type Bush and Cheney have apparently structured—"centralized, highly secretive, its clean direct lines of authority unencumbered by information or consultation"[73] and not much constrained by the existing law. A major lesson of the Bush-Cheney administration is that something significant needs to be done to keep that from happening again, no matter which party is in power. The evolution of the presidency, along with changes in the party system and Congress, suggest that the current American constitutional order may no longer be fully adequate to that task.

Notes

I would like to thank Andrew Rudalevige, who provided insightful comments and helpful suggestions for revising the initial draft of this chapter.

1. All quotes from *Federalist* 51 in Alexander Hamilton, John Jay, and James Madison, *The Federalist* (New York: Modern Library, 1937), 336–337. There is controversy about whether No. 51 was written by Hamilton or Madison.
2. Richard E. Neustadt, *Presidential Power* (1960; repr., New York: Wiley, 1980), 26–29, 73–78. See also Charles O. Jones, *The Presidency in a Separated System,* 2nd ed. (Washington, D.C.: Brookings Institution Press, 2005).
3. William G. Howell, *Power without Persuasion* (Princeton: Princeton University Press, 2003); Kenneth R. Mayer, *With the Stroke of a Pen* (Princeton: Princeton University Press, 2001); Phillip J. Cooper, *By Order of the President* (Lawrence: University Press of Kansas, 2002).

4. Richard Nathan, *The Plot That Failed: Nixon and the Administrative Presidency* (New York: Wiley, 1975), 8.

5. See the brief discussion of the George W. Bush presidency in Joel D. Aberbach and Bert A. Rockman, *In the Web of Politics: Three Decades of the U.S. Federal Executive* (Washington, D.C.: Brookings Institution Press, 2000), 38–39.

6. Andrew Rudalevige, *The New Imperial Presidency* (Ann Arbor: University of Michigan Press, 2005), 261–262.

7. See the chapter by David A. Yalof in this volume.

8. Joel D. Aberbach, "The State of the Contemporary American Presidency," in *The George W. Bush Presidency: Appraisals and Prospects,* ed. Colin Campbell and Bert A. Rockman (Washington, D.C.: CQ Press, 2004), 46–72; and Joel D. Aberbach, "The Political Significance of the George W. Bush Administration," *Social Policy and Administration* 39, no. 2 (April 2005): 130–149.

9. "Bush Defends Embattled Rumsfeld," BBC News, April 18, 2006, http://news.bbc.co.uk/1/hi/world/americas/4919650.stm (accessed December 4, 2006).

10. The quotes are from Clay Johnson, "The 2000–2001 Presidential Transition: Planning, Goals, and Reality," *PS: Political Science and Politics* 35, no.1 (March 2002): 51, 53.

11. See A. Farris, R. P. Nathan, and D. J. Wright, "The Expanding Administrative Presidency: George W. Bush and the Faith-Based Initiative," Roundtable on Religion and Social Welfare Policy, Rockefeller Institute of Government, August 2004, www.Religionand SocialPolicy.org (accessed September 30, 2004).

12. J. Brinkley, "Out of Spotlight, Bush Overhauls U.S. Regulations," *New York Times,* August 14, 2004, www.nytimes.com (accessed August 16, 2004).

13. Charlie Savage, "Bush Challenges Hundreds of Laws: President Cites Powers of His Office," *Boston Globe,* April 30, 2006, www.boston.com (accessed December 5, 2006).

14. See the running tally at Kelley's Web site, www.users.muohio.edu/kelleycs/.

15. Quoted in American Bar Association, Task Force on Presidential Signing Statements and the Separation of Powers Doctrine, *Report,* 2, www.abanet.org (accessed July 25, 2006).

16. American Bar Association Task Force, *Report,* 7, 10.

17. Phillip J. Cooper, "George W. Bush, Edgar Allan Poe, and the Use and Abuse of Presidential Signing Statements," *Presidential Studies Quarterly* 35, no.3 (September 2005): 515–532.

18. Cooper, "George W. Bush," 517.

19. The quote is from a 1994 memo by Walter Dellinger, then head of the White House Office of Legal Counsel, cited in the American Bar Association Task Force, *Report,* 13.

20. American Bar Association Task Force, *Report,* 15.

21. "President Signs Justice Appropriations Authorization Act," signed by George W. Bush and released by the Office of the Press Secretary, November 4, 2002, www.whitehouse.gov (accessed February 24, 2006).

22. See pages 18–19 of the American Bar Association Task Force, *Report.*

23. Cooper, "George W. Bush," 530.

24. Charlie Savage, "Bush Could Bypass New Torture Ban: Waiver Right Is Reserved," *Boston Globe,* January 4, 2006, www.boston.com (accessed February 15, 2006).

25. Ibid.

26. American Bar Association Task Force, *Report,* 19.

27. Ibid., 27. As Andrew Rudalevige suggested to me, it would be very useful to know the full extent to which the administration has followed through on its claims, that is, how many provisions of law objected to in signing statements have actually not been enforced. The point is well taken, though that would be extraordinarily difficult to ascertain under the best of circumstances, and the Bush administration's penchant for secrecy compounds the difficulty.

28. Sheryl Gay Stolberg, "Justices Tacitly Backed Use of Guantanamo, Bush Says," *New York Times,* July 8, 2006, www.nytimes.com (accessed July 14, 2006).

29. Charles Lane, "High Court Rejects Detainee Tribunals," *Washington Post,* June 30, 2006, www.washingtonpost.com (accessed June 30, 2006).

30. Peter Baker and Michael Abramowitz, "Governing Philosophy Rebuffed: Ruling Emphasizes Constitutional Boundaries," *Washington Post,* June 30, 2006, www.washingtonpost.com (accessed June 30, 2006).

31. Julian E. Barnes, "Military Fought to Abide by War Rules," *Los Angeles Times,* June 30, 2006, www.latimes.com (accessed June 30, 2006).

32. Ibid.

33. For a good general account of the controversy and the political forces behind it, see Edward Luce, "For America's 'Decider' the Laws of War Still Apply: Power Play: Why Bush Is Facing a Backlash against His 'Imperial' Presidency,' " *Financial Times,* July 6, 2006, 13.

34. CNN News, "Bush Defends NSA Spying Program," January 1, 2006, http://cnn.worldnews.printhis.clickability.com (accessed December 7, 2006).

35. My thanks to Andrew Rudalevige for suggesting the use of the phrase "framework statute" to describe FISA. As he noted in private correspondence, "The phrase 'framework statute' is one that University of Chicago legal scholar Gerhard Casper has used. The idea is that these are laws designed only in part to solve a particular problem but also 'to support the organizational skeleton of the Constitution by developing a more detailed framework for governmental decision making. . . . and attempt[ing] to stabilize expectations about the ways in which governmental power is exercised.' " See Gerhard Casper, "The Constitutional Organization of the Government," *William and Mary Law Review* 26 (Winter 1985): 187–188.

36. Eric Lichtblau, "Despite a Year of Ire and Angst, Little Has Changed on Wiretaps," *New York Times,* November 25, 2006, www.nytimes.com (accessed November 27, 2006).

37. "A Crack in the Stone Wall," *New York Times,* November 30, 2006, www.nytimes.com (accessed November 30, 2006).

38. Lichtblau, "Despite a Year of Ire and Angst."

39. Barton Gellman, "Daschle: Congress Denied Bush War Powers in U.S.," *Washington Post,* December 23, 2005, www.washingtonpost.com (accessed December 23, 2005).

40. Beth Nolan et al., "On NSA Spying: A Letter to Congress," *New York Review of Books,* February 9, 2006, www.nybooks.com/articles (accessed December 7, 2006). For a defense of the NSA program, see U.S. Department of Justice (DOJ), "Legal Authorities Supporting the Activities of the National Security Agency Described by the President," January 19, 2006, www.usdoj.gov (accessed December 7, 2006). On page 1 the DOJ paper talks about "the President's well-recognized inherent constitutional authority as Commander in Chief and sole organ for the Nation in foreign affairs to conduct warrantless

surveillance of enemy forces for intelligence purposes to detect and disrupt armed attacks on the United States." Page 2 describes the administration's case under the AUMF (Authorization for the Use of Military Force) resolution.

41. See, among others, Aberbach and Rockman, *In the Web of Politics,* especially chap. 4.

42. Eric Schmidt, "Pentagon Contradicts General on Iraq Occupation Force's Size," *New York Times,* February 28, 2003, www.globalpolicy.org (accessed December 7, 2006). The author of this statement was Paul D. Wolfowitz, then the deputy secretary of defense.

43. Quoted in Thom Shanker, "New Strategy Vindicates Ex-Army Chief Shinseki," *New York Times,* January 12, 2007, www.nytimes.com (accessed January 12, 2007).

44. Ibid.

45. Andrew C. Revkin, "Bush vs. the Laureates: How Science Became a Partisan Issue," *New York Times,* October 19, 2004, www.nytimes.com (accessed October 18, 2004).

46. James Hansen, "The Threat to the Planet," *New York Review of Books,* July 13, 2006, 12.

47. Revkin, "Bush vs. the Laureates."

48. Alan C. Miller, "EPA Director Hangs Back on Ordering Mercury Studies," *Los Angeles Times,* November 7, 2004, www.latimes.com (accessed November 8, 2004).

49. Dafna Linzer, "Bolton Faces Allegations That He Tried to Fire Analysts," *New York Times,* April 15, 2005, www.washingtonpost.com (accessed April 15, 2005).

50. See Robert Pear, "Inquiry Confirms Medicare Chief Threatened Actuary," *New York Times,* July 7, 2004, www.nytimes.com (accessed September 1, 2004).

51. Thomas E. Mann and Norman J. Ornstein, *The Broken Branch: Why Congress Is Failing America and How to Get It Back on Track* (New York: Oxford University Press, 2006).

52. "Institutional patriotism" is the term that well-known scholar Donald Matthews used in a book published in 1960 to describe one of the norms then prevalent in the Senate. Mann and Ornstein (*The Broken Branch*) argue that House members had a "heavy dose of institutional patriotism" (146) as well. By the early 1990s, they say, institutional patriotism in Congress was fading fast in the face of negative views about congressional service by many new members and "the growing indifference of committee and party leaders to the history and independent role of their own institutions" (148).

53. Mann and Ornstein, *The Broken Branch,* 158.

54. In the words of Mann and Ornstein, "The institutional rivalry designed by the framers gave way to a relationship in which Congress assumed a position subordinate to the executive. Party trumped institution"; *The Broken Branch,* 139.

55. Ibid., 161.

56. American Bar Association Task Force, *Report,* 24.

57. Signing statement of November 2, 2002, quoted in the American Bar Association Task Force, *Report,* 24–25.

58. Ibid., 25.

59. "Profiles in Cowardice," *Washington Post,* October 1, 2006, www.washingtonpost.com (accessed October 9, 2006).

60. Scott Shane and Adam Liptak, "Detainee Bill Shifts Power to President," *New York Times,* September 30, 2006, www.nytimes.com (accessed September 30, 2006).

61. In February 2007, the U.S. Court of Appeals for the District of Columbia upheld the part of the Military Commissions Act that "stripped Guantanamo detainees of their right

to . . . habeas corpus petitions." An appeal to the Supreme Court was expected. The quote is from Josh White, "Guantanamo Detainees Lose Appeal: Habeas Corpus Case May Go to High Court," *Washington Post,* February 21, 2007.

62. Charles Babington and Jonathan Weisman, "Senate Approves Detainee Bill Backed by Bush," *Washington Post,* September 29, 2006, www.washingtonpost.com (accessed October 11, 2006).

63. Specter's amendment failed by a 51–48 vote. Five Republicans voted for it, but only one (Senator Chafee of Rhode Island) voted against the final bill. See Babington and Weisman, "Senate Approves Detainee Bill," for details.

64. From the decision by Judge Anna Diggs Taylor, quoted in Lichtblau, "Despite a Year of Ire and Angst."

65. Both quotes are from Lichtblau, "Despite a Year of Ire and Angst."

66. Jonathan Weisman and Carol D. Leonnig, "No Compromise on Wiretap Bill," *Washington Post,* September 27, 2006, www.washingtonpost.com (accessed September 27, 2006).

67. "Bipartisanship on Hold," editorial, *New York Times,* November 10, 2006, www. nytimes.com (accessed November 10, 2006).

68. At this writing (early March 2007), the extent of the Democratic-controlled Congress's leverage over the Bush administration in the last two years of its term is not immediately clear. There will, without a doubt, be ample opportunities for oversight. However, barring the unforeseen, the administration will often be in a good position, should it so desire, to resist much of what Congress may want, especially given the less than two years that remain before the next presidential election and the fact that the Democratic majority is quite slim.

69. Executive Office of the President, Office of Management and Budget, *The President's Management Agenda,* www.whitehouse.gov/omb/budget/fy2002/mgmt.pdf (accessed December 9, 2006).

70. "The Facts about the President's Management Agenda," October 3, 2006, www.white house.gov/results/agenda (accessed October 9, 2006).

71. James P. Pffifner, "The First MBA President: The Public Administration Legacy of George W. Bush," *Public Administration Review* 67 (January/February 2007), no. 1: 6–20 (the quote appears on 8).

72. "The Real Agenda," editorial, *New York Times,* July 16, 2006, www.nytimes.com (accessed July 17, 2006).

73. Mark Danner, "Iraq: The War of the Imagination," *New York Review of Books,* December 21, 2006, 87.

CHAPTER 7

"The Decider"
Issue Management and the Bush White House

Andrew Rudalevige

IN SPRING 2005 PRESIDENT George W. Bush was asked to describe the office he held. He responded, "It is a decision-making job. When you're dealing with a future president, you ought to say, 'How do you intend to make decisions? What is the process by which you will make large decisions and small decisions? How do you decide?'" It was a formulation to which Bush would return frequently, sometimes in shorthand form—as most famously in spring 2006, when he declared that the president is "the decider."[1]

Decisions are, indeed, a critical part of the president's job; and their quality has broad implications for a president's legacy. Still, they are rarely made alone. On one side, as other chapters in this volume make clear, the president finds himself in an institutional context surrounded by other competing power centers—the president is sometimes just "a," not "the," decider. On the other, understanding presidential decision making also requires us to consider the president's staff and staff structure: issue management is closely aligned with staff management. If decisions are at the heart of the presidency, information is at the heart of how presidents make them—and information is a function of how an administration is organized to provide for the flow of advice.[2] What information actually reached the president, of the nearly infinite amount that could in prospect do so? Did the president get the facts he needed? Did calculations that might have changed his mind get lost somewhere en route to the White House? Were bad data somewhere finessed and made good?

History suggests that styles of White House issue management can have a dramatic effect on the ways decisions are conceived and made. Early in John F. Kennedy's term, for example, he agreed to a proxy invasion of Cuba at the Bay of Pigs, a quick decision shaped largely by a small circle of its advocates who never questioned, nor pushed the president to question, the unrealistic assumptions on which it was based. In October 1962, in contrast, when the Cuban missile crisis broke out, Kennedy convened a special staff group, including domestic advisers and retired diplomats, to make sure all options and outcomes were fully considered.

Twenty years later, Ronald Reagan's first term "troika" system empowered three largely coequal staffers, whose fierce competition ensured that policy possibilities reaching the president received strict scrutiny, and thus protected Reagan's interests. But in Reagan's second term, the troika was replaced by a strict pyramid topped by chief of staff Donald Regan. Entrepreneurial national security aides made an end-run around the hierarchy to funnel profits from sales of weapons to Iran into support for the Nicaraguan contras. The president's own investigatory commission later concluded that the pursuit and failure of those policies "resulted in large part from the flaws in the manner in which decisions were made."[3]

George W. Bush's staffing and management styles have been alternately lauded and assailed. Admirers highlight the president's decisiveness, his ability to build a team of advisers, and his confidence in delegating complex policy analysis to them, reserving final judgment for himself. "Bush," wrote one observer, "is the very model of a modern MBA president."[4] Detractors counter that the president is incurious, trapped in a "bubble" that echoes back his own preconceived preferences, thus denying him a full range of options or a sense of their likely real-world outcomes. In this sense, they argue, "Bush may be the most isolated president in modern history."[5]

In this chapter I explore these competing views. After laying out some basic considerations for assessing decision making, I examine the development of the Bush advisory system in the White House and cabinet, from the truncated, post-2000 election transition period to the early part of 2007, as the president struggled to adapt to new Democratic majorities in Congress. The evolving characterization of the administration by Washington *uber*-insider Bob Woodward, in his 2002, 2004, and 2006 books about the war on terror, is instructive.[6] The same decision-making process that Woodward lauded early on proved to harbor important weaknesses as policy needs changed but the policy process (and in some cases the policies themselves) did not.

In short, President Bush created a system that enabled him to extract desired information from a disciplined hierarchy. But it was a system through which he was less likely to encounter alternative analyses that might have made him change his mind about what information he desired in the first place. As early as February 2002, a senior administration official made a telling comment along these lines. President Bush, he said, "finds out what he *wants* to know. But he does not necessarily find out what he might *need* to know."[7]

The difference, perhaps, is the difference between short-term, tactical success and long-term governance. And the sum, perhaps, is the Bush legacy in issue management.

Thinking about Decision Making

Suspended in the checks and balances of American governance, the president must seek to expand his influence over governmental outcomes: this is the very definition of presidential power.[8] Contemporary presidents have a wide range of tools for the purpose, both cooperative and unilateral. Whatever tools they choose, and whether they seek legislative sanction or purely administrative action, presidents need to manage issues in a way that gives them the information they need about policy options and outcomes. "Rumsfeld's rules"—the tenets compiled by George W. Bush's first defense secretary after his experiences in the Nixon and Ford White Houses—say the job of staff is "to help identify the choices and see that [the president] is aware of the real differences at the heart of the issues he must address." As Rumsfeld went on to caution, "Staff will not necessarily do this automatically." Staff members, he noted—and these days there are a lot of them in the White House orbit—will always stay busy; but whether they are busy working in the *president's* interest is not to be assumed.[9]

Presidents face an odd information problem: Given the simple constraints of time and human cognitive capacity, not too little, but too much, information is available to them. The job of the presidents' advisers is to serve as the screen that reduces a sea of fact and estimation to a manageable puddle. Already a possible problem arises. Information must be lost as it moves toward the president—but what information? Harry McPherson, an aide to Lyndon Johnson, put the challenge this way:

> The real danger was that we [LBJ's advisers] would weigh it wrong. The very process of reducing a dozen position papers and committee meetings to a three page memorandum for the President required that we exclude some arguments and data, and emphasize others. We tried to give him both sides, but our judgments colored what we wrote. . . . [T]he danger of bias or omission is always there, and it is unavoidable so long as Presidents make twenty decisions a day on the basis of information they can only receive through the filter of other men's convictions.[10]

Presidents need advice that is relevant, tied to real-world policy and political realities; that is comprehensive; and that comprehends diverse starting assumptions about possible outcomes. Thus presidents must construct that "filter of other men's convictions" in a way that best serves them, that protects their prerogatives of choice and minimizes (since it cannot eliminate) the danger of ignoring information salient to a particular policy decision. Dwight Eisenhower's comments on staff management are often quoted but worth remembering: "Organization cannot make a genius out of an incompetent . . . [but] disorganization can scarcely fail to result in inefficiency and can easily lead to disaster."[11]

If staff help is not automatic, how can presidents enhance its utility? How can they avoid "disaster"? Generally presidents have followed two sets of strategies for organizational leadership. The first deals with the careful selection of personnel—the idea being, as the Reagan administration aphorized, that "personnel is policy."[12] Presidents bent on politicizing the executive branch staff it with people loyal to the president and his program, making bureaus better attuned, and more responsive, to Oval Office preferences. After all, cabinet members often have divided loyalties and are eager to court not only Congress's favor (especially in times of divided government) but also that of the constituencies intertwined with their department's mission. Richard Nixon's efforts to combat this centrifugal force led him briefly to designate "supersecretaries" who held joint appointments as White House staffers. The Reagan team systematically removed every holdover from the Carter administration and centrally vetted appointees at both the cabinet and subcabinet levels for ideological purity. One internal memo concerning the search for a cabinet secretary cautioned that candidates must "have [a] clear understanding that being responsive to the White House is critical. Need someone loyal. . . . Need someone who can deflect criticism and controversies away from White House."[13]

Careful recruitment and indoctrination, however, do not solve every problem. Finding loyalists who are also administratively competent is often time-consuming, when it is possible. And presidents should keep in mind that even subordinates who do not mirror their preferences can be useful advisers, so long as the bias of each is understood and weighted when their advice is considered. Indeed, a focus on loyalty can be problematic if disloyalty is defined generically as disagreement, resulting in groupthink among a united front of advisers who have already hashed out any discord. Presidents should empower at least some advisers strong enough to say no. "The wider the advisory net is cast, the more likely that the emperor's wardrobe will receive the scrutiny it deserves."[14]

Even then the president may not know what to ask, or know whether an option is missing from the menu he receives, especially when the policy under consideration is technically complex. Alexander George's seminal work on executive decision making warns against a broad range of potential problems, such as avoidance of certain logical options; a lack of follow-up on dissenting proposals; overdependence on a single channel of information; and failure to secure review of key premises by parties not already wedded to them.[15] Thus a second, complementary strategy deals with structure—with how personnel are arrayed to make sure that important debates are pushed to the top of the staff pyramid. Presidents need to arrange their staff institutions so as to be alerted to key issues and to ensure that their resolution is not preempted by lower-level officials.

The underlying theme of the literature on this topic is that presidents should protect themselves by "institutionalizing distrust."[16] One way to do that is to build advisory structures based on broad function, rather than limited by policy area. In this model, narrow specialists are assigned to issues as just one part of a wider decision stream centered on what Richard Neustadt called ongoing "action-forcing processes," such as the compilation of a presidential policy program, budgeting, legislative liaison, presidential appointments (both of people and on his calendar), and communication.[17] Compartmentalized policy advice channels may not produce the key information about how different problems interact across policy areas that can highlight both intended and unintended consequences of policy choice. Organizing things this way leads to some duplication of effort, to be sure. But it also means that different types of expertise will be brought to bear on a problem.[18]

Another, conceivably reinforcing strategy is to create multiple channels of information—what organization theorists call "parallel processing." Some presidents, such as Franklin Roosevelt, have preferred to give their staff overlapping assignments, in the expectation that such competition would improve the quality of the advice received.[19] Another of "Rumsfeld's rules" likewise tells future chiefs of staff to "work to assure adequate access."[20] Empowering diverse viewpoints helps to avoid groupthink, by ensuring consideration of the downsides of policy proposals.

Third, although a disciplined, centralized hierarchy can have real advantages—it provides a wide reach across even obscure issues, gives staffers clear jurisdictions, and eliminates extraneous data—its downside is that personnel on the hierarchy's upward slope may make the wrong decisions about which data are extraneous to the president's needs. This suggests that presidents will get better information about policy matters when they have effective monitoring mechanisms that allow them to spot-check lower-level decision processes. John F. Kennedy, for example, was well known for his proclivity to call on bureaucrats at all levels of the organizational chart to find out additional information about an issue. President Clinton had hundreds of "FOBs"—friends of Bill—whom he used as extra eyes or brains.[21]

Using these strategies will give the president better information, on average, but they take time and have their own managerial costs.[22] Creating overlapping jurisdictions or tracking lower-level decision processes forces a wealth of information to the president and ensures that he maintains final control over decisions. But either requires that the president invest a good deal of personal energy in managing the system and may lead him to be overwhelmed by minutiae. Finding a balance between ignorance and overload is part of the job of every "decider."

The Bush Administration: Centralized Politicization

How did George W. Bush arrange his staff to seek this balance? Following from the discussion above, this section will summarize personnel choices and the way in which the White House staff and cabinet were organized. The next section will assess what those choices meant for information flow.

Appointment Strategies

As Joel Aberbach notes earlier in this volume, the Bush transition team took a page from the 1980 Reagan model in seeking to control appointments at even the subcabinet level. The transition director (and subsequent head of the presidential personnel office), Clay Johnson, was charged with finding appointees who were competent but also loyal to presidential preferences.[23]

Bush, then, clearly followed a strategy of committed "politicization" as described above. Although that term is often given a negative connotation, the idea is simply to make the far-flung executive branch more immediately responsive to presidential dictate, ensuring that core programmatic functions receive consistent support across the government. For instance, as chief of staff Andrew Card told an interviewer, "I made sure our communications team is not just a team in the White House. It is a communications team for the executive branch of government. Our legal team is a legal team for the government."[24] Thus key positions within each department and agency received special scrutiny—not just the secretary at the top of the pyramid, but the deputy secretary (who often handles departmental administration), the general counsel, the legislative liaison, and the head of the press office.[25] After cabinet members were selected they were given a choice of subordinates already vetted by the White House personnel and political teams. In short, as one staffer later put it, the president sought to "implant his DNA throughout the government"—and he did so systematically.[26]

Many of the administration's original appointees came from Texas, of course, and more than a third had worked on the campaign, but even more came from Washington, D.C.: 43 percent had worked for President George H. W. Bush. Another 20 percent came from trade associations or lobbying firms. The Interior Department, for example, included new officials who had lobbied for mining, cattle, and oil and gas development interests. Such appointments indicated the importance the new president attached to regulatory policy, with an eye most often toward deregulation. For example, during the president's first term, the Occupational Safety and Health Administration (OSHA) canceled five times as many pending rules as it completed, and it began not a single major rule-making process. The Environmental Protection Agency (EPA) refused even to consider regulating carbon dioxide emissions as pollutants, earning a 2007 rebuke from the Supreme Court, which ruled such inaction incompatible with EPA's statutory mandate.[27]

Another, related emphasis was to subject government functions (and thus jobs) to "competitive sourcing." This process had the potential advantage of shrinking the number of nonresponsive permanent employees while making the performance of those remaining more efficient. While the number of regular civil service employees held steady or diminished, the number of outside contractors performing government services rose dramatically over the course of the administration, creating something of a "blended" workforce in areas ranging from information technology to military interrogation. Contractors billed the government some $400 billion in 2006, up from $207 billion in 2000.[28]

The Cabinet

The original Bush cabinet appointments were generally lauded for their collective "high-wattage" experience and gravitas.[29] That was especially true in foreign affairs, where Vice President Dick Cheney, himself a former secretary of defense, was joined by Colin Powell (retired four star general, former national security adviser, and former chair of the Joint Chiefs of Staff) as secretary of state and Donald Rumsfeld (former secretary of defense, NATO ambassador, and White House chief of staff) at the Pentagon. At Treasury was Paul O'Neill, CEO of Alcoa and one of the most widely respected government managers when he was at the Office of Management and Budget in the 1970s. Other notables in the cabinet included Wisconsin governor Tommy Thompson at Health and Human Services and New Jersey governor Christine Todd Whitman at the EPA. More controversial was the new attorney general, John Ashcroft, who had just been defeated for reelection to the U.S. Senate from Missouri.

The Bush cabinet was quite stable during the first term. O'Neill left first, at the end of 2002, replaced by railroad executive John W. Snow. Whitman resigned in spring 2003 and was succeeded by Utah governor Michael Leavitt. Most of the rest, however, stayed in their posts through the 2004 election, and some stayed beyond.

Cabinet members, however, had little influence over early administration policy proposals. In part the reason was that the president's program faithfully tracked the campaign platform—tax cuts, education reform, aid to faith-based organizations—and could thus be sent to Congress nearly off the shelf. Furthermore, although the cabinet secretaries were in place, their political subordinates mostly were not, for reasons including both lengthy background checking and disclosure processes and Senate dawdling (or due diligence, depending on one's perspective). The White House also was slow to forward names to the Senate in the first place. By mid-June 2001, the White House had made just under 193 nominations for the top five hundred political jobs in the administration. Some observers were concerned. "There is no way a tiny cadre of Bush appointees and a handful of aides working with them can put their stamp on what a big sprawling department is doing," warned Chester E. Finn, an assistant secretary of education in the Reagan administration.[30]

Still, it was not clear that the White House cared much what the departments were doing. Policymaking was largely centralized. As Whitman lamented, "There is a palace guard [in the White House], and they want to run interference for him." Paul O'Neill would soon vent at book length about the lack of departmental expertise in policymaking.[31] By no coincidence, these two were the first to depart the cabinet.

At the same time the White House strengthened its ability to monitor agency behavior. The Office of Management and Budget (OMB) and its Office of Information and Regulatory Affairs (OIRA) had subjected proposed regulations to centralized review since the early 1980s, but their cost-benefit analyses became particularly rigorous under new OIRA head John Graham. Graham took a strict line on scientific claims made by agencies, rejecting them when they did not meet OMB standards of "quality, objectivity, utility, and integrity." Critics complained that OMB was ignoring agency expertise and rejecting conclusions that did not match the administration's policy preferences.[32]

Later, when the administration became worried that agencies were evading regulatory clearance by issuing "guidance documents" that laid out statutory interpretations without engaging in the formal rule-making process, the president issued an executive order on "regulatory planning and review" that specified guidance documents as within OIRA's purview. The new order also emphasized that regulations should address a specific "market failure." Although a 1993 Clinton executive order had required agencies to designate a "regulatory policy officer," the new Bush order required the officer to be a presidential appointee and dictated that unless directly authorized by the agency head, "no rulemaking shall commence nor be included" in agency regulatory plans without that officer's approval.[33]

OMB's oversight of agency management more generally was upgraded by the August 2001 President's Management Agenda (PMA). Among other initiatives, OMB developed a Program Assessment Rating Tool (PART) that could be used to evaluate individual agencies and programs and inform subsequent funding decisions. By most accounts, agencies paid closer and more sustained attention to PART, and PMA generally, than to most of the management reform efforts that have periodically gripped Washington.[34]

In short, then, as a senior White House aide put it, this was not to be "a presidency under which there's a lot of freelancing within the cabinet. It's a very tight team, very regimented, very tight message discipline, and I think the cabinet officers realize a large part of their job is to be shields."[35]

The White House Staff

A variety of models for organizing the White House staff have been assayed since Franklin D. Roosevelt's Brownlow Commission concluded in 1937 that "the president needs help." Through the Johnson administration in the late 1960s, presidents sometimes used a formal hierarchy culminating in a chief of staff, sometimes a less-layered, spokes-of-the-wheel model with themselves at the hub.[36] Since Nixon every president has had a chief of staff; Jimmy Carter was the exception that proved the rule when he abandoned his effort to re-create the "spokes" model in 1979.

Carter's about-face seems to have cemented the trend into what political scientists have called a "standard model" of White House organization.[37] Its basic template reflects both the expectations of political observers regarding the proper structure and functions of the Executive Office of the President (EOP) and the growth in its size and scope as the skeletal EOP of the 1930s has been fleshed out. The EOP now includes not only the White House Office, but the Office of Management and Budget and an array of policy staff serving the National Security Council (NSC), the Domestic Policy Council (DPC), and the National Economic Council. It has acquired press and communications functions; liaisons to Congress, interest groups, and local governments; travel services; and even a small law office with the president as its chief client. All of these are now normal parts of the White House apparatus.[38]

Thus, although George W. Bush tweaked the structure of his predecessors' White House—eliminating the Office of Women's Initiatives and Outreach, creating an Office of Faith-Based and Community Initiatives, emphasizing long-term planning with an Office of Strategic Initiatives, enhancing the role of the Office of the Vice President—in important ways the "deep structure" of the White House was more or less continuous and performed functions similar to those in previous administrations.[39] One study showed that "the same units" in the early Bush White House were "found in the Clinton White House." The Bush transition team's plan to wipe out the Office of Intergovernmental Affairs, for example, was revised after fierce protest from state and city officials.[40]

Bush did move more quickly, and to better purpose, than Bill Clinton had eight years earlier to put his team in place. Clinton's cabinet construction after the 1992 election was so time-consuming that he wound up aggregating a White House staff nearly on the fly, which in turn necessitated a major reorganization in late 1993. Bush, by contrast, made his initial White House staff appointments in advance of his cabinet choices. Chief of staff Andrew H. Card Jr.'s appointment was announced on November 26. Indeed, Clay Johnson told one interviewer that decisions about the organizational structure and top aides were in place by early December 2000—even before *Bush v. Gore* finally brought closure to the chad-littered election.[41]

Starting with Card, Bush's top aides had long experience working with him, working in Washington, or both. Nearly 30 percent of the new EOP staffers were from Texas, and more than 80 percent had worked on the Bush campaign in 2000. The president, Card indicated, "liked old, comfortable shoes."[42] Loyalty was a key credential. For instance, deputy chief of staff for policy Joshua Bolten had worked in the financial industry but also as a staffer to the Senate Finance Committee, counsel to the U.S. Trade Representative, a White House aide for legislative liaison, and policy director for the 2000 Bush campaign. Bolten's counterpart for administration, Joseph Hagin, had been George H. W. Bush's personal aide, or "body man," before becoming his White House appointments secretary and then George W. Bush's deputy campaign manager. White House counsel Alberto Gonzales had held the parallel position under Governor Bush.[43]

The policy councils, too, were directed by aides very familiar to the president. The National Security Council staff was led by Condoleezza Rice, a Stanford political scientist who had worked in the George H. W. Bush administration. At her old boss Brent Scowcroft's recommendation she became George W. Bush's foreign policy adviser during the 2000 campaign. The domestic side was overseen by Margaret (La Montagne) Spellings, who was political director for Bush's first gubernatorial campaign in 1994 and then served six years in his administration working on education issues; she would head the Office of Policy Development. In that role, she was a key architect of the elementary and secondary education proposal that would become the landmark No Child Left Behind Act. At the National Economic Council (NEC) was Lawrence B. Lindsey, a Harvard economics professor who had worked for Presidents Reagan and Bush I before spending five years as a member of the Federal Reserve Board of Governors. From late 1999 on, he served as the chief economic adviser to the Bush campaign. He helped design the multiple, massive tax cuts that became law in 2001 and 2002.[44]

Card himself was a Bush family loyalist dating to his days as a state representative in Massachusetts in the late 1970s; he served as deputy chief of staff and later secretary of transportation under George H. W. Bush.[45] Two other veteran Bush aides, political adviser Karl Rove and campaign press secretary Karen R. Hughes, also reported directly to the president. Rove and Hughes had worked together, and with Bush, since his first run for governor in 1994. In fact Rove's experience with the Bush family went back to his college Republican days in the 1970s; he then became famous (or infamous) as a hard-nosed political consultant in Texas before selling his consultancy to work for George W. Bush full time in 1999. Rove, given the title "senior advisor to the president," headed the new Office of Strategic Initiatives as well as the political affairs staff and served as a general political troubleshooter and policy sounding board. He developed a system of contacts in those areas, from members of Congress to election strategists to scholars at sympathetic think tanks.[46]

Hughes, a former television reporter, became counselor to the president and de facto director of the White House communications operation, including speechwriting and media affairs. Her portfolio was extended by forty-five staff members and what Card called her "mystical bond" with George W. Bush. She was often described as the single person closest to, and most trusted by, the president—"The two share what may be the closest thing to the Vulcan mind-meld," said an Austin-based journalist early in the 2000 campaign.[47]

This three-headed hierarchy was intended to avoid the problem that Bush's father had faced when his own chief of staff, the former New Hampshire governor John Sununu, sought to dominate White House decision making. (Card knew all about this, having been tabbed to fire Sununu back in 1991.) The three aides formed a troika similar in structure to Reagan's, but they were on much more congenial terms with one another than Reagan's trio had been. As a result they were far more disciplined in preventing infighting from becoming public. As in Reagan's operation, the elevation of Rove and Hughes provided a mechanism for integrating political and communications concerns into the White House decision-making process. Each, for instance, had a role in signing off on the subcabinet appointments mentioned above. However, the correspondence was not exact. For one thing, Card was (in Rove's own phrasing) "first among equals"; as Card put it, it was his job to "stan[d] on the middle of the seesaw" between Rove and Hughes to provide balance between them. And Card had policy responsibilities that Jim Baker, for example, had not formally exercised in the early Reagan years (though substantively, one could argue, the imbalance went the other way—Baker had more of a hand in policy development than Card normally chose to have).[48]

The door to the Oval Office was open wider than the troika analogy suggests, since Rice, Gonzales, and Vice President Cheney also had direct access to the president. Cheney played an especially critical role, given his immense experience in government and his unusually large, seasoned staff, so integrated with the president's own that its top aides were given the title "assistant to the president" in conjunction with their jobs in the vice president's office. The detail-oriented vice president quickly became a quiet but effective broker in a variety of policy areas. At the other end of Pennsylvania Avenue, Cheney had an office in the House as well as that befitting his constitutional role as president of the Senate. He also led a working group developing energy policy for the administration. That endeavor, as it turned out, itself became a test of executive power, for when legislators sought to ascertain the role of industry insiders in the formulation of its recommendations, the White House refused to open its books. That claim to privilege was in keeping with Cheney's strong belief that post-Watergate Congresses had overstepped their bounds in seeking to rein in presidential discretion and that executive authority needed to be restored—a view that grew in influence after September 11. After the attacks on the World Trade Center and the Pentagon, Cheney's long experience in national security policy came to the fore. He participated actively in the formulation and implementation of the war on terror both abroad and within the United States. Even then, however, Cheney normally sought to avoid public scrutiny, offering his advice to the president on a wide range of policy issues behind the scenes.[49] The centralized unilateralism that he encouraged was a crucial aspect of the Bush management style vis-à-vis both Congress and the wider bureaucracy.

Revolution, Evolution

One mockingly bright morning in September 2001 would catapult new issues onto the national agenda, transform the president's worldview, and rework White House issue management. After September 11, the National Security Council and various permutations of a "war cabinet" began to meet daily or more often. Cheney, Rumsfeld, Rice, Powell, and CIA director George Tenet were among the principals, but decision making was often ad hoc. In Paul Light's phrase, it was "an organized anarchy," with "more dotted lines" on the organizational chart "than on a dress pattern." Decisions about the military direction of the war, for example, had to be supplemented by legal decisions about the status of detainees captured on Afghan battlefields and the extent of presidential war powers at home and abroad. Cheney (through his counsel, David Addington) and attorneys in the Justice Department's Office of Legal Counsel (OLC) played important parts, with the State Department and even the NSC staff generally less influential. In this context the roles of Hughes and Rove were not as prominent, but domestic and communications concerns clearly remained salient. Bush's halting response to the September 11 attacks from the Oval Office that evening was quickly superseded by impressive formal and informal appearances at "Ground Zero" in New York, at Washington's National Cathedral, and on September 20 before a joint meeting of Congress. Communications served to shape policy in important ways, not just reflect it.[50]

"Organized anarchy" worked as a response to crisis, but as that crisis became part of normal life, structure morphed to match it. Most immediately it took the form of an Office of Homeland Security (OHS) under Pennsylvania governor Tom Ridge. As director, Ridge was to be a cabinet-level "fixer," running a new council that was supposed to coordinate the forty-plus agencies with some role in reassuring a homeland that felt distinctly insecure. OHS, however, had a small staff and little bureaucratic clout—no control over budgets, for example, or personnel. Thus it was unable to do much coordinating, nor Ridge any directing. Ridge would subsequently serve as the first secretary of the Department of Homeland Security (DHS) after it was created in late 2002, bringing together in statute what OHS had failed to bring together by moral suasion.

Card's "seesaw" job was made harder when Hughes left Washington in July 2002. Worried about the need for a counterbalance to Rove, he told a reporter that "we have a serious problem of replacement costs." And in fact, although Hughes remained in close touch with the president and was active in the 2004 campaign, she was not replaced on the White House staff. To be sure, her assistant, communications director Dan Bartlett, was promoted, and Card himself occasionally took on a more direct role in policymaking. For instance, he secretly convened a small group in the White House basement to draw up an administration version of the legislation creating DHS. At the same time, Rove's reach into policy grew more systematic, even as he successfully piloted the president's involvement in the 2002 elections that bucked the "law" of midterm loss to restore Republican control of the Senate and expand the party's House majority. As jobs opened, younger staff on the outskirts of the inner circle began to move up, as the president clearly preferred promoting from within. One result was to enhance the authority of the remaining senior staff.[51]

The Second Term Shifts

President Bush's reelection in 2004 marked a natural transition point for personnel and prompted a reshuffling of the cabinet and the White House staff. Nine of fifteen cabinet secretaries left. They included attorney general John Ashcroft, who was replaced by Alberto Gonzales, and Rod Paige at the Department of Education, replaced by Margaret Spellings. There were changes, too, at the Agriculture, Commerce, Energy, Health and Human Services, and Veterans Affairs Departments, as well as at Homeland Security, where federal circuit court judge Michael Chertoff replaced Ridge.[52]

Perhaps the most notable departure was that of Colin Powell who, after a frustrating four years, had planned to retire but at a time of his own choosing. He was disappointed in being asked to resign soon after the election. At the least, Powell had felt that Rumsfeld should also be replaced, in view of the continued insurgency in Iraq and other, related issues (the Abu Ghraib prisoner abuse scandal, for example, broke publicly in April 2004). The president rejected that suggestion. Rice would succeed Powell at State.[53]

The strategies of centralization and politicization were applied sequentially here, rather than simultaneously. That is, together with the Gonzales and Spellings appointments, the choice of Rice represented a systematic shift of key White House staff to crucial posts in the wider bureaucracy, creating what one former Bush aide called "a true kitchen cabinet" that could help the White House ride herd on the bureaus. For example, given Spellings's role in crafting No Child Left Behind, moving her to the Education Department meant having a trusted hand on site to oversee its implementation. Likewise moving Gonzales, the overseer of the administration's aggressive legal strategy in the war on terror, to the Justice Department meant that that strategy and other administration priorities would be defended and maintained by what Gonzales's chief of staff would call "loyal Bushies."[54]

At the same time the job of secretary to the cabinet, along with the Office of Cabinet Affairs, was effectively eliminated. This suggested that the White House expected informational input from the departments to diminish in volume or cease. Indeed, said a senior aide to the president after the 2004 election, "the function of the Bush cabinet is to provide a chorus of support for White House policies, and technical support for implementing them."[55]

At the White House itself, trusted aide Bartlett moved up again to become counselor to the president; gifted speechwriter Michael Gerson, key to Bush's second inaugural vision of global democratization, became a policy and strategic planning adviser. Rice's deputy, Stephen Hadley, moved up to become assistant for national security. Spellings's domestic turf was downsized, at least in relative terms, occupied uneventfully by Claude Allen, then by the American Enterprise Institute's Karl Zinsmeister. Longtime Bush attorney and aide Harriet Miers, who was serving as deputy chief of staff for policy (taking over for Josh Bolten, who had become director of OMB in 2003), became White House counsel; from there she would become, briefly, a nominee to the Supreme Court in 2005. Rove's command of the policy coordination process, from homeland security to tax reform, was formalized. He was named to Miers's deputy slot while holding onto his political portfolio.[56]

After the election, Card had offered his resignation to the president. By all accounts the move was sincere; but it was declined. However, after a tenure second only to that of Eisenhower's Sherman Adams—but also after the debacle of Hurricane Katrina, the indictment of Cheney aide I. Lewis Libby on perjury charges, the flap over the Dubai Ports management proposal, and the widely panned Miers nomination—Card left the administration in April 2006. He was replaced with OMB's Bolten, his deputy at the start of the administration. Bolten brought his own deputy, Joel Kaplan, to oversee the policy development process, bumping Rove; White House aides had complained of "sclerosis" in the policy shop under both Miers and Rove. To sell that policy, Bolten made another change in the press room, replacing press secretary Scott McClellan with Fox News personality Tony Snow.[57] Karen Hughes also returned to Washington, but to the State Department as the undersecretary for public diplomacy.

Many in Washington, not all of them Democrats, had pushed for a new staff chief with stature independent of the president. Their role model was Howard Baker, who was widely credited with righting the Reagan presidency after it was nearly capsized by the Iran-contra scandal in 1987. President Bush, however, preferred "somebody [he] knows well, and . . . knows how he operates."[58] Over time, as the president's political prospects continued to languish, most notably with the Democrats' impressive performance in the 2006 midterm elections, further changes occurred. Frustrated that he was not getting sufficient credit for a strong economy, Bush replaced Treasury secretary Snow with Goldman Sachs CEO Henry Paulson in late spring 2006. Soon after the election—the timing hugely irked many Republicans, who felt that Iraq policy had cost them their congressional majorities— Defense Secretary Rumsfeld was fired and replaced by George H. W. Bush's intelligence director (and member of the Baker-Hamilton Commission), Robert Gates. An additional internal change was less noted but perhaps equally important: Republican "wise man" Fred Fielding, whose service to the presidency dated back to the Nixon administration, was brought back for a third stint in the counsel's office, replacing Harriet Miers. Fielding's experience was deemed necessary to deal with potentially hostile congressional committees seeking information and administration officials' testimony at hearings.[59] These appointments marked an intriguing expansion of what had heretofore been a fairly small circle of trusted advisers. What remained in question was how much influence they would have.

Issue Management in Practice

The Bush style of staff management—and thus issue management—is therefore marked by both strong politicization and centralization. How do these strategies compare to the discussion of information flow laid out at the start of the chapter? And how did they play out in practice?

Personnel Selection

"If I have any genius or smarts," President Bush commented in 2002, "it's the ability to recognize talent, ask them to serve and work with them as a team." As traced above, the Bush administration took staff selection and placement very seriously. Its personnel operation will be carefully studied by future administrations. Whereas other White House staffs have served as a sort of representative coalition of various factions within the president's party, "team Bush" was devoted to the president himself. Taking its cue from the president, the White House ran its meetings strictly on time, and in suits; the extended bull sessions and casual Fridays of the Clinton administration vanished, replaced by what one admirer called "the rhythm of executive leadership."[60] The team was also unified around its goals, which were correspondingly ambitious. Drastic cuts in taxes; dramatic changes in Social Security, Medicare, and education; and, most radical, preemptively spreading democracy worldwide—all were part of the agenda. As a first term speechwriter, David Frum, later wrote, the president's "vision was large and clear."[61]

Out in the departments, teamwork meant subordination to this vision, as well as White House-dictated stratagems for implementing it. Those who were disgruntled by this, such as Paul O'Neill and Christine Todd Whitman, did not stay with Bush for long. Those who were not, prospered in an operation reminiscent of the second-term Nixon cabinet, which favored low-profile managers who owed their positions to the president and not to any independent constituencies. Indeed, one White House official told the *Washington Post* that he liked that analogy, with one caveat: "It's like the Nixon cabinet, without the scandal."[62]

Yet some kinds of scandal were made more probable by such a strategy. One disadvantage, of course, was that unquestioning commitment created an "echo chamber" where dissenting views were not so much ignored as weeded out in the hiring process.[63] Some argued that aggressive politicization had the potential effect of downgrading independent expertise; the scientific community grew particularly exercised about this, especially in the environmental arena. Early in 2007 additional questions arose at the Justice Department over the dismissals of eight (Republican) U.S. attorneys, purportedly for insufficient loyalty to the president and attorney general.[64] The expanded role of government contractors raised different concerns. Even with the best intentions, the flow of government decisions through institutions more responsible to shareholders than to the electorate could raise concerns. How might intelligence analysis be affected, for example, when more than half of budgeted CIA positions were filled by contract employees rather than permanent civil servants? How would a Federal Emergency Management Agency (FEMA) hollowed out of experienced personnel respond to massive natural disaster? The answer to the last question at least, Hurricane Katrina showed, was "poorly."

Generalist Structures

People work through structures, and one hypothesis proffered above posits that generalist, functional structures serve the president better than "stovepipe" structures defined by policy specialization. In many ways, the early Bush administration followed this pattern, and it often served the president well as he turned his 2000 campaign platform into a tangible legislative and regulatory agenda. Politics and policy were not artificially partitioned. As one aide noted regarding Karl Rove's prominence, "I'd rather have good people with real judgment rather than people with foreign policy Ph.D.'s."[65] Thus the administration was not browbeaten by subject-matter specialists who might not share the president's broader bargaining perspective. This enabled problems to be considered in all of their interactions rather than in isolation. Asking questions of and pushing back against experts—perhaps especially military experts—is a valuable asset to a president.

That said, it is important to ask the right questions. Bush himself showed little interest in that most fundamental of action-forcing general functions, the annual aggregation of the federal budget.[66] And the Bush troika was balanced more heavily toward selling, than toward formulating and assessing, policy. The policy councils (DPC, NEC, NSC) are a structural mechanism for merging cabinet expertise with the White House's wider perspective. Thus they arguably should have been headed by coordinators charged with collating divergent views and sharpening disagreements for presidential consideration and resolution. Instead those positions were filled with advocates for a given point of view. Along these lines, the role of Condoleezza Rice at NSC attracted criticism in the wake of the Iraq war and insurgency. It was charged that Rice's ardent support of the invasion meant she could not impartially manage the interagency process.[67] As a result, charged longtime foreign policy adviser Richard Perle, the president was not really in a position to make decisions: "The machinery of government that he nominally ran was actually running him."[68]

On the domestic side, Bush's key, generalist aides certainly dealt with the meat of substantive issues. But developing and selling a new domestic agenda after the objectives of the 2000 campaign were largely attained proved challenging. The reasons seem attitudinal but also organizational. The goal of integrating politics and policy is to prevent the former from being subsumed, but it is equally important to avoid the opposite extreme. In some cases, important presidential communications were not vetted by departments for factual accuracy or feasibility.[69] As professor-turned-Bush-staffer John DiIulio observed, "In eight months I heard many, many staff discussions, but not three meaningful, substantive policy discussions. . . . Even quite junior staff would sometimes hear quite senior staff pooh-pooh any need to dig deeper for pertinent information on a given issue." The advisory processes, he added, "have been . . . organized in ways that make it hard for policy-minded staff . . . to get much West Wing traction, or even get a non-trivial hearing." Ideology ran the risk of standing in for fact. An exception was issues on which the president was personally knowledgeable and very much engaged, especially the No Child Left Behind education initiative throughout his presidency and immigration reform in the second term.[70]

After September 11, of course, the role of foreign policy specialists expanded dramatically, shutting out (at least in tactical decision making) more overtly political advice. Still, the lead-up to the attack on Afghanistan was impressively deliberative, grounded in a "war cabinet" that met frequently and incorporated a wide range of input.[71] By contrast, when the war cabinet stopped its regular meetings, multiple advocacy also stopped. Defense Secretary Rumsfeld and his high-powered staff of neoconservative strategists kept control of a separate stovepipe of advice to the president, as the possibility of war with Iraq moved to the front burner.[72]

Other fronts of the war on terror were also handled by discrete groups of specialists when wider input might have led to wiser decisions. Most of the president's information on issues of interrogation, for example, came from the groups managed by White House counsel Gonzales, which were dominated by the Justice Department's Office of Legal Counsel and the vice president's office. The final decision to create military tribunals for noncitizen terror suspects was made without substantive input from military lawyers in the Judge Advocate General corps, the State Department, the criminal division of the Justice Department, or even Rice and the NSC staff. Gonzales's January 2002 memo recommending that detainees from Afghanistan be categorized as "unlawful enemy combatants" outside the reach of the Geneva Conventions noted strong State and Defense Department objections to the idea but did not present them in detail. (Secretary Powell was moved to write his own dissenting memo.) Later in 2002 Gonzales solicited a memo from OLC on the legal definition of torture, again without canvassing military or State Department experts. Such a process certainly did not cause widespread abuses in CIA and military prison facilities, but the odds of such abuses' occurring might have been calculated, and they might have been forestalled, by better advising.[73]

On these issues and elsewhere Vice President Cheney proved an important freestanding center of power within the White House. As the material released during the trial of Cheney staffer Lewis Libby revealed, the vice president's office was one side of a continuing informational cleavage, with its own direct line to the president (who, for example, declassified portions of a National Intelligence Estimate at Cheney's request without informing other senior staff). Cheney also ensured that only ideologically vetted civilians were allowed to serve in the Iraqi reconstruction effort, even where that meant passing over more qualified personnel.[74] Indeed, when reporter Karen deYoung asked Colin Powell whether "a different NSC, under more deft and decisive leadership, would have made a difference" to the policymaking process, "Powell shrugged. . . . 'Probably not.' " Why not, she asked? His reply: "Cheney."[75]

Open Doors and Closed Minds?

"A president must give people access," the president noted, and his chief of staff faithfully implemented "an open door in a relatively flat organizational chart. . . . I maintain a chain of command," Card said, "but I do not limit access."[76] As that suggested, Bush clearly understood the limits that a single line of approach potentially imposed on his capacity to make choices. And he worried about the potential for groupthink: "If everybody had the same opinion and the same prejudices and the same belief structure," he observed in 2002, ". . . I would not get the best advice." As he added in 2005, "They walk in here and they get just overwhelmed by the Oval Office and the whole atmosphere and the great beauty of this place, and they say, 'Man, you're looking good, Mr. President.' So I need people walking in here saying, 'You're not looking so good.' "[77]

It was less clear that the president worked to overcome that syndrome—or to ensure that the open door was accompanied by open minds. Sen. Carl Levin claimed that the president preferred "people around him who will not challenge him but will give him the ammunition which he needs or wants in order to achieve some more general goal." Even Bush strategist Matthew Dowd later complained of the president's "my way or the highway" approach and that he was "secluded and bubbled in." As the "stovepiping" noted above makes clear, some debates were kept tightly confined. Other, traditionally open settings saw little robust debate: Treasury Secretary O'Neill described cabinet meetings as literally "scripted," with participants assigned the order and substance of their comments in advance.

Certainly dissent expressed publicly was quickly rebuked. When NEC chair Lindsey suggested that the cost of the Iraq war might approach $200 billion (it has since passed $500 billion), he was dismissed. When General Eric Shinseki told Congress that "several hundred thousand soldiers" would be needed to provide postwar security in Iraq, he was publicly scolded by deputy secretary of defense Paul Wolfowitz, and his replacement as Army chief of staff announced more than a year before his scheduled retirement.[78]

Some censorship was self-imposed. For example, in the final meeting that the first U.S. administrator in Iraq, Jay Garner, had with the president, Garner "had not mentioned the problems he saw, or even hinted at them. . . . Once again, the aura of the presidency had shut out the most important news—the bad news." Nor did the president seek to elicit that news. Indeed, some argue that the sorts of questions Bush favors discourage detailed answers and prevent the discussion from moving in a way that might open up new questions or unwelcome options. Even when the president made public appearances billed as "town meetings," or "conversations," guests were normally screened to ensure that they were supportive of the president generally and of his preferences concerning the policies on the event's agenda.[79]

Certainly in the lead-up to the Iraq invasion, dissenters from the small-foot-print, "shock and awe" battle plan preferred by Rumsfeld and Cheney, and drawn to their specifications by General Tommy Franks, were not welcome at the table. An August 2002 U.S. Central Command briefing reviewing "how we got here," made public in early 2007, stated, "POTUS/SECDEF [i.e., the president and secretary of defense] directed effort; limited to a very small group."[80] A series of recent books elaborate that group's decisions, which need not be detailed here.[81] But they suggest in the aggregate a wide array of the advisory dysfunctions that Alexander George identified, both in the formulation of the plan and in its public presentation. The two are, of course, related—most dramatically by the briefing given to the British cabinet in summer 2002, in which the head of the British MI6 intelligence service recounted that "military action was now seen as inevitable. Bush wanted to remove Saddam, through military action, justified by the conjunction of terrorism and WMD. But the intelligence and facts were being fixed around the policy."[82]

If accurate, that suggests that the decision to go to war long preceded debate over whether it was a good idea, indeed foreclosed the need for it. This in turn suggests that the president either did not heed, or did not seek out, competing arguments on a variety of questions central to the conduct of the war and its aftermath. Additional information was readily accessible. For instance, extensive estimates of the challenges and costs of occupying Iraq had been produced by State and Defense Department analysts; far higher troop levels had been urged by the uniformed military. Difficulties with existing plans for interim Iraqi governments, and the real possibility that CIA chief Tenet's promised "slam dunk" (with regard to Iraq's weapons of mass destruction) would turn out to be an air ball instead, could also be gleaned from information available in the executive branch.[83]

Manufacturing Alternative Views

That conclusion suggests the potential importance of the "parallel processing" and monitoring mechanisms noted earlier. They provide a means of double-checking the existence and credibility of dissenting views when they are not presented directly. As Deputy Defense Secretary Wolfowitz observed, for example, there is "a phenomenon in intelligence work, that people who are pursuing a certain hypothesis will see certain facts that others won't, and not see other facts that others will."[84]

Parallel processing does not appear to have been much practiced during the first Bush term. After all, it is by its nature decentralized—and arguably inefficient, if you trust the advice you are getting. The president's own conversations tended instead to be efficient, and brief. Even the "PDB," the president's daily report of the most immediate intelligence matters, was limited to one page in length. "He least likes me to say, 'This is complex,'" Rice has noted, and parallel processing often brings out the nuances of policy choice.[85] Furthermore, because competition among advisers tends to cause friction, and thus media coverage, it is not a strategy likely to be favored by a leak-averse administration. Interestingly, one example from the period leading up to the Iraq war—the Pentagon's Office of Special Projects (OSP)—shows not only the use but the potential misuse of parallel processing.

OSP was set up in part to explore whether CIA estimates regarding Iraq and other aspects of the war on terror were reliable. Given the intelligence community's recent track record, this seemed reasonable. As it transpired, though, the OSP was used to build evidence that led only in one direction—data that would justify an invasion of Iraq and overcome the intelligence community consensus that doubted Saddam Hussein's links to al Qaeda and September 11. At least at times, its conclusions were not used to compete with alternative data but to overwrite them (e.g., in a July 2002 memo titled "Iraq and al-Qaida: Making the Case"). The Pentagon's inspector general said in February 2007 that such work was "inappropriate."[86]

More generally Bush tended not to see the need to search for outside advice or to manufacture dissenting views. "I appreciate people's opinions," he told an interviewer, "but I'm more interested in news. And the best way to get the news is from objective sources. And the most objective sources I have are people on my staff who tell me what's happening in the world." As a result, "I have no outside advice. Anybody who says they're an outside adviser of this Administration on [the war on terror] is not telling the truth."[87]

Such a view obviously contrasts sharply with the notion of "institutionalizing distrust." Yet the utility of the strategy of institutionalizing distrust was highlighted by the difficulties the administration faced in responding to Hurricane Katrina in late August 2005. The scope of the storm's damage did not sink in at the White House for some four days. When the hurricane struck, one journalist concluded, "It appears there was no one to tell President Bush the plain truth: that the state and local governments had been overwhelmed, that the Federal Emergency Management Agency was not up to the job." FEMA itself had been moved into the Department of Homeland Security, a shift that made sense on the organization chart but made it difficult to move information and approvals through additional levels of hierarchy. As a White House aide noted, "The extremely highly centralized control of the government—the engine of Bush's success—failed him this time."[88] As with the levees of New Orleans itself, there was no backup system in place.

Legacies and Limits

The 2006 elections brought divided government back to Washington and calls for bipartisanship and collaboration back to the president's lexicon. The administra-

tion made a show of reaching out for new advice and advisers, even as new problems (Iran, the condition of the veterans health care system, the conviction of
Cheney aide Lewis Libby, the prosecutors' firings) crowded onto the agenda next
to old ones (Iraq, Afghanistan, Katrina) and the 2008 campaign threatened to dis-
tract attention from White House initiatives altogether.

Still, as his rejection of the Iraq "out" proffered by the Baker-Hamilton Commission and the subsequent troop surge into Baghdad suggested, the president's
decision-making style had likely changed only at the margins. "I don't need people
around me who are not steady," the president had told Bob Woodward in 2005,
and some combination of steadiness and stubbornness remained central to his
White House and his legacy.[89] After all, unlike the George H. W. Bush administration, the second Bush administration had the "vision thing" in spades. And it
could make a strong case that carrying out that vision required a particular discipline. Its strategy of centralization presupposed a healthy disdain for its agenda by
the expert naysayers in the bureaucracy and the academy. And politicization, in
turn, assumed that implementing the agenda would require some force if the usual
bureaucratic norming process were not to sand down the blunt impact of those
policies. In this sense the Bush style of issue management echoed Nixon aide John
Ehrlichman's memo to OMB some three decades earlier, defining public administration as the means to "get-the-Secretary-to-do-what-the-President-needs-and-
wants-him-to-do-whether-he-likes-it-or-not."[90]

Still, as David Gergen, who worked in four administrations over three decades,
has observed, "top-down leadership . . . can yield strong short-term results but turn
sour over time."[91] The Bush approach shows both the strengths and limits of its
complementary strategies. They enable immediate effectiveness in an institution
rarely known for that trait. But by failing to draw on deliberative collaboration and
technical expertise, they make long-term change less likely to take hold. They work
to move government forward when you know what you want to do; they are less
useful, perhaps, in showing you what you *should* want to do. Clear goals have real
value to leadership; but clarity in itself does not make a goal consistent with the
public interest. Politics is about inspiration; but political leadership in the end is
judged by facts on the ground.

The balance between decisiveness and knowledge in the Bush administration
was clearly weighted toward decisiveness. As the president told a group of Craw-
ford, Texas, schoolchildren, "If you know what you believe, decision making is
pretty easy." Thus the marginal cost of garnering additional information was rarely
worth the price. As Bob Woodward saw it, "Once on a course, he directed his
energy at forging on, rarely looking back, scoffing at—even ridiculing—doubt."[92]
As a result, for George W. Bush as for few presidents, leadership and management
were of a piece, both marked by a stinging polarity. Someone could be with the
president (and in the right), or against him (and, too often in the administration's
rhetoric, America).

Yet neither choice nor success is always binary. And thus presidential staffing institutions must force their chiefs to ask and answer hard questions, including those of failure and nuance, assumption and implementation. Facts can be as stubborn as any individual, and presidential "deciders," no matter how much they hate to admit to error, are not infallible. The key is whether their management institutions help them learn from their mistakes—to gain fresh advice, fresh choices, and perhaps fresh staff—or whether the mistakes themselves become institutionalized. The MBA president might benefit from recent MBA curricula that urge the creation of flat, decentralized decision-making structures that reach out widely to foster debate and build consensus, as well as the use of "situational" leadership that allows for changing goals and methods. In a perverse way, the questions at hand are too important to be sure about; for as a wise political scientist once said, democracy is "a political system for people who are not too sure that they are right."[93] If so, then doubt and dissent are not weaknesses but the soul of self-governance.

Notes

1. Bush quoted in Alexis Simendinger, "Bush's 'Aha!' Moments," *National Journal,* July 23, 2005, 2358; "President Bush Nominates Rob Portman as OMB Director," Office of the White House Press Secretary, April 18, 2006.

2. At least in the modern presidency, starting (by most accounts) with Franklin Roosevelt. See, for example, Norman Thomas, "Presidential Advice and Information: Policy and Program Formulation," *Law and Contemporary Problems* 35 (1970): 540–572; Patricia D. Witherspoon, *Within These Walls: A Study of Communication between Presidents and Their Senior Staffs* (Westport, Conn.: Praeger, 1991).

3. Arthur Schlesinger Jr., *A Thousand Days: John F. Kennedy in the White House* (Greenwich, Conn.: Fawcett, 1965), chap. 10, 30–31; John Tower, Edmund Muskie, and Brent Scowcroft, *The Tower Commission Report* (New York: Times Books, 1987), 62. See, more generally, Andrew Rudalevige, "The Structure of Leadership: Presidents, Hierarchies, and Information Flow," *Presidential Studies Quarterly* 35 (June 2005): 333–360.

4. Donald F. Kettl, *Team Bush: Leadership Lessons from the Bush White House* (New York: McGraw-Hill, 2003), 31; see too James Bennet, "C.E.O., U.S.A.," *New York Times Magazine,* January 14, 2001; Richard L. Berke, "Bush Is Providing Corporate Model for White House," *New York Times,* March 11, 2001.

5. Evan Thomas and Richard Wolffe, "Bush in the Bubble," *Newsweek,* December 19, 2005; see also Mike Allen, "Management Style Shows Weaknesses," *Washington Post,* June 2, 2004, A6; Carl Cannon, "Trapped in the Mirror," *National Journal,* October 29, 2005, 3348–3349.

6. Bob Woodward, *Bush at War* (New York: Simon and Schuster, 2002); *Plan of Attack* (New York: Simon and Schuster, 2004); *State of Denial* (New York: Simon and Schuster, 2006).

7. Dan Balz and Bob Woodward, "Bush Awaits History's Judgments," *Washington Post,* February 3, 2002, A1; emphasis added.

8. At least according to Richard E. Neustadt, *Presidential Power and the Modern Presidents* (New York: Free Press, 1990).

9. Donald Rumsfeld, "Rumsfeld's Rules," revised December 17, 1976, James A. Baker III Papers, Princeton University, Box 60, "Office/Desk Files 1981."

10. Harry McPherson, *A Political Education: A Washington Memoir* (Boston: Houghton Mifflin, 1988), 292; for a more recent (and less elegant) take, see Dick Morris, *Behind the Oval Office* (New York: Random House, 1997), 100–102.

11. Dwight D. Eisenhower, *The White House Years: Mandate for Change, 1953–56* (New York: Doubleday, 1963), 114.

12. See Thomas J. Weko, *The Politicizing Presidency: The White House Personnel Office, 1948–1994* (Lawrence: University Press of Kansas, 1994), 89. Broad treatments of this strategy can be found in Terry Moe, "The Politicized Presidency," in *New Directions in American Politics,* ed. John Chubb and Paul E. Peterson (Washington, D.C.: Brookings Institution Press, 1985); and David E. Lewis, *Politicizing Administration* (Princeton: Princeton University Press, forthcoming).

13. See Joel Aberbach's chapter in this volume, as well as Dick Kirschten, "White House Strategy," *National Journal,* February 21, 1981, 302; Martin Anderson, *Revolution: The Reagan Legacy,* expanded ed. (Stanford: Hoover Institution Press, 1990), 193–205; Andrew Rudalevige, "The President and the Cabinet," in *The Presidency and the Political System,* 8th ed., ed. Michael Nelson (Washington, D.C.: CQ Press, 2006). The memo quoted is from Dennis Thomas to Don Regan, "Secretary of HHS," October 25, 1985, Ronald Reagan Library, W. Dennis Thomas papers, Box 7, "Regan Memorandum July–Dec 1985 (2 of 2) OA 14161."

14. Irving Janis, *Groupthink,* 2nd ed. (Boston: Houghton Mifflin, 1982); Andrew Rudalevige, "Pro: A President's Cabinet Members Should Have a Larger Role in the Formation of Public Policy," in *Debating the Presidency,* ed. Richard Ellis and Michael Nelson (Washington, D.C.: CQ Press, 2006), 150.

15. Alexander L. George, *Presidential Decisionmaking in Foreign Policy: The Effective Use of Information and Advice* (Boulder: Westview Press, 1980), chap. 6.

16. Richard Rose, "Organizing Issues In and Organizing Problems Out," in *The Managerial Presidency,* ed. James P. Pfiffner (Pacific Grove, Calif.: Brooks/Cole, 1991), 108. This is also one conclusion of a series of articles by Thomas Hammond, including "Toward a General Theory of Hierarchy," *Journal of Public Administration Research and Theory* 3 (1993): 120–145.

17. Neustadt, "Statement before the Subcommittee on National Security Staffing and Operations of the Senate Committee on Government Operations, March 25, 1963," in *The National Security Council: Jackson Subcommittee Papers on Policy-Making at the Presidential Level,* ed. Henry M. Jackson (New York: Praeger, 1965); see also Neustadt, *Presidential Power,* 221.

18. Foreign and domestic issues, after all, as longtime presidential confidant W. Averell Harriman argued, are only "different aspects of the same national purpose." See Emmet John Hughes, *The Living Presidency* (New York: Coward, McCann and Geoghegan, 1973), 349.

19. Matthew J. Dickinson, *Bitter Harvest: FDR and the Growth of the Presidential Branch* (New York: Cambridge University Press, 1997), 74–76, 206–208.

20. Rumsfeld, "Rumsfeld's Rules." As detailed below, he seems to have been less enamored of this rule from his seat in the Pentagon.

21. Schlesinger, *A Thousand Days,* 627–628; Morris, *Behind the Oval Office,* 100.

22. For a more detailed discussion of these trade-offs see, for example, Roger Porter, *Presidential Decisionmaking: The Economic Policy Board* (New York: Cambridge University Press, 1980); Doris A. Graber, *The Power of Communication: Managing Information in Public Organizations* (Washington, D.C.: CQ Press, 2003).

23. Sheryl Gay Stolberg, "Bush Friends, Loyal and Texan, Remain a Force," *New York Times,* February 21, 2007. Johnson himself clearly fit that bill; he had ties to the president extending back to prep school and had served a similar vetting role in Bush's governorship.

24. Martha Joynt Kumar, "Recruiting and Organizing the White House Staff," in *The White House World: Transitions, Organization, and Office Operations,* ed. Martha Joynt Kumar and Terry Sullivan (College Station: Texas A&M Press, 2003), 368.

25. This strategy was consistent with, and perhaps drawn from, those of earlier presidents as well. Consider Nixon chief of staff H. R. Haldeman's handwritten notes from a 1972 meeting with the president: "Loyalty up is the most important thing," he noted. The administration needed to "control the key posts: press, legal, personnel, Congressional, Deputy." He would add, darkly: "Loyalty much more important than competence." Quoted in Andrew Rudalevige, *Managing the President's Program* (Princeton: Princeton University Press, 2002), 38.

26. James A. Barnes, "Bush's Insiders," *National Journal,* June 23, 2001; James A. Barnes, "Selecting the Players," transcript of an interview with Clay Johnson, NationalJournal.com, June 25, 2001 (accessed March 7, 2007); Mike Allen, "Bush to Change Economic Team," *Washington Post,* November 29, 2004, A1; Shirley Anne Warshaw, "The Administrative Strategies of President George W. Bush," *Extensions: Journal of the Legislative Studies Section,* Spring 2006, 19–20; Warshaw, "Ideological Conflict in the President's Cabinet," in *The Presidency of George W. Bush and the War on Terrorism,* ed. Richard S. Conley (Upper Saddle River, N.J.: Pearson Prentice Hall, 2005).

27. Barnes, "Bush's Insiders," *National Journal,* June 23, 2001; Warshaw, "The Administrative Strategies," 20; *Massachusetts v. EPA,* decided April 2, 2007.

28. Scott Shane and Ron Nixon, "In Washington, Contractors Take on Biggest Role Ever," *New York Times,* February 4, 2007, A1.

29. See, for example, Alexis Simendinger, "Stepping into Power," *National Journal,* January 26, 2001.

30. Finn and figures (from a Brookings Institution study) cited in Crystal Nix Hines, "Lag in Appointments Strains the Cabinet," *New York Times,* June 14, 2001.

31. Ron Suskind, *The Price of Loyalty: George W. Bush, the White House, and the Education of Paul O'Neill* (New York: Simon and Schuster, 2004); Whitman quoted in Mike Allen and David S. Broder, "Bush's Leadership Style: Decisive or Simplistic?" *Washington Post,* August 30, 2004.

32. Amy Goldstein and Sarah Cohen, "Bush Forces a Shift in Regulatory Thrust," *Washington Post,* August 15, 2004, A1; Rick Weiss, "'Data Quality' Law Is Nemesis of Regulation," *Washington Post,* August 16, 2004, A1; Warshaw, "The Administrative Strategies."

33. E.O. 13422, issued on January 18, 2007.

34. Jonathan D. Breul, "Three Bush Management Reform Initiatives," *Public Administration Review,* January/February 2007, 21–26; author's interviews with OMB staff. Generally, see Paul C. Light, *Tides of Reform* (New Haven: Yale University Press, 1997).

35. Todd S. Purdum, "Mr. Heat Shield Keeps Boss Happy," *New York Times,* December 6, 2001, B7.

36. See, for example, Richard Tanner Johnson, *Managing the White House* (New York: Harper and Row, 1974).

37. Karen M. Hult and Charles E. Walcott, *Empowering the White House: Governance under Nixon, Ford, and Carter* (Lawrence: University Press of Kansas, 2004), chap. 2.

38. And many more entities besides; for a very comprehensive accounting, see Bradley Patterson, *The White House Staff* (Washington, D.C.: Brookings Institution Press, 2000).

39. The phrase is Hugh Heclo's; see "The Changing Presidential Office," in *The Managerial Presidency,* 2nd ed., ed. James P. Pfiffner (College Station: Texas A&M Press, 1999), 24. See too Karen M. Hult, "The Bush White House in Comparative Perspective," in *The George W. Bush Presidency: An Early Assessment,* ed. Fred I. Greenstein (Baltimore: Johns Hopkins University Press, 2003).

40. Kumar, "Recruiting and Organizing," 369.

41. Ibid., 361; and see Terry Sullivan, "Assessing Transition 2001," in *The Nerve Center: Lessons in Governing from the White House Chiefs of Staff,* ed. Terry Sullivan (College Station: Texas A&M University Press, 2004), 128. *Bush v. Gore* (531 U.S. 98) was decided on December 12, 2000.

42. Barnes, "Bush's Insiders"; Kathryn Dunn Tenpas and Stephen Hess, "Organizing the Bush Presidency," in *Considering the Bush Presidency,* ed. Gary L. Gregg II and Mark J. Rozell (New York: Oxford University Press, 2004), 39. Card cited in Woodward, *State of Denial,* 354.

43. Kumar, "Recruiting and Organizing"; Richard L. Berke, "This Time, Dissent Stops at the White House Door," *New York Times,* December 2001, IV:3; Elisabeth Bumiller, "An Invisible Aide Leaves Fingerprints," *New York Times,* January 6, 2003; Jeff Birnbaum, "Yosh!" *Stanford Lawyer,* Summer 2004, 16–21; John Burke, "The Institutional Presidency," in *The Presidency and the Political System,* 8th ed., ed. Michael Nelson (Washington, D.C.: CQ Press, 2006).

44. Spellings, as assistant to the president for domestic policy, oversaw the Domestic Policy Council, though it was formally directed by deputy assistant John Bridgeland, another former congressional and campaign aide.

45. Dana Milbank, "A Loyalist Calls White House to Order," *Washington Post,* February 20, 2001, A1.

46. Thomas B. Edsall and Dana Milbank, "White House's Roving Eye for Politics," *Washington Post,* March 10, 2003, A1.

47. Robert Bryce, "The Loyal Lieutenants," *Austin Chronicle,* March 17, 2000; Card quoted in Ron Suskind, "Mrs. Hughes Takes Her Leave," *Esquire,* July 2002, 103.

48. Rove quoted in John P. Burke, "The Bush Transition," in *Considering the Bush Presidency,* ed. Gary L. Gregg II and Mark J. Rozell (New York: Oxford University Press, 2004), 31; Card quoted in Suskind, "Mrs. Hughes," 110.

49. Greg Hitt, "Out of Sight, Cheney Is Power," *Wall Street Journal,* December 9, 2003; Richard W. Stevenson and Elisabeth Bumiller, "Cheney Exercising Muscle on Domestic Policies," *New York Times,* January 18, 2005; Kenneth T. Walsh, "The Cheney Factor," *U.S. News and World Report,* January 23, 2006, 40–48.

50. Light quoted in Dana Milbank, "With a Crisis, More Fluid Style at the White House," *Washington Post,* October 10, 2001; see also Woodward, *Bush at War;* the documentary

record regarding the treatment of detainees in Karen Greenberg and Joshua Dratel, eds., *The Torture Memos* (New York: Cambridge University Press, 2005).

51. Suskind, "Mrs. Hughes," 107; Richard L. Berke and David E. Sanger, "Some in Administration Grumble as Aide's Role Seems to Expand," *New York Times,* May 13, 2002, A1; Matt Bai, "Rove's Way," *New York Times Magazine,* October 12, 2002; Mike Allen, "Bush Fills Key Slots with Young Loyalists," *Washington Post,* May 29, 2003, A1.

52. Chertoff's nomination followed that of former New York police commissioner Bernard Kerik, who withdrew from consideration after various irregularities in his personal and professional lives became public.

53. Woodward, *State of Denial,* 364–366; Karen deYoung, *Soldier: The Life of Colin Powell* (New York: Knopf, 2006), 508–511.

54. Amy Goldstein and Dan Eggen, "Prosecutor Posts Go to Bush Insiders," *Washington Post,* April 1, 2007, A1.

55. David E. Sanger and Steven R. Weisman, "Cabinet Choices Seen as Move for More Harmony and Control," *New York Times,* November 17, 2004, A1; Dana Milbank, "Bush Seeks to Rule the Bureaucracy: Appointments Aim at White House Control," *Washington Post,* November 22, 2004, A4; Jim VandeHei and Glenn Kessler, "President to Consider Changes for New Term," *Washington Post,* November 5, 2004, A1. Interestingly, the president soon required cabinet members to spend at least part of each workweek at the Eisenhower Executive Office Building near the White House. Whether this arrangement allowed them to participate in policymaking or simply to receive marching orders was unclear.

56. Allen's tenure at the Domestic Policy Council was notable mostly for its conclusion: He resigned in advance of shoplifting charges filed in early 2006. See Milbank, "A Loyalist Calls White House to Order." On Card, Rove, and other changes in White House staffing, see Anne E. Kornblut and Elisabeth Bumiller, "White House Using Cuts to Shuffle and Shoo Staff," *New York Times,* February 8, 2005; Peter Baker, "Rove Is Promoted to Deputy Staff Chief: Job Covers a Broad Swath of Policy," *Washington Post,* February 9, 2005, A21; Woodward, *State of Denial,* 354–358.

57. Alexis Simendinger, "Stirred, Not Shaken," *National Journal,* April 22, 2006, 42–43.

58. Former commerce secretary Don Evans, quoted in David E. Sanger, "Top Aide Leaves White House Job; Budget Chief In," *New York Times,* March 29, 2006.

59. Peter Baker, "Bush Picks Reagan White House Counsel Fielding to Replace Miers," *Washington Post,* January 9, 2007, A4.

60. Anonymous political strategist quoted in Kettl, *Team Bush,* 104.

61. David Frum, *The Right Man: An Inside Account of the Bush White House,* paperback ed. (New York: Random House, 2005), 91; and see Fred Barnes, *Rebel-in-Chief: Inside the Bold and Controversial Presidency of George W. Bush* (New York: Crown, 2006).

62. Bush quoted in Woodward, *Bush at War,* 74; VandeHei and Kessler, "President to Consider Changes."

63. Allen, "Bush Fills Key Slots with Young Loyalists."

64. David Johnston and Eric Lipton, "'Loyalty' to Bush and Gonzales Was a Factor in Prosecutors' Firings," *New York Times,* March 14, 2007.

65. Berke and Sanger, "Some in Administration Grumble."

66. Internal accounts suggest that Bush spent only a small fraction of the time Clinton did on budget deliberations. Bush delegated the task to a Budget Review Board made up of the

vice president, the directors of OMB and NEC, the White House chief of staff, the Treasury secretary, and the chair of the CEA. Author's interviews with OMB staff, July 10, 2006.

67. On the policy councils generally, see Hult, "The Bush White House." On Iraq and NSC, see Woodward, *State of Denial,* esp. 329–330, 420; James Fallows, *Blind into Baghdad: America's War in Iraq* (New York: Vintage, 2006); Chitra Ragavan, "Who Lost Iraq?" *U.S. News and World Report,* November 27, 2006, 38–39. For NEC, see Noam Scheiber, "Bush's War on Honest Economics," *New Republic,* May 6, 2002.

68. Quoted in David Rose, "Neo Culpa," *Vanity Fair,* January 2007. Some argue that the NSC's focus on such issues as missile defense before September 11 meant that the terrorist threat posed by al Qaeda received too little attention. Counterterrorism staffer Richard Clarke reported to the deputy national security adviser, rather than to Rice directly. As Rice herself testified, the famous August 2001 brief titled "Bin Ladin Determined to Strike in U.S." was viewed as a "historical memo. . . . [The president] was told this is historical information and there was nothing actionable in this." See the testimony of Richard Clarke and Condoleezza Rice, collected in *The 9/11 Investigation* (New York: Public Affairs Reports, 2004), 174ff; Woodward, *State of Denial,* 49–51.

69. See, for example, Suskind, "The Price of Loyalty," 107–109. Likewise, the second inaugural was supposedly the first time Secretary of State Rice had heard of its dramatic new emphases in American foreign policy.

70. DiIulio's memo to Ron Suskind, dated October 24, 2002, and titled "Your Next Essay on the Bush Administration," was the basis for Suskind, "Why Are These Men Laughing?" *Esquire,* January 2003. More generally, on the difficulty presidents have had in giving policy formulation sufficient stress, see Karen M. Hult, "Strengthening Presidential Decision-Making Capacity," *Presidential Studies Quarterly* 30 (March 2000): 27–46. On education reform, see Andrew Rudalevige, "Forging a Congressional Compromise," in *No Child Left Behind?* ed. Paul E. Peterson and Martin West (Washington, D.C.: Brookings Institution Press, 2003); on immigration, see Kenneth T. Walsh, "Q & A with White House Deputy Chief of Staff Joel Kaplan," August 17, 2006, *U.S. News and World Report* Web site, www.usnews.com/news/articles/060817/16kaplan.htm (accessed August 18, 2006).

71. James P. Pfiffner, "Presidential Leadership and Advice about Going to War," paper presented at the Conference on Presidential Leadership, Richmond, Virginia, September 9–10, 2005; Warshaw, "Ideological Conflict"; Woodward, *Bush at War.*

72. Warshaw, "Ideological Conflict," 76–81; Woodward, *Bush at War,* 205.

73. R. Jeffrey Smith and Dan Eggen, "Gonzales Helped Set the Course for Detainees," *Washington Post,* January 5, 2005, A1; Greenberg and Dratel, *The Torture Memos;* Jane Mayer, "The Hidden Power: The Legal Mind behind the White House's War on Terror," *New Yorker,* July 3, 2006. For a strongly dissenting view by one of those involved in the decision making, see John Yoo, *War by Other Means* (New York: Atlantic Monthly Press, 2006).

74. Amy Goldstein, "Libby Trial Offered Glimpses of Way White House Worked," *Washington Post,* March 8, 2007, A4; Rajiv Chandrasekaran, *Imperial Life in the Emerald City* (New York: Knopf, 2006).

75. DeYoung, *Soldier,* 520.

76. Bush in Woodward, *Bush at War,* 255; William Douglas, "Andrew Card Keeps a Low Profile at the Center of the Storm," *Knight-Ridder Newspapers,* March 10, 2006.

77. Quoted in Bob Woodward, "A Course of 'Confident Action,'" *Washington Post,* November 19, 2002; transcript of January 2005 *Washington Times* interview, available at www.washingtontimes.com/national/20050111-114349-9789r.htm (accessed March 10, 2007).

78. Suskind, *The Price of Loyalty,* 147–149; Fallows, *Blind into Baghdad*; Levin quoted in Woodward, *State of Denial,* 416; Jim Rutenberg, "Ex-Aide Says He's Lost Faith in Bush," *New York Times,* April 1, 2007, A1.

79. Garner in Woodward, *State of Denial,* 224; Thomas and Wolffe, "Bush in the Bubble"; Dan Froomkin, "White House Briefing: Should Tax Dollars Fund Bush Bubble?" *Washington Post.com,* February 8, 2005, www.washingtonpost.com/wp-dyn/articles/A7880-2005Feb8.html (accessed March 10, 2007).

80. "Tab I, Slide 2: Background," POLO STEP planning group briefing for Central Command, August 2002, as reproduced in National Security Archive Electronic Briefing Book No. 214, www.gwu.edu/~nsarchiv/NSAEBB/NSAEBB214/index.htm (accessed March 7, 2007).

81. See, for example, Chandrasekaran, *Imperial Life in the Emerald City*; Fallows, *Blind into Baghdad*; Michael R. Gordon and Bernard E. Trainor, *Cobra II: The Inside Story of the Invasion and Occupation of Iraq* (New York: Pantheon, 2006), 503–504; George Packer, *Assassin's Gate: America in Iraq* (New York: Farrar Straus and Giroux, 2005); Thomas E. Ricks, *Fiasco: The American Military Adventure in Iraq* (New York: Penguin, 2006); James Risen, *State of War: The Secret History of the CIA and the Bush Administration* (New York: Free Press, 2006). A useful summation is contained in James P. Pfiffner, "The First MBA President: George W. Bush as Public Administrator," *Public Administration Review,* January/February 2007, 9–11.

82. "The Downing Street Memo," July 23, 2002, reprinted in Mark Danner, *The Secret Way to War* (New York: New York Review Books, 2006), 88–90.

83. See, for example, Murray Waas, "What Bush Was Told about Iraq," *National Journal,* March 4, 2006, 40–42. An earlier reconstruction by Fallows in *The Atlantic,* reprinted as the title chapter in *Blind into Baghdad,* concludes that the president was probably "exposed to only a narrow range of options worked out by the contending forces within his Administration. If this interpretation proves to be right, and if Bush did in fact wish to know more, then blame will fall on those whose responsibility it was to present him with the widest range of choices: Cheney and Rice" (available at www.theatlantic.com/doc/200401/fallows).

84. Eric Schmitt and Thom Shanker, "A CIA Rival: Pentagon Sets up Intelligence Unit," *New York Times,* October 24, 2002, A1.

85. Evan Thomas, "How Bush Blew It," *Newsweek,* September 19, 2005; "The Silent President," editorial, *New York Times,* April 12, 2004, A22; Rice quoted in Nicholas Lemann, "Without a Doubt," *New Yorker,* October 14–26, 2002, 177.

86. Beyond the sources on Iraq noted above (perhaps especially Packer), see Mark Hosenball, Michael Isikoff, and Evan Thomas, "Cheney's Long Path to War," *Newsweek,* November 17, 2003, 36; David S. Cloud and Mark Mazzetti, "Prewar Intelligence Unit at Pentagon Is Criticized," *New York Times,* February 9, 2007; R. Jeffrey Smith, "Hussein's Pre-War Ties to Al-Qaeda Discounted: Pentagon Report Says Contacts Were Limited," *Washington Post,* April 6, 2007, A1.

87. Bush interview with Brit Hume of Fox News, September 22, 2003; transcript at www. foxnews.com/story/0,2933,98006,00.html (accessed March 7, 2007); Nicholas Lemann, "Remember the Alamo," *New Yorker,* October 18, 2004, 158.

88. Adding to the difficulty was the performance of the head of FEMA, Michael Brown, a polit- ical appointee with a limited background in emergency management. Thomas, "How Bush Blew It"; "key adviser" quoted in Mike Allen, "Living Too Much in the Bubble?" *Time,* Sep- tember 12, 2005. For a useful overview, see Pfiffner, "The First MBA President," 15–17.

89. Woodward, *State of Denial,* 326.

90. John Ehrlichman to Cap Weinberger, June 26, 1972, White House Subject Files,[CF] FG 6-16 Folder, Nixon Presidential Materials Staff, College Park, Maryland.

91. Quoted in Cannon, "Trapped in the Mirror," 33.

92. Frum, *The Right Man,* 91; Woodward, *Bush at War,* 256.

93. John Maggs, "Yes, He's Back," *National Journal,* February 17, 2007, 32–36; E. E. Schattschneider, *Two Hundred Million Americans in Search of a Government* (New York: Holt, Rinehart, and Winston, 1969), 53.

CHAPTER 8

Living (and Dying?) by the Sword
George W. Bush as Legislative Leader

Barbara Sinclair

WHEN WE CONSIDER A PRESIDENT'S legacy, one of the first things we think about is his record of legislative leadership. During the twentieth century, and especially with the presidency of Franklin Roosevelt, legislative leadership came to be seen as central to the office of president; Americans came to expect their president to propose a legislative agenda for the Congress and to engineer its enactment into law.[1]

A U.S. president attempts to exert legislative leadership within a governmental system that makes the president dependent on an independently elected Congress for success. The Constitution created a national government of separate branches sharing power and, by doing so, established a relationship of mutual dependence between the president and Congress. In terms of policymaking, it put the president in the weaker position.[2] The legislative power is vested in Congress; the president cannot even compel Congress to consider—much less pass—his legislative program. The president is dependent on Congress not just for new programs but also for money to carry out already existing programs, for approval of top-level personnel to staff the administration, and for acquiescence in many of the decisions the president makes that Congress, through legislation or less-formal means, could hinder. The only specifically legislative power the Constitution gives the president is the power to sign or veto legislation—and vetoes can be overridden.

Because the president cannot command Congress, the *context* in which the president acts and the *resources* the president commands as a result of that context are the most important determinants of presidential success. Skill can make a difference, and we rightly judge presidents on whether they extracted the maximum advantage from a given context. But to understand a president's legislative record, we need to understand the context—and sometimes, as is certainly the case with George W. Bush, the multiple contexts—in which he operated.

The Contextual Determinants of Presidential-Congressional Relations

Understanding the relationship between a particular president and Congress and the policy outputs that ensue requires understanding how incentives and behavior are shaped by the constitutional, institutional, and political contexts. The Constitution and the undisciplined and decentralized party system that it fostered provide the president with no basis for commanding Congress, but they do give him leverage. Through the veto, control of the executive branch, and access to the news media, the president can advance or hinder the goals of members of Congress. Because of the president's dependence on Congress, his inability to command but potential to influence, every president needs a strategy for dealing with Congress— a plan or approach for getting Congress to do what he wants and needs it to do to accomplish his goals.

A president's strategies vis-à-vis Congress are shaped and constrained by his legislative goals and by the resources—the political capital, in George W. Bush's terminology—that he commands. The extent to which a president's policy preferences and those of a congressional majority coincide or conflict influences how a president sets out to get what he wants, as well as the probability of success. So, too, do the resources the president commands for eliciting support beyond that based purely on policy agreement.

Even in the weak U.S. party system, members of a party tend to share policy preferences; consequently, when members of the president's party make up the congressional majority, they and the president often agree at least on the general thrust of policy, providing a basis for presidential-congressional cooperation.[3] The ideological homogeneity of the congressional parties has varied over time; sometimes, as at present, the extent of agreement on what constitutes good public policy within one or both parties is great. Additionally, the members of his party have an interest in the president's success that transcends any specific legislative battle. Because many of those members believe that a strong president will be able to help them attain various of their goals in the future, they may be willing to support the president even when their policy preferences do not coincide with his. To the extent that presidential success in the legislative arena breeds a perception of strength, which translates into future success, a member of the president's party may believe that supporting the president today will pay off in the passage of preferred legislation in the future. To the extent that presidential success has an electoral payoff— increasing the chances of the party's holding the White House or increasing its seats in Congress—a fellow party member has an incentive to provide support for the president beyond that based purely on policy agreement.

Congressional leaders of the president's party are especially likely to see presidential success as in their best interest; they must concern themselves with the party's image and are likely to be judged by their success in enacting the president's program.⁴ Thus, when the president's party is in the majority, the very considerable institutional and procedural advantages of control of one or both chambers—such as control over the legislative agenda—are usually available to the president.

Members of the other party, in contrast, are likely to see a strong, successful president as a threat to their electoral and policy goals. When policy differences between the parties are not very great, or the opposition party is ideologically diverse, the president may gain significant support from opposition-party members solely on the basis of their agreement with his policy stances. However, for the president to elicit support from members of the opposition party beyond that based purely on policy agreement, such members must be persuaded that the costs of opposing the president are higher than the costs of supporting him. That is likely to occur if opposing the president presents a threat to the member's personal reelection chances. Circumstances that make that threat credible provide a president with significant resources for influencing Congress; their absence leaves a president with little leverage for persuading opposition-party members to support him.

When the same party controls both the presidency and Congress, cooperation is the dominant strategy for the president and the congressional majority. However, while the incentives to support the president are ordinarily considerable for members of his party, incentives to defect may also be present. Neither of the major parties is monolithic; on any issue, some members will disagree with the president. Furthermore, electoral priorities differ. Members of Congress want to see their party do well in congressional and presidential elections, but their own reelection is their first priority. If the vote required to bring about the president's success would hurt a member's reelection chances, that direct cost may well outweigh the benefits to the member of presidential success. A member's best reelection strategy may dictate voting against a president of his own party on some major issues. The political context determines whether incentives to defect dominate and for how many members.

Consequently, although cooperation with and reliance on the members of his party are the best strategy for a president whose party controls the Congress, the strategy does not necessarily ensure success. Depending on the issue, the party's cohesion, and the size of the partisan majorities, the president may need to reach across the aisle. The issue and the political context determine whether that is likely to succeed.

The Bush Agenda and the Initial Context

Any judgment about a president's legislative success must take into account his legislative goals. George W. Bush, according to Karl Rove, his most influential political adviser, campaigned on six key issues in 2000: tax cuts, education standards, military upgrades and a missile defense shield, federal support for faith-based charities, partial privatization of Social Security, and Medicare reform and prescription drug coverage for seniors.⁵ Although he billed himself as "a compassionate conservative" and promised to be "a uniter not a divider," Bush's proposals put him squarely in the strongly conservative camp. His agenda was ambitious—not in size but in the magnitude of the change in policy direction he proposed.

The political context in which Bush began his presidency did not seem particularly favorable for nonincremental policy change. Bush received fewer popular votes than his Democratic opponent; his narrow Electoral College majority depended on a five-to-four decision by an ideologically split Supreme Court. His party lost seats in both chambers of Congress. Republicans held onto control of the House of Representatives by a razor-thin majority of 221–211,[6] and the Senate, which before the elections was 54–46 Republican, emerged from the 2000 elections with an even split. Democrats and impartial commentators would not find credible any claim that the voters had given Bush a mandate for his program.

Yet Bush did enjoy unified partisan control of both chambers of Congress, and the Republicans in Congress that Bush would be working with were ideologically homogeneous and cohesive. In the 1990s (1991–2000) the average Republican voted with his party colleagues on 88 percent of party votes in the House and on 87 percent in the Senate. Party votes—those on which a majority of Republicans voted against a majority of Democrats—were much more frequent in the 1990s than before. In the 1990s, 58 percent of the roll call votes in the House and 57 percent in the Senate were party votes. In contrast, in the 1960s and 1970s (1961–1980), Republican and Democratic majorities opposed each other on 40 percent of the recorded votes in the House and 42 percent in the Senate.[7]

Congressional Republicans were eager to work with Bush. Republicans had won control of Congress in the 1994 elections but had been stymied by President Clinton in effectuating the sort of sweeping, conservative policy change they wanted. The largely conservative Republican congressional party supported Bush's agenda and saw much of it as their own.

Despite their narrow margin, House Republican leaders were in a good position to aid Bush. In the House, a reasonably cohesive majority can work its will; minorities lack effective ways of blocking action. The Speaker of the House, who is the chamber's presiding officer and the leader of the majority party, exercises considerable power if backed by a majority. As the parties became more ideologically homogeneous and more polarized in the 1980s, and then even more so in the 1990s, the House majority-party leadership became stronger and more actively engaged in all aspects of the legislative process. The leadership now commands procedural, organizational, and informational resources invaluable for passing legislation.[8]

Because the vice president of the United States is the president of the Senate and as such casts the tie-breaking vote, the Republicans would be able to organize and thus control the Senate. Yet the Senate would certainly present greater challenges for Bush than the House, and not just because of its 50–50 seat split. The Senate has always operated under highly permissive rules—amendments to most legislation need not be germane, and cutting off debate over any senator's objection requires a supermajority. In the 1950s and early 1960s, senators were quite restrained in using their prerogatives, but by the 1970s that restraint had given way to an activist style that saw senators as individuals much more willing to offer multitudes of amendments on the floor and to use extended debate.[9] The 1990s saw these prerogatives increasingly employed by the parties, especially, of course, by the minority party.[10]

The leader of the majority party in the Senate becomes the Senate majority leader and by precedent gains the right of first recognition, through which he or she manages the floor schedule. However, because motions to proceed to consider legislation (as well as legislation itself) can be filibustered, true control of the Senate agenda, much less of outcomes, requires sixty votes.

Goals, Context, and Strategy

George W. Bush's legislative strategy, referred to here as the "partisan strategy" for reasons that will quickly become apparent, can be summarized in four maxims:

- Focus on a few big things—limit your agenda in size, but be ambitious.
- Don't negotiate with yourself—don't compromise unless and until you absolutely must.
- The House first and to the right—rely on the House to go first and to set a mark well to the right on the spectrum for negotiations with the Senate.
- Go public—take the campaign to pass legislation beyond closed-door negotiations among officials, to the public and outside Washington.

Bush took from the Reagan presidency the lesson that, to be successful, a president should focus on a few big things, concluding, as do many political observers, that a president who has too many priorities really has none at all and squanders his political resources.[11] Unlike Reagan, however, Bush had no credible claim to a popular mandate. Bush's first strategic choice was whether to respond to his narrow and disputed election by moderating his ambitious agenda. In retrospect, we can see that most of his other strategic choices flowed from that decision. Bush and his advisers decided that any retreat would be seen as an admission of weakness and would likely alienate his core supporters in Congress and the country. They decided instead to act as if they had a mandate.

That decision dictated heavy reliance on his own partisans in Congress and little real attempt to build bipartisan consensus on legislation. Within the ideologically polarized Washington political community, a commitment to compromising only as a last resort precluded working with mainstream Democrats. Republican and Democratic notions of what constitutes good public policy were just too far apart.

Refusing to moderate or compromise until late in the legislative process meant relying on the House of Representatives and its Republican leadership to do the "heavy lifting." Because a Speaker leading a cohesive party can engineer passage of major legislative with a bare majority, Bush could count on the House to pass bills in a form that would advantage his position in bargaining with the less easily controlled Senate. Usually that required the House to take very conservative positions. Because House Republicans, with few exceptions, ranged from conservative to far right, asking them to pass legislation quite far right on the spectrum actually put less strain on the party than asking them to compromise would have done.

The strategy of going public also follows from the initial strategy decision. Going public consists, in Sam Kernell's words, of "a class of activities that presidents engage in as they promote themselves and their policies before the American public," with the aim of "enhance[ing their] chances of success in Washington."[12] A president who aims to bring about nonincremental policy change with narrow congressional majorities is almost forced to appeal to the public over the heads of his congressional opponents. However, as I suggest below, Bush's use of the strategy may well have had an intention, and certainly had an effect, different from that usually attributed to going public.

Domestic Policy before 9/11

Bush chose tax cuts and education reform as his initial domestic priorities, and on those issues the administration employed diametrically opposite approaches. The process on the tax bill illustrates the dominant, aggressively partisan strategy that Bush was to employ, especially on domestic legislation, throughout the first six years of his presidency. In contrast, Bush's strategy on education reform was characterized by compromise and bipartisanship. That case provides some clues to why Bush so seldom pursued that strategy.

Big tax cuts were the number-one priority of a great many Republicans. Congressional Republicans had passed massive tax-cutting bills several times in the 1990s only to see them killed by a Clinton veto. Democrats opposed cuts as large—and as skewed to the well-off—as Republicans wanted, but with the economy slowing in early 2001 they were amenable to some reductions in the cause of economic stimulus. Bush's decision to stick with his full package of across-the-board cuts in income tax rates, repeal of the estate tax, alleviation of the "marriage penalty," new charitable giving deductions, and some lesser provisions, estimated to cost $1.6 trillion over ten years, meant that he opted for a partisan strategy.

Going public was a key part of the Bush strategy on the tax cut, as it would be on most of his domestic priorities. The administration launched "a massive public relations campaign on behalf of his priority initiatives" when it entered the White House.[13] Each of the first four weeks was dedicated to one priority—the faith-based initiative, education, tax cuts, and defense. Curiously, however, Bush confined his campaign on the tax cut mostly to areas of the country in which he had done very well in the election and to already-supportive audiences. He might, thus, put some pressure on Democratic senators from "red" states, but he was unlikely to persuade the public beyond his base. As George Edwards shows, Bush's efforts did not move public opinion, and yet this remained Bush's modus operandi at least through the 2004 elections. Bush's public relations strategy seems to have had the effect, if not the intention, of solidifying and mobilizing his base.

At every stage, the legislative process in the House was intensely partisan. The majority leadership used its procedural and organizational tools to muscle through the Bush proposal in the form he wanted. The normal budget process requires that both chambers first pass a budget resolution to set guidelines for future legislative action, including possibly a tax cut. Then the chambers would be expected to pass a reconciliation bill that actually enacts into law the instructions set out in the budget resolution. Bush and House Republican leaders decided, however, to pass the biggest part of the Bush tax cut—the across-the-board cut in income tax rates—in the House even before the budget resolution was passed. The majority-party leadership's control over the House floor schedule, and over the special rules that govern floor consideration of legislation, made this possible. The leadership wanted to establish momentum, but by flouting the normal process they infuriated Democrats. The House Way and Means Committee, working from a draft bill that had been negotiated through a purely partisan process, approved the legislation on a party-line vote. The leadership brought up the bill for consideration on the House floor under a special rule that waived the budget rules against considering the tax bill before the budget resolution; the rule allowed only one Democratic substitute and no other amendments, thus protecting the legislation from possible killer amendments. The bill passed without amendments on a vote of 230–198, with all Republicans but only ten Democrats voting for it.

Unless the tax cut was passed as part of the budget process, it could be filibustered in the Senate. Unlike most legislation, reconciliation bills are protected from a filibuster in the Senate and thus require only a simple majority, not sixty votes, to pass. House Republicans therefore quickly moved their budget resolution, required to make a reconciliation bill in order, through the Budget Committee on a party-line vote and passed it on the floor with only three Democrats and two Republicans defecting from their party's position.

In the Senate the 50–50 party split had forced the Republicans to enter into a power-sharing agreement with Democrats that specified equal numbers of members on every committee. Republicans would, however, chair committees. The evenly split Senate Budget Committee was unable to agree on a budget resolution, so majority leader Trent Lott, Miss., bypassed the committee and brought a Republican resolution directly to the floor. The Senate majority leader is not, however, able to protect even budget measures from floor amendments, as House leaders are.

On the second full day of debate, liberal Democrat Tom Harkin, Iowa, offered an amendment reducing the tax cut by $488 billion and shifting the money to education and debt relief. When three Republican moderates—Lincoln Chafee, R.I., Jim Jeffords, Vt., and Arlen Specter, Pa.—deserted their party, the amendment passed. Vice President Dick Cheney and other administration officials scurried to figure out how to reverse the setback. But the vote just broke the dam, and before the budget resolution passed, a number of other amendments altering the president's program had been added.

Republicans hoped to recoup some of their losses in conference with the House. When Democrats complained about being excluded from the conference negotiations, Senate Budget Committee chair Pete Domenici, R-N.M., baldly replied, "We don't expect you to sign [the conference report], so we don't expect you to be needed."[14] The administration focused on getting the support of just enough moderate Senate Democrats to pass the conference report in the Senate. That dictated not substantially increasing the Senate's tax cut figure, but it did allow other changes, including cutting the Senate's figure for discretionary spending. The partisan strategy resulted in largely party-line votes on the budget resolution conference report in both chambers. It passed the House 221–207, with six Democrats and three Republicans crossing party lines. The Senate vote was 53–47. Fifteen Democrats had supported the budget resolution, as amended, when it passed the Senate, but only five supported the conference report. That was enough, however, to offset the two Republican defections.

With a budget resolution calling for tax cuts in place, the Senate could now proceed to write a tax bill, assured that it would be protected by budget rules from a filibuster. The chair and ranking minority member of the Finance Committee worked together and produced a compromise measure that won committee approval on a 14– 6 vote, with all Republicans and four of the ten Democrats voting for it. A majority of both Republicans and Democrats, including the party leaders on both sides, were dissatisfied with the bill; their committee leaders had given away too much in the negotiations, they believed. When the bill got to the floor, neither liberal Democrats nor conservative Republicans had the votes to move it significantly in their preferred direction. In the end, twelve Senate Democrats joined all fifty Republicans to pass the tax-cutting legislation.

Under pressure from Bush, the conference committee moved with unusual speed to approve a compromise bill. The result was legislation that largely tracked the Senate bill: it called for a somewhat smaller tax cut than Bush's initial request; it distributed the reductions somewhat differently, giving more to those in the lower income brackets; it provided immediate tax rebates to stimulate the economy; and it "sunsetted," that is, automatically repealed, the entire bill in 2010.[15] Nevertheless, enactment represented a huge victory for Bush. Not only had the largest tax cut since Ronald Reagan's first year in office become law, but it included many of the provisions—across-the-board rate cuts, alleviation of the "marriage penalty," and eventual ending of the estate tax—that Bush had advocated and that the Republican base had long desired. Furthermore, the real size of the tax cut was likely to exceed what the budget resolution specified; conferees phased in some tax cuts and set early expiration dates for others so as to fit them into the budget figure—a "gimmick," some analysts claimed, as Congress would be likely to extend many of the tax cuts before they expired. The partisan strategy seemed to pay off. If Bush had gone for less, if he had been willing to compromise earlier in the process, if the House had not set such a strongly conservative mark, the result might well have been much further from Bush's initial proposal.

From the beginning, the administration pursued a completely different strategy on education reform, though this issue also split the parties. To be sure, there was considerable agreement that more accountability for results should be required in return for federal education funds, that that required some sort of testing, and that at least some more money would be needed. Yet a number of ideologically charged issues divided the parties and in some cases split moderate from conservative Republicans as well. Conservative Republicans strongly advocated vouchers for children in failing schools to use at a school, even a private school, of their choice; Democrats strongly opposed vouchers as taking money away from already-underfunded public schools, and many moderate Republicans agreed. Republicans wanted to give states much more freedom to use federal education funds as they saw fit, so long as they showed results; Democrats opposed such block grants, concerned that less money would go to the children and schools that needed it most. Republicans who were social conservatives opposed nationally mandated testing as a mechanism of accountability, fearing too much federal intrusion into education. Bush's education reform program included vouchers, flexibility, some increase in funding, and a heavy emphasis on periodic testing.

With Bush's blessing, House Education and the Workforce Committee chair John Boehner, R-Ohio, although himself a strong conservative, worked closely with his minority counterpart, liberal George Miller, D-Calif., to reach a bipartisan compromise on legislation to present to the committee. The bill the committee approved increased funding for education, severely weakened the block grant provisions, and did not include vouchers. It was approved by a big, bipartisan vote, with six of the seven "no" votes in committee cast by conservative Republicans, who were extremely unhappy with the compromises that had been made. The House passed the bill 384–45, with thirty-four of the "no" votes cast by Republicans.

The process was bipartisan in the Senate as well, with the committee reporting out a moderate bill on a twenty-to-nothing vote. The White House negotiated with Senate education leaders of both parties, Ted Kennedy, D-Mass., prominent among them, on the Senate bill, which passed after lengthy floor consideration 91–8. Negotiations to resolve House-Senate differences were also bipartisan, and both chambers approved the conference report by big votes.

The No Child Left Behind Act that Bush signed, with smiling Democrats and Republicans behind him, was truly a bipartisan product. It included much more funding than Bush had originally requested and excluded both vouchers and the strong flexibility provisions he had asked for. Yet its passage was clearly a big win for Bush. He got many of the testing and accountability measures he requested. He could—and did—brag that he had delivered on a top priority and had done so in a bipartisan fashion. The victory allowed Bush to reach out beyond his base to voters concerned about issues on which Democrats usually have an advantage and to those put off by intense partisanship.

Thus, in the early months of his presidency, Bush pursued divergent strategies on his two highest legislative priorities, and in both cases, the strategy employed was successful. But the partisan strategy became the norm; the bipartisan strategy proved to be an aberration. Why?

Examination of the costs that the two strategies entailed suggests some answers. The successful bipartisan strategy on the education bill required making much greater substantive compromises than the partisan strategy on the tax bill. In the case of No Child Left Behind, the concessions necessary to get a bipartisan deal seemingly did not cost Bush much personally; apparently he is much more committed to testing than to vouchers. The conservative base of the Republican Party, both in the country and in Congress, saw the compromise very differently, however. Vouchers and flexibility, which had been traded away, were their priorities; they regarded federally mandated testing with suspicion at best. A conservative Republican House member explained conservatives' votes for Bush's education bill: "He had a very narrow win, and we don't want to do anything to jeopardize his number-one initiative. But that doesn't mean we like it."[16]

Yet the costs of the partisan strategy might seem higher. In late May 2001, Sen. Jim Jeffords left the Republican Party because, he explained, he differed with the president on "very fundamental issues." Jeffords's defection turned control of the Senate over to the Democratic Party, depriving Bush of one of his greatest resources—Republican control of both houses of Congress. Furthermore, the perception of Bush as a partisan leader extended well beyond the politically attentive. Bush began his presidency with unusually low approval scores from Democrats—not surprising, considering the contested election. Public opinion polls showed that Bush had made little headway in building support among those—half of all voters—who had not voted for him.

By the congressional recess in August 2001, Bush's prospects for further legislative success did not look promising. His public opinion poll numbers were mediocre and sliding, certainly not at a level that would provide him with the ammunition to scare Democrats, who now controlled the Senate, into supporting his programs. Bush's attempts to use the bully pulpit had yielded little success beyond his base.

September 11 and a New Political Context

The shocking attacks of September 11, 2001, transformed Americans' concerns and so elected officials' priorities. Foreign crises tend to produce a "rally round the flag" effect,[17] and private citizens and public officials alike responded to the horrendous attacks on U.S. soil by rallying around the president and vowing solidarity. Democratic congressional leaders quickly pledged their support. "We are shoulder to shoulder. We are in complete agreement and we will act together as one. There is no division between the parties, between the Congress and the president," House Minority Leader Dick Gephardt said. "The world should know that the members of both parties in both houses stand united," reiterated Senate Majority Leader Tom Daschle, D-S.D.[18]

Bush reached out and conferred with members of Congress. Democrats, whom Bush had seldom consulted, were now included in White House meetings on security issues. The new political context that 9/11 created greatly increased Bush's political capital; his job approval rating soared, and more important, the public clearly wanted Congress to give the president what he said he needed to protect Americans. Members of Congress are loath to weaken a president vis-à-vis foreign adversaries, and they certainly do not want to be perceived by voters as doing so. During a time of crisis, members are even more sensitive than usual to the potential policy and political costs. Holding a greatly strengthened hand, Bush saw no need to compromise significantly. Bush's and Vice President Dick Cheney's desire to reassert executive authority vis-à-vis Congress also prompted them to extract the maximum possible advantage from the new context.

Acting with speed and unity, Congress on September 14 approved a resolution authorizing the president to "use all necessary and appropriate force against those nations, organizations or persons he determines planned, authorized, committed or aided the terrorist attacks on September 11, 2001, or harbored such organizations or persons."[19] On the same day both houses passed an emergency supplemental appropriations bill providing $40 billion for recovery and antiterrorist efforts. One vote was cast against the use-of-force resolution; none against the money bill. The Senate approved by voice vote the previously controversial nomination of John Negroponte as U.S. ambassador to the United Nations. House Republicans, who had opposed paying dues that the United States owed to the UN backed down so as to facilitate Bush's efforts to build an antiterrorism coalition. On October 25, only six weeks after the attack, Congress sent Bush the USA Patriot Act, a far-reaching antiterrorism bill that made it easier for law enforcement to track Internet communications, detain suspected terrorists, and obtain nationwide warrants for searches and eavesdropping.[20] Congress did force some narrowing of the breathtakingly broad grants of power the administration requested in each of these legislative measures, but Bush got much of what he asked for.

On national security and war-on-terrorism-related issues, the story was largely the same until 2007. Effectively using rhetorical strategies to make vocal opposition by members of Congress politically risky, the Bush administration got from Congress most of what it asked for, including, most fatefully, the use-of-force resolution against Iraq. Occasionally, when a battle allowed Bush's opponents to position themselves as the more assiduous protectors of the homeland, they could best him. Thus, Democrats defeated Bush and House Republicans on the issue of federalizing airport screeners; the safety of government control trumped arguments based on free enterprise. Congress stopped the administration-supported deal to allow a Dubai company to run a number of American ports. In a few instances, especially as the Iraq war became increasingly unpopular, Congress forced into law provisions that Bush strongly opposed. Sen. John McCain's, R-Ariz., anti-torture amendment is perhaps the most notable instance.[21] But with American troops committed to both Iraq and Afghanistan, Congress had little choice but to provide funding. The way in which the Bush campaign used Democratic nominee John Kerry's late-2003 votes against $87 billion in supplemental war spending in the 2004 election campaign reinforced many Democrats' wariness of confronting Bush on such issues. All presidents attempt to use their advantages on issues of foreign and defense policy to pressure Congress to follow their lead, and, certainly in modern times, doing so has involved "going public." Often the administration's rhetoric implicitly charges the president's opponents with being less concerned with the country's welfare—if not less patriotic—than the president.

Although the Bush administration employed that strategy from 9/11 forward, the fight over creating a department of homeland security demonstrates how aggressively the Bush forces were willing to use it. Senate Democrats had proposed bringing the far-flung agencies with security responsibilities into a single cabinet department, so as to alleviate the coordination problems that seem to have contributed to the 9/11 debacle. Bush had initially opposed a new department but, in early June, changed his mind and called on Congress to create a new cabinet department of homeland security. The House passed Bush's plan largely intact, but Senate Democrats balked at some of the provisions that Bush requested that would weaken worker rights. Senate Republicans filibustered the Democratic bill, preferring an election issue to a compromise. Republicans then used the issue in the 2002 elections, charging that Senate Democrats chose to protect selfish special interests even at the expense of the country's security. Ads charged Sen. Max Cleland, D-Ga., a Vietnam veteran and triple amputee running for reelection in Georgia, with, in essence, a lack of patriotism. Cleland lost, and some Democrats were intimidated. In the lame-duck session after the election, Bush got what he wanted in the homeland security department bill. The tactic embittered Democrats and increased the hostility between the parties.

Domestic Policy and Politics in the Aftermath of 9/11

Although 9/11 elevated security and foreign policy issues in priority, domestic policy continued to make up much of Congress's legislative workload, as it always does. Did the Bush strategy on such issues change? The Democratic takeover of the Senate had not led to a significant shift in presidential strategy. Fearing they would be seen as grievously weakened by the loss of the Senate, Bush and White House officials aggressively asserted that the switch would not change their agenda or their approach, and in the few months between Jeffords's defection and 9/11 they made little attempt to cultivate the Senate Democratic leadership.

Some commentators believed that 9/11 would usher in a sustained period of bipartisanship encompassing the full range of issues, but that was never realistic. Bush and congressional Republicans, believing themselves in a strengthened position politically, pursued the same domestic agenda they had before the crisis. If Bush was unwilling to "negotiate with himself" or compromise "preemptively" when he was far weaker politically, why should he do so now? As domestic issues that evoke deeply held ideological beliefs resurfaced, so did partisan debate and jockeying. Bush and congressional Republicans tried to sell everything from trade promotion authority to drilling in the Arctic National Wildlife Refuge (ANWR) as national security matters. But despite Bush's sky-high popularity, polls and visits home showed Democrats that their constituents did not expect them to support Bush on such issues. Bush's strong public support on security allowed him to extract support even from members who disagreed with him on policy substance on those issues. But the public continued to split along partisan lines on Bush's domestic agenda, and so Democrats felt free to oppose his proposals and, in the Senate, to promote their own.

The result was mostly stalemate on domestic legislation during the remainder of the 107th Congress. Bush's energy legislation was stuck in conference because the two chambers' bills were too different to reconcile. The bill the Democratic Senate had passed was much more tilted toward conservation than Bush wanted, and it did not include drilling in ANWR, a high Bush priority. The House passed the faith-based initiative, a fetal protection bill, welfare reauthorization with a substantially increased work requirement, and a ban on human cloning—all measures Bush strongly supported—but none of them reached the Senate floor. When the Democratic Senate passed a medical patients' bill of rights in a form Bush vehemently opposed, he and the Republican House leadership had to pull out all the stops to prevent the House from passing a similar bill and confronting the president with the unpalatable choice of vetoing a popular measure or letting what they considered bad public policy become law.

In fall 2002 Bush faced a choice: compromise with Senate Democrats on the spending bills, his homeland security bill, and other domestic legislation or gamble on taking control of both chambers in the midterm elections and gaining a stronger hand to play. Bush decided to put all his chips on the electoral strategy. After the Iraq resolution passed in early October, he took to the campaign trail with an intensity unprecedented for a sitting president at midterm. Bush raised more than $140 million, campaigned for dozens of Republican candidates, and dispatched Cheney, cabinet officers, and White House officials to do the same. In the week before the election, Bush visited fifteen states.

The gamble paid off. Republicans gained a majority in the Senate and increased their majority in the House. Bush's effort translated his popularity into strong turnout among core Republican voters. Although Iraq does not appear to have been the biggest motivator for voters, the media attention it received seems to have prevented domestic issues from becoming salient in a way that might have helped Democrats.

Unified Republican Government 2003–2004

With his political capital greatly increased by the election victory, for which he was given credit, Bush again saw no need to alter his legislative strategies. He proposed another big tax cut and won much of what he asked for through a partisan strategy. In fact, the process on the 2003 tax cut was largely a replay of that on the 2001 tax bill. Bush's proposal was ambitious: $726 billion over eleven years. The House acted first and set the mark by including the full Bush request in the budget resolution. The Senate, though now with a narrow Republican majority, again proved more difficult; moderate Republicans combined with Democrats to trim the figure. The conference committee, from which Democrats were largely excluded, restored a considerable proportion of the reductions through creative sunsetting.

In 2003 Congress also passed a massive bill reforming Medicare and adding a prescription drug benefit. This was an even more impressive accomplishment. The legislation could not be passed as a reconciliation bill, and so a filibuster was possible in the Senate. Additionally, a great many conservatives had deep doubts about the drug benefit, inasmuch as it constituted a new entitlement, so the issue had party-splitting potential. The budget process aided the measure's proponents by setting aside in the budget resolution $400 billion over the next decade to fund a drug benefit.

Bush had campaigned on providing a drug benefit to seniors; his political advisers believed that delivering on the promise would allow Republicans to appropriate one of the Democrats' best issues and make it their own. In addition, Bush and congressional Republicans saw this as an opportunity to inject private sector competition into the Medicare program, which they believed would control costs. Bush's initial proposal made the drug benefit contingent on a senior joining a private health care plan. That proved to be so unpopular, with Republicans as well as

Democrats, that Bush released not a full plan but rather a conceptual "framework" and allowed Congress to work out the details.

On this legislation, House and Senate acted almost simultaneously but otherwise played their appointed roles in the Bush strategy. The House process was thoroughly partisan: Only Republicans were allowed to participate in the negotiations that produced the bills considered by the two committees with jurisdiction, and both committees approved their bills on partisan votes. Republican Party leaders and the chairs of the two committees then negotiated a postcommittee compromise on the legislation before taking it to the floor. Over the course of several days, the party leaders met with small groups of members, attempting to persuade them to vote for the bill and, when necessary, negotiating changes to get their votes. President Bush also got into the act, inviting groups of members to the White House to urge them to support the bill. The Republican leadership took the Medicare/drug benefit measure to the floor under a highly restrictive rule that allowed only one amendment, a Democratic substitute. They thus protected the bill—and their members—against politically attractive amendments that would cause problems down the road. The rule also allowed consideration of a bill expanding private medical savings accounts, right before HR 1, the Medicare/prescription drug bill, and specified that if both it and HR 1 passed, the medical savings account bill would be added to HR 1 and they would be sent to the Senate as a package. The medical savings account bill, which would cost $174 billion over ten years, had not been considered and reported by a committee. House Speaker Dennis Hastert, Ill., agreed to bring it up and include it in the rule in return for the votes of a number of conservatives who were unhappy with a new entitlement.

The bill passed the House on a highly partisan vote, but only after Hastert had stretched the normal fifteen minutes for a recorded vote to almost an hour. Getting the votes for passage required considerable pressure on members who disliked the bill but who did not want to see the president and the party lose. Although conservatives were leery about setting up a new entitlement and believed that there was not enough private sector competition in the measure, it did constitute a significant change in policy direction in the Medicare program by requiring direct competition between private plans and traditional Medicare starting in 2010, and it thereby set a conservative mark.

With a filibuster a possibility, the process in the Senate was much more bipartisan. The leaders of the Finance Committee worked together to come up with a draft that Sen. Ted Kennedy praised as a good beginning. The legislation passed both in committee and in the full Senate with bipartisan majorities. The big majority for passage—seventy-six strong—was fragile, however. Many Republicans wanted to require Medicare to compete with private plans, a provision the Senate bill did not include; many Democrats believed that the drug benefits were far too stingy and confusing.

In conference, the House provision forcing traditional Medicare to compete with private plans was most controversial. However, forty-two House Republicans had told their leadership that if this provision was removed in conference, they would not vote for the resulting bill. Senate Democrats also considered the provision a deal breaker. In early July, Ted Kennedy drafted, and thirty-six Democrats, including Minority Leader Tom Daschle, signed, a letter to President Bush stating their bottom line. "We will oppose a conference report that forces seniors to choose between giving up their doctor or facing higher premiums to stay in the current Medicare program," they wrote.[22]

In the end, the conference allowed Bush and conservative Republicans to recoup much, though far from all, of what they had lost in the Senate. Republicans had excluded from the conference negotiations all the Democratic conferees except two Senate moderates, Max Baucus, Mont., and John Breaux, La. Even then, it took intervention by Speaker Hastert and Senate Majority Leader Bill Frist, Tenn., to get a resolution. They worked out a deal that cut back the full-fledged competition provision in the House bill to an experiment instead.

Democrats believed that the compromise jettisoned much of what they had won in the Senate—already barely adequate from their perspective. What remained, they argued, was a bill that benefited drug companies and HMOs at the expense of the elderly. Conservative Republicans, many of whom thought the original House bill was not strong enough, judged the compromise considerably worse. On the other hand, the scaling back of the competition provision induced the AARP, the largest senior lobbying group, to support the bill.

The conference report passed the Senate on a party vote. Even with AARP support, the number of Democrats voting for the bill shrank from thirty-five to eleven; nine conservative Republicans opposed it. In the House, the Republican leadership held the vote open for three hours before they were able to obtain enough votes for passage. Ernest Istook, Okla., chair of an appropriations subcommittee, a position recently made subject to approval by the leadership-dominated Steering Committee, changed his vote from nay to yea. Nick Smith, a conservative Republican from Michigan who was retiring, refused to switch, though he later said he was offered inducements to do so. Bush, who had been actively engaged in the persuasion process, was awakened at 5 a.m. and set to calling recalcitrant conservatives on their cell phones to argue for a "yes" vote. On the vote to approve the conference report, 204 Republicans voted "yea" and 25 "nay"; Democrats voted against the bill 189 to 16.

On other legislative battles, the partisan strategy did not work as well. The energy bill, caps on medical malpractice damage awards, legislation restricting class action litigation, overhaul of the bankruptcy law, the reauthorizations of the welfare program and Head Start (both with conservative alterations), and the faith-based initiative all failed to pass before the 2004 election. Most of these measures passed the House—in strongly conservative form and by partisan majorities in committee and on the floor. Senate Democrats used the considerable power that Senate rules give the minority to stop them. In some cases—medical malpractice, for example—they successfully blocked the motion to proceed to consider the legislation. In others—the welfare reauthorization, for instance—their threat to offer nongermane amendments persuaded the majority leader to keep the bill off the floor. In still others—the faith-based initiative, for example—Democrats blocked the bill from going to conference to protest their exclusion from conference negotiations. Democrats successfully filibustered to kill the energy bill conference report that had been drafted without their participation.

The standoff extended to judicial nominations. Senate Democrats successfully filibustered to block confirmation of ten Bush appellate court nominees. Democrats believed the ten were out of the mainstream and had been chosen to cater to the extreme right of the Republican Party. Bush and the Republicans claimed the president should be given wide leeway in his judicial choices and that only competence, not judicial philosophy, should be considered in the confirmation process. Bush, congressional Republicans, and conservative interest groups mounted multiple public relations offensives to pressure Senate Democrats. But although the tone became more and more shrill and extreme, Senate Democrats held firm. Meanwhile, in its approval of Bush's job performance, as in its support for his domestic agenda, the public increasingly divided along party lines. The voters that congressional Democrats counted on for reelection certainly were not pressuring them to support Bush; they, like Democratic activists, were more likely to punish them for voting in favor of right-wing judicial nominees or drilling in ANWR than for voting against.

If Bush's legislative strategy did not translate into across-the-board legislative success on domestic policy, it almost always protected him from costly defeats. Early in his first term, Bush had forged a strong working relationship with Speaker Hastert. With the formidable tools possessed by a House Speaker leading a unified majority, Hastert was able to play his assigned offensive role in the "House first and to the right" strategy over and over again, and he also played effective defense for Bush. "[Hastert] made it clear that they would not allow bills that would be vetoed to reach the president's desk," according to Nick Calio, Bush's first head of congressional liaison.[23] An amendment that had prompted a Bush veto threat was removed from the Trade Promotion Authority legislation in conference. Attempts to overturn new Federal Communications Commission media ownership rules, to lift the ban on travel to Cuba, to prevent the administration from revising overtime rules to deprive some of those currently eligible of overtime pay, to delay military base closings, to allow concurrent receipts for veterans, and to block the administration's efforts to outsource federal jobs to private companies—all approved as amendments to appropriations bills—were watered down or removed in conference. Hastert stopped a transportation bill that his own members wanted but that Bush, calling it a budget buster, had threatened to veto. Bush did not veto a single bill during his first term—the only president in over a century to cap his veto pen for that long.

In a few cases, political calculations induced Bush to sign bills he disliked. Despite a mighty effort, Hastert was unable to stop a popular campaign finance reform bill in the House, and with Democrats in control of the Senate, the strategy of killing it in conference failed. Majority leader Tom Daschle engineered Senate acceptance of the House bill, preventing a conference. Enron and other corporate accounting scandals induced Congress to pass a strong corporate accountability bill; reversing his position, Bush claimed credit for that measure, which he signed with great fanfare. With many of the closest Senate races, whose outcomes would determine partisan control of the Senate, in farm states in 2002, Bush signed a farm bill that was much more expensive than he had originally wanted. These, however, were the exceptions; by and large, Bush did not use the veto during his first term because Republican congressional leaders made sure that unacceptable legislation did not reach his desk.

The 2004 Elections and the Second Term: The Limits of the Partisan Strategy

"I earned capital in the campaign, political capital, and now I intend to spend it," George W. Bush declared on November 4, 2004. As Bush had won reelection with a majority of the popular vote, and Republicans had picked up four seats in the Senate and three in the House, his claim seemed justified. Yet Bush's victory had been the narrowest of any reelected president, and his approval ratings were anemic, hovering around 50 percent. Public approval of his job performance—overall and on a host of specific issues—was sharply bifurcated with Republicans continuing to support him strongly but Democrats and an increasing number of independents disapproving. Most ominous, overall support for the war in Iraq and Bush's handling of the situation was slipping badly.[24]

The gain in Senate seats did pay off in 2005. Bankruptcy overhaul and restrictions on class action lawsuits passed quickly after having long been stymied. Both bills had been moderated over time, but both were significant Republican victories. Several of the Bush appellate court nominees that Democrats had blocked were approved after a bipartisan group of senators reached a pact that avoided a showdown on the "nuclear option" in the Senate (see David Yalof's chapter in this book). A bit later in the year, an energy bill finally became law. Senate Republicans abandoned the partisan strategy that had led to stalemate in the 107th and 108th Congresses; they worked with Democrats and produced a compromise measure. Although drilling in ANWR was not included, Bush claimed victory. The Senate handily approved two conservative Bush nominees to the Supreme Court, Chief Justice John Roberts and Associate Justice Samuel Alito Jr.

Bush's most daring use of his political capital was on Social Security. Altering the program to allow workers to set up private accounts and invest part of their Social Security taxes in the stock market was one of Bush's big campaign issues in 2000. Newly reelected, Bush made it his top domestic legislative priority in 2005. The administration and its interest group allies invested in an enormous public relations campaign to persuade the public. During the week of February 21, a coalition of business lobbies made over a quarter of a million phone calls. The "60 Stops in 60 Days" campaign saw thirty-one administration officials make 166 appearances in 127 cities to promote the private accounts proposal.[25] Bush's massive public relations campaign—and those of his opponents—certainly succeeded in raising the visibility of the issue, but the more people heard about Bush's plan, the less they liked it. Democrats and their interest group allies, especially labor, publicized the downside of the Bush proposal and found an attentive audience.

Although a substantial majority of congressional Republicans favored private accounts on policy grounds, no legislation emerged from any congressional committee. To this point, Republicans had supported Bush's legislative proposals at very high levels because they usually agreed with him on policy grounds, and because their voters supported Bush as a leader and at least did not oppose his programs. Bush had occasionally asked some Republican members to support him with their votes against their policy preferences, as he had on No Child Left Behind and on the drug benefit. He had occasionally asked some to cast a vote that was likely to hurt them at home, as he did on "fast-track" trade authority. Now, however, he was asking them to take on an enormously popular program in what would be a highly visible battle. Not inclined to commit political suicide, congressional Republicans needed an appreciable number of Democrats to support the proposal to provide them with cover. But most Democrats would support the Bush approach only if he could threaten their reelection by producing public pressure. In this case, Bush needed to influence general public opinion, not just rev up his base, and that he was not able to do.

The failure of the Bush Social Security proposal marked the end of the solid Republican phalanx of support in Congress. The drumbeat of bad news from Iraq, the bungled government response to Hurricane Katrina, and the consequent precipitous slide in Bush's job approval rating sent congressional Republicans scurrying to save themselves. When the administration approved the previously mentioned Dubai Ports deal, Republicans joined Democrats in vociferously condemning the agreement and forced the administration to withdraw its assent. Privately Republicans vehemently questioned the administration's "political deaf ear."

Responding to constituent concern about illegal immigrants, in December 2005 House Republicans passed a harsh, enforcement-only immigration bill that they knew the president opposed. Big business, a core component of the Republican coalition, favored a bill with a guest worker program and a route to legal status for the millions of undocumented workers currently working in the United States. Bush also feared that a punitive approach would alienate Latino voters. With the Republican base split between the two approaches, Senate Republicans also split, but a bipartisan coalition managed to pass a bill acceptable to Bush in the Senate in mid-2006. However, House Republicans, who had repeatedly fallen in line behind Bush, refused to go along. Instead of agreeing to a conference to work out differences between the two bills, House Republicans scheduled a flurry of public hearings on illegal immigration, in Washington and around the country, with the intention of pressuring the Senate and the president to consent to a bill emphasizing enforcement. Shortly before the 2006 elections, both chambers passed, and Bush signed, a bill to build a seven-hundred-mile fence along the U.S.-Mexican border.

Responding to their base, conservative Republicans also began to complain vocally about the enormous deficits run up under the Bush administration. In July 2006, Congress passed legislation, which Bush had repeatedly said he opposed, allowing government funding of stem cell research, and the president cast his first veto. Pressure by moderate Republicans as well as Democrats had forced the issue to the floors of both chambers. Though the House failed to override the veto, Bush's having to cast it showed how much his position had weakened.

The 2006 elections were a stinging rebuke to Bush and congressional Republicans. Democrats regained majority status in both the House and the Senate, picking up thirty seats in the House and six in the Senate (including wins in "red" Virginia, Montana, and Missouri). The Iraq issue and a pervasive sense that the government in Washington was failing both ethically and in policy terms drove voters. Even before the elections it was clear that, unless Bush could somehow replenish his political capital, further major domestic legislative victories that pushed policy nonincrementally in a conservative direction were unlikely. Although Bush and congressional Republicans continued to agree on many issues, the sense of shared electoral fate had dissipated. Congressional Republicans no longer believed that supporting Bush would pay off for them in electoral terms—often just the opposite. In 2006 congressional candidates welcomed fund-raising help, and the president and vice president appeared at many private fund-raisers, but few candidates wanted to appear publicly with Bush or Cheney. In campaign ads, many Republican incumbents emphasized their independent voting records.

The 110th Congress, the last of the Bush presidency, sees a weakened president confronting a House and Senate controlled by Democrats whom the president had done little to court and much to antagonize in the preceding six years. Following the elections, Bush and Democratic congressional leaders pledged cooperation and bipartisanship. They agreed that voters are "sick and tired of the needless partisanship in Washington," as Bush put it.[26] But the new Democratic majority came in with its own agenda, grounded in items that Bush strongly opposed, for example, loosening restrictions on stem cell research and having the government negotiate

Medicare prescription drug prices directly. Democrats promised vigorous oversight of the administration, a task that they charged Republican majorities had neglected. And most Democrats believed that opposition to the war in Iraq and Bush's policies there had contributed greatly to the party's victory; their strongest supporters would expect them to do something about the war. In February 2007, the House passed a nonbinding resolution expressing disapproval of Bush's plan to increase the number of U.S. troops in Iraq, and although Senate Republicans blocked a vote, more than a majority of senators were on record as supporting it. In both chambers, Democrats were almost unanimous in opposing Bush.

Bush's Legislative Legacy: Strategy and Record in Retrospect

Despite multiple and major shifts in context during the first six years of his presidency, Bush did not modify his legislative strategy significantly. When changes in the political context increased his political capital, as 9/11, the 2002 election results, and to a lesser extent, the 2004 elections did, Bush employed that political capital, usually aggressively. Thus the post-9/11 public concern about security issues and his own high popularity were wielded to get much of what he wanted from Congress on foreign policy and on foreign and domestic security. They were also used, though with less success, in the public relations battles over domestic issues. When events such as the drawn-out Iraq war and the government's response to Hurricane Katrina eroded his political capital, Bush did not significantly adjust his legislative strategies, either. All of the president's formidable public relations resources were deployed for damage control, but Bush did not move toward a more accommodating and bipartisan stance.

We expect purposive actors to adjust their strategies to the context in which they pursue their goals. Bush seems not to have done so. An explanation may lie in those aspects of the context that did not change and perhaps in the character of Bush's goals themselves. By pursuing a few big things, compromising only late in the process and when absolutely necessary, and having the House go first and to the right, Bush got more of what he wanted on those bills that passed than he would have with a more accommodating strategy. The 2001 and 2003 tax cuts and the Medicare/prescription drugs bill, Bush's signature domestic accomplishments, would have looked very different if Bush had pursued accommodation and compromise. His strategy did have legislative costs: More major legislation died—for example, capping medical malpractice awards, a Bush priority, never made it out of the Senate. An additional cost, and potentially a greater one, is the extent to which the policy changes wrought by Bush's signature legislative achievements remain contested. The Medicare/prescription drug bill, many of the tax cuts—in particular, the termination of the estate tax—and even the No Child Left Behind Act continue to excite great controversy, the latter because Democrats and many state officials claim Bush reneged on funding promises. These major policy departures have not become broadly accepted.

A president determined to make nonincremental policy changes for which no broad public support exists, and with only a narrow congressional majority, almost certainly had little choice but to pursue the partisan strategy. With the public divided, Bush needed to keep his conservative base firmly in his camp. His strategy of going public may have been aimed primarily at ensuring intense support from his base and perhaps also at blunting the effects on the general public of opposition attacks.

When members of Congress are sharply divided along partisan lines in their notions of what constitutes good public policy—as they currently are—and when margins of control in the chambers are narrow, so that control is up for grabs in the next election—as it has been for over a decade—the politics of the domestic policymaking process will inevitably be characterized by fairly intense partisanship. This context helped shape Bush's legislative strategy, but his partisan strategy, as well as that of the Republican congressional leadership, amplified the partisan hostility that was so evident on both sides of the Hill. The militantly conservative Republican membership in the House would have pushed Bush toward employing the partisan strategy even if he had not been so inclined. Still, a president who relies mostly on his base and pursues a partisan strategy almost exclusively finds that when adversity strikes, he has little good will beyond his base—in Congress or in the country.

Sobered by the loss of Republican congressional majorities in the 2006 elections, Bush may sincerely attempt to change his legislative strategy and become more accommodating. Bush has not heretofore experienced such a deleterious change in the political environment. House Democrats showed their cohesion and discipline by passing the "one hundred hours agenda" on which they ran, with few defections from their own ranks and time to spare. Bush faces a formidable competitor in the Democratic-controlled House. The Senate, so often the problem during his first six years, may with its supermajority requirements prove to be a major bargaining asset for Bush. In any case, the new Democratic majorities will have to work with him on legislation necessary to keep the government functioning, especially on the appropriations bills that fund government programs. Bush endorsed the Democrats' minimum wage increase proposal, one of their top priorities, though he advocated coupling it with tax breaks for small business. Opportunities for genuine cooperation and compromise may well arise in areas such as education, an alternative fuels energy program, and immigration. But the parties remain polarized; Bush and mainstream Democrats have very different notions of what constitutes good public policy. With his insistence on keeping troops in Iraq, and even increasing their numbers, Bush has confronted Democrats with a policy they bitterly oppose. The shadow of the 2008 presidential election hangs over everything, inevitably influencing the calculations of all the major political actors.

Presidents often run low on political capital in their last two years in office, and Bush's political capital has never been so depleted. His legislative strategy has left a residue of deep distrust among Democrats in Congress and the country.[27] Whether a change in strategy now will pay off in terms of Bush's legislative legacy is open to question. Having lived by the sword of a highly partisan strategy, can he avoid also dying by the sword?

Notes

1. See Andrew Rudalevige, "The Executive Branch and the Legislative Process," in *The Executive Branch,* ed. Joel Aberbach and Mark Peterson (New York: Oxford University Press, 2005); Stephen J. Wayne, *The Legislative Presidency* (New York: Harper and Row, 1978); and Paul C. Light, *The President's Agenda: Domestic Policy Choice from Kennedy to Clinton,* 3rd ed. (Baltimore: Johns Hopkins University Press, 1998).
2. Charles O. Jones, *The Presidency in a Separated System,* 2nd ed. (Washington, D.C.: Brookings Institution Press, 2005).
3. Jon Bond and Richard Fleisher, *The President in the Legislative Arena* (Chicago: University of Chicago Press, 1990).
4. Barbara Sinclair, *Majority Leadership in the U.S. House* (Baltimore: Johns Hopkins University Press, 1983); Barbara Sinclair, *Legislators, Leaders and Lawmaking* (Baltimore: Johns Hopkins University Press, 1995).
5. George C. Edwards, *Governing by Campaigning* (New York: Pearson Longman, 2007), 158.
6. The House contained one vacancy and two independents who usually split their votes between the parties.
7. In the 1980s (1981–1990) the percentage of party votes rose to 51 percent in the House and 45 percent in the Senate. Data are from *Congressional Quarterly Almanacs,* various dates.
8. Sinclair, *Majority Leadership* and *Legislators, Leaders and Lawmaking*; David Rohde, *Parties and Leaders in the Postreform House* (Chicago: University of Chicago Press, 1991).
9. Barbara Sinclair, *The Transformation of the U.S. Senate* (Baltimore: Johns Hopkins University Press, 1989).
10. Barbara Sinclair, *Unorthodox Lawmaking,* 2nd ed. (Washington, D.C.: CQ Press, 2000); Barbara Sinclair, "The New World of U.S. Senators," in *Congress Reconsidered,* 7th ed., ed. Lawrence C. Dodd and Bruce I. Oppenheimer (Washington, D.C.: CQ Press, 2001).
11. James P. Pfiffner, *The Strategic Presidency: Hitting the Ground Running,* 2nd rev. ed. (Lawrence: University Press of Kansas, 1996), 118ff.
12. Samuel Kernell, *Going Public,* 3rd ed.(Washington, D.C.: CQ Press, 1997), ix. See also Edwards, *Governing by Campaigning.*
13. Edwards, *Governing by Campaigning,* chap. 3.
14. *CQ Weekly,* April 28, 2001, 904.
15. *CQ Weekly,* May 26, 2001, 1251–1254.
16. *CQ Weekly,* May 5, 2001, 1010.
17. John Mueller, *War, Presidents and Public Opinion* (New York: John Wiley, 1973); Richard A. Brody, *Assessing the President* (Stanford: Stanford University Press, 1991).

18. *CQ Weekly,* September 15, 2001, 2116.

19. Ibid., 2158.

20. *CQ Weekly,* October 27, 2001, 2533.

21. When Bush signed the bill he issued a signing statement in which he, in effect, reserved the right to ignore the provision. See Joel Aberbach's chapter in this book.

22. *Roll Call,* July 8, 2003.

23. *Roll Call,* December 15, 2003.

24. Gary Jacobson, *A Divider Not a Uniter: George W. Bush and the American People* (New York: Pearson Longman, 2007).

25. Edwards, *Governing by Campaigning,* 232–233.

26. *Washington Post,* December 20, 2006.

27. See Jacobson, Fiorina, in this volume; see also Jacobson, *A Divider,* chaps. 8 and 9.

CHAPTER 9

In Search of a Means to an End

George W. Bush and the Federal Judiciary

David A. Yalof

WHEN PRESIDENT GEORGE W. BUSH first took office in January 2001 there was little suggestion that he would make the appointment of extremely conservative jurists one of the central pillars of his presidency. As governor of Texas from 1995 through 2000, Bush had sponsored tort reform, increased education funding, set higher standards for schools, and reformed the criminal justice system. In pressing for $2 billion in tax cuts for Texans, he cultivated his reputation as a pro-business conservative in his home state. By contrast, Governor Bush had moved rather cautiously in the area of judicial appointments, nominating four moderate judges to the Texas Supreme Court during his six years in office, including a young lawyer named Alberto Gonzales.[1] Social conservatives who backed his presidential bid were no doubt heartened by some of the programs Bush had sponsored as governor, including initiatives that allowed "faith-based" religious entities to compete for government contracts to deliver social services and the designation of "Jesus Day" in Texas, when all Texans were asked to "answer the call to serve those in need." But they could be only guardedly optimistic about President Bush's promise that he would appoint strict constructionists like Antonin Scalia and Clarence Thomas to the federal bench. Was this newly elected president a "true believer," or would he fall into a pattern similar to that of his father? A one-time social moderate, George H. W. Bush seemingly viewed conservative judicial appointments as smart politics, but little more.

Looking back, such fears on the part of social conservatives have proved unfounded. In crafting his approach to judicial appointments, "Bush 43" borrowed far more from the playbook of President Ronald Reagan than he did from "Bush 41." During his own presidency, Reagan unabashedly promised to transform the constitutional landscape through his appointments of lower court judges and Supreme Court justices. He accomplished that to a great degree, by hiring lawyers who were passionate and enthusiastic advocates of a more conservative judiciary and then giving them all the resources they needed to conduct comprehensive reviews of potential judicial candidates across the country. The Reagan administration virtually revolutionized the judicial appointment process by seeking to fulfill not just political goals but ambitious ideological goals as well.[2]

The Reagan example provided George W. Bush and his administration with a template for making conservative appointments to the federal bench. Although Bush was perhaps less inclined than Reagan to argue for dramatic shifts in doctrine in the course of Supreme Court litigation, he was just as enthusiastic as the fortieth president in his efforts to remake the judiciary. Indeed, when one considers some of the obstacles facing Bush that were not present during the Reagan administration— a polarized Senate controlled by the opposition party for nearly half his presidency, recalcitrant Senate Democrats determined to exact revenge for the delays met by President Bill Clinton's nominees, and so on—Bush's success in appointing conservative jurists seems even more impressive. Add to that a record of appointing nontraditional, diverse candidates to the federal bench that far outdid the records of previous Republican presidents, and one quickly comes to a surprising conclusion: that a president likely to be remembered in history for his foreign policy initiatives in fact may have embedded his most enduring legacy deep within the federal judiciary.

Changes in the Judicial Appointment Process

George W. Bush could claim only the narrowest of electoral mandates from the presidential election of 2000. Despite that, his White House aggressively seized control of the nation's domestic policy agenda, including the nomination of especially conservative jurists to the federal bench. The opportunity to do so was clearly before him: Nearly one hundred judicial vacancies awaited President Bush when he arrived at the White House in January 2001, and several hundred more were expected in the years to follow.

From the outset, Bush sought to expand the discretion afforded the chief executive in the appointment process. Because of the Constitution's mandate that presidents appoint judges only with the "advice and consent of the Senate," the White House was obviously prepared to consult with senators. But in a break from the status quo, the Bush administration sought to reduce the influence of "senatorial courtesy"— meaning the traditional power wielded by senators to suggest some nominees and to block others for judicial vacancies in their home states—in two important ways. First, President Bush continued to afford great weight to senatorial courtesy in the selection of district court judges but differentiated that process from the selection of appeals court judges, where senatorial courtesy would receive less weight. In recent decades presidents of both parties had begun placing increased emphasis on filling the circuit courts with ideologically compatible individuals as part of an overall strategy to transform the judiciary. The Reagan administration was particularly adept at this strategy. But even so, given the Senate's near-absolute control over the confirmation process, senatorial courtesy remained an important factor in appeals court appointments throughout the remainder of the twentieth century.[3] Ignoring those traditions, the George W. Bush administration actively treated the two types of federal judgeships quite differently.[4]

Second, Bush administration officials all but cut off the influence of Democratic senators in helping to choose lower court nominees. To be sure, senators of the opposition party have always had more limited influence in the process than senators of the president's own party. Still, modern presidents have learned that such cross-party consultations can smooth the way considerably in the confirmation process. President Clinton, for example, consulted with Sen. Orrin Hatch, R-Utah, about lower court nominations and even Supreme Court nominations. By contrast, no such cross-party dialogue was forthcoming during President Bush's first term.

How did the Bush administration avoid suffering reprisals in the confirmation process for such breaks with Senate tradition? Individual senators had long enjoyed disproportionate influence over the appointment process through the strategic deployment of so-called blue slips. By tradition, whenever a judicial nomination arrived from the White House, the Senate Judiciary Committee has routinely issued blue slips to the two home state senators, regardless of party. If the two senators support the judicial nomination in question, they indicate their support on the light blue sheets of paper provided and return the slips to the committee. If one or both of the home state senators withheld their blue slip, the Judiciary Committee chairman frequently chose to let the nomination die at that point.[5] Senators' strict adherence to the blue slip system meant that if the president ever ignored one or both home state senators' preferences in choosing a judicial nominee, a withheld slip would inevitably follow, causing serious problems for the nomination in question.

In practice, the blue slip system managed more often to delay nominations rather than defeat them outright.[6] According to one study of the process by political scientist Elliot Slotnick, the blue slip had preserved consensus and harmony among senators by offering them the equivalent of an early warning system of potential difficulties. Yet by institutionalizing senatorial courtesy through the blue slip system, which dated to the middle of the twentieth century, the Senate Judiciary Committee was able to check presidents with designs on wrestling discretion away from senators.[7]

President Bush was determined to write a different ending to the story. Immediately upon assuming office he found an ally in Senator Hatch, chair of the Senate Judiciary Committee since 1995. Anticipating opposition from Senate Democrats to some of Bush's more conservative nominees, Hatch announced in early 2001 his plan to heed their preferences only when *both* home state senators withheld their blue slips in a timely fashion.[8] Later in Bush's first term, Hatch went even further: Without any formal announcement he decided that, on a case-by-case basis, he would consider sending some nominations forward even when two blue slips were withheld.[9] The first change in the blue slip system had an immediate impact on the fate of nominees slated to fill appeals court judgeships in states, such as Illinois and Oregon, where the two Senate seats were split between the two parties. The second change had the potential to end the blue slip system in its current form if applied more than occasionally. Both changes would add muscle to Bush administration efforts to exert greater control over appointments to the appellate courts. They also afforded the White House even more discretion in determining whether and under what circumstances to consult with Senate Democrats about judicial vacancies in the first place.

These changes in the appointment process were orchestrated by Republican senators, often acting behind the scenes. President Bush also directly authorized at least one high-profile reform. This time the administration's target was the American Bar Association (ABA), whose ratings of judicial nominees had become a staple of the appointment vetting process going back to the 1950s. Beginning in the 1970s, conservative interest groups began accusing the ABA of hypocrisy, as the organization took liberal positions on public policy issues such as abortion, while at the same time claiming to be neutral in rating judicial nominees on a spectrum from "not qualified" to "highly qualified." In late 1971, President Richard Nixon accused the ABA of leaking the names of several Supreme court nominees under consideration by his administration; sixteen years later, Reagan aides grew exasperated when a majority of the fifteen-member ABA panel rated high court nominee Robert Bork merely "qualified" despite his credentials as a law professor, solicitor general, and member of the federal bench.

Although modern presidents no longer submit the names of Supreme Court nominees to the ABA in advance, recent administrations continued to provide the ABA with the names of lower court nominees prior to their formal submission to the Senate. That changed early in Bush's first term, when White House Counsel Alberto Gonzales informed the ABA that the president would no longer give it the names of potential lower court nominees in advance. The ABA would now learn the names along with everyone else, after the president had made his selections public.[10]

The change proved mostly symbolic. The ranking Senate Democrat, Patrick Leahy, D-Vt., along with other Democrats on the Senate Judiciary Committee, indicated that the committee would not vote on judicial candidates without first considering the ABA's views. One member of the committee, Sen. Charles Schumer, D-N.Y., even hinted that the change might actually slow down the confirmation process for Bush's nominees, as senators would be forced to wait that much longer for the ABA's evaluation. Accordingly, Assistant Attorney General Viet Dinh established a procedure, consistent with the administration's new policy, whereby nominations would be sent to the Senate and the ABA concurrently, so that the ABA could start its review process with as little delay as possible.[11] Still, Gonzales's declaration served as a public denunciation of the ABA, whose officials criticized the policy as "substituting politics for competence" in the review of judges. At the same time, it immediately endeared the new administration to social conservatives frustrated with a process that had allowed the ABA's voice to be heard "before and above all others."

Bush administration officials stated that the White House opposed giving the "ABA or any other group" a "preferential, quasi-official role" in the judicial appointment process. In reality, however, the administration did encourage the ascension of at least one organization into a position of considerable influence in the process. Founded in 1982, the Federalist Society began as a student organization dedicated to challenging the "orthodox liberal ideology" that was prominent in many law schools. By 2001 the society had opened chapters at nearly every law school in the country, though its influence was limited primarily to the academy, where it often sponsored symposia and speakers. Federalist Society members were now slated to play prominent roles in the Bush administration. Counted among its members were at least three cabinet secretaries: attorney general John Ashcroft, interior secretary Gale Norton, and energy secretary Spencer Abraham. Once obscure, the Federalist Society had risen to the heights of influence in the nation's capital.[12]

Documenting the Federalist Society's actual influence over the Bush administration's appointment process is a tricky proposition; its influence remains informal, a product of networking more than anything else. Still, no one doubts that the Federalist Society has become an important vetting agent for Republican presidents. As the *National Journal* described it, "The organization attracts conservative minds, and anyone who would surprise a conservative president is unlikely to be a member."[13]

A Switch in Time Puts the Democrats in Control: Lower Court Appointments during the 107th Congress

The tense environment that President Clinton's judicial nominees had to navigate during the late 1990s, when Senate Republicans ruled the appointment process with an iron hand, was fresh in the minds of Senate Democrats when President George W. Bush took office. Against some of Clinton's more liberal nominees Republicans had employed numerous delaying tactics that were unusual and in some cases unprecedented. The Republican-controlled Senate achieved an effective slowdown of the appointment process by (1) refusing to hold hearings for some nominees; (2) subjecting other nominees to a second round of hearings, and (3) instituting a system whereby Republican senators could place "secret holds" on nominations, effectively denying them hearings.[14] In the final tally, fewer than 60 percent of President Clinton's nominees for the circuit courts were confirmed, the lowest confirmation rate to that point for appellate court nominees of any presidency in the postwar period (see Table 9.1).[15]

TABLE 9.1   Judicial Confirmation Rates for Lower Court Nominees, 1945–2005

Administration	Percentages of nominees confirmed	
	Appellate courts	District courts
Geo. W. Bush	53	87
Clinton	59	81
Geo. H. W. Bush	76	77
Reagan	89	92
Carter	93	93
Ford	85	83
Nixon	96	99
Johnson	95	96
Kennedy	95	99
Eisenhower	100	91
Truman	100	87

Source: Sarah Binder, Forrest Maltzman, and Alan Murphy, *New York Times,* May 19, 2005, A27.
Note: Data updated through May 19, 2005.

As the minority at the start of the 107th Congress, Senate Democrats could not hope to offer the same level of opposition to President Bush's nominees. Immediately after the inauguration, Vice President Dick Cheney broke the Senate's fifty-fifty deadlock in favor of the Republicans, and united party government reigned for the first time since 1994. President Bush moved quickly on the judicial appointments front. Borrowing once again from the playbook of the Reagan administration, he reestablished the Office of Legal Policy in the Justice Department. Lawyers in that office joined with members of the White House Counsel's Office to staff a Judicial Selection Committee, with the resources to comprehensively research potential nominees to the federal bench.[16]

The committee began meeting on a near-weekly basis early in 2001 to identify potential judicial candidates. Summaries of the committee's work were quickly prepared for the president, who announced his first eleven judicial nominees on May 9, 2001. Included on the list were two peace offerings to the Democrats: One was Roger Gregory, a recess appointment by President Clinton, who was currently serving as the first African American judge in the history of the Fourth Circuit. The list also included Barrington Parker, appointed by President Clinton to the district court seven years earlier and now nominated to the U.S. Court of Appeals. But the list also included several extremely conservative nominees, including Miguel Estrada (nominated to the D.C. Circuit), Dennis Shedd (nominated to the Sixth Circuit), and Texas Supreme Court justice Priscilla Owen (nominated to the Fifth Circuit).

Little did the White House realize that just as the Senate Judiciary Committee was preparing to schedule hearings on these nominees, the already tense confirmation environment was about to be turned on its head.

The key event occurred a little more than two weeks after President Bush's May 9 announcement. On May 24, Sen. Jim Jeffords, R-Vt., announced that he was leaving the Republican Party to become an independent and, of greater significance, would caucus with the Democrats. Jeffords's switch shifted control of the Senate back into Democratic hands, transferring the Senate Judiciary Committee gavel to Senator Leahy. At least for the remainder of the 107th Congress, Democrats would control the upper house.

The impact of Jeffords's switch was felt immediately in the judicial appointment process. Instead of rushing ahead with hearings, the Senate Judiciary Committee effectively slowed down the confirmation process. That summer Senator Schumer of New York—now chairman of the Senate Judiciary Committee's Subcommittee on Administrative Oversight—held hearings on the question of whether ideology should matter in judicial nominations. He and other Democratic senators used the hearings as a platform to argue that consideration of the ideologies of judicial candidates was appropriate. Renewing his support for the traditional blue slip system, Leahy announced that he would defer to the wishes of just one senator, Barbara Boxer, D-Calif., who planned to withhold a blue slip on one of President Bush's nominees, Christopher Cox. In the late 1980s, Cox had served as a senior associate counsel to Reagan's White House. He then was elected to Congress, where he became a highly partisan member of the House Republican Policy Committee. Boxer's action denied Cox a hearing, and he eventually withdrew his name from active consideration. Dennis Shedd's nomination stalled as well, along with that of Priscilla Owen, whose nomination had the support of Texas's two Republican senators. Committee Democrats also opposed Ninth Circuit nominee Carolyn Kuhl, who as a Reagan administration lawyer had argued hard for tax-exempt status for the racially discriminatory Bob Jones University.[17] Only four of President Bush's judicial nominees were confirmed before the Senate adjourned for the summer. Meanwhile, Bush continued to nominate more lower court judges, including some that liberal interest groups viewed as conservative extremists. In all, Bush made thirty-two nominations to the circuit courts and ninety-eight to the district courts during his first two years in office.

The Democrats retained the procedural power to delay the controversial nominations indefinitely, in committee or on the Senate floor. Though they had a slight overall majority, the Democratic leadership could not risk a floor vote, as several moderate Democratic senators, including Zell Miller, D-Ga., and Ben Nelson, D-Neb., had expressed willingness to vote in favor of the nominees on the merits. A handful of nominees soon joined Shedd and Owen in appointment limbo, including Miguel Estrada, Charles Pickering (Fifth Circuit), Terrence Boyle (Fourth Circuit), Deborah

Cook and Jeffrey Sutton (Sixth Circuit), and Kuhl (Ninth Circuit). Some nominees did receive hearings: Senate minority leader Trent Lott, R-Miss., successfully pressed for hearings on his close friend Pickering, for example. But on March 14, 2002, the Judiciary Committee voted ten to nine, along party lines, to refuse to move Pickering's nomination forward for a vote in the full Senate.

Several other nominees also received hearings, only to suffer the same fate as Pickering. Priscilla Owen's hearings, held on July 23, 2002, were televised by C-SPAN and featured an extended discussion of Owen's views on abortion. Democratic senators homed in on one especially high-profile case, in which Owen's former colleague (and now the White House counsel) Alberto Gonzales had castigated her for undue activism, ruling on an issue where it was not necessary. The news media also paid extra attention to the nomination of Estrada, who appeared at hearings held on September 26. The interest in Estrada's nomination was perhaps understandable. An immigrant child of a family from Honduras, Estrada had been an editor of the *Harvard Law Review*, secured a Supreme Court clerkship, and served as a lawyer in the Justice Department in both Republican and Democratic administrations. Instead of focusing solely on Estrada's conservative views—the presumed basis of their opposition—Senate Democrats made Estrada's nomination a test case for challenging the Bush administration's refusal to turn over Justice Department documents that he had written. Specifically, the committee demanded documents from Estrada's time as an assistant solicitor general during the Clinton administration. The Bush administration refused the request, citing executive privilege. Estrada's nomination quickly fell into limbo as well.

The final tally of judicial appointments during the 107th Congress was mostly positive. Of President Bush's 131 lower court nominations, the Democrat-controlled Senate Judiciary Committee held hearings for 103, voted on 102, and approved 100. (The only two candidates that the committee rejected outright were Owen and Pickering.) All 100 nominations the committee approved were also approved by the full Senate. Among those confirmed were some of President Bush's more controversial nominations, including Dennis Shedd and Michael McConnell (a nominee to the Tenth Circuit). But most of the media's attention continued to focus on the nominees who had yet to receive up-or-down votes by the full Senate during the 107th Congress. Joining Owen and Estrada on the list of nominees whose fate remained in limbo was a name that would become especially prominent during President Bush's second term: John G. Roberts Jr. (see Table 9.2).

Renominations, Filibusters and Sleep-Ins: Lower Court Appointments during the 108th and 109th Congresses

The 2002 midterm elections shifted control of the Senate back into Republican hands, this time by a 51–48 margin. Basking in their newfound control of the various

TABLE 9.2 U.S. District and Circuit Court Nominations during the First Two Years of a Presidency, 1981–2002

Congress	Years	President	District court nominations confirmed	District court nominations withdrawn, returned, or rejected	Circuit court nominations confirmed	Circuit court nominations withdrawn, returned, or rejected
97th	1981–1982	Reagan	69	2	19	1
101st	1989–1990	Geo. H. W. Bush	48	3	22	1
103rd	1993–1994	Clinton	108	11	19	3
107th	2001–2002	Geo. W. Bush	83	35	17	44

Source: Congressional Research Service.

Senate committees, Republican leaders geared up to push more aggressively for the swift confirmation of even Bush's more controversial judicial nominations. Forsaking any notion that Republicans might make a peace offering to the Democrats, on January 7, 2003, President Bush resubmitted all fifteen circuit court nominations that had failed to get a vote on the merits from the full Senate during the 107th Congress. The Republican-controlled Senate Judiciary Committee, chaired once again by Orrin Hatch, would now get its own crack at confirming the nominations of Pickering, Owen, and Estrada, among others.

Certainly several nominations that had failed under divided government during the previous Congress might now succeed. Hearings were held for a number of previously stalled nominations beginning in January 2003. Jeffrey Sutton—whose advocacy of states' rights had incurred the wrath of Democrats concerned with how he might limit the reach of federal statutes—now made it through committee and was confirmed by the full Senate on April 29. He was joined a week later on the Sixth Circuit by another controversial nominee, Deborah Cook. Democrats remained wary of John Roberts's expansive views on executive power, but they consented to his confirmation to the D.C. Circuit by a voice vote on May 8.

At least one social scientist had correctly predicted that because the confirmation process had deteriorated so much in recent years, a return to unified government might not improve the situation.[18] True to form, a handful of nominees continued to draw significant fire from Senate Democrats in the minority, with no apparent end in sight. Once again the ranking Democrat on the Senate Judiciary Committee, Senator Leahy declared that committee Democrats would continue to oppose a handful of nominees with extreme conservative views, including Estrada, Boyle, Owen, Pickering, and Kuhl. Two freshly nominated candidates also drew the Democrats' opposition: Eleventh Circuit nominee William Pryor, whose negative comments about homosexuality and abortion incited Democratic charges that he was a judicial "activist," and D.C. Circuit nominee Janice Rogers Brown, who was accused of advocating pre-1937 views of the Constitution that would severely limit state and federal power to enact economic regulations.

With Hatch in control, every single one of the president's nominees now received hearings. Yet for the defeated Democrats, all that had changed was the locus of the battle—they now took their fight to the Senate floor, where the minority has various tools at its disposal, including the threat of a filibuster. Senators had only rarely deployed filibusters in earlier judicial appointment wars. Most notably, in 1968 Lyndon Johnson withdrew Justice Abe Fortas's bid for promotion to chief justice of the United States after a vote to invoke cloture failed 45–43.[19] Senate Republicans, led by Strom Thurmond, S.C., and Robert Griffin, Mich., were determined to prevent a full Senate vote on Fortas, and Fortas asked President Johnson to withdraw his name. During the Clinton administration, Republican senators employed the filibuster to delay the confirmation of two of his nominees for much of the second term. (The two, Judge Richard Paez and attorney Marsha Berzon, were ultimately confirmed during Clinton's final year in office.)

Formerly employed only rarely against nominations of any kind, the filibuster quickly became a lightning rod for controversy. During spring 2003, Senate Republicans tried to bring the more controversial nominees up for a vote on the floor, only to run up against the filibuster. Needing sixty votes to invoke cloture and end debate, Republicans were easily defeated by the votes of forty-five of the forty-eight Senate Democrats. Attempting to distinguish these tactics from filibustered nominations of the past, Senate Republicans argued that the minority was using the filibuster here when it did not have enough votes to defeat the nominee on the floor; Senate majority leader Bill Frist, R-Tenn., also reminded reporters that the two nominees stalled during the Clinton administration did eventually receive a vote on the merits. With united party government unable to break the logjam, Frist and the Senate Republican leadership began to consider more drastic solutions to the problem— namely, a Senate rules change to prevent filibusters on judicial nominations. Any such motion to change the rules and compel a vote on judicial nominations—if treated as a mere procedural change by the presiding officer of the Senate—could in theory be approved by a simple majority vote.[20] Law professor Stephen Calabresi, a cofounder of the Federalist Society, argued on behalf of the proposal that the Constitution alone specifies all areas where supermajorities are absolutely required.[21] Senate Democrats quickly labeled Frist's proposal the "nuclear option" because they planned to treat any such move as an all-out declaration of war, halting much of the routine legislative business of the chamber, which was usually conducted via unanimous consent agreements that could readily be withheld.[22]

This back-and-forth between Senate Republicans and Democrats continued throughout fall 2003, with few offers of compromise forthcoming. Frustrated by twenty-eight months of waiting for a Senate vote, Miguel Estrada asked the Bush administration to formally withdraw his circuit court nomination on September 4. A Republican-sponsored "sleep-in" during late October—in which the Senate Republicans conducted around-the-clock debates on the stalled nominations, complete with portable cots outside the Senate chamber doors—changed few minds.[23] President Bush stoked the fire in January 2004 when he named William Pryor and Charles Pickering as recess appointments to the U.S. Courts of Appeals for the Fifth and Eleventh Circuits, respectively. Recess appointments are authorized by Article II, Section 2 of the Constitution: The chief executive may fill vacant positions while the Senate is in recess, although such an appointment lasts only until the end of the next congressional session. Given the vitriol surrounding the Pickering and Pryor nominations, their appointments were likely to be interpreted as acts of defiance rather than acts of necessity. A pre–Memorial Day agreement between the White House and the Senate leadership headed off the possibility of future recess appointments, in return for which the White House secured from Senate Democrats the promise to allow votes on twenty-five less-controversial nominations that were being held up for retaliatory purposes only.

The looming presidential election of 2004 put off the final showdown for a short period. But the 2004 election results made Republicans more determined to carry through on their threat of a rules change. Not only did President Bush secure his own reelection, but Republicans saw their numbers in the Senate increase from a bare majority of fifty-one, to fifty-five, the party's high-water mark of Senate power dating back to the 1930s. Less than two weeks after the 2004 elections, Senator Frist prepared to give his official blessing to the "nuclear option." Even so, Senate Democrats (though now down to forty-four) still had the votes to delay the controversial nominations. President Bush again stoked the flames by renominating twenty candidates to lower court judgeships, including Owen, Pryor, and Brown. All of Capitol Hill braced for the high-stakes game of "chicken" that seemed sure to follow.

The nuclear option was only sidelined by an unlikely coalition of moderate senators reacting to opinion polls that showed the public rejecting the use of extreme measures to resolve the judicial appointments battle.[24] While Frist was busy posturing after the election, a "centrist coalition" of Republican and Democratic senators started meeting to discuss ways to head off a showdown. By early 2005 the coalition had grown into the "Gang of Fourteen," consisting of seven Republican and seven Democratic senators, reportedly led by Senator Nelson and Sen. John McCain, R-Ariz.[25] With a looming battle over the nomination of Priscilla Owen scheduled for May 24, the coalition crafted a compromise by which Democrats agreed that they would (1) allow immediate cloture votes on three of the most controversial nominees (Pryor, Brown, and Owen) and (2) reserve future filibusters for only "extraordinary circumstances." In return, Senate Republicans promised they would not attempt to amend the current filibuster rules.

The compromise benefited Republicans more than Democrats in the short term, as moderate Democrats of the Gang of Fourteen refused to recognize the existence of "extraordinary circumstances" in several high-profile cases during the remainder of the 109th Congress. Thus despite considerable Democratic opposition to President Bush's third Supreme Court nominee, Samuel Alito Jr., efforts by Sen. John Kerry, D-Mass., to lead a filibuster on his nomination fell well short of the necessary forty-one votes. Nelson and the other coalition members made clear their position that ideology alone would not normally constitute the "extraordinary circumstances" necessary to support a filibuster.

Naturally, the 2006 midterm elections dramatically altered the environment for lower court appointments yet again. The 110th Congress convened on January 4, 2007, with the Democrats in charge of both houses, including a narrow two-seat margin in the Senate. But at least two factors rendered the Democrats' hold on the upper chamber in early 2007 even more precarious than it had been during the latter half of 2001 and throughout 2002. Sen. Joseph Lieberman, I-Conn., caucused with the Democrats to give them a majority but served notice to his colleagues that he could not be taken for granted to vote the party line. Sen. Tim Johnson, D-S.D., suffered a brain rupture in December 2006, and after a successful operation his return to the Senate was not expected for months. Still, Democrats' control of the Senate Judiciary Committee, chaired once again by Leahy, promised rough going for President Bush's judicial nominees during the remainder of his presidency. When the White House renominated Federalist Society cofounder Peter Keisler to the D.C. Circuit just weeks after the 2006 midterm elections, Leahy re-articulated his position that only "consensus nominees" would be confirmed by the new Democratic majority in the 110th Congress.

George W. Bush's Lower Court Appointments Record, 2001–2006

The first six years of George W. Bush's presidency witnessed perhaps the most tumultuous period for lower court appointments in American history. The conflict was ignited in part by an administration determined to make the constitutional landscape more conservative through the appointment of extremely conservative jurists. To press their cause in a legislative body structured to protect the minority's interests, Senate Democrats joined the battle by discarding two traditional norms that had governed the confirmation process in the past: (1) they challenged some highly experienced, qualified nominees strictly for their ideological positions, and (2) they employed the threat of a filibuster, which had seldom been used before then to challenge nominations of any kind. The absence of even one Supreme Court vacancy during the president's first term added to the tensions on both sides, as lower court appointments became the primary venue where political battles over federalism, abortion, and religion were waged.

By any measure, obstruction and delay have become a more prominent aspect of lower court appointments in recent years. According to political scientist Sheldon Goldman, although the proportion of nominees confirmed has fluctuated from year to year, by empirically measurable indicators delay has generally increased since the 97th Congress of 1981–1982, and this trend has continued whether there has been divided or unified government.[26]

As of September 2006, President Bush had successfully brought the federal judiciary up to 95 percent capacity. The Sixth Circuit provides a case in point. Perennially under strength since the 1990s, the circuit had six Bush-appointed full-time judges by the end of 2006, leaving only two vacancies. By the end of the 109th Congress, President Bush was responsible for the appointment of forty-six judges to the U.S. Courts of Appeals and 203 judges to the federal district courts, amounting to nearly three in ten judges sitting on those two levels of the federal judicial system. By the time he leaves office in 2009, more than one in three federal judges may owe their appointments to President George W. Bush. These numbers compare favorably to those of other recent, two-term presidents such as Ronald Reagan and Bill Clinton, each of whom successfully appointed an average of forty-five lower court judges per year during his eight years in office.[27]

As important as simply staffing the courts, President Bush generally succeeded in appointing judges who were extremely conservative. According to a study of judicial outcomes by scholars Robert Carp, Kenneth Manning, and Ronald Stidham, Bush's judicial appointees (through the summer of 2004) had amassed a record of conservatism that was matched during the past half-century only by President Reagan's appointees.[28] Their data indicated that 36 percent of the decisions of the George W. Bush jurists were decided in a liberal direction, compared with 45 percent by Bill Clinton's nominees and 37 percent by the appointees of George H. W. Bush. Reagan's nominees voted on the liberal side in 35.8 percent of cases. In civil liberties and civil rights cases in particular, George W. Bush's nominees voted for the liberal result less than 28 percent of the time, a significantly lower percentage than that recorded even by the Reagan appointees (36 percent). Of course it may be decades before the true ideological impact of President Bush's nominees can be assessed. Moreover, the standards by which we analyze ideology are constantly changing— such hot-button issues as abortion, gay rights, and affirmative action were barely blips on the radar screen when President Richard Nixon appointed his four justices to the Supreme Court. Still, Bush's success by current standards must be considered significant.

A final standard by which to judge President Bush's success is based on a goal that he rarely acknowledged in public: the need for a more diverse federal bench. "Nontraditional" nominees include not just minorities such as African Americans and Hispanics, but female appointees as well. One may infer President Bush's interest in maintaining diversity from some of his other actions. As a candidate for reelection as governor of Texas in 1998, George W. Bush promised to make Hispanics a more significant part of the state government. As president, he was willing to disappoint some of his core constituencies with a more cautious approach to racial preferences. For example, in staking out his administration's position in two landmark affirmative action cases from the University of Michigan, *Gratz v. Bollinger*[29] and *Grutter v. Bollinger*,[30] President Bush approved an *amicus curiae* brief to the Supreme Court with a mixed message. On one hand, his administration argued that the University of Michigan's racial quotas were unconstitutional. Yet the administration made clear in its brief in *Grutter* that it also had no objection to race-conscious admissions per se, so long as there were no disguised quotas.[31] The administration's refusal to argue that the Supreme Court should break new ground and hold that race should never be a factor in admissions clearly disappointed some of President Bush's more con-servative constituents.

President Bush's immediate predecessor, Bill Clinton, had broken significant new ground in diversifying the lower courts: Approximately half of Clinton's district court judges (47.6 percent) and circuit court judges (50.8 percent) could be classified as nontraditional.[32] Bush did not come close to Clinton's record in this regard. Of Bush's first 204 lower court appointments, 43 were women, 15 were African Americans, and 21 were Hispanic. Despite Bush's high-profile attempts to confirm such nontraditional circuit court nominees as Miguel Estrada, Priscilla Owen, and Janice Rogers Brown, his administration increased by just one the absolute number of racial and ethnic minorities on the courts of appeals during his first term in office.[33]

President Bush increased the gender diversity of six courts of appeals, but he decreased the overall number of women on four other circuits. Moreover, although he diversified two of thirteen courts of appeals, his appointments decreased diversity on five others.[34] Bush did only marginally better on the district courts, where he increased the gender diversity on twenty-six courts and the racial diversity on sixteen. But once again there were also courts that became less diverse under his watch. Bush appointments decreased gender diversity on eighteen district courts and decreased racial diversity on sixteen. As expected, Bush appointments increased the number of Hispanics on the federal bench, but those gains generally came at the expense of other racial minorities. In summarizing President Bush's first-term appointments, Rorie Solberg observed that "men and whites lost no ground, despite the administration's commitment to diversity."[35]

The Long Wait Ends: Second Term Opportunities on the U.S. Supreme Court

As a candidate for the White House, George W. Bush spoke of Antonin Scalia and Clarence Thomas as his model justices, causing speculation that his election might eventually transform the constitutional landscape through his Supreme Court appointments. The last Supreme Court justice to leave office had been Harry Blackmun, in 1994. High court vacancies seemed inevitable—perhaps more than one during President Bush's first term alone. Speculation about retirements focused primarily on Chief Justice William Rehnquist, who turned seventy-six years old just weeks before Bush's election. Ruth Bader Ginsburg, a more liberal appointee of Bill Clinton, was sixty-seven at the time of President Bush's first inauguration. Sandra Day O'Connor, the frequent swing vote, who had frustrated social conservatives by casting liberal votes in abortion and Establishment Clause cases, was then sixtynine.[36] And if the most liberal member of the Court, eighty-year-old John Paul Stevens, were to retire, even a moderate conservative substitute likely would produce a marked shift by the Court to the right.

Yet as the lower court confirmation wars heated up during President Bush's first four years, no word of any retirements was forthcoming from the U.S. Supreme Court. Defying many expert predictions, O'Connor stayed put. The chambers of Stevens, Ginsburg, and Rehnquist remained quiet as well. Soon the Court approached one of its own historic milestones for stability: By fall 2004 the same nine justices had been serving together for more than a decade, the longest period without a vacancy since the James Monroe administration. To escape the ignominy of becoming only the second elected president in history to serve at least one full term without a Supreme Court appointment (Jimmy Carter was the first), George W. Bush needed to secure reelection to a second term. Once that feat was accomplished, rumors began about Chief Justice Rehnquist's failing health. At the start of Bush's second term, Clarence Thomas, fifty-six, was the only justice under sixty-five. It seemed as if the floodgates of Supreme Court retirements were about to explode.

Finally there came word from Justice O'Connor. Immediately after the Supreme Court's 2004–2005 term concluded, O'Connor announced her retirement from the court on July 1, 2005, "effective upon the confirmation of [her] successor." As expected, President Bush moved quickly to name her replacement and on July 19 announced his selection of Judge John G. Roberts Jr. Although Roberts, fifty, had been a judge on the U.S. Court of Appeals for the D.C. Circuit for just two years, his name had appeared on nearly every list of potential nominees to the Court that had circulated in the media and around Washington, D.C., since the beginning of Bush's presidency.

Of course other names appeared as well. Far more experienced federal appeals court judges, such as Samuel Alito, Edith Jones, J. Harvie Wilkinson, Emilio Garza, and J. Michael Luttig, were available. Attorney General Alberto Gonzales, forty-nine, was not just a close personal friend of the president but had been a justice on the Texas Supreme Court, and he offered the extra advantage of making history as the first Hispanic justice. If President Bush wanted to challenge the high wall of separation built by the Supreme Court in its interpretation of the Establishment Clause, U.S. Court of Appeals judge Michael McConnell boasted an impressive background of scholarship on the subject. And if he leaned toward replacing Sandra Day O'Connor with another female justice, there were many conservative women available in the pool: in addition to Edith Jones, speculation revolved around Judge Karen Williams of the Fourth Circuit and Judge Edith Brown Clement of the Fifth Circuit.

With such an esteemed and diverse pool, how did John Roberts's candidacy vault past the others? In truth, Roberts met nearly every criterion deemed most important by the president and his aides. His legal credentials seemed beyond reproach: Harvard Law School graduate, a Supreme Court clerkship (under Rehnquist), associate White House counsel to President Reagan, deputy solicitor general, ten years in private practice, and recent service as a D.C. Circuit Court judge. According to one measure of nominee qualifications constructed by scholars Jeffrey Segal and Lee Epstein, Roberts places among the ten most qualified Supreme Court candidates formally nominated since the New Deal.[37] Roberts also possessed an unusual amount of experience litigating before the Court. He had argued thirty-nine Supreme Court cases in all and had prevailed in twenty-five of them. At fifty years old, he was young; among the other most frequently mentioned candidates for the high court, only McConnell and Gonzales were younger. And because Roberts had been serving on the federal bench for only two years, he had written only a limited number of judicial opinions. He had rendered no decisions on abortion, school prayer, or some of the other issues that had tripped up Robert Bork almost two decades earlier. Many assumed that as a practicing Roman Catholic he would oppose abortion. Yet there was no judicial opinion on record to confirm that Roberts's personal beliefs translated into his views on abortion's place in the Constitution.

Roberts's overall conservative views of the law were no doubt heavily influenced by the time he spent as a government lawyer in the Reagan and George H. W. Bush administrations. Numerous conservatives from those two administrations had worked closely with Roberts and could vouch for his conservative views on a number of subjects. In particular, White House aides expected that Roberts would become a classic advocate of broad executive authority and thus that he would pose no significant barrier to the administration's war-on-terrorism initiatives. At the same time, Roberts had cultivated a reputation within legal circles as a cautious craftsman of the law. In an article published in July by the *New Republic,* Jeffrey Rosen offered the expectation that Roberts was more likely to be a "bottom-up, conservative incrementalist," as opposed to the more "top-down judges" who are "willing to overturn decades of precedent that clash with their vision."[38] Noted judicial scholar Cass Sunstein agreed, finding in Roberts's limited judicial background evidence of "minimalism in action: an unwillingness to speak broadly and a desire to proceed with careful attention to particular facts and arguments."[39]

Clearly Roberts's candidacy posed a number of challenges for potential detractors. After law school and his two clerkships, Roberts had cut his teeth as a young government lawyer serving as an advocate for the Reagan administration in the courts. Accordingly, liberal interest groups reviewed his record as a litigator for clues to his legal philosophy. Yet the carefully worded memos and briefs he wrote to his superiors during the late 1980s and early 1990s could not fairly be understood as representing his own personal views of the law; rather, they were his best arguments on behalf of his client administration. Senate Democrats would thus have a tough time gaining traction against Roberts's candidacy because it did not offer the "smoking guns" that might outrage larger segments of the public.

Finally, opposing Roberts's nomination would force many Senate Democrats to confront charges of hypocrisy. After Roberts's nomination to the court of appeals had remained in limbo from 2001 to 2003, the newly Republican controlled Senate of 2003 quickly moved his renomination forward to committee hearings. The Senate Judiciary Committee approved Roberts's nomination by an overwhelming 16–3 vote, with several Democrats (including Leahy, the ranking Democrat) voting in favor. With his confirmation to the court of appeals a forgone conclusion, the full Senate had given its assent to his nomination by a unanimous-consent voice vote. Thus with the exception of the three senators who had voted against Roberts in committee, Senate Democrats would be hard-pressed to explain why they should now oppose his promotion to the U.S. Supreme Court.

As expected, the opposition to Roberts was muted. Groups such as the Leadership Conference on Civil Rights opposed Roberts on principle. Yet all signs pointed to a relatively painless confirmation process, highlighted by committee hearings scheduled for the first week in September. A new wrench was thrown into the process on September 3, 2005, with the announcement of Chief Justice Rehnquist's death at the age of eighty. In early July Bush administration officials had focused on filling the O'Connor vacancy under the assumption that nothing else was forthcoming. With the chief justiceship now available, that dynamic changed. For the previous six weeks Roberts had been scrupulously vetted in the media and by Senate Democrats, and nothing troubling had emerged. Indeed, Roberts had seemingly accomplished the impossible: Senators from both sides of the aisle were praising his credentials. Shrewdly capitalizing on the aura of inevitability surrounding Roberts's appointment, President Bush raised the stakes just a bit with the announcement on September 6 that he was renominating Roberts for the Court's center seat.

Delayed by just a week, Roberts's hearings proceeded with barely a hiccup. On direct questioning, Roberts raised some eyebrows among conservative senators such as Sam Brownback, R-Kan., and Tom Coburn, R-Okla., when he offered that the repeated affirmation of a precedent over time should make judges more reluctant to overturn it. Yet if Roberts was signaling that he was not an automatic vote to overturn *Roe v. Wade,* the hint he provided was so ambiguous and heavily qualified that it never really threatened to disrupt his nomination.

Sen. Joseph Biden, D-Del., who would eventually declare his interest in seeking the Democratic presidential nomination in 2008, led the attack on Roberts for his refusal to indicate whether he thought a statute banning all abortions would be constitutional. Roberts calmly responded that he was following the rule established by Justice Ruth Bader Ginsburg at her hearings twelve years earlier: "No hints, no forecasts, no previews." Roberts proved so unflappable during his four days of testimony that he drew praise for his performance even from some of his most heated Democratic antagonists. In a radio interview conducted several weeks later, Senator Schumer called Roberts a "legal rock star," who could have weathered the Democrats' questioning successfully no matter how long it had continued. Consistent with his negative vote on Roberts's earlier nomination to the D.C. Circuit, Schumer voted against his appointment to the Supreme Court. But Schumer's voice was lost even among the forty-four-person Democratic caucus, which split down the middle (22–22) on confirmation. The final Senate tally of 78–22 was narrow by historical standards, but was an overwhelming victory given the rancor and politicization that had characterized appointment politics throughout the Bush administration.

In seeking another candidate to fill Sandra Day O'Connor's seat, the administration faced a more daunting set of challenges. First, the stakes seemed higher. Replacing the conservative Rehnquist with a conservative nominee would only marginally shift the Court's balance of power. Replacing O'Connor, the quintessential swing vote of the past decade, with a conservative would have a far greater impact on Court doctrines. Interest groups quieted by the less-controversial Roberts nomination were now spoiling for a fight over O'Connor's successor. Second, O'Connor was one of only two women serving on the high court; with the chief justiceship going to another white male, pressure now increased on Bush to appoint a woman to maintain the Court's current gender balance. Third, Roberts had coasted through the confirmation process because his record defied the argument that he was a fire-breathing, extreme conservative. With this next vacancy, social conservatives wanted one of their own—a "sure thing" on issues such as abortion and school prayer. More-conservative Republican senators were ready to join them in this regard. Navigating these various crosswinds would require a delicate touch indeed.

The Bush administration stumbled badly in its initial effort to fill the seat. On October 3, 2005, President Bush introduced as his next choice, White House counsel Harriet Miers, whose close association with Bush dated back to the early 1990s in her home state of Texas. Among her various duties, Miers, sixty, had been assisting in the selection of judges just prior to her nomination. Still, her selection caught nearly everyone by surprise. Unlike Roberts, her name had not been on many people's lists of potential nominees for the Court.

Miers's credentials for the Supreme Court were unusual to say the least. In 1970 she graduated from Southern Methodist Law School; after a clerkship she worked at a Dallas law firm for the better part of three decades. Certainly Miers was well known in Texas legal circles: In 1986 she had become the first female head of the Dallas Bar Association, and in 1992 she became the first female to head the state bar of Texas. Yet aside from a two-year term on the Dallas city council, Miers had limited experience in government before joining the White House as staff secretary in 2001. Whereas Epstein and Segal had found Roberts to be among the most qualified nominees since the 1930s, Miers's limited credentials placed her among the least qualified. In fact, only six justices placed lower than Miers, with two of the six (Clement Haynsworth and G. Harrold Carswell) rejected by the Senate and one other (Douglas Ginsburg) withdrawing before a formal Senate vote. President Bush's claim that he appointed one of the most qualified nominees to the Court simply did not hold up in the case of Miers.

Even more problematic was Miers's lack of judicial experience at any level. To be sure, many notable justices of the past had no judicial service before arriving on the Court: John Marshall, Felix Frankfurter, Robert Jackson, and Earl Warren, to name a few. Yet each of those individuals could boast some other impressive legal accomplishments that had won them national acclaim and exalted stature prior to becoming a Supreme Court justice. John Marshall had been a congressman and secretary of state; Felix Frankfurter was a well-respected law professor who had famously defended the anarchists Sacco and Vanzetti. Robert Jackson had gained fame as a young attorney in New York, and after becoming Franklin Roosevelt's attorney general in 1940 he was seen by many as a leading contender for the Court. Earl Warren had been elected to three terms as governor of California and was the Republican Party's candidate for vice president in 1948. Miers, by contrast, was a relative unknown.

Conservatives in particular were most troubled because Miers's positions on hot-button legal issues were unclear. Christian fundamentalists may have been encouraged that Miers was a devout evangelical protestant, but would her religious faith influence her jurisprudence? As she had written no judicial opinions and held no high executive office where important decisions were made, there was no way to tell. One of the few public positions Miers did take concerned abortion: while head of the Texas bar in the early 1990s she had joined an unsuccessful effort to have the ABA maintain its official position of neutrality on the issue. That was not enough evidence to convince social conservatives that Miers was not a potential "David Souter in the making," a reference to George H. W. Bush's Supreme Court appointee who became a moderate-to-liberal justice. Certainly Miers fell far short of the "sure thing" they were hoping for to replace O'Connor.

The announcement of Miers's nomination on October 3 set loose a chain of events that culminated just twenty-four days later when she requested that her nomination be withdrawn. Miers gained the instant support of Senate Minority Leader Harry Reid, D-Nev., but publicly most others withheld judgment. Privately Miers's nomination was being undermined from the outset. Conservative critics, including Pat Buchanan, George Will, and the defeated Supreme Court candidate Robert Bork, complained that Miers's nomination was a clear example of political cronyism, as she lacked the judicial experience of so many other candidates. Some Senate Democrats may have relished the opportunity to see Republicans fighting among themselves, but even Senator Leahy complained that many of Miers's answers to interrogatories about the Constitution had been inadequate and needed to be redone. When the Senate Judiciary Committee demanded that the White House turn over Miers's internal memos on constitutional matters, the White House stood firm against the request, thus creating the pretext for her withdrawal, which Bush accepted on October 27.

What led President Bush to stumble so badly with the Miers nomination? Perhaps he miscalculated the degree to which the political environment had turned against him since his reelection. In the meantime the administration's mishandling of Hurricane Katrina and the steadily worsening situation in Iraq had combined to drub the president's approval rating and weaken the power of his bully pulpit. Perhaps it was also a case of hubris: even when conservatives had disagreed with

President Bush in the past, on issues such as affirmative action, they had never before failed to support his decisions publicly during his four-and-a-half years as president. Bush was convinced that Miers would be conservative on the issue that mattered most to him—executive branch discretion. But he could not persuade social conservatives of her positions on the issues that mattered most to *them*. The Miers nomination thus marked a real turning point in the George W. Bush presidency, after which the White House could never again take social conservatives' support for granted.

Just four days after Miers's withdrawal, the administration turned back to one of the names that had been frequently mentioned earlier: Judge Samuel A. Alito, 55, of the U.S. Court of Appeals for the Third Circuit. In many ways Alito was the exact opposite of Miers. Educated at Yale Law School, he had extensive experience working in government, both as a member of the Solicitor General's Office and later as the U.S. Attorney for the District of New Jersey. More important, he had spent the previous fifteen years on a circuit court, giving him more judicial experience than any other Supreme Court nominee since Benjamin Cardozo. Perhaps most crucially for conservatives, Alito's brand of judicial conservatism was not a matter of guesswork. His many years on the federal bench featured a number of controversial opinions covering free speech, the Establishment Clause, and civil rights. Unlike Roberts, Alito had actually expressed his opposition to *Roe v. Wade*. For example, in a job application to attorney general Edwin Meese in 1985, Alito wrote that "the Constitution does not protect a right to an abortion" and stated, "I personally believe very strongly" in that legal position.[40] That revelation inflamed many liberals and opened a debate in Washington about how seriously to take the hyperbole found in nearly every job application. Yet it also warmed social conservatives to Alito's candidacy at a time when they were still smarting from the Miers nomination.

Alito's confirmation did not go as smoothly as Roberts's. During his four days of testimony Alito became exasperated at times by the intense questioning he received from Senate Democrats. By the end of each day he looked worn out and frustrated, in marked contrast to the optimistic and controlled front Roberts had presented several months earlier. At one point the nominee's wife, Martha-Ann Alito, became so distraught at the harsh questioning of her husband that she left the hearing room in tears. Yet Judge Alito never gave his opposition the ammunition to defeat his candidacy. When asked by Senator Schumer whether the views he expressed on abortion as a job applicant in 1985 remained his views twenty years later, Alito ducked the question by promising that he would engage in the "judicial process" to determine whether a precedent such as *Roe v. Wade* should be overruled. Answers such as these did not satisfy Senator Schumer and other Senate Democrats, but they did not generate any sustained political momentum to defeat Alito. And any remaining hopes for a filibuster were dashed when every senator in the Gang of Fourteen voted for cloture of debate on the Alito nomination on January 30, 2006 (the final cloture vote was 72–25, fifteen votes short of the forty-one needed to sustain a filibuster). Several members of the Gang of Fourteen still voted against Alito on the merits, but the Senate confirmed his nomination on January 31 by a vote of 58–42.

George W. Bush and the Federal Judiciary: Evaluating the Legacy

George W. Bush's historical legacy may well depend on the outcome of America's war in Iraq. Yet in defining his administration's most important and long lasting contributions to the political system, Bush's influence over the makeup of the federal judiciary, and with it the future direction of constitutional law, is no less significant.

Conservatives must be more than satisfied by Bush's carefully constructed program of appointing fellow conservatives to the federal bench. Like Reagan, Bush invested significant resources in conducting comprehensive research about potential candidates for the bench at all levels. Just as President Reagan focused on the lower courts as a means of transforming the constitutional landscape over the long haul, so too did President George W. Bush take seriously the appointment of lower court judges, investing his administration's political capital to see them confirmed.

As expected, the concerted effort to put ideological conservatives on the courts of appeals, in particular, led to confrontations with Senate Democrats, and some nominations suffered long delays as a result, especially during the eighteen months when Democrats controlled the Senate Judiciary Committee in 2001 and 2002. Yet by the end of 2006 President Bush had successfully installed all but a handful of his chosen candidates for the lower courts, and as a group they stand among the most conservative judicial cohorts in modern times. Considerations of senatorial courtesy, which had hemmed in previous presidents when selecting federal judges, also gave way to Bush during the first six years of his presidency. Bush's plummeting approval ratings in early 2007, combined with the presence of a Democratic Senate majority in the new 110th Congress, may well restore senatorial courtesy to its traditional place in the process. Yet even that possibility remained an open question at the time this volume went to press.

As for President Bush's first two Supreme Court appointments, conservatives were "quietly optimistic and perhaps even secretly gleeful" at the appointment of Roberts and Alito.[41] Writing in the conservative magazine *The National Review,* law professors Nelson Lund and Craig Lerner argued that Bush did not actually fulfill his pledge to appoint Supreme Court justices in the mold of Scalia and Thomas. Neither Roberts nor Alito professed a belief that the intentions of the Founders should be the primary consideration in interpreting the Constitution, as Scalia and Thomas often do in their opinions. Instead, the White House presented Roberts and Alito in a quite different light, as models of respect for precedent and the judicial process.[42] Even if the two do not become the conservative judicial activists that many conservatives were hoping for, they should still be loyal foot soldiers in the revolution to transform the constitutional landscape along more conservative lines.

Moreover, whether or not either Roberts or Alito is willing to assist in the effort to overturn *Roe v. Wade, Lawrence v. Texas,* and other controversial precedents, these two "deferential conservatives" are almost certain to extend their brand of deference to broad exercises of executive branch discretion in fighting the war on terrorism and other matters. In speeches he gave prior to his arrival on the Supreme Court, Alito forthrightly endorsed a "unitary executive" theory, which denied to Congress the authority to put law enforcement power in administrative agencies not directly accountable to the president. Consider also both justices' involvement in the 2006 case of *Hamdan v. Rumsfeld,*[43] in which the detention of so-called unlawful combatants was challenged as unconstitutional before the Supreme Court. Chief Justice Roberts recused himself from the case because when the same case had been before the D.C. Circuit, he had sided with the federal government. Alito cast his vote as associate justice squarely with the U.S. government.

The votes of Roberts and Alito in *Hamdan,* along with the other votes that Bush's lower court appointees will cast in the war on terror, may constitute the most important Bush legacy of all. Although close assessment of the Bush nominees reveals varying measures of social conservatism at the time of their respective nominations, the unifying thread in the administration's selection of judges has been its overriding concern that judges be deferential to claims of expansive executive branch authority. The restraint shown by Roberts and Alito in such instances may be seen as a sign of timidity by social conservatives, but it marks unambiguous success from the point of view of the nation's commander in chief.

Notes

1. Robert S. Greenberger, "Texas Justices Named by Bush Show Moderate Mien," *Wall Street Journal,* March 20, 2001, A24.
2. For a detailed account of the Reagan administration's process for selecting Supreme Court nominees, see David Yalof, *Pursuit of Justices: Presidential Politics and the Selection of Supreme Court Nominees* (Chicago: University of Chicago Press, 1999), 133–167. The most authoritative account of Reagan's lower court selection process is found in Sheldon Goldman, *Picking Federal Judges: Lower Court Selection from Roosevelt through Reagan* (New Haven: Yale University Press, 1999), 285–345.
3. By contrast, the Reagan administration enjoyed relatively greater discretion to place such ideologically conservative luminaries as Robert Bork, Antonin Scalia, and James Buckley on the D.C. Circuit because there were no senators from D.C. to stand in its way.
4. Sheldon Goldman et al., "W. Bush's Judiciary: The First Term Record," *Judicature,* May–June 2005, 246–247.
5. Lee Epstein and Jeffrey Segal, *Advice and Consent* (New York: Oxford University Press, 2005), 77.

6. Brannon Denning, "The Judicial Confirmation Process and the Blue Slip," *Judicature,* March–April 2002, 222.

7. Slotnick's study is cited in Denning, "The Judicial Confirmation Process and the Blue Slip," 221. Although the exact date of the blue slip system's establishment is unknown, a memorandum prepared by the Judiciary Committee staff in 1979 noted that the blue slip system had been around for more than a quarter of a century. Denning, "The Judicial Confirmation Process and the Blue Slip," 220. See also Stephen B. Burbank, "Politics, Privilege and Power: The Senate's Role in the Appointment of Federal Judges," *Judicature,* July–August 2002, 28–33.

8. The switch to a Democratic-controlled Senate Judiciary Committee in May 2001 put Hatch's changes on hold for the time being. But when he reassumed the chair of the committee in 2003, he was determined to follow this new practice. Specifically, Hatch proceeded to hold hearings on the nomination of Carolyn Kuhl to the Ninth Circuit, despite objections (and a withheld blue slip) by Sen. Barbara Boxer, D-Calif. The senior Democratic senator from California, Dianne Feinstein, announced her opposition to Kuhl only later in the process.

9. The first instance of this practice occurred in 2004, when the Judiciary Committee proceeded to a vote on the nomination of Henry Saad to the U.S. Court of Appeals for the Sixth Circuit. Saad was opposed by both of Michigan's senators, Carl Levin and Debbie Stabenow, both Democrats.

10. Amy Goldstein, "Bush Curtails ABA Role in Selecting U.S. Judges," *Washington Post,* March 23, 2001, A1.

11. Sheldon Goldman et al., "W. Bush Remaking the Judiciary: Like Father Like Son?" *Judicature,* May–June 2003, 290.

12. Thomas B. Edsall, "Federalist Society Becomes a Force in Washington," *Washington Post,* April 18, 2001, A4.

13. Siobhan Gorman, "White House Calculus," *National Journal,* December 11, 2004, 3666.

14. David M. O'Brien, "Judicial Legacies: The Clinton Presidency and the Courts," in *The Clinton Legacy,* ed. Colin Campbell and Bert Rockman (New York: Chatham House, 2000).

15. Sarah Binder et al., "Op Chart: Judicial Confirmation Rates," *New York Times,* May 19, 2005, A27.

16. Gorman, "White House Calculus."

17. Viveca Novak, "The GOP's Judiciary Showdown," *Time,* April 26, 2003.

18. Sheldon Goldman, "The Senate and Judicial Nominations," *Extensions: A Journal of the Carl Albert Congressional Research and Studies Center,* Spring 2004, 9.

19. Bruce Allen Murphy, *Fortas: The Rise and Ruin of a Supreme Court Justice* (New York: William Morrow, 1988), 525.

20. Of course many previous attempts to change the Senate filibuster rule had been defeated in part "because the attempts themselves are vulnerable to filibuster." Norman Ornstein, "The Debate to End All Debate," *New York Times,* May 14, 2003.

21. Norman Ornstein, "Filibuster Redux: Reform Is Needed, but Tread Carefully," *Roll Call,* May 21, 2003.

22. Exhaustive research on "nuclear options" can be found in Gregory Koger, "The Majoritarian Senate: Nuclear Options in Historical Perspective," paper delivered at the 2003 Meeting of the American Political Science Association, Philadelphia.

23. David Yalof, "It's the Supreme Court, Stupid," *Atlanta Journal-Constitution,* November 6, 2003.

24. Daniel Eisenberg, "The Posse in the Pulpit," *Time,* May 16, 2005. A *Time* poll conducted in early May 2005 found that close to 40 percent of respondents said courts had too much power, but almost 60 percent said the filibuster of nominees should not be eliminated.

25. The Gang of Fourteen included twelve senators in addition to Nelson and McCain: Republicans Graham, Warner, Snowe, Collins, DeWine, and Chafee and Democrats Lieberman, Byrd, Landrieu, Inouye, Pryor, and Salazar.

26. Sheldon Goldman, "Assessing the Senate Judicial Confirmation Process: The Index of Obstruction and Delay," *Judicature,* March–April 2003, 257.

27. Binder et al., "Op Chart."

28. Robert Carp, Kenneth Manning, and Ronald Stidham, "The Decisionmaking Behavior of George W. Bush's Judicial Appointees," *Judicature,* July–August 2004, 20–28.

29. 539 U.S. 244 (2003).

30. 539 U.S. 306 (2003).

31. See *Brief for the United States as Amicus Curiae supporting the Petitioner, Grutter v. Bollinger* (U.S. Supreme Court No. 02-241), filed January 2003.

32. For a more general discussion of Clinton's record appointing nontraditional judges, see Rorie Spill and Kathleen Bratton, "Clinton and Diversification of the Federal Judiciary," *Judicature,* March–April 2001, 256–261.

33. Rorie Spill Solberg, "Diversity and George W. Bush's Judicial Appointments: Serving Two Masters," *Judicature,* May–June 2005, 276–283.

34. Ibid., 279–280.

35. Ibid., 280.

36. Speculation about Justice O'Connor's plans only intensified when it was reported that at an election night party in 2000, she had uttered, "This is terrible," in reaction to one network's announcement (as it turns out, a premature one) that the Democrat Al Gore Jr. had won the state of Florida.

37. See Epstein and Segal, *Advice and Consent.* The updated scores for President George W. Bush's first three nominees can be found at http://ws.cc.stonybrook.edu/polsci/jsegal/qualtable.pdf (accessed March 6, 2007).

38. Jeffrey Rosen, "Bottoms Up: Incremental Changes on the Court," *New Republic,* August 1, 2005, 12.

39. Cass Sunstein, "Minimal Appeal," *New Republic,* August 1, 2005, 19.

40. Bill Sammon, "Alito Rejected Abortion as a Right," *Washington Times,* November 14, 2005.

41. That assessment comes from James R. Stoner, "Constitutional Resistance," *Claremont Review of Books* 6 (Summer 2006): 42.

42. Nelson Lund and Craig S. Lerner, "Precedent Bound? We've Stopped Hearing about 'Justices in the Mold of Scalia and Thomas'—and That Could Be Good," *National Review Online,* March 6, 2006.

43. *Hamdan v. Rumsfeld* (U.S. Supreme Court Case No. 05-184, decided June 29, 2006).

CHAPTER 10

Grand Strategy as National Security Policy

Politics, Rhetoric, and the Bush Legacy

Raymond Tanter and Stephen Kersting

THE TERM "GRAND STRATEGY" DESCRIBES how a country plans to use military, political, economic, and ideological means to promote its national interests. Grand strategy as national security policy in the George W. Bush administration has as its rationale to prevent potential attacks on the American homeland from states and nonstate actors with weapons of mass destruction and to protect others against such devastation.[1] Grand strategy as national security policy is bound to occupy a central place in the Bush presidential legacy in foreign affairs because of the September 11, 2001, attacks on the twin towers of the World Trade Center and the Pentagon, hot wars in Afghanistan and Iraq, and sectarian strife and insurgency in Iraq, as well as the Iranian regime's subversion of Iraq and its efforts to acquire nuclear weapons.

Iraq and Iran are central players in the drama of the Bush presidency; hence we give them special attention in this chapter. Important aspects of President Bush's legacy will depend on how he handles these two countries, even more than how he manages the threat from al Qaeda. Although al Qaeda occupied a central place in the U.S. national security debate after 9/11, the relative ease with which the organization has been disrupted and the lack of a serious attack on the U.S. homeland since relegate al Qaeda to a secondary place in the Bush legacy, behind the more enduring problems of state-based threats in Iraq and Iran. Thus far, U.S. policy in Iraq is increasingly seen as a failure, and the likelihood of Iran's acquiring a nuclear weapon is becoming more palpable. North Korea ranks as a lower-order threat compared with Iraq and Iran, but Pyongyang's success in acquiring nuclear weapons further undermines the Bush legacy. Because the imperative of nonproliferation was so vigorously voiced in the rhetoric of the White House, the failure to prevent North Korea's acquisition of nuclear weapons is particularly damaging. However, the spring of 2007, six-party and bilateral talks with North Korea advanced a road map for eventual denuclearization of the Korean peninsula and normalization of U.S.–North Korea relations. If successful, this plan would mitigate the damage done to the Bush legacy. The outcome of U.S. policy in Iran and Iraq should have more important implications for the role of future presidents in the foreign policy arena. The die is cast with respect to failures in Iraq, but the outcome of U.S. policy regarding Iran will depend on President Bush's national security bureaucracy during his last years in office. Hence this analysis of the Bush legacy not only evaluates past decisions but also assesses future policy choices.

Factors that shape doctrine and legacy include (1) the international security environment; (2) the domestic milieu, including bureaucratic, congressional, and public opinion; and (3) presidential leadership in word and deed.

The International Security Environment

Grand strategy emerges from situations: Events drive the policy process. International crises, as high-threat, rapidly evolving, surprise situations, act as policy-forcing events. The perceived magnitude of the danger requires a corresponding response. Short time to respond to a rapidly changing milieu demands immediate action.[2] The shock of surprise allows presidents to cut through the red tape of bureaucratic politics and congressional constraints and to shape public opinion with new strategic doctrine. But presidents must take advantage of the moment afforded by the high-threat, short-time, surprise situation to develop grand strategy. Major crises do not produce grand strategy unless presidents seize the opportunity.

Grand strategy or doctrine plays a substantial part in the legacies of prior presidents.[3] Indeed, the Bush doctrine may be understood in the context of other presidential grand strategies. These have changed as a result of shifts in the milieu. Since the 1930s, the international security environment has evolved from hot wars to cold wars, from state actors to nonstate actors, and from conventional to unconventional threats.

The surprise attack at Pearl Harbor was a high-threat, short-time event that resulted in a hot war. It produced a major transformation of strategy during the administration of President Franklin D. Roosevelt. Though FDR had favored intervention in Europe earlier, the majority of the foreign policy elite only realized after December 7, 1941, that America's geographic isolation did not secure the homeland from attack by foreign aggressors. Roosevelt used the shock of Pearl Harbor to rally American public opinion around the war, not only in Asia but in Europe. Taking the country to war in several theaters was based upon a forward-leaning strategy that reversed the isolationism of the interwar period.

President Truman capitalized upon the momentum of the Roosevelt experience in World War II to transform U.S. defense and intelligence institutions via the National Security Act of 1947. It created the National Security Council, the Department of Defense, and the Central Intelligence Agency. In addition, Truman seized on the Soviet-initiated cold war to craft a strategic doctrine of containment. Instead of retreating into the isolationism of the interwar years, Truman made the case for sustained American involvement around the world as a bulwark against the spread of communism. This strategic posture required the kind of budgetary commitment to defense spending that would have been unthinkable just a decade before. The perception of a high threat at the outset of the cold war allowed Truman to fashion a grand strategy that led public opinion and overcame bureaucratic and congressional hurdles.

As the cold war continued, doctrines enunciated by Presidents Dwight D. Eisenhower and Jimmy Carter stressed containment via deterrence and prevention. In 1957 Eisenhower, as Truman had done, pledged military and economic assistance to anticommunist governments—Europe in the Truman period and the Middle East in the Eisenhower era. President Carter initially rejected the urgency of containment that motivated prior presidents, saying, "We are now free of that inordinate fear of communism which once led us to embrace any dictator who joined us in that fear."[4] But by the fourth year of Carter's presidency in 1980 he extended containment to the Middle East, in what became known as the Carter doctrine: "An attempt by any outside force [the USSR] to gain control of the Persian Gulf region will be regarded as an assault on the vital interests of the United States of America, and such an assault will be repelled by any means necessary, including military force."[5] A 1980 Soviet Command Post Exercise, simulating an invasion of Iran following Moscow's invasion of Afghanistan in 1979, played a role in heightening President Carter's perception of the Soviet threat to the gulf, prompting him to issue the deterrent threat, create a rapid deployment force, and build up American forces in the area.[6]

President Reagan expanded the containment strategy of the Carter approach to emphasize remedy and cure. He provided economic and political support for insurgent movements in an effort to roll back Marxism. Reagan provided aid to anticommunist "freedom fighters" in Afghanistan and Nicaragua. According to the Reagan doctrine, Moscow had to be convinced that Washington would not break faith with those attempting to counter Soviet aggression. Thus, for Roosevelt, Truman, Eisenhower, Carter, and Reagan there was, more or less, a fit between their grand strategies and actions—evidence of coherent presidential leadership.

As the cold war declined, there has been a gradual shift from a superpower-dominated international system to one characterized by rogue regimes and hostile nonstate actors and a corresponding transformation from conventional to unconventional threats. Because there was not a single overarching threat to characterize the post–cold war era, national security policy became a lower-priority item and received proportionately fewer resources. The radicalism behind the 9/11 attacks, however, provided a peril equivalent to the fascist threat during the interwar years and the communist danger during the cold war. As with the Reagan doctrine, the

George W. Bush approach to grand strategy stands for treatment as much as deterrence. President Bush's "cure" consists of actively confronting—even preempting—rogue nations that might acquire weapons of mass destruction and spread them to hostile nonstate entities and/or sponsor terrorism, as opposed to relying solely on deterrence. Reagan intended to reverse Soviet advances in Afghanistan by supporting freedom fighters there; Bush explicitly brought about regime change by toppling the Taliban in Afghanistan and Saddam Hussein in Iraq. Moreover, Bush implicitly called for regime change in Iran, by announcing his support for the Iranian people to determine their own future in his 2006 State of the Union address and pledging to fight against Iranian interference in Iraq in a January 2007 speech on Iraq.

Although there is a gap between doctrine and actions, George W. Bush has instigated the broadest reformulation of U.S. grand strategy since the presidency of Franklin D. Roosevelt, again based on the shock of a surprise attack. Indeed, 9/11 may have been an even greater shock than Pearl Harbor because the assaults occurred against civilian targets on the mainland of America, as opposed to the earlier attack on Hawaii military installations. September 11 made clear that the United States was threatened, even within its own territory, and rendered moot several strategic reassessments occurring at the time. It called for a radical reevaluation of strategy, the outcome of which was the Bush doctrine.

The 9/11 attacks demonstrated that religiously inspired terrorists seek to kill unlimited numbers of civilians, a departure from past terrorism in which groups calibrated their violence to avoid a backlash. The coincidence of rogue nations hostile to the United States building weapons of mass destruction (WMD) dramatically increased the urgency of this new threat of global terrorism.

The George W. Bush administration, accordingly, has expanded the use of "rogue state" language, largely to justify missile defense and mobilize democratic allies and friendly states in the war on terrorism. This approach is in many ways a return to the ideologically charged language of Ronald Reagan and the cold war idiom of anticommunism. Although the Soviet nuclear threat to the United States was orders of magnitude greater than that posed by rogue states, the latter peril may be more dangerous because rogue leaders might not be as deterrable as the Soviet leadership was.

The Domestic Milieu

In addition to the international security environment, domestic considerations help shape strategic doctrine. Despite an increase in the attention President Bush paid to foreign affairs after the 9/11 attacks and the spike in his ideological rhetoric, he relied more on his cabinet principals for decision making than many prior occupants of the Oval Office. He was more of a rhetorical warrior, leaving it to strong cabinet officials to implement that hot rhetoric. In view of the president's lack of information and inattention to foreign affairs, discussion of the Bush legacy should take into account bureaucratic politics as part of the domestic milieu.

Bureaucratic Politics

Bureaucratic rivalry between the Departments of State and Defense is legendary. Although the State Department has authority for the formulation of foreign policy and use of diplomacy, Defense has the resources to create and execute security policy, especially when military forces may be used. The Pentagon is inclined to focus on locating and destroying enemy forces, whereas Foggy Bottom prefers that resources be directed toward reconstruction. But without strong leadership from 1600 Pennsylvania Avenue, there is a vacuum at the intersection of diplomacy and force.

The bureaucracies of State and Defense are large and demonstrate a high degree of inertia. Those who head the Departments of State and Defense have enormous tasks in coordinating their own bureaucracies, have little incentive to coordinate with one another, and often see one another as rivals. In the context of strong coordination by the National Security Council (NSC) staff in the Executive Office of the President, contentious relationships between State and Defense can be mediated to produce effective decision making. Without such coordination, however, dire consequences are likely.

Bureaucratic rivalry is a product of the structure of the U.S. government and is, when controlled, helpful in representing a spectrum of opinion on a given issue. After taking into account conflicting views, the key to managing this relationship is to decide on a course of action and bring organizations to heel in its execution. The only authority that can successfully exercise such leadership is the White House, though it does not always do so.

Like President Bush, President Clinton had little experience with foreign affairs and preferred to focus on the economy. And like Bush, Clinton also failed to coordinate issues of diplomacy and force. He considered the State Department and secretary of state Madeleine Albright the "first among equals" in the National Security Council. However, President Clinton's secretary of defense, William Cohen, would later say that Secretary Albright's judgment regarding the use of aerial bombing to coerce Serbia to halt its campaign against ethnic Albanians in Kosovo was unrealistic.

According to the view of Secretary Albright and her bureaucratic allies, Serb leader Slobodan Milosevic would surrender after only three days of bombing; but the war dragged on for over seventy days. Secretary Cohen argued that the State Department's desire to please NATO allies dictated the more limited mission, while his warnings to the contrary were disregarded. Instead, the U.S. military quietly had to draw up more comprehensive bombing plans out of sight of NATO's reluctant members.[7] Had there been better White House coordination between State and

Defense, perhaps a cost-effective plan for the execution of the air campaign might have emerged. Clinton's tilt toward Albright probably precluded the diversity of opinion necessary to facilitate effective policymaking.

Lack of effective management would soon recur in the Bush administration. Bush's aloofness had a greater negative effect because the stakes were higher during his tenure. When competing opinions from secretary of state Colin Powell and secretary of defense Donald Rumsfeld were aired during National Security Council meetings, there often was no resolution of differences. *Washington Post* editor Bob Woodward describes National Security Council sessions in which Powell and Rumsfeld talked past one another and never debated the issues, while the president's "legs often jiggled under the table."[8] General Tommy Franks, former commander of the U.S. Central Command, lamented that if anything could have been done differently, it would have been for Secretaries Powell and Rumsfeld to have their departments work more closely, implying the need for strong White House direction. As Richard Perle laments, "Bush did not make decisions, in part because the machinery of government that he nominally ran was actually running him."[9]

After the 9/11 attacks there was enough urgency to overcome some of the bureaucratic rivalries and converge on a more-or-less coherent rhetorical approach to national security policy and on the necessity of ousting the Taliban in Afghanistan, though there were serious differences between Defense and the CIA on the conduct of the Afghanistan war.

In the case of Iraq, where there was less urgency and where long-term goals were far less clear than in Afghanistan, very different conceptions of ends and means germinated among different bureaucracies. After September 11, 2001, Secretary Powell took a different perspective from the other principals regarding Iraq. Within the first days after the 9/11 attacks, it was Secretary Powell's efforts that persuaded the war cabinet to forgo regime change in Iraq and focus on Afghanistan. Iraq became the focal point of the fissure between Secretary Powell and others in the war cabinet. There was a high degree of tension between Powell and a subcabinet official, deputy secretary of defense Paul Wolfowitz, who conceived of the war on terror as the vehicle for spreading democracy by force. Powell, in the realist tradition, opposed making the spread of American values via force a pillar of foreign policy. He recognized the goal as both inappropriate and unachievable.

There was also disagreement over how the United States conducted diplomacy before going to war with Iraq, with Powell often the only dissenting voice in the National Security Council. Many in the Bush administration had written off the United Nations for its ineffectiveness in dealing with Iraq in the past and did not want the pursuit of UN approval to interfere with war plans. Powell, along with his British counterpart, Jack Straw, exerted maximum pressure to forestall the beginning of the war to build whatever consensus was possible at the UN. Powell's efforts to build consensus were at times undermined. The secretary of state insisted that a call for a new resolution demanding Iraq's compliance with the United Nations be included in President Bush's address to the UN on September 12, 2002, despite the objections of Vice President Dick Cheney, who was aligned closely with Secretary Rumsfeld within the Bush administration. Powell was shocked as he read through the speech that morning to find that the agreed-upon language regarding further resolutions had been deleted.[10]

Powell was also the lead dissenter on the treatment of al Qaeda and Taliban prisoners. Vice President Cheney, Secretary Rumsfeld, and the White House legal counsel did not believe the prisoners should be protected under the Geneva Convention, since they did not fight as uniformed military personnel. Powell pointed out the danger that could befall U.S. troops in the future if the United States denied Geneva protections. On the detainee decision, the president overruled his secretary of state, but Powell was vindicated by the Supreme Court's decision in *Hamdan v. Rumsfeld,* in June 2006, and when the Bush administration modified its detainee policies in the face of the midterm elections of November 2006. In *Hamdan v. Rumsfeld,* the Supreme Court ruled that the special military tribunals established to try detainees at Guantanamo Bay were illegal and violated both the Uniform Code of Military Justice and the 1949 Geneva Convention.[11]

Such differences at the highest level became disastrous in the execution of the Iraq war. Contrasting priorities resulted in a mismatch of goals and means. Despite his reluctance to spread democracy by the sword, Secretary Powell argued that if the U.S. government were to authorize an invasion of Iraq, reconstruction was absolutely necessary. Powell's evaluation is summed up in the notorious Pottery Barn rule: "You break it, you buy it." If the United States was going to remove the existing government of Iraq, Powell argued, Washington would be obligated to devote the resources necessary to rebuild the country and put an effective government in place. Two interdependent themes underlie Powell's thinking. The first is the principal aspect of what became known as the Powell doctrine—if a decision was made to intervene militarily, overwhelming force must be deployed and employed. The second is implicit in the first principle—when disproportionately large force is used, existing institutions in a target country will be destroyed, and the United States must be prepared to engage in postwar reconstruction.

Cheney and Rumsfeld never quite accepted such a broad nation-building mission. In any event, U.S. government planning for postwar Iraq had been disorganized and insufficient until December 2002. According to Bob Woodward, Rumsfeld only accelerated postwar planning when he was informed that a failure to exercise leadership over the postwar planning process could cost President Bush reelection, and even then, he did a poor job of it.[12] Secretary Rumsfeld sharply disagreed with those in the military, such as army chief of staff Eric Shinseki who, in agreement with the Powell doctrine, suggested that more troops were necessary to saturate Iraq with enough forces to prevent disorder in the aftermath of the war.

President Bush's reluctance to overrule National Security Council principals allowed Rumsfeld, with the Secretary of Defense's superior resources and command over the military, to proceed largely as he saw fit. Rumsfeld's freedom of action was enhanced by Vice President Cheney's support. When the need to continue most of the rank-and-file Iraqi military personnel on the payroll after the fall of Saddam Hussein came to the president for decision, he shrugged off the issue, indicating that the choice was up to Rumsfeld.[13] The decision to disband the Iraqi military was later recognized as a serious mistake that created a critical mass of former soldiers with grievances against both the Coalition Provisional Authority and, later, the government of Iraq.

President Bush essentially had three choices in the execution of the Iraq war. He could have accepted the broad mission that Powell argued was necessary, taken the advice of the uniformed military, and overruled Rumsfeld by deploying more U.S. troops. Second, Bush could have sided with Rumsfeld's narrower definition of the mission, approved the corresponding force levels, and overruled Powell by avoiding the sort of large occupation that could provoke an Iraqi backlash. Bush took a third choice, which amounted to not choosing at all. He trumpeted the lofty goals of democratizing and reconstructing Iraqi society, and yet he allowed Rumsfeld to devote insufficient resources and planning. The result of that failure to choose is an Iraq that is vulnerable to Iranian-inspired violence and moving away from the goals of stability and democracy, with hundreds of thousands of U.S. soldiers at risk. Although Powell and Rumsfeld have been blamed by supporters of each official, the buck really stops at the Oval Office, where the president neither reined in his cabinet officers nor chose among them in a way that would allow for a consistent strategy.

Public Opinion and Congressional Politics

Besides bureaucratic politics, other domestic constraints within which presidents must navigate are public opinion and congressional politics. As President Bush delivered his State of the Union address of January 23, 2007, a *Washington Post*/ABC News poll found confidence in his leadership at an all-time low. At 33 percent, the president's overall approval rating matched the lowest it had been in such polls since he took office in 2001. He had an overall disapproval rating of 65 percent. It is noteworthy that 51 percent of Americans polled strongly disapproved of his performance in office, the worst rating of his presidency. Only 17 percent strongly approved of the manner in which Bush handled the presidency as of January 2007. By way of comparison, only two other presidents have had lower approval ratings on the eve of a State of the Union address: Harry S. Truman was at 23 percent in January 1952, because of disapproval of the Korean War; Richard Nixon was at 26 percent in 1974, seven months prior to resigning because of the Watergate scandal.[14]

President Bush's poor public opinion ratings redounded to the benefit of the Democrats in the November 2006 midterm elections. In control of both houses of Congress since January 2007, congressional Democrats are seeking to constrain President Bush's leeway regarding foreign policy generally and Iraq in particular.

Presidential Leadership: Hot Words and Ineffective Deeds

A third driver of strategic doctrine is presidential leadership, in particular the fit between rhetoric from the White House and implementing actions by the bureaucracy. At the time he was deciding to run for president, Governor George W. Bush had a limited knowledge of foreign policy. His lack of experience contrasted sharply with the background of his father, George H. W. Bush, who was a seasoned diplomat and former director of central intelligence. After recruiting Stanford professor Condoleezza Rice as his principal foreign policy adviser for the 2000 presidential campaign, Governor Bush reportedly told her, "I don't have any idea about foreign affairs. This isn't what I do."[15] Initially in the Bush administration, the president seemed content to allow the foreign policy team he had assembled, the self-described "Vulcans," to run national security policy with little intervention.[16] For example, although reform of the Defense Department was a major aspect of President Bush's campaign, the mechanics were left almost completely to Secretary of Defense Rumsfeld. As with presidents past, a high-threat, short-time, and traumatic surprise event was an invitation for strong presidential leadership, which came in the form of words but not deeds.

The sense of urgency created by the 9/11 attacks and emergence of a new, unpredictable, terrorist threat from radical Islamists potentially armed with weapons of mass destruction allowed the Bush administration to reformulate U.S. national security policy in a way that would not otherwise have been possible. To thwart a second attack, President Bush and his national security team crafted a new strategy that emphasized preemption: The United States will act, either in concert or alone, to neutralize threats to its security before they can fully materialize. Outlined in the 2002 *National Security Strategy of the United States of America,* this approach, more commonly known as the Bush doctrine, has four principal components:

- It allows for preemptive military action against hostile states and terrorist organizations.
- It calls for American military primacy to be maintained: The United States will not allow its military power to be challenged.
- While expressing America's commitment to multilateralism, it nevertheless cautions that the United States will act unilaterally if circumstances warrant.
- It declares America's goal of promoting democracy and human rights.[17]

The most significant and controversial features of the Bush doctrine, and those that distinguish it from previous national security policies, are its insistence on the right of the United States to "anticipatory self-defense," or preemption, and the need to spread democracy, by force if necessary. Both of these features are highly contentious, in large part because they appear to reject realism as well as diplomacy and to espouse unilateralism. They are a crux of debate among pundits and theorists.

An example is the debate between journalist Charles Krauthammer and political scientist Francis Fukuyama about the manner in which American values are promoted in the interest of national security. Krauthammer's "democratic realism" approach to foreign policy holds that the use of military force to depose despots and promote democracy is the way to uproot conditions that foster radical ideologies. Although Krauthammer acknowledged in a 2004 American Enterprise Institute lecture that the Iraq war "may have been a bridge too far," he also maintains that the war was absolutely necessary. The establishment of comprehensive democracy in Iraq may be an unlikely outcome of American efforts, but Krauthammer argues that deposing Saddam Hussein was the only viable alternative to allowing despotism in the Middle East to continue fueling radicalism.[18]

In contrast, Fukuyama is one of the most emphatic critics of the Bush doctrine, and he takes particular issue with Krauthammer. Fukuyama believes that so-called neoconservatism, or what Krauthammer would call "democratic realism," is hopelessly optimistic regarding the prospects for spreading democracy via military power. Though Fukuyama believes that the promotion of democratic ideals is worthwhile, he argues that using force toward such ends is counterproductive. Iraq is his case in point: Not only has the establishment of democracy been incomplete, to say the least, but admiration of America around the world has been set back.[19]

From the perspective of the Bush administration, preemption and democracy promotion are vital to American national security; they are essential instruments to combat Islamist terrorism and the proliferation of WMD, as well as to compensate for the inefficacy of international organizations, which lack the resolve and capabilities the United States possesses. Preemption prevents potential threats from coming to fruition; spreading democracy aims to eliminate those factors that feed Islamism by creating additional pro-American governments that also are ideologically aligned with the United States. In this respect, the Bush doctrine is a slight departure from policies of prior administrations.

Yet the Bush approach to outlaw states also builds on previous presidential doctrines and hence benefits from continuity of purpose and wide public understanding of its concepts. The Bush doctrine's ambitious words call for replacing states that engage in weapons proliferation and sponsor terrorism with peaceful democracies, in keeping with democratic peace theory: democracies rarely do battle with each other.[20] And given the significant benefits and minimal costs of employing "rogue state" language, as well as the promise of democratic peace, the Bush administration is likely to continue using such rhetoric, difficulties of the Iraq war notwithstanding.

During George W. Bush's first term, administration officials tended to treat states in general rather than specific terms. They defined "rogue regimes" as state sponsors of international terrorism and/or proliferators of weapons of mass destruction. The use of "axis of evil" terminology, while providing the advantages of charged rhetoric, was a slight misnomer, as Iraq under Saddam Hussein, the Islamic Republic of Iran, and North Korea were governed by different types of regimes that require different approaches. Although North Korea and Iran share similarities, there are also differences. One is a totalitarian communist state; the other Islamist-fascist; yet they both deserve harsh language. No longer is Tehran to be labeled a "rogue regime" purely because of terrorism and proliferation of WMD. An extremist ideology—Islamism—reinforces terrorist sponsorship and proliferation to make the Iranian regime an unacceptable threat. Although North Korea has developed a nuclear capacity and has used terrorism in the past, North Korea is much less of a threat because of its record of using WMD development only as a bargaining chip and its departure from terrorist activities since the 1980s.

More broadly, the Bush doctrine has become part of an intense international debate about America's role in the world. Its opponents cite poll data that indicate growing international disapproval of U.S. foreign policy. According to a January 2007, BBC poll, "Across the 25 countries polled, 49 percent of respondents said the U.S. played a mainly negative role in the world." Furthermore, "29 percent of people said the U.S. had a positive influence, down from 36 percent last year and 40 percent two years ago."[21] International disapproval of American foreign policy is a problem to be managed, but it does not completely discredit elements of the Bush doctrine. Being unpopular in the short term may be a necessary consequence of the proactive, sometimes unilateral requirements of the war on terrorism in general and Iraq in particular. Furthermore, not all Bush administration policies are met with the same level of disapproval. The Iraq war stands out as the most distasteful of U.S. policies in the BBC poll, indicating that administration mismanagement is partly responsible for the international backlash, not only the unilateralist elements of the Bush doctrine.

At stake is the overall U.S. strategy for protecting and promoting its security, values, and national interests. President Franklin D. Roosevelt was able to devise a grand strategy that played down unilateralism and preemption but established unilateral prerogatives through a multilateral framework to institutionalize American wartime dominance. Citing historical antecedents, cold war historian John Lewis Gaddis notes that "when President George W. Bush warned, at West Point in June 2002, that Americans must be ready for preemptive action when necessary to defend our liberty and to defend our lives, he was echoing an old tradition rather than establishing a new one. Adams, Jackson, Polk, McKinley, Roosevelt, Taft, and Wilson would all have understood it perfectly well."[22]

The manner in which American values are promoted in the pursuit of national interests, whether unilaterally or multilaterally, whether preemptively or not, will help define the foreign policy legacy of President Bush. Presidential speeches are windows into the policies by which the occupant of the Oval Office leaves a mark on history; they are signals to both domestic and international audiences. As such, speeches offer analysts an opportunity to look within the policymaking process. It is worth examining, then, the language that President Bush has used in his public remarks.

Analysis of Bush Doctrine Language

Major foreign policy speeches are vehicles for enunciating new foreign policy priorities or reinforcing existing ones. The following analysis is a quantitative study of foreign policy statements of President George W. Bush. For the study the authors combed State of the Union and other speeches for certain terms, such as "terrorism" and "rogue state." We assumed that the frequency of these terms corresponds to the priority given them by the Bush administration.[23] Thus, by measuring their frequency over time, and taking context into account, we can shed light on how the Bush administration's view of the world has changed. Context is important regarding the use of such phrases as "axis of evil." That term occurs only once in a major speech of the president; nonetheless phrases like these are critical for defining the threat perception of the Bush administration because they single-handedly illustrate a broad shift in policy toward several adversaries.

State of the Union 2001.   In President Bush's first State of the Union address of February 2001, before 9/11, he focused lightly on national security issues, such as war, defense, and terrorism. The president spoke of "emerging threats," ranging from "terrorists who threaten with bombs to tyrants in rogue-nations intent upon delivering weapons of mass destruction." Although the president's use of "rogue nations" suggested a tough approach to dealing with dangerous governments and countries, his rhetoric reflects a pre-9/11 mindset. He did not systematically link rogue regimes to terrorists, and the threat of weapons of mass destruction stems more from nation-states than terrorist networks. Yet that would soon change with the September 11, 2001, attacks.

The 9/11 Address.   The assaults of September 11, 2001, shocked the world and allowed President Bush to ratchet up his rhetoric. As a starter, the president used the word "terror" or its variants thirty-three times in the September 20 speech to the nation about these events. When speaking about what motivates terrorists he also introduced a concept that he termed "Islamic extremism," which would evolve over the course of his presidency. Bush implied, but did not state explicitly, that such extremism—Islamism as used here—is the main threat to the United States. Bush also named the terrorist group he thought responsible for the atrocities of 9/11, mentioning al Qaeda six times in his speech, though he referred to Osama bin Laden by name only once. Such reticence might be prudent, to refrain from overplaying the importance of bin Laden versus states that provided him safe harbor and those that might transfer weapons of mass destruction. The White House downplayed bin Laden's importance as an individual and focused on state sponsors.

The president introduced the nation to the idea that the United States is entering a "war on terror." Bush framed this war by explaining that the "enemies of freedom committed an act of war" against the United States. He noted that enemies in this war on terror are the "radical network of terrorists, and every government that supports them." Bush explained that in the war on terrorism any nation that provides "aid or safe haven to terrorism" or "continues to harbor or support terrorism" or "supports them [terrorists]" will be regarded as a "hostile regime."

Initially, Bush treated the ideology that motivates terrorists in general terms. He spoke about other "murderous ideologies of the twentieth century," such as fascism, Nazism, and totalitarianism. He framed the battles with terrorists in terms of previous conflicts; indeed, as detailed below, he only began to describe more fully the ideology that drives the terrorists he faces in speeches during 2005.

State of the Union 2002–2007.   For an illustration of the proportion of words that constitute the Bush grand strategy, see Figure 10.1. It contains the frequency of occurrence for key concepts mentioned in the State of the Union addresses of 2002, 2006, and 2007. The president's rhetoric in the State of the Union of 2002 focused on the war on terror. In contrast to its counterpart a year earlier, which devoted very little space to war, defense, and terrorism, approximately three-quarters of the post-9/11 State of the Union address was devoted to such issues. The rhetoric in this speech shared several similarities in language with the 9/11 speech and introduced one important new concept, the "axis of evil."

The president used the word "terror" or its variants thirty-six times in the State of the Union of 2002. Speaking of Iran, Iraq, and North Korea, the president said that states "like these, and their terrorist allies, constitute an axis of evil, arming to threaten the peace of the world."[24] Bush's remarks thus brought to mind the Axis of World War II—Nazi Germany, fascist Italy, and imperial Japan—as well as President Ronald Reagan's description of the Soviet Union as an "evil empire."[25]

The 2002 State of the Union marked the first time President Bush targeted Iran directly in a major speech. Although just one sentence long, the president's language was direct and strong when he stated, "Iran aggressively pursues these weapons [of mass destruction] and exports terror, while an unelected few repress the Iranian

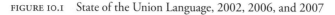

FIGURE 10.1   State of the Union Language, 2002, 2006, and 2007

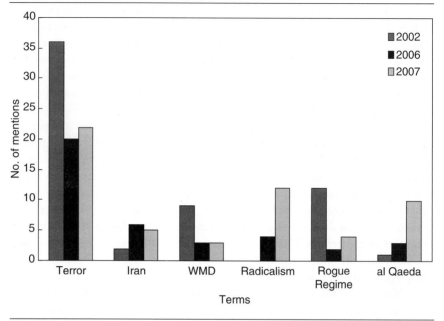

people's hope for freedom." Just as in the case of "axis of evil," which only occurred once in a major speech, mention of Iran only one time in a speech registers low on frequency but has high relevance to the president's characterization of the threat because of its stark contrast to previous statements regarding Iran.

The president reiterated hostile rhetoric toward the Iranian regime in the State of the Union of 2003: "In Iran, we continue to see a government that represses its people, pursues weapons of mass destruction, and supports terror." But he took it further than before in speaking of supporting Iranian "aspirations to live in freedom." Although not suggesting how the United States would support the Iranian people, this speech marked the first time the president at least vaguely expressed solidarity with Iranians against the regime, implicitly calling for change of the regime in Tehran. But unless he also calls for empowering the Iranian people by enabling their main opposition groups to function against the regime, this lofty rhetoric does not translate into democratic regime change in Tehran.

In the 2004 State of the Union address, the president dropped references about standing with the Iranian people. Instead, Bush demanded that "Iran meet its commitments and not develop nuclear weapons." He further noted that "America is committed to keeping the world's most dangerous weapons out of the hands of the most dangerous regimes," an implicit reference to Iran and North Korea. In 2005 he mentioned "working with European allies to make clear to the Iranian regime that it must give up its uranium enrichment program and any plutonium reprocessing, and end its support for terror." In this formulation, the president prefers to work with allies but retains the option of unilateral action. This shift in language from 2004 to 2005 may be due to increased influence of regional specialists at the Department of State, who reflect the views of European allies in dealing with Iran during 2005. Enhanced reliance on diplomacy to prevent a nuclear-armed Iran from coming into being may result as well from the perceived weak strategic position of the United States, in the face of growing insurgency and sectarian violence in Iraq.

Nonetheless, as 2007 begins, speculation abounds about possible military action against the Iranian regime because of its successful efforts to destabilize Iraq via aid to radical militias responsible for killing American and British soldiers. The 2005 formulation, "standing with the Iranian people," returned in the 2007 State of the Union address, in which the president promised, "As you [the Iranian people] stand for your own liberty, America stands with you." Regime change for Iran is back on the table.

Speech at the National Endowment for Democracy, October 6, 2005. The National Endowment for Democracy address provided a strong expression of the Bush doctrine. The speech linked Iran and Syria with al Qaeda because these two countries allow foreign fighters to enter Iraq, some of whom are associated with al Qaeda. The speech was recognition that Iraq's insurgency does not exist in a vacuum but is partly a consequence of the actions of troublesome neighbors. The address implied that the way to stabilize Iraq is to clean up the neighborhood. The speech states that the United States is "determined to deny radical groups the support and sanctuary of outlaw regimes." In addition, the president argued, "State sponsors like Syria and Iran have a long history of collaboration with terrorists and they deserve no patience from the victims of terror. The United States makes no distinction between those who commit acts of terror and those who support and harbor terrorists, because they are equally guilty of murder." That sentence from the National Endowment for Democracy (NED) address is a threat to bring about regime change in Damascus and Tehran by extending the Bush doctrine against terrorist groups to state sponsors of terrorism.

But the 2005 NED address may not reflect the views of the permanent bureaucracy at State, Defense, and the CIA; if not, it is doubtful that the speech represented a change from existing policies. The address then would only represent views of globalists and speechwriters at the White House, rather than policy input from the bureaucracy, which comprises realists and regionalists. As suggested above, this tug-of-war between globalists at the White House and realists in the departments and agencies is typical of other presidencies, but such pulling and hauling is especially apparent in the administration of George W. Bush because of his strong ideological stance. An offer to Tehran of direct negotiations with the European allies over its nuclear program is also evidence of a division between regionally oriented bureaucrats and global thinkers. In this regard, globalists were quick to blame under secretary of state for political affairs R. Nicholas Burns, for being "too ready to compromise with Iran."[26]

In the NED speech, rhetoric about the war on terror evolved dramatically. New vocabulary was introduced such as "militant Jihadism," "Islamist-fascism," and "militants." Conversely, vocabulary that had almost vanished saw a resurgence. For example, the president mentioned "radical beliefs" twelve times in the National Endowment for Democracy speech, whereas during the previous four years he mentioned this phrase only four times in total. The same October 2005 speech also contains the second presidential use of the term, "Islamo-fascism," which we call in this chapter "Islamist fascism." The global war on terrorism, then, is redefined as a war against extremism and terrorism, as well as "outlaw regimes," which are linked not through active ties as much as via radical ideologies. "The followers of Islamic radicalism are bound together by their shared ideology," the president said, "not by any centralized command structure."

Furthermore, in his rhetoric the president brought together this global war and the Bush administration's democracy initiatives in the Middle East: "We are denying the militants future recruits by advancing democracy and hope across the broader Middle East."[27] In so doing, Bush revised the "axis of evil" group from the original list: North Korea, Iraq replaced by Syria, and Iran serving double duty: "In pursuit of their goals, Islamic radicals are empowered by helpers and enablers. They are sheltered and supported by authoritarian regimes—allies of convenience like Syria and Iran—that share the goal of hurting America and moderate Muslim governments, and that use terrorist propaganda to blame their own failures on the West, America, and Jews."

National Security Strategy 2002 and 2006.   Another rhetorical evolution takes place in administration documents. President Bush's *National Security Strategy* of 2006 builds on, yet differs from, his plan laid out in 2002. Most notably, in 2006 Bush gives far more attention to Iran, ideology, and rogue regimes than in 2002. With the more frequent use of adversary-related language in 2006, Bush's perceptions of threat were made more explicit. For instance, in 2006 Bush stated, "Yet a new totalitarian ideology now threatens, an ideology not grounded in a secular philosophy, but in the perversion of a proud religion."[28] This identification of Islamist fascism as a threat to the United States stands in stark contrast to the 2002 *National Security Strategy,* which downplayed ideology. In 2002 Bush had stated, "The enemy is not a single political regime or person or religion or ideology."[29] Bush's perception evolved from ignoring the threat posed by radical, religiously fueled ideology to identifying outright the intersection of totalitarianism with radical Islam as the threat of the day. This threat perception signified the rise of Islamist fascism as a major concern of the White House. Furthermore, although Bush mentioned Iran only a single time in 2002, he named Iran sixteen times in 2006 and al Qaeda ten times. To these totals add the many instances where political rhetoric did not favor directly identifying threats by name and where the president identified Iran and al Qaeda as "terrorists" or "rogue regimes."

From 2002 to 2006, Bush increased his use of the word "terror" by roughly 44 percent, from eighty-six mentions in 2002 to 124 in 2006. However, Bush increased his use of "rogue regime"–type language by 252 percent from 2002 to 2006, increasing from twenty-three mentions in 2002 to eighty-one in 2006. By all indicators, the Iranian regime has progressively grown as a danger in the judgment of the White House. Such quantitative increases reinforce qualitative analysis of single statements made by Bush that openly denounce Iran as a grave threat. Indeed, whereas in 2002 Iran received only one, less-ominous mention, Bush escalated his rhetoric dramatically in 2006. "We may face no greater challenge from a single country," the president intoned, "than from Iran."[30]

January 2007 Address to the Nation on Iraq.   In the 2005 National Endowment for Democracy address, President Bush had targeted Iran and Syria as sources of post-Saddam instability in Iraq, laying down a marker for his subsequent speech to the nation on Iraq on January 10, 2007. In that speech, the president upped the ante again:

> Succeeding in Iraq also requires defending its territorial integrity and stabilizing the region in the face of extremist challenges. This begins with addressing Iran and Syria. These two regimes are allowing terrorists and insurgents to use their territory to move in and out of Iraq. Iran is providing material support for attacks on American troops. We will disrupt the attacks on our forces. We'll interrupt the flow of support from Iran and Syria. And we will seek out and destroy the networks providing advanced weaponry and training to our enemies in Iraq.[31]

The president's language in the January 2007 address on Iraq went beyond the vague descriptions of Iranian and Syrian threats in earlier speeches and documents. It identified Iranian and Syrian interference in the operational context of violence in Iraq. Linking Iran to "extremist challenges" was a further step in the direction of labeling the Iranian regime Islamist-fascist, though Bush weakened the ideological case for such designation by placing Syria (a secular authoritarian regime) and Iran in the same category.

The January 2007 address came on the heels of a U.S. raid of the Baghdad compound belonging to Abdul Aziz al-Hakim, leader of the Supreme Council of the Islamic Revolution in Iraq. Along with eight Iraqis, two Iranian nationals were arrested by U.S. forces.[32] The address was also followed almost immediately by the arrest by U.S. Special Operations Forces of several Iranian members of the Qods (Jerusalem) Force of the Islamic Revolutionary Guards Corps in the Iraqi city of Irbil, who were alleged to be involved in fueling sectarian conflict.[33] President Bush's speech and corresponding actions by U.S. forces indicate a greater awareness of the Iranian threat and an enhanced willingness to confront agents of the Iranian regime in Iraq.

State of the Union 2007.   Just two weeks after the Iraq speech, on January 23, the president took another firm line on Iraq and Iran in his 2007 State of the Union address. As in the Iraq speech the president singled out Iran for its destabilizing role in Iraq: "Radical Shia elements, some of whom receive support from Iran, formed death squads. The result was a tragic escalation of sectarian rage and reprisal that continues to this day." President Bush went on to advocate a surge of more than 20,000 U.S. soldiers to Iraq, mostly to Baghdad, to help the Iraqis counter such radicals.[34]

Despite the president's commitment to a troop surge for Iraq, domestic constraints may again prevent rhetoric from being translated into effective action. Out of about sixty interruptions by applause, only six came during the president's remarks on Iraq, which represented about one-quarter of the speech.[35] Furthermore, the next day (January 24) the Senate Foreign Relations Committee formalized its opposition in a resolution declaring that the suggested troop surge was not in "the national interest."[36] Although such a resolution could not block the president's deployment of additional troops to Iraq, it exerts a great deal of pressure on him to ensure that the surge of forces achieves results quickly.

The Bush Doctrine: Looking Forward

This analysis reveals evolution in the themes underlying the Bush doctrine, especially in recognizing the ideology motivating terrorists and its connection to rogue states. Take, for example, the description in the October 2005, National Endowment for Democracy address:

> Some call this evil Islamic radicalism; others, militant Jihadism; still others, Islamo-fascism. Whatever it's called, this ideology is very different from the religion of Islam. This form of radicalism exploits Islam to serve a violent, political vision: the establishment, by terrorism and subversion and insurgency, of a totalitarian empire that denies all political and religious freedom.

A president that questions Israel's right to exist, a president that denies the Holocaust cannot think that Germany has even the slightest degree of tolerance. We have learned from our history.

Looking back to the German history in the early 1930s when National Socialism was on the rise there were many outside Germany who said it is only rhetoric[;] don't get excited. There were times when people could have reacted differently, and in my point of view, Germany is obliged to do something at the early stages.[40]

If a U.S. president were to take as bold a stand as the German chancellor, such rhetoric may be the first step in American action to empower the Iranian people to change the Iranian regime.

Conclusions

Analysis of words and deeds underlying the Bush doctrine suggests that the 9/11 attacks, threats from weapons of mass destruction in the hands of failed and rogue states, as well as suicide terrorism, all provide a rationale for the Bush grand strategy. Assaults in New York and Washington, as well as the March 11, 2004, train bombing in Madrid, attacks in London, and assaults in Turkey, Indonesia, and the Philippines are evidence of a deadly and growing threat. The danger comes not only from fanatical terrorist groups, but also from tyrannies that support terrorism, as well as those that seek weapons of mass destruction. The willingness of terrorists to carry out attacks causing mass casualties—in the case of 9/11, directed at two of the most powerful symbols of America's commercial and government life—poses a great and unambiguous danger. Terrorist organizations, such as al Qaeda, are an immediate threat to the United States, are not deterred by fear of U.S. retaliation, and would seize the opportunity to kill millions of Americans if WMD could effectively be used on American soil. Thus 9/11 explains the need for a proactive campaign to eliminate terrorists and a proclaimed approach toward state sponsors of terrorism that would deter those states from pursuing WMD or cooperating with terrorists in the first place.

President Bush's involvement in foreign policy has varied from active leadership, in the formation of the Bush doctrine, to passivity, and that passive approach is partly responsible for failures in Iraq and an uncertain approach toward Iran. As Iraq continues to slide into chaos, George W. Bush's legacy in foreign policy suffers as well. Because U.S. policy regarding the Iranian regime strongly influences whether Iraq moves toward stability or instability, failure to deter and coerce Tehran harms the Bush legacy. Assume both that the United States "loses" Iraq and that Iran attains a nuclear weapons capability: then, the Bush legacy would suffer catastrophic decline.

Thus far, Washington's effort to deter and coerce the Iranian regime falls short due in part to a high degree of infighting within the Bush administration, not much different from bureaucratic warfare about Iraq. The State Department's approach has evolved from subcontracting to Europeans to negotiate with Tehran to fostering multilateral sanctions by the UN Security Council; meanwhile, the Department of Defense has reportedly drawn up war plans for dismantling Iran's nuclear weapons program.[41] There are in addition American military plans for destroying the terrorist infrastructure that Tehran maintains in Iraq and for engaging in raids across the Iraqi border to eliminate the supply of sophisticated roadside bomb technology manufactured in Iran. Based on the inability of the White House to fashion a coherent policy toward Iraq, however, there is reason to suspect that bureaucratic politics will thwart effective policymaking toward the Iranian regime.

The Democratic Party's victories in the 2006 congressional elections reflected a low point in public support for President Bush's handling of foreign policy. The subsequent resignation of Secretary of Defense Rumsfeld and the selection of Robert Gates as his replacement demonstrate the degree to which Congress can impinge on traditional presidential domination of the national security policy process in hot-button cases such as Iran and Iraq. Congressional constraints on the president in the national security policy process are substantial when public discontent mounts because of the perception of administration failures, as has happened with respect to Iraq. For the final two years of Bush's presidency, the White House will be similarly constrained regarding policy toward Iran. The United States will be unable credibly to threaten military action for the purpose of coercion, which in the short term may embolden Tehran and in the long run may necessitate problematic U.S. military action.

If diplomacy fails to rein in Iran, U.S. military strikes also are unlikely to be effective. U.S. intelligence is severely lacking on the Iranian regime's nuclear programs. The large capability of Tehran to retaliate with terrorism outweighs the small chance that military strikes could disable a meaningful segment of Iranian nuclear sites. Instead of just setting back the Iranian regime's acquisition of nuclear weapons by three to five years with air strikes, there is a need for a long-term transformation of the Iranian regime toward a constitutionally constrained democratic government.

Developing an approach that does not embolden the regime in Tehran or rely on improbable military strikes will require strong presidential leadership. President Bush has already demonstrated rhetorical leadership on the subject when he spoke directly to the Iranian people in his 2005 State of the Union address, saying, "As you stand for your own liberty, America stands with you." In 2006 he added, "We respect your right to choose your own future and win your own freedom. And our nation hopes one day to be the closest of friends with a free and democratic Iran." Now is the time for the president to match his strong words with deeds that would reinforce the diplomatic option yet keep the military alternative on the table.

One way of closing the gap between rhetoric and action is to develop a third option regarding Iran, between failing diplomacy and challenging military strikes. Empowering democratic forces both inside and outside of Iran would be a step toward creating such a third option that puts pressure on the Iranian regime to rethink its pursuit of nuclear weapons and sponsorship of terrorism, before resorting to military action. Such a third alternative also would help to dampen sectarian violence in Iraq and to persuade the Sunni insurgents that they have more to gain from cooperating with the United States than from facilitating enhanced Iranian political control of Iraq, which is an inadvertent result of the Sunni insurgency in Iraq. Otherwise President Bush's rhetoric will be grand strategy that has little effect on the regime in Tehran.

The international security environment in which President Bush has operated gave him an opportunity to fashion a grand strategy. Before 9/11, the domestic milieu, including bureaucratic, congressional, and public opinion, did not favor the development of doctrine. When 9/11 occurred, it allowed the president to create a strategy proportional to the perceived threat. But his failure to impose order on the national security bureaucracy made it difficult to translate rhetorical doctrine into effective practice with applications in Iraq and Iran.

The good news is that formulation of the Bush doctrine coincides with the absence of another 9/11 within the United States. The bad news is the escalation and expansion of the Iraq war, continuing fighting in Afghanistan, and an inability to arrest the movement of Iran toward nuclear weapons status. On one hand, the grand strategy of the Bush administration may be an effective rationale to defend the U.S. homeland against potential attacks with weapons of mass destruction and to protect others against such devastation. On the other hand, North Korea's success in acquiring nuclear weapons, the increasing likelihood of insurgency and sectarian violence turning into a full-scale civil war in Iraq, and the growing prospect of a nuclear-armed Iran are likely to doom the legacy of the Bush presidency in national security affairs.

Ultimately, a president has to decide between competing conceptions of strategy and be sufficiently involved to supply the logistical necessities to fulfill the chosen strategy. Although President Bush has proclaimed himself to be "the decider" on national security policy, it is precisely his lack of involvement in the decision-making process that has resulted in a chasm between grand rhetoric and operational capacity.

Notes

1. Robert J. Lieber, "A New Era in U.S. Strategic Thinking: September 11, One Year Later," (Washington, D.C.: U.S. Department of State, September 2002). The authors are most grateful to Professor Lieber for his constructive critique of earlier drafts.

2. Charles Hermann, ed., *International Crises: Insights from Behavioral Research* (New York: Free Press, 1972). While Hermann defines crisis as high threat, short time, and surprise, Ned Lebow considers crisis as characterized by high threat, heightened anxiety, expectation of violence, and belief that actions will have far-reaching consequences. See Ned Lebow, *Between Peace and War: The Nature of International Crisis* (Baltimore: Johns Hopkins University Press, 1981).

3. John Lewis Gaddis, "Grand Strategy in the Second Term," *Foreign Affairs,* January/February 2005, www.foreignaffairs.org/20050101faessay84101/john-lewis-gaddis/grand-strategy-in-the-second-term.html?mode=print.

4. Jimmy Carter, "Human Rights and Foreign Policy," commencement address at Notre Dame University, June 1977, http://usinfo.state.gov/usa/infousa/facts/democrac/55.htm.

5. Jimmy Carter, State of the Union Address, Washington, D.C., January 23, 1980, www.jimmycarterlibrary.org/documents/speeches/su80jec.phtml.

6. Raymond Tanter, *Rogue Regimes: Terrorism and Proliferation* (New York: St. Martin's Griffin, 1999), 295.

7. PBS, "Frontline 1812: War in Europe," February 22 and 29, 2000, www.pbs.org/wgbh/pages/frontline/shows/kosovo/.

8. Bob Woodward, *State of Denial* (New York: Simon and Schuster, 2006), 241.

9. David Rose, "Neo Culpa: Politics and Power," *Vanity Fair,* January 2007, www.vanityfair.com/politics/features/2007/01/neocons200701?printable=true&currentPage=all.

10. Karen DeYoung, *Soldier: The Life of Colin Powell* (New York: Knopf, 2006), 410–411.

11. Supreme Court of the United States, *Hamdan v. Rumsfeld, Secretary of Defense, et al.,* June 29, 2006.

12. Woodward, *State of Denial,* 103; James Fallows, "Blind into Baghdad," *Atlantic Monthly,* January/February 2004, www.theatlantic.com/doc/prem/200401/fallows.

13. Woodward, *State of Denial,* 164.

14. Dan Balz and Jon Cohen, "Confidence in Bush Leadership at All-Time Low, Poll Finds," *Washington Post,* January 22, 2007.

15. Woodward, *State of Denial,* 6.

16. See James Mann, *Rise of the Vulcans: The History of Bush's War Cabinet* (New York: Viking, 2004) for a description of the Vulcans. The name comes from a Vulcan statue that over-looks Secretary Rice's hometown of Birmingham, Alabama.

17. Cf. Robert J. Lieber, *The American Era: Power and Strategy for the Twenty-First Century* (New York: Cambridge University Press, 2005).

18. Charles Krauthammer, "Fukuyama's Fantasy," *Washington Post,* March 28, 2006, www.washingtonpost.com/wp-dyn/content/article/2006/03/27/AR2006032701298_pf.html; "In Defense of Democratic Realism," *National Interest,* September 24, 2004.

19. Francis Fukuyama, "After Neoconservatism," *New York Times,* February 16, 2005, www.nytimes.com/2006/02/19/magazine/neo.html?ei=5090&en=4126fa38fefd80de&ex=12980 05200&pagewanted=print; Paul Berman, review of *America at the Crossroads,* by Francis Fukuyama, *New York Times,* March 26, 2006, www.nytimes.com/2006/03/26/books/review/26berman.html?ei=5088&en=eb57b7ea9f3e9a07&ex=1301029200&partner=rssnyt&emc=rss&pagewanted=print.

20. R. J. Rummel, *Power Kills: Democracy as a Method of Nonviolence* (New Brunswick, N.J.: Transaction, 1997).

21. BBC, "View of US's Global Role Worse," January 23, 2007, http://news.bbc.co.uk/1/ hi/world/americas/6286755.stm.

22. John Lewis Gaddis, *Surprise, Security, and the American Experience* (Cambridge: Harvard University Press, 2004).

23. For extensive studies of presidential rhetoric and policy, see Robert Shogan, *Bad News: Where the Press Goes Wrong in the Making of the President* (Chicago: Ivan R. Dee, 2001); and Roderick P. Hart, *The Sound of Leadership: Presidential Communication in the Modern Age* (Chicago: University of Chicago Press, 1989), the latter of which analyzes over 10,000 presidential speeches.

24. David Frum and Richard Perle, *An End to Evil: How to Win the War on Terror* (New York: Random House, 2003).

25. Raymond Tanter, "How Much of an Axis, and How Evil?" *PolicyWatch,* no. 602, Washington Institute for Near East Policy, February 7, 2002, www.washingtoninstitute.org/ templateC05.php?CID=1480.

26. Paul Richter, "Rice's Offer to Iran Spurs Unease from Right," *Los Angeles Times,* June 12, 2006.

27. The National Endowment for Democracy address also resumes mention of Osama bin Laden's name, which the president had virtually dropped from his vocabulary when it looked increasingly likely that bin Laden would not be quickly found and when the White House refrained from giving him inordinate publicity.

28. George W. Bush, *The National Security Strategy 2006,* March 2006, 1, www.whitehouse. gov/nsc/nss/2006/.

29. George W. Bush, *The National Security Strategy 2002,* September 2002, 5, www.whitehouse. gov/nsc/nss/2002/index.html.

30. Bush, *The National Security Strategy 2006,* 20.

31. The President's Address to the Nation on Iraq, January 10, 2007, www.whitehouse.gov/ news/releases/2007/01/print/20070110-7.html.

32. James Glanz and Sabrina Tavernise, "U.S. Is Holding Iranians Seized in Raids in Iraq," *New York Times,* December 25, 2006, www.nytimes.com/2006/12/25/world/middleeast/ 25iraq.html?ei=5088&en=57bbb45f8e61b7ba&ex=1324702800&partner=rssnyt&emc=rss &pagewanted=print.

33. James Glanz, "The Reach of War; G.I.s in Iraq Raid Iranians' Offices," *New York Times,* January 12, 2007.

34. For a comparison of all the language used in each of President Bush's State of the Union addresses, see "The Words That Were Used: The 2007 State of the Union Address," *New York Times,* January 24, 2007, www.nytimes.com/ref/washington/20070123_STATEOF UNION.html.

35. Peter Baker and Michael Abramowitz, "Bush Urges Congress, Nation to Give His Iraq Plan a Chance," *Washington Post,* January 24, 2007, www.washingtonpost.com/wp-dyn/ content/article/2007/01/23/AR2007012300700_pf.html.

36. Jonathan Weisman, "Senators Rebuff Bush on Troop Plan," *Washington Post,* January 24, 2007, www.washingtonpost.com/wp-dyn/content/article/2007/01/24/AR2007012400181_ pf.html.

37. See Iran Policy Committee, *What Makes Tehran Tick: Islamist Ideology and Hegemonic Interests* (Washington, D.C.: Iran Policy Committee, 2006), on Islamist fascism and the

nature of the Iranian regime, as well as for evidence on Iranian perception of threat and expression of hostility regarding Israel.

38. Christopher Hitchens is one of the first to use the term, "fascism with an Islamic face." *Nation Magazine,* October 8, 2001, www.thenation.com/doc/20011008/hitchens20010924. Walter Mead describes the post-9/11 threat of Islamist militancy as "Arabian fascism," although Islamists advocate religious rather than ethnic solidarity. See Walter Mead, *Power, Terror, Peace, and War: America's Grand Strategy in a World at Risk* (New York: Knopf, 2004).

39. James A. Baker III and Lee H. Hamilton, *The Iraq Study Group Report* (Washington, D.C.: U.S. Institute of Peace, 2006).

40. Paul Ames, "Merkel Says Nazi Past Shows Need for Early Action against Iranian Extremism but Rules out Military Option," Associated Press, February 4, 2006.

41. Seymour M. Hersh, "The Coming Wars," *New Yorker,* January 24 and 31, 2005, www.newyorker.com/printables/fact/050124fa_fact.

CHAPTER 11

Ideology Meets Reality
Managing Regime Change in Iraq and the Transformation of the Military

Colin Campbell

GEORGE W. BUSH'S PRESIDENCY is remarkable for its ideologically driven character, its emphasis on crisis inflation, and its unwillingness to subject its ideas to scrutiny before putting them into action—action that, given those characteristics, likely leads to failure. In this chapter I detail how those characteristics led the United States into the war in Iraq and how that, in turn, sabotaged one of the administration's expressed goals, namely, the transformation of the Pentagon. That transformation had been going on prior to the advent of the Bush administration and the stewardship of Donald Rumsfeld over the Defense Department (DoD), but it has been impeded by the deepening morass of the commitment in Iraq and the inadequate consultations with the military establishment that preceded the invasion.

The Personal Nature of the American Presidency

Before he became president, Woodrow Wilson highlighted the distinctive constitutional position of the American chief executive in comparison to British prime ministers. Key elements of the American president's power that stem from the incumbent's being simultaneously head of state, head of government, and commander in chief combine to give presidents leverage beyond what prime ministers enjoy. In Wilson's words:

> The president is at liberty, both in law and conscience, to be as big a man as he can; . . . he is the only national voice in affairs. Let him once win the admiration and confidence of the country, and no other single force will withstand him. . . . His office is anything he has the sagacity and force to make it.[1]

Wilson proved overoptimistic about "sagacity" in the presidency. Few presidents have brought to the office Wilson's own depth of understanding of leadership and world affairs. Indeed, one might ask just how much more incumbents' grasp of issues—as opposed to their talent for public relations and political maneuver—must decline before the public begins insisting upon a higher standard. The "personal presidency," in fact, may be contributing to the problem. Arguably it has led to steady decline of the dynamics within administrations that could possibly compensate for presidents' lack of sagacity by pooling the acumen of advisers and submitting the stances that they press on presidents to validating scrutiny and refinement. In the absence of conditions that foster more judicious decisions, presidents are apt to resort to "crisis inflation," hyperbole, and public relations, which in turn pave the way for unrestrained ideological entrepreneurship. When acting as ideological entrepreneurs, presidents operate from certitude yet delegate almost entirely the difficult work of devising options.

To be sure, *policy* entrepreneurship is important work. John W. Kingdon underscores the importance and legitimacy of this function among government officials. From Kingdon's perspective, officials get policy innovation rolling initially through a pre-decision process of identifying available alternatives.[2] They then position themselves for the opportunity to drive home their case, like a surfer waiting for the perfect wave. However, the policy entrepreneur may often find it hard to maintain a balance between the advocacy inevitably associated with entrepreneurship and a thorough canvassing of the possible implications of the options that he or she has chosen to promote. One way of resolving this tension is to emphasize loyalty to the will of the president through opting for "responsive competence" among presidential appointees. "Responsive competence" implies that the role of administration officials is merely to advance the administration's political support and the president's will, even if that comes at the expense of "neutral competence"— the idea of taking what a relatively detached assessment would suggest is the best course of action among a plausible set of options defined by presidential goals.[3] Sometimes a sufficiently probing review of alternatives may suggest a revision of those goals.

Differentiating *ideological* from *policy* entrepreneurship is not easy. Ideologically based policy, however, usually entails a very strong and deep adherence that makes compromise difficult. It also often caters to a narrowly defined, yet politically leveraged, segment of a president's perceived base. Finally, advocates frequently display exceptional, even dogged persistence on behalf of their goals; they are largely resistant to countervailing evidence.

Ideological entrepreneurship becomes "unrestrained" within an administration when two conditions prevail:[4] (1) when the selection of political appointees has been influenced to a substantial degree by the ideological commitments of nominees, and (2) when an administration's decision-making process fails to ensure that policy proposals are tested through intense countervailing review. Unrestrained ideological entrepreneurship stands in sharp contrast to "multiple advocacy," which gained great currency through the work of Alexander George and Roger Porter. George pointed to the benefits of providing a level playing field for the advocacy of ideas from different vantage points within an administration.[5] Porter, a former White House aide, analyzed multiple advocacy at work in economic policy formulation during the Ford administration.[6]

Dwight Eisenhower and Ronald Reagan exemplify presidents who implemented multiple advocacy to some degree. Eisenhower, for instance, brought to policy deliberations a strong requirement of inclusion, consistent with his experience in the Pentagon and his exposure to a collective approach to decision making during World War II.[7]

Reagan, too, differed substantially from George W. Bush in the practice of decision making during his first term (but not his second). The principles behind Reagan's policy views became widely known even before he attained the presidency. His former domestic policy adviser, Martin Anderson, coedited a collection of papers that reveal that a great deal of thought and effort, if not a high degree of intellectual sophistication, went into Reagan's speeches before he became president.[8] Furthermore, while governor of California, Reagan had become enamored of structures for collective consultation among cabinet secretaries.[9]

In his first term Reagan imposed a strict "roundtable" norm, whereby cabinet secretaries usually could not bring matters directly to him without their going first to the relevant cabinet council.[10] In addition, Reagan frequently would chair those bodies when they had reached the critical decision point on administration policies. Significantly, however, Reagan and his closest aides let the roundtable norm lapse substantially during the second term, primarily because the president was then becoming somewhat detached from reviewing the details of policy. An additional factor was that James A. Baker III, the first term White House chief of staff, who was a firm believer in the roundtable norm, switched positions in Reagan's second term with Donald Regan, the first term Treasury secretary, who viewed the White House job as a command position rather than a collegial one.[11]

The notorious Iran/contra affair stands almost as a monument to the consequences of the decline of roundtabling during Reagan's second term. It involved a scheme, concocted and driven from within the National Security Council staff, which had the U.S. government arranging through third parties to send weapons to Iran in exchange for funds that were then funneled covertly to the U.S.-supported contra forces seeking to overthrow a leftist regime in Nicaragua. The episode ultimately became a debacle for the administration's credibility.[12] The Tower Commission report on the affair placed the blame squarely at the feet of a president who had become overindulgent of the machinations of his immediate White House advisers.[13]

In the George W. Bush administration, we have seen once again a high degree of presidential detachment from the "heavy lifting" of policymaking. We find as well no evidence of decisional conventions, such as a roundtabling norm and its associated structures, that might compensate for any shortfall in presidential engagement.

In their media appearances early in the administration, two chroniclers of the Bush II administration's first innings, the *Washington Post's* Bob Woodward and Bush's own former speechwriter, David Frum, time and again found themselves defending the president's intelligence.[14] George W. Bush's obvious tactical intelligence, especially in the realm of political maneuver, does not seem to translate into the consistent concentration and rigor required for grasping the key elements of policy issues and the processes through which they might be resolved. This lack of deliberative effort should cause concern, especially at moments when the president is receiving strong external reinforcement for his performance, such as high approval ratings, gains for his party in midterm elections, and his own renewed electoral mandate in 2004. Such reinforcement might easily have lulled an inattentive executive into excessive docility toward the advice bubbling up from his most trusted aides. One general result is that the Bush II presidency has had little engagement with the apparatus of government and has largely failed to encourage discussion and mediation of differing views.

President Bush's inability to express the reasons for his positions unless heavily scripted exacerbates concerns that he has acquired little authentic mastery of the issues.[15] Institutions, including bureaucracies, can be helpful to presidents. Discussion, give-and-take, and appreciation of the requirements of implementation can enable presidents to avoid egregious errors in decision making. But a president, or someone acting on behalf of his administration, must want to be helped. Bush and many of his key players, such as Rumsfeld, Cheney, and their legions of neoconservative ideologues, showed little sign of wishing for that, unless the advice was helpful to political imaging. Straightforward confidence (which makes for good reelection posturing) has been unfettered by doubt or skepticism concerning extraordinarily ambitious ideas. This weakness is both personal—a function of who Bush is as a leader—and institutional, inasmuch as staffing in the presidency is a reflection of the incumbent president.

The Administration, the War on Terrorism, the War in Iraq, and the Pentagon

I now turn to how these traits and trends have affected a crucial agency—the Department of Defense—and the Bush presidency's relation to it. I examine two dimensions of the dynamic between the administration and the department most central to formulating and implementing the administration's response to the terrorist attacks of 9/11. The first dimension is the decision chain that led ultimately to the invasion of Iraq as part of that response. The response to 9/11 received the title the "global war on terrorism" (GWOT) and in many respects completely refocused the Pentagon and the individual military services. The second dimension concerns the path of the administration's commitment to "transform" the military services through strategic commitments that would skip a generation of technology. Though the notion of transformation predated the 9/11 attacks, the impact of those attacks—or, more accurately, the administration's response to them—has had important ramifications for how transformation has been (and can be) carried through. One legacy, in short, affects another.

Iraq and the GWOT

I address two questions that are crucial to evaluating the George W. Bush presidency: First, did the president establish and lead a rigorous dynamic for the review of policy issues? Second, to what degree has Bush revealed an aptitude for steering effective discourse within his administration over policy? Insofar as the answers to these two questions appear to be respectively "no" and "little," we might expect fertile soil for unrestrained ideological entrepreneurship within the administration.

The Bush administration's response to 9/11 showed a loosely run national security process and a lack of direction from the president (see, e.g., the Tanter and Kersting chapter in this book), as well as a strong element of crisis inflation. This mix of elements owed largely to the porous boundary between political operations and policymaking in the administration. Bush's popular appeal has ebbed and flowed in almost complete unison with public concerns about the terrorist threat. Linking the necessity of regime change in Iraq to that country's putative possession of weapons of mass destruction (WMD) and Saddam Hussein's alleged support of al Qaeda performed two vital functions: It kept the 9/11 balloon aloft, and it provided crucial justification for a long-standing neoconservative objective.

Until September 2005, after Hurricane Katrina, assessments of the Bush administration's performance were relatively mild. The president's approval soared and then stabilized at about the level he had when he arrived in office, enabling him to win a narrow but solid reelection victory. After all, in early spring 2003 the United States led a relatively efficient invasion of Iraq, mounted with minimal support (except for Britain) from a number of allies, many of them blips on a map. America's major allies (again, save the UK and, to a lesser degree, Italy and Spain—for a time) were either notably absent from the fray, having indicated their displeasure at the administration's unilateralism, or were minimally and largely symbolically involved. This assortment of forces, many of them noncombatant, was dubbed the "coalition of the willing" by the Bush administration—implying that the "unwilling" would be dealt with later for their disloyalty.

Despite one tense week during which the U.S. force's advance overstretched its supply lines, the operation proceeded with surprising precision, resulting in far fewer civilian casualties than had been feared. Soon after toppling Saddam Hussein's government, however, the administration began to appear very much like the dog that caught the bus. That is, it seemed not to know what to do next—how to advance its stated goal of establishing a stable democracy without running the risk of ensnarling itself in chaos. At a minimum, the circumstances on the ground in Iraq pointed to a long and tortuous road toward the envisioned transformation of Baghdad into a beacon for democracy in the Arab world. By spring 2007, the situation appeared far worse still, with Iraqis embroiled in a seemingly multi-headed civil war. The administration displays little comprehension of this conflict (admittedly, it is not easy to comprehend) and even less capability to halt it. How did the United States end up in this apparently open-ended commitment that runs the risk of draining its military of both morale and capability?

The persistent surfer. Unrestrained ideological entrepreneurship was a fundamental element of the administration's commitment and resolve to invade Iraq. Immediately after 9/11, Paul Wolfowitz, then deputy secretary of defense, pressed for making regime change in Iraq a centerpiece of the war against terrorism.[16] Indeed, Wolfowitz advocated his position so strenuously at a Camp David meeting on September 15 that the White House chief of staff, Andrew Card, had to admonish him not to interrupt defense secretary Donald Rumsfeld. Wolfowitz, who was under secretary for defense policy during the George H. W. Bush administration, had, as a young Pentagon analyst, led the development of a secret 1979 document warning of the emerging Iraqi threat to Middle East security.[17] During the 1991 Gulf War, when the televised "highway of death" images had begun to trouble the Bush I administration, Wolfowitz adamantly opposed the chairman of the Joint Chiefs of Staff, Colin Powell, and the top general in the Persian Gulf campaign, H. Norman Schwarzkopf, in their determination to abruptly end the allied attack. The visuals being transmitted around the globe had even induced qualms back home in the United States. Still, Wolfowitz argued, continued pressure could prompt a coup in Iraq that would lead to Saddam Hussein's ouster even without the ground war having to continue on to Baghdad.[18] The tension between Wolfowitz and Powell would play a significant role during the buildup to the 2003 invasion of Iraq, as well.

Although at the Camp David meeting following 9/11 George W. Bush cut short consideration of an invasion-of-Iraq option,[19] the idea apparently intrigued him. Indeed, *New York Times* journalist Bill Keller asserted that when Wolfowitz registered his concerns privately to the president during a break in the discussions, Bush had admonished him to speak up.[20] As Keller notes, Wolfowitz was well positioned to spread his perspective widely within the administration.[21] For one thing, he shared a mentor with Richard Perle—chair, until 2003, of Rumsfeld's Defense Advisory Board—in that both men had received their socialization as neoconservatives under the tutelage of the late Sen. Henry M. "Scoop" Jackson, D-Wash.

Wolfowitz, in turn, had nurtured a generation of neoconservatives by mentoring two critically placed administration hawks. While at Yale he taught I. Lewis "Scooter"

Libby, who had since 2001 been Dick Cheney's chief of staff and who aligned himself soon after 9/11 with those seeking regime change in Iraq.[22] Then, in the Pentagon during the Bush I administration, Wolfowitz had supervised Stephen J. Hadley, Condoleezza Rice's deputy in the first term and later her successor, who chaired the crucial National Security Council deputies' committee, which met several times a week to prepare issues for cabinet-level consideration. One level down in the NSC staff at the time of 9/11 was another Wolfowitz protégé in Zalmay Khalilzad, Rice's senior director for Southwest Asia, Near East, and North African Affairs. Close to both Rumsfeld and Cheney—he headed Rumsfeld's transition team—Khalilzad was the administration's most senior Muslim and strongest proponent of the view that a democratized Baghdad would become the beacon for the transformation of the Arab world.[23] In 2005 Khalilzad became U.S. ambassador to Iraq, after occupying the same position in Afghanistan.[24]

Ideological entrepreneurship becomes "unrestrained" when the selection of appointees allows for pockets of officials who share strongly held programmatic commitments and when the administration does not sufficiently test those advocates' views through countervailing ones. Given Rumsfeld's and Cheney's reflexes, Colin Powell stood almost alone in the way of Wolfowitz and his cohorts in their determination to use the war on terrorism as a pretext for going after Saddam Hussein. What resulted was a skewed process that preordained flawed implementation.[25]

The initial response. In its immediate response to the 9/11 attacks, the Bush administration made a great show of slamming the barn door shut, so that future terrorists intent on attacking U.S. targets would find it much more difficult to get in and out of the country or to operate within it. In reality, the administration (along with the rest of the political system) displayed both parsimony in actually meting out resources for homeland security and hesitancy in imposing rationality in their use.[26] But a truly jarring irony rests on the proposition that whereas before 9/11 the Bush administration had been intent on not personalizing the antiterrorism effort, it suddenly focused its sights on getting Osama bin Laden "dead or alive."[27] Edward Cody, at the time the deputy foreign editor at the *Washington Post,* and a highly regarded observer of the Islamic world, writing with colleagues, filed two prescient reports in fall 2001.[28] Both outlined exactly how circumstances in Afghanistan and, relatedly, in Pakistan would make the Bush II administration's designs on bin Laden difficult, if not impossible, to achieve. The reports' skepticism rested on two facts: Pakistan's Inter-Service Intelligence Agency controlled access to the lawless, tribal regions of Afghanistan and eastern Pakistan, and that agency would have to reverse a culture deeply supportive of the Taliban and al Qaeda before it could help U.S. forces track down bin Laden. In the meantime, the porousness of the border areas would allow bin Laden to maneuver with sufficient freedom to avoid capture.

Ultimately, the U.S. Special Forces outsourced the effort to flush out bin Laden from Tora Bora—where he was thought to have fled in an effort to reach Pakistan—

to Afghan guerrillas, who apparently proved more intent on humoring their American patrons than on thwarting bin Laden's escape. The al Qaeda leader vanished into western Pakistan sometime in December 2001,[29] and he soon all but disappeared from the administration's rhetoric as well. The administration turned its focus instead toward "rogue regimes" it thought capable of unleashing weapons of mass destruction (WMD)—Iraq, Iran, and North Korea, which it styled the "axis of evil." Subsequently, two key National Security Council aides responsible for counterterrorism resigned their positions, registering, in one case publicly, their dismay over the administration's shift of focus from al Qaeda to Iraq.[30]

The axis of evil. A rhetorical flourish that had issued from the keystrokes of a White House speechwriter captured the impulse that would lead eventually to the U.S. invasion of Iraq in March 2003. As the speechwriter, David Frum, recounted, he had mulled over the "fascism" of some Middle Eastern regimes and movements and had come up with the concept that they composed an "axis of hatred."[31] According to Frum, this turn of phrase caught fire not just with Condoleezza Rice and her deputy, Stephen Hadley, but with the president as well. The president's January 2002 State of the Union address eventually spoke of the three countries as the "axis of evil."

The adoption of the axis image (evocative of the World War II alliance of Germany, Italy, and Japan) and its galvanizing impact are an excellent example of what former Bush faith-based initiatives adviser John DiIulio characterized as "on-the-fly policymaking by speech-making."[32] The rhetoric of crisis inflation also provided a timely vehicle for the neoconservatives who were bent on invasion of Iraq, giving an immense boost to those in the administration who wanted to cast the conflict with rogue states in black and white rather than in shades of gray.[33] Chris Patten, the European Union's external affairs chief, noted the dangers of such a posture in facilitating the impetuous assertion of power, remarking, "The Afghan war [has] perhaps reinforced some dangerous instincts: that the projection of military power is the only basis of true security; that the U.S. can rely on no one but itself; and that allies may be useful as optional extras."[34] The events that unfolded between the State of the Union address and the U.S. invasion of Iraq seemed to justify Patten's concerns. They also provide evidence of the lengths to which the Bush administration would go to keep the public mood toward global challenges inflamed.

The administration's initial attempt to follow through on its rhetoric on Iraq proved abortive. In March 2002, Vice President Cheney embarked on an eleven-nation tour of the Middle East in an effort to obtain support for a confrontation with Iraq. However, Arab frustrations over the lack of progress toward resolving the Israeli-Palestinian conflict made it impossible for Cheney to stay on message in discussions with Arab leaders.[35]

This roadblock turned some minds in the administration, during spring 2002, toward rejoining the languishing peace process. (Certainly, that was something British prime minister Tony Blair had pushed hard on his American ally.) But since his inauguration Bush had studiously avoided entanglement in the Israeli-Palestinian struggle on the grounds that Bill Clinton had become excessively mired in the issue.[36] When prompted to engage the issue therefore, he encountered an exceedingly sharp learning curve. Moreover, his advisers divided deeply on the matter.[37] The result was less-than-optimal coherence, just when clarity was most needed. Thus a Mideast mission by Colin Powell was stillborn before the Secretary of State even reached the region.[38] Bush I's national security adviser, Brent Scowcroft, opined that the administration was "in real danger of being overextended." James B. Steinberg, a senior fellow at the Brookings Institution and a former deputy national security adviser under Clinton, saw peril in the prospect of an administration that was deeply divided on ideological grounds trying to address quotidian issues in black-and-white terms. As Steinberg put it,

> Below [cabinet] level, it's not working at all. You have people with intense ideological convictions and such trench warfare . . . that it's hard for them to get anything done. . . . They have this . . . grand Bush doctrine to fight evil, but they haven't developed an elaborate set of policies on the second order problems. If it can't be fit into the template of counterterrorism and the fight against evil, they haven't any strategies.[39]

The continued intractability of the Middle East peace process, ironically, cleared the field for still more aggressive advocacy by administration proponents of regime change in Iraq. The hawks' arguments emphasizing the putative ripeness of Iraq for conversion to democracy[40] had lodged the idea with near religious certainty in the president's mind after 9/11.[41] Even staunch supporters of the invasion voiced concerns about the way Bush tended to eschew explaining his position on Iraq and to present his views as articles of faith.[42] The president's uncommunicativeness suggested, again, that he had not gone through an elaborate thought process before embracing the views put forward by the neoconservatives. That faith turned into policy: In general, after all, once it is known that a president has taken a strong position, there is certainty about the outcome. A career Office of Management and Budget official's account of why his agency rarely won conflicts with the Pentagon during the Reagan administration illustrates the point: "Now the biggest hawk in the administration happens to be the president himself. So, when the issue goes that far, the outcome is predictable."[43]

As Bush flirted with the invasion option, his obvious lack of interest in a thoroughgoing canvassing of alternatives gave opponents a sense that the neoconservatives would prevail no matter what. Glenn Kessler of the *Washington Post* quoted an official close to the deliberations, who described the resignation that seized skeptics of regime change: "The issue got away from the president. He wasn't controlling the tone or the direction. . . . [He was being influenced by people who] painted him into a corner because Iraq was an albatross around their necks." Kessler also reported an awkward, July 2002 meeting between Condoleezza Rice and Richard N. Haass, the State Department's director of policy planning, who left the administration in June 2003 to head the prestigious Council on Foreign Relations. When Haass inquired of Rice whether they should discuss the pros and cons of confronting Iraq, Rice apparently replied, "Don't bother. The president has made a decision."[44] The consequences were real: As James Risen later wrote, "An attitude took hold among many senior CIA officials that war was inevitable—and so the quality of the intelligence on weapons of mass destruction didn't really matter."[45]

By summer 2002, the administration notably intensified its focus on planning an invasion of Iraq.[46] In mid-August, however, formidable Republicans in the foreign policy community began to air both privately and publicly their reservations about the haste with which the president appeared to have opted for an invasion over further diplomatic efforts. Key among them was Brent Scowcroft, who registered his concerns in a *Wall Street Journal* op-ed piece on August 16. Because Scowcroft had served as Bush I's national security adviser, observers believed that he would not have gone public with his concerns without conferring first with the former president.[47] (Indeed, shortly before the actual invasion, George H. W. Bush himself publicly lodged his preference for multilateral approaches to threats such as those posed by Iraq.)[48]

Although the vice president countered almost immediately with strenuous defenses of preemptive action,[49] the concerns that Republican foreign policy experts expressed clearly raised a formidable challenge to the administration's strategy. James A. Baker III—a White House chief of staff and Treasury secretary under Reagan and secretary of state and chief of staff under Bush I—had directly questioned the rationale for preemptive action in his own August op-ed piece, which some also believed to have been prompted by Bush I.[50] Baker urged the president to "do his best to stop his advisers and their surrogates from playing out their differences publicly." He then outlined the costs associated with military confrontation with Iraq, in his mind inevitable, and stressed that they would increase exponentially if the United States were to act alone. In an eerily insightful premonition of the difficulty of seeking regime change militarily, Baker said that the invasion would have to include sufficient ground troops to get the job done, and not simply try to get by "on the cheap," that the occupation could prove challenging, and that Saddam Hussein might elude capture.

The concerted efforts of the Olympians from the Bush I administration succeeded in resurrecting Colin Powell's preference for a multilateral approach. By late September, Powell had worked out a deal with the hawks whereby they would support seeking an additional UN resolution and a rigorous regime of inspections, and he would promise to support an invasion should Iraq remain defiant.[51] By November, observers were hailing Powell's diplomatic coup in negotiating through the UN

Security Council a resolution calling for Iraq to eliminate its weapons of mass destruction and submit to comprehensive inspections.[52] No sooner had the ink dried on that resolution, however, than neoconservatives, and eventually the president, began questioning the likelihood that Iraq would comply.[53] This set the stage for a single-minded campaign by the administration to find Iraq in "material breach" of the resolution.

The failure to achieve UN support for preemptive intervention against Iraq left the administration with two problems. First, without the UN imprimatur the United States exposed its actions to serious questions about legitimacy and legality from the standpoint of just war. Second, and related, it could not muster sufficient international support for an effective alliance to sustain not just an invasion, but perhaps more importantly, an occupation.[54]

From crisis inflation to faith-based invasion. Whatever one's views of the decision to invade Iraq nearly unilaterally, unrestrained ideological entrepreneurship in the administration's approach to pursuing the war was clear. I offer three examples of how the administration's judgment appears to have been clouded during the buildup to the invasion of Iraq.

The first example concerned the effort to persuade Turkey to grant access to the Army's 4th Infantry Division, so that the U.S. forces could invade Iraq from the north as well as from the south. The negotiations collapsed, with recriminations all around, when a Turkish parliamentary resolution failed on a technicality, and it became clear that the United States would have to pay much more than had been offered for the access. The Turks maintained that the outcome would have been different had U.S. representatives not behaved in such a heavy-handed manner.[55] When the Bush I team successfully gained access for U.S. forces through Turkey in 1990, during the first Persian Gulf crisis, its effort included three visits to Turkey by James Baker and upwards of fifty-five telephone calls by President George H. W. Bush.[56] By contrast, Colin Powell failed to visit Turkey even once during the buildup to the invasion of Iraq, and President George W. Bush logged a total of three calls or meetings with Turkish leaders.

The second case arose in the determination of the structure and size of the force that would be required to carry off the invasion. To be sure, as discussed in more detail below, then-defense secretary Donald Rumsfeld styled himself a staunch advocate of the "transformation" of the military. Before the rise of terrorism and insurgency, that term tended to refer to the adjustments that the Pentagon had to make in its medium- and long-term resource commitments to position itself for the emergence of a peer competitor to the United States—most likely China—that would be able to operate with a large exclusionary zone. That is, the peer competitor would control air space and the seas so far beyond its shores (say 1,000 miles) that it would make warfare from U.S. bases in its region, aircraft carriers, fighters, and ground attacks much more difficult than now.[57] Rumsfeld's version of transformation, in contrast, hewed more closely to the "reinvention" movement of the 1990s (notably the commission to reform public management headed by Vice President Gore in 1993), which stressed management efficiency and streamlining. That is, political leaders expected to do the same things as before—but for less money.[58]

This conception of reinvention came through loud and clear even at the beginning of discussions with the military about what would be required to invade Iraq. When, in summer 2002, the military pegged the figure at as many as 300,000 troops, the administration countered with a "Baghdad first" strategy whereby it would land 80,000 to 100,000 troops in Baghdad and have them fan out from there to pacify Iraq.[59] In the end, about 145,000 U.S. and coalition troops were initially on the ground in Iraq. Even before the loss of the northern salient through Turkey, military analysts had expressed concern that the war plan placed too much stress on a speedy advance to Baghdad that might overreach supply lines.[60] Once the invasion began—certainly during the second week, when major supply problems emerged—those concerns became known through remarks made by retired generals, who were doubtless acting as surrogates for serving military leaders who could not go public.

Indeed, a recent assessment of the invasion claims that a major dispute arose between General Tommy Franks, the commander overseeing the invasion from the Central Command, and his field generals on the ground in Iraq.[61] It derived from the assessment that Iraqi soldiers had abandoned their uniforms to mount guerrilla disruption in areas purportedly under U.S. control and centered on whether the U.S. forces should delay their advance to Baghdad to clean out the resistance. The retired generals' public statements, and those of other former leaders, reflected concerns on the ground with the strategic consequences of the fact that Rumsfeld's force was inadequate for the task and also concerns that the administration had seriously hobbled the armed forces by its failures in diplomacy, especially regarding access to Turkey and the use of bases in Saudi Arabia.[62]

Observers noted that Rumsfeld's determination to conduct the war on the cheap extended to unprecedented involvement in appointments to top positions on the Joint Staff—the operating arm of the Joint Chiefs of Staff—as well as parsimonious management of the Pentagon's deployment plan.[63] By May 2003, tensions between Rumsfeld and the army leadership had reached the point where a bipartisan group of senators wrote the secretary to express concern that he was encountering too much difficulty finding successors for the army chief and vice chief of staff.[64] Within ten days, Rumsfeld ended the speculation about the reasons behind the delayed transition by appointing a three-year retiree, after at least two serving army generals had declined to serve under him as chief.[65]

Once the U.S. force captured Baghdad, much of the criticism of the actual war plan subsided. Soon, however, a third issue—the influence of ideology in planning for the occupation of Iraq—became salient. The invading force began to encounter difficulties not only in the pacification of Iraq but also in securing important sites such as hospitals, archaeological treasures, oil industry infrastructure, munitions sites, and most crucially, nuclear facilities.[66] To add to the disarray, the occupation force seemed suddenly unable to locate convincing evidence of the weapons of mass destruction whose alleged proliferation and readiness for deployment had served as the administration's primary justification for the invasion.[67]

Even neoconservative members of the Defense Policy Board, including then-chair Richard Perle and former Speaker of the House Newt Gingrich, had raised alarm (in October 2002) over the lack of preparations for occupation of Iraq.[68] Much of the difficulty appeared to stem from conflicts between the State and Defense Departments over how to foster a successor to Saddam Hussein's regime. The vice president seemed to have taken control of the planning by January 2003—personally attending to many details.[69] Then, once the administration decided its game plan for the occupation, it was up to Paul Wolfowitz to defend it against critics. Wolfowitz took especially strong exception to the congressional testimony of General Eric Shinseki, the outgoing army chief of staff, to the effect that a force of "several hundred thousand" troops would be needed to return stability to Iraq.[70] Just as events subsequently flew in the face of the vice president's March prediction that "from the standpoint of the Iraqi people, my belief is we will . . . be greeted as liberators,"[71] they also seemed to demolish Wolfowitz's claim that Shinseki's testimony was "far off the mark" because Iraq had no history of ethnic strife comparable to that in Bosnia or Kosovo.[72] Once again, unrestrained ideological entrepreneurship had clouded key aides' judgments about a crucial dimension to regime change in Iraq.

From Iraq to the Pentagon

A presidential administration is not exclusively composed of a president's direct actions but is rather the composite of all of those who speak and act under the authority of the president. To the extent that a president gives wide range to one of his key officials, it indicates that the president either supports the agenda of that official or simply is indifferent to its implications.

Donald Rumsfeld, returning to the Pentagon in 2001 (he also served as defense secretary in the Ford administration), was given immense leeway. And few secretaries of defense have brought with them as focused an agenda as he did. Few have brought with them such an "in-your-face" style of confronting the military professionals under his command. Few, if any of them, have thought that "the enemy within"—meaning bureaucratic resistance—was the greatest enemy facing America's national security. Rumsfeld intended to streamline the military and transform the Pentagon to achieve greater efficiencies. That most affected the army. Rumsfeld wanted a smaller, lighter army able to deploy quickly and move quickly once deployed. Thus he resisted the army's requests for heavy-duty weaponry that he thought ran counter to his version of the new, lightening-quick strike force.

Again, from early 2001 until his removal after the 2006 midterm elections, Rumsfeld had substantial freedom at the Pentagon to implement that vision. How did the Iraq regime change experience affect Rumsfeld's determination to transform the military?

The short answer is, substantially—even fatefully. To begin with, the project no longer focuses on the emergence of China as a near-peer competitor. The prospect of continued challenges from rogue states and individuals has shifted attention away from traditional conflicts with states to "irregular" threats such as counterinsurgency, "catastrophic" attacks (such as the oft-cited danger of a dirty bomb being exploded in Times Square), and the "disruptive" potential of an adversary interfering with critical infrastructure.

Second, the operational tempo of, and the frustrations emerging from, the occupation of Afghanistan and Iraq have made it difficult for the military branches, especially the army and marines, to focus on transformation at all. Becoming mired in the here and now naturally constricts the latitude for skipping a generation of technology.

Finally, virtually all of the Vietnam veterans have retired from the upper echelons of the military establishments in the Pentagon and the combatant commands. Those not seared by direct experience of failure against insurgency have tended toward greater optimism about the prospects of winning the "global war on terror."

Purple and gray suits. These shifts have taken place against a broader backdrop of change in the Pentagon, which has sought organizationally to emphasize joint thinking and coordination. This has both muted the distinctiveness of service colors and facilitated dialogue between the leaders of the uniformed services and the political leaders to whom they report in responding to current and future challenges. The colors of the uniformed services are thus no longer distinctly blue or green: "jointness" and coordination of command have blurred them to purple. Hence, the military at the Pentagon may be thought of as "purple suits," as against their civilian superiors' traditional gray.

One result is that capabilities-based planning in the Pentagon and all of the branches involves plans that try to impose service neutrality about how precisely a required strike against a target is actually going to be delivered. We could conceive of ordnance against an enemy arriving via a navy missile, an air force bomber, a marine fighter jet, or army artillery. Neutrality about which of these "platforms" delivers the strike allows greater agility all through the military's strategic, budgetary, and operational decision trees. It also allows for the elimination of redundant programs and systems. Although the implementation of capabilities-based planning is by no means complete, or even entirely on track, and has been made considerably more difficult by the current wars in Afghanistan and Iraq, it has worked a considerable adjustment of mindsets among those seeking greater innovation in the military.

FIGURE II.I   U.S. Military Challenges

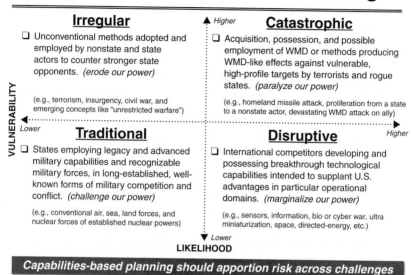

Security Environment: Four Challenges

Irregular	▲ Higher	Catastrophic

Irregular
- ❏ Unconventional methods adopted and employed by nonstate and state actors to counter stronger state opponents. *(erode our power)*

(e.g., terrorism, insurgency, civil war, and emerging concepts like "unrestricted warfare")

Catastrophic
- ❏ Acquisition, possession, and possible employment of WMD or methods producing WMD-like effects against vulnerable, high-profile targets by terrorists and rogue states. *(paralyze our power)*

(e.g., homeland missile attack, proliferation from a state to a nonstate actor, devastating WMD attack on ally)

Lower ◀ ·························· ▶ Higher

Traditional
- ❏ States employing legacy and advanced military capabilities and recognizable military forces, in long-established, well-known forms of military competition and conflict. *(challenge our power)*

(e.g., conventional air, sea, land forces, and nuclear forces of established nuclear powers)

Disruptive
- ❏ International competitors developing and possessing breakthrough technological capabilities intended to supplant U.S. advantages in particular operational domains. *(marginalize our power)*

(e.g., sensors, information, bio or cyber war, ultra miniaturization, space, directed-energy, etc.)

VULNERABILITY

▼ Lower
LIKELIHOOD

Capabilities-based planning should apportion risk across challenges

The gray-suited civilian personnel who currently direct strategic planning and budgeting in the Pentagon have been able to operate much more collectively and in consultation with the purple suits than did their predecessors, Paul Wolfowitz, the former deputy secretary, and Douglas Feith, the former under secretary for policy during the Bush administration's first term. Neither Wolfowitz nor Feith displayed much interest in either collective decision making with their colleagues or consultation with the military leadership. Furthermore, neither took a strong interest in middle-term, much less long-term, strategic and budgetary matters. With the arrival of Gordon England as Wolfowitz's successor as deputy secretary, and the leadership provided by Feith's principal deputy as Feith transitioned out of the Pentagon, the connectivity among the political appointees in the Pentagon and the links with the uniformed military leadership in the building began to improve significantly.

New vectors for transformation. The administration used the process leading toward the 2006 Quadrennial Defense Review to establish new vectors for transformation of the military. The Bush administration believes that the U.S. military faces challenges from four discrete sectors.[73] The quadrants fit along a low-high vulnerability axis that intersects with a low-high likelihood axis (Figure II.I). In the upper-left-hand quadrant, irregular challenges offer comparatively little direct threat to the United States but occur with relative frequency. Cumulatively, they erode U.S. credibility. Such occurrences include terrorism, insurgency, civil war, and the "emerging concept" unrestricted warfare. The current challenges in Iraq and Afghanistan fall within this quadrant.

To the upper right, characterized by high likelihood and U.S. vulnerability, are catastrophic challenges. These include such dangers as homeland missile attacks, nuclear proliferation from a state to nonstate actors, or even a devastating WMD strike on an ally. Threats in this quadrant could work paralytic effects on American power.

In the lower-left quadrant, traditional threats—using long-established, well-known forms of military competition and conflict—seem remote. They pose little current danger because of the status of the United States as the only superpower. However, we could imagine the emergence within the next twenty years or so of a near-peer competitor (China? Russia?) that could challenge U.S. power.

Finally, in the lower-right quadrant are disruptive challenges characterized by low likelihood but high lethality to the United States should they arise. That is, they could marginalize U.S. power. Such challenges would rely heavily on advanced technology, including space-based sensors; information, biological, or cyber warfare; ultraminiaturization, and directed energy (lasers). As with the possible emergence of a near-peer competitor, China serves as the most likely candidate for development of disruptive capabilities sufficient to begin to undermine U.S. global power.

The administration has specifically embraced capabilities-based planning as a method for balancing risk across these four quadrants and, on the basis of those assessments, setting "priorities among competing capabilities."[74] The latest Quadrennial Defense Review, issued by the Bush administration on February 6, 2006, encapsulated the ways in which the administration planned to align platforms, systems, and capabilities in relation to the four challenges depicted in Figure 11.1. The illustration in Figure 11.2 reflects its dedication to the principle of greater balance in the distribution of capabilities from the traditional challenge quadrant to the others.

This process readily risks focusing excessively on one type of threat over the others. Indeed, Clayton M. Christensen and Michael E. Raynor assert that mainstream organizations find such balancing very difficult to achieve.[75] First, the rules for success in one market sector often run directly counter to those prevailing in another. Second, an organization under intense pressure within one area will take its gaze from the long-term view by focusing more on immediate threats than on future opportunities and challenges.[76] And, in the process of its coping, a bias will emerge toward augmentation of legacy platforms and systems—for instance, adding armor to Humvees rather than developing new alternatives to them.

Efforts to shift emphasis from the traditional to other quadrants fall most clearly within the compass of the effects of 9/11 and the global war on terrorism on civilian

FIGURE 11.2   The Effort to Balance Capabilities among the Four Types
of Security Challenges

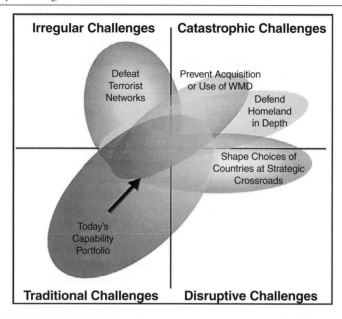

Irregular Challenges | Catastrophic Challenges

Defeat
Terrorist
Networks

Prevent Acquisition
or Use of WMD

Defend
Homeland
in Depth

Shape Choices of
Countries at Strategic
Crossroads

Today's
Capability
Portfolio

Traditional Challenges   Disruptive Challenges

Note: As the diagram shows, the department is shifting its portfolio of capabilities to address irregular, catastrophic, and disruptive challenges while sustaining capabilities to address traditional challenges.

and military leaders' perceptions of the current and future national security challenges faced by the United States. Indeed, that the administration assigns such prominence to catastrophic and irregular threats derives very substantially from the shocks associated with the 9/11 attacks and the difficulty of pursuing the GWOT. Some strategists, however, suggest that the American military culture fostered poor institutional learning in the "irregular" quadrant in Vietnam; a British brigadier, Nigel Aylwin-Foster, similarly argued that many of those cultural impediments to performance in the area have manifested themselves in the U.S. performance in Iraq.[77] The army chief of staff, General Peter J. Schoomaker, found Aylwin-Foster's critique so cogent that he circulated it to all of his generals. If a military culture proves maladroit at adaptability in this quadrant, should it persist and seek to adapt, or alternatively, try to avoid entanglements of this sort? Of course, these choices came to a boil in the Vietnam era with wrenching consequences for the national psyche, bringing some comprehension of the limits of counterinsurgency tactics.

The effects of capabilities-based planning. Clearly, the Bush II administration has placed great stock in the utility of capabilities-based planning in devising and balancing programmatic priorities. Given the issues raised above, has the emphasis succeeded?

In seeking to answer that question we should focus on the Office of the Secretary of Defense (OSD) as the engine of the innovation process. In this regard, the extent to which OSD instituted capabilities-based planning to further adjust mindsets among Pentagon officials can be examined. Are we able to say that the efforts of OSD facilitated the balancing of strategic vision and investments among the quadrants? If they have, to what can we attribute that success? If not, to what can we attribute the failure? Again, the assessment here—based partly on multiple interviews with key participants in, and observers of, strategic planning and resource allocation in the Pentagon[78]—simply tries to ascertain the current situation with respect to shifts in mindsets. Figure 11.2's commitments themselves serve at this stage only as indicative objectives, rather than definitive decisions. But we can examine how relevant actors in DoD reflect the degree to which institutional and cultural shifts might underpin the administration's intent.

OSD encompasses an immense bureaucracy in its own right. It provides central guidance and coordination to the Department of Defense and policy and management support to the secretary of defense. With respect to capabilities-based planning, the critical elements of OSD include the deputy secretary of defense, the under secretary for policy, and the director for program analysis and evaluation. Importantly, the deputy secretary position remained vacant during much of the development of the 2006 Quadrennial Defense Review (QDR)—that is, from Paul Wolfowitz's departure in spring 2005 to his formal succession by Gordon R. England in January 2006, through a recess appointment. England did provide oversight of the QDR process while serving in an acting capacity as deputy secretary. However, his failure initially to obtain Senate confirmation hampered his institutional leverage.

The under secretary for policy, Douglas Feith, also departed the administration in August 2005. Ryan Henry, Feith's principal deputy, took much of the lead for the 2006 QDR. He developed the administration's quadrant chart depicting the four challenges of the security environment, which provided the intellectual focal point for the QDR. However, several respondents noted that the lack, until mid-2004, of a deputy assistant secretary for plans and resources under Henry led to significant delay in OSD's development of guidance for the QDR. Meanwhile, the Directorate for Program Analysis and Evaluation, under Ken Krieg, did preparatory work on many of the central program issues vying for attention as the QDR unfolded. Krieg left the directorate in June 2005 to become under secretary of defense for acquisition, technology and logistics.

The resulting delay in providing guidance about the capabilities that the administration wished to promote proved exceedingly frustrating for uniformed officers committed to implementing capabilities-based planning. A great deal of contestation naturally surfaces around the resource issues that emerge in any effort to align programmatic with strategic commitments. Conventionally, the branches have pressed their cases for reordering investments within and across branches on the basis of analyses of projected costs and benefits. For members of Congress and senators, however, such assessments typically include costs and benefits to their districts. Regardless of how thoroughly those in the Pentagon take on the program-agnosticism that capabilities-based planning prescribes, legislative politicians will cling to platforms that translate into jobs in their respective districts and states. Still, an ethos has emerged at the Pentagon whereby planners and budgeters try to prove their cases with rigorous analysis. They become frustrated when those higher up in branch staffs, the Joint Staff, or OSD civilian leaders override analytically based recommendations for seemingly political reasons.

With these conceptual and analytic strictures in mind, it does not come as a surprise that respondents failed to ascribe great significance to OSD with respect to aligning plans and resource commitments *within* the four challenge environments. However, another crucial role for OSD is to balance commitments *between* the environments; and to the administration's credit, the OSD leadership has invested considerable effort in providing machinery for addressing and reconciling conflicting elements of both strategic plans and resource commitments. (As we might expect, however, those actually working in OSD were more sanguine about its effectiveness in this role than were those outside the secretary's inner sanctum.)

At the outset of the administration Donald Rumsfeld thought, perhaps naïvely, that he could bring about the requisite "trading" between priorities through a Senior Executive Council (SEC). Rumsfeld conceived of this group as having a function similar to that of a corporate board of directors. The membership included the secretary; the deputy secretary; and the under secretary for acquisition, technology and logistics; plus the three service department (Army, Navy and Air Force) secretaries. But the SEC never functioned as Rumsfeld intended.

Purple suits or not, the three service secretaries continued to carry baggage from the service departments that they headed. Furthermore, the uniformed chiefs of the military branches, not their corresponding civilian branch secretaries, bear the legal authority for advising on organizing, training, and equipping their branches. This leads the military branch secretaries to defer to their uniformed chiefs, which hardly helps the service secretaries to overcome their predispositions to wrap themselves in the colors of their branches.

Given this obstacle to joint planning and coordination, Rumsfeld decided early on to widen his consultative compass with a much larger body than the SEC. This broader group he styled the Senior Leadership Review Group (SLRG). SLRG was chaired by Rumsfeld and included a wider array of Pentagon officials, as well as more actors from OSD, namely, the deputy secretary of defense and the five OSD under secretaries, as well as the chairman and vice chairman of the Joint Chiefs of Staff, all four branch chiefs, and the secretaries of the army, navy, and air force. On occasion, SLRG meetings would also include the four star combatant commanders responsible for the regional and functional elements of joint global operations.

In theory SLRG's inclusiveness provided a one-stop marketplace for trade-offs with respect to strategic and resource commitments, but its size often proved cumbersome. Nonetheless, the SLRG dynamics and rules for deliberation had sufficiently separated the branch chiefs from their reflex to fight for their service interests that they began to open their minds to very substantial trades in the fulfillment of capabilities.

Powerful, service-based impediments to transformations based on strategic or tactical outputs remain. The services tend to focus on technologies that fit their mission. However, increasingly, aspiring flag officers (beginning with rear admirals and brigadier generals) pass through an intensive "joint" socialization, with required tours in the Joint Staff and combatant commands as well as courses operating under the direction of the Joint Staff. Thus, the emerging cadres of flag and general officers do think "purple" much more than their counterparts in previous generations. In addition Rumsfeld, at the beginning of the administration, adopted the practice of interviewing each candidate for full or lieutenant general. Until Rumsfeld's departure toward the end of 2006, a very significant proportion of assignments were made directly from Rumsfeld's personal staff or the Joint Staff into the leading positions in combatant commands. Early in 2006, these included the heads of the Northern, Southern, Strategic, and Transportation Commands.

Rumsfeld's tenure at DoD was intended to accentuate strategic planning objectives that were established prior to his incumbency. But Rumsfeld chose to do this largely by ignoring the service chiefs and their respective cultures—a strategy bringing to mind, in some ways, Robert McNamara's tenure under Presidents Kennedy and Johnson. The Senior Leadership Review Group that Rumsfeld instituted did at least acknowledge that civilian officials and service chiefs needed to converge in a single forum for the various responsible individuals in the Pentagon to begin working in concert.

With increased institutionalization of capabilities-based planning and new leadership approaches among political appointees at the Pentagon, it was vital for balance among commitments to be at the forefront of defense concerns. In times of stress, organizations risk becoming so fixated on one nettlesome set of challenges that they lose sight of the need for adaptability both in their traditional activities and when different challenges emerge in other sectors.

The Rumsfeld team could not have faced a clearer requirement for agility than that presented by the invasions and occupations of Afghanistan and Iraq. The focal point at the Pentagon for planning and budgeting has shifted from concern of a potential near-peer competitor (China) to counterterrorism. Yet we seem now to face a further transition to a possible long-term footing of global, or at least Middle Eastern, counterinsurgency. Rumsfeld, as have other "powerful" secretaries of defense, sought to augment the power and strategic control of the center. A new secretary, Robert Gates, and a changed team of political appointees (notably Deputy Secretary England) may have learned that they cannot run the Defense Department and the military services without giving due regard to the views of the uniformed officers. Paying attention to what they and other stakeholders at the Pentagon think could bring to the current Quadrennial Defense Review renewed intellectual rigor and analytic robustness, and thus a momentous readjustment of mindsets in the Pentagon and the military branches. That positive legacy can be achieved—but only by tuning in to the voices of key individuals, not tuning them out, as was too often the case during the Rumsfeld years at DoD and the George W. Bush presidency.

Conclusion

This chapter has analyzed the George W. Bush administration's relationship with the Pentagon, especially through Donald Rumsfeld's stewardship of the Defense Department. It centers on two areas: first, on the dynamics of the decision to invade Iraq, from the standpoint of the type of leadership the administration provided in connection with an intervention extremely difficult for the military to plan and implement; and second, on the progress of the overarching administration commitment to transformation of the military. The two are, of course, intertwined: the institutionalization of capabilities-based planning at DoD must be considered in relation to insights derived from the invasion and occupation of Iraq and changes in the leadership in the Pentagon during the past three years.

With respect to Iraq, the analysis suggests the extent to which the administration's advisory system proved to be a breeding ground for unrestrained ideological entrepreneurship—a result both of President Bush's seeming detachment from open discourse about the crucial issues he faced and of the surfeit in the administration generally of doctrinaires. The consequence was that little effort was given to ensuring that policy initiatives would receive intense collegial scrutiny; very little structure was in place to do so. The especially porous boundary between political operations and policy development in the administration exacerbated the dysfunctions that stemmed from poor issue management. That allowed free rein to those, especially Paul Wolfowitz, who were inclined to resort to crisis inflation. The political impasse created by the administration's failure to capture Osama bin Laden in Afghanistan left the road open for Wolfowitz (and his confederates, placed strategically in the Executive Office of the President, who had long been interested in overthrowing Saddam Hussein) to change the subject and press for regime change in Iraq. This gambit played so well to the president's natural reflexes that it gained primacy within the political executive without a rigorous examination of the complexities of its implementation or the potential damage that it could do to U.S. standing in the global community.

However, even worse for the Bush legacy, the intramural conflicts between political appointees in the Pentagon and the uniformed leadership proved devastating to the uniformed military. As a result, the invasions occurred with a woeful lack of consideration of the consequences of poor planning, inadequate force structure, and insufficient latitude for operational commanders to adjust strategy and tactics.

In the end, haphazard decision making, without adequate vetting or accounting for worst-case consequences, not only can bog the nation down in costly and uncertain ventures, but also can create difficulties for organizational planning and adjustment.

It remains to be seen whether the task of transformation can be achieved in such circumstances. Secretary Rumsfeld's Senior Leadership Review Group—even though not deployed from the outset, and in some respects inclusive to a fault—at least acknowledged head-on that all colors of "suits" must be able to converge in a single forum for the various powers in the Pentagon to begin working cooperatively.

With the increased institutionalization of capabilities-based planning and new personnel and leadership approaches among political appointees, balance among commitments has to take center stage. Given the stakes, it is to be hoped that one legacy of the Bush administration will be to empower the new leadership at the Pentagon to make that balance work.

Notes

1. Woodrow Wilson, *Constitutional Government of the United States* (New York: Columbia University Press, 1908), 70–71.
2. John W. Kingdon, *Agendas, Alternatives, and Public Policies,* 2nd ed. (New York: Harper-Collins, 1995), 94.
3. Terry M. Moe, "The Politicized Presidency," in *The New Direction in American Politics,* ed. John E. Chubb and Paul E. Peterson (Washington, D.C.: Brookings Institution Press, 1985).
4. For a detailed discussion of this notion, see Colin Campbell, "Unrestrained Ideological Entrepreneurship in the Bush II Advisory System," in *The George W. Bush Presidency: Appraisals and Prospects,* ed. Colin Campbell and Bert A. Rockman (Washington, D.C.: CQ Press, 2004), 73–80, from which the subsequent discussion is drawn.
5. Alexander L. George, *Presidential Decisionmaking in Foreign Policy: The Effective Use of Information and Advice* (Boulder: Westview Press, 1980), 193–194.
6. Roger B. Porter, *Presidential Policy-Making: The Economic Policy Board* (Cambridge: Cambridge University Press, 1980).
7. Fred I. Greenstein, *The Hidden-Hand Presidency: Eisenhower as Leader* (New York: Basic Books, 1982), 113–116.
8. Kiron K. Skinner, Annelise Anderson, and Martin Anderson, eds., *Reagan in His Own Hand: The Writings of Ronald Reagan That Reveal His Revolutionary Vision for America* (New York: Free Press, 2001).

9. Colin Campbell, *Managing the Presidency* (Pittsburgh: University of Pittsburgh Press, 1986), 72.

10. Ibid., 73.

11. Ibid., 108–111.

12. John P. Burke, *The Institutional Presidency: Organizing and Managing the White House from FDR to Clinton,* 2nd ed. (Baltimore: Johns Hopkins University Press, 2000), 153–154.

13. According to the Tower Commission Report, "The President's management style is to put the principal responsibility of policy review and implementation on the shoulders of his advisors. Nevertheless, with such a complex, high-risk operation and so much at stake, the President should have ensured that the NSC system did not fail him. He did not force his policy to undergo the most critical review of which the NSC participants and the process were capable. . . . the most powerful features of the NSC system—providing comprehensive analysis, alternatives and follow-up—were not utilized." President's Special Review Board (Tower Commission), *Report* (New York: Bantam Books, 1987), 79–80.

14. Bob Woodward, *Bush at War* (New York: Simon and Schuster, 2002); and David Frum, *The Right Man: The Surprising Presidency of George W. Bush (An Inside Account)* (New York: Random House, 2003).

15. Mark Crispin Miller, *The Bush Dyslexicon: Observations on a National Disorder* (New York: Norton, 2001).

16. Woodward, *Bush at War,* 49, 83–85.

17. Michael R. Gordon and General Bernard E. Trainor, *The General's War: The Inside Story of the Conflict in the Gulf* (Boston: Little, Brown, 1995), 6.

18. Ibid., 418, 424, 448.

19. Woodward, *Bush at War,* 83–85.

20. Bill Keller, "The Sunshine Warrior," *New York Times Magazine,* September 22, 2002, 52.

21. Ibid., 54, 84.

22. Judith Miller and Lowell Bergman, "Calls for New Push into Iraq Gain Power in Washington," *New York Times,* December 13, 2001.

23. Barrie McKenna, "The Pashtun Prophet Who Shapes U.S. Policy," *Toronto Globe and Mail,* March 1, 2003.

24. In February 2007, Khalilzad was nominated to become U.S. ambassador to the United Nations.

25. For a detailed discussion, see George Packer, *The Assassins' Gate* (New York: FSG, 2004).

26. Phil Shenon, "Threats and Responses, Domestic Security: Ridge Discovers Size of Home Security Task," *New York Times,* March 3, 2003; Bill Keller, "Defense! Defense! Defense!" *New York Times,* April 19, 2003; and Ceci Connolly, "Readiness for Chemical Attack Criticized," *Washington Post,* June 4, 2003.

27. Woodward, *Bush at War,* 100–102; and Jane Perlez, David E. Sanger, and Thom Shanker, "A Nation Challenged: The Advisers," *New York Times,* September 23, 2001. See also Judith Miller, Jeff Gerth, and Don Van Natta Jr., "Planning for Terror but Failing to Act," *New York Times,* December 30, 2001; and Barton Gellman, "A Strategy's Cautious Evolution before Sept. 11," *Washington Post,* January 20, 2002.

28. Edward Cody and Kamran Khan, "U.S. Struggles to Revive Crucial Cold War Alliance," *Washington Post,* October 17, 2001; and Molly Moore and Edward Cody, "Hunting bin Laden: U.S. Stymied by Slippery Target," *Washington Post,* November 4, 2001.

29. Edward Cody, "Manhunt Uncovers No Traces of Bin Laden," *Washington Post,* December 26, 2001. See also Eric Schmitt and Michael R. Gordon, "New Priorities; Hunt for bin Laden Loses Steam as Winter Grips Afghan Caves," *New York Times,* December 30, 2001; Barry Bearak, "Sanctuary; Tribal Area of Pakistan Gives Refuge to Qaeda Fighters Fleeing Caves," *New York Times,* December 31, 2001; and Eric Schmitt, "The Dragnet: Tribes Balking at Cave Hunt, Pentagon Says," *New York Times,* January 17, 2002.

30. Barton Gellman, "Anti-Terror Pioneer Turns in Badge," *Washington Post,* March 13, 2003; Karen DeYoung and Peter Slevin, "Counterterror Team's Turnover Continues," *Washington Post,* March 20, 2003; and Laura Blumerfeld, "Former Aide Takes Aim at War on Terror," *Washington Post,* June 16, 2003.

31. Frum, *The Right Man,* 235.

32. National Desk, "Ex-Aide Insists White House Puts Politics ahead of Policy," *New York Times,* December 2, 2002. See also Ron Suskind, "Why Are These Men Laughing?" *Esquire,* January 2003.

33. David E. Sanger, "Bush Aides Say Tough Tone Put Foes on Notice," *New York Times,* January 31, 2002; and Michael R. Gordon, "Cheney Rejects Criticism by Allies over Stand on Iraq," *New York Times,* February 16, 2002.

34. Gordon, "Cheney Rejects Criticism."

35. Karen DeYoung and Alan Sipress, "A Rush to Act on the Mideast," *Washington Post,* March 14, 2002; and Alan Sipress, "Cheney Plays Down Arab Criticism over Iraq," *Washington Post,* March 18, 2002.

36. Richard Cohen, "The Undoing of Mideast Diplomacy," *Washington Post,* April 19, 2001.

37. Dan Balz and Dana Milbank, "Bush Doctrine Begins to Blur," *Washington Post,* April 3, 2002; and Dana Milbank and Karen DeYoung, "The Birth of a Balancing Act," *Washington Post,* April 6, 2002.

38. Steven R. Weisman, "President Bush and the Middle East Axis of Ambiguity," *New York Times,* April 13, 2002; Elisabeth Bumiller, "Seeking to Stem Growing Political Fury, Bush Sends Conservative to Pro-Israel Rally," *New York Times,* April 16, 2002; and Patrick E. Tyler, "A Rising Toll for Bush: No Peace, More Blame," *New York Times,* April 18, 2002.

39. Karen DeYoung and Walter Pincus, "Crises Strain Bush Policies," *Washington Post,* April 21, 2002.

40. George Parker, "Dreaming of Democracy," *New York Times Magazine,* March 2, 2003.

41. Dana Milbank, "Bush Links Faith and Agenda in Speech to Broadcast Group," *Washington Post,* February 10, 2003; and Jackson Lears, "How a War Became a Crusade," *New York Times,* March 11, 2003.

42. See Richard Cohen, "The Crude Crusader," *Washington Post,* February 10, 2003; and "Kirkpatrick Was Right," *Washington Post,* May 8, 2003.

43. Campbell, *Managing the Presidency,* 70.

44. Glenn Kessler, "U.S. Decision on Iraq Has Puzzling Past," *Washington Post,* January 12, 2003.

45. James Risen, *State of War: The Secret History of the CIA and the Bush Administration* (New York: Free Press, 2006), 113–115.

46. Thom Shanker, "Bush Hears Options Including Baghdad Strike," *New York Times,* August 7, 2002.

47. Elisabeth Bumiller, "President Notes Dissent on Iraq," *New York Times,* August 17, 2002.

48. James Dao, "Senior Bush Defends '91 Decision on Iraq," *New York Times,* March 1, 2003.

49. Dana Milbank, "Cheney Argues for Preemptive Strike on Iraq," *Washington Post,* August 26, 2002; and Howard Kurtz, "Cheney Rattles His Saber," *Washington Post,* August 27, 2002.

50. James A. Baker III, "The Right Way to Change a Regime," *New York Times,* August 25, 2002. See also Neil Lewis and David E. Sanger, "Bush May Request Congress's Backing on Iraq," *New York Times,* August 29, 2002.

51. Patrick Tyler, "U.S. and Britain Drafting Resolution to Impose Deadline on Iraq," *New York Times,* September 26, 2002.

52. Michael O'Hanlon, "How the Hard-Liners Lost," *Washington Post,* November 8, 2002; and Steven R. Weisman, "How Powell Lined Up the Votes, Starting with the President's," *New York Times,* November 9, 2002.

53. Dana Milbank, "Conservatives Wary of Arms Inspections," *Washington Post,* November 14, 2002; and "U.S. Voices Doubts on Iraq Search," *Washington Post,* December 2, 2002.

54. Even the British had grave doubts about the legal legitimation of the invasion. See the documents collected in Mark Danner, *The Secret Way to War* (New York: New York Review Books, 2006).

55. Dexter Filkins, "Turkish Deputies Refuse to Accept American Troops," *New York Times,* March 2, 2003; and "Turkey Will Seek a Second Decision on a G.I. Presence," *New York Times,* March 3, 2003.

56. Glenn Kessler and Mike Allen, "U.S. Missteps Led to Failed Diplomacy," *Washington Post,* March 16, 2003.

57. Michael Barzelay and Colin Campbell, *Preparing for the Future: Strategic Planning in the U.S. Air Force* (Washington, D.C.: Brookings Institution Press, 2003).

58. See, for instance, David Osborne and Ted Gaebler, *Reinventing Government: How the Entrepreneurial Spirit Is Transforming the Public Sector* (Reading, Mass.: Addison-Wesley, 1992). A critique of reinvention that highlights the need for political leaders to frame transformation more generally within the context of policy guidance is found in Joel D. Aberbach and Bert A. Rockman, *In the Web of Politics: Three Decades of the U.S. Federal Executive* (Washington, D.C.: Brookings Institution Press, 2000), esp. 187.

59. Shanker, "Bush Hears Options."

60. Eric Schmitt and Thom Shanker, "War Plan Calls for Precision Bombing Wave to Break Iraqi Army Early in Attack," *New York Times,* February 2, 2002.

61. Michael R. Gordon and Bernard E. Trainor, *Cobra II: The Inside Story of the Invasion and Occupation of Iraq* (New York: Pantheon, 2006).

62. Thomas E. Ricks, "War Could Last Months," *Washington Post,* March 26, 2003; and Merrill A. McPeak, "Shock and Pause," *Washington Post,* April 2, 2003.

63. Vernon Loeb, "Rumsfeld Faulted for Troop Dilution," *Washington Post,* March 29, 2003; and Seymour M. Hersh, "Annals of National Security: Offense and Defense," *New Yorker,* April 7, 2003.

64. Vernon Loeb, "Rumsfeld Queried on Nominees," *Washington Post,* May 31, 2003.

65. Bradley Graham, "Retired General Picked to Head Army," *Washington Post,* June 11, 2003.

66. R. W. Apple Jr., "A New Way of Warfare Leaves behind an Abundance of Loose Ends," *New York Times,* April 20, 2003; Elizabeth Becker, "Baghdad Hospitals Face a Crisis, Groups Warn U.S.," *New York Times,* May 3, 2003; Douglas Jehl and Elizabeth Becker,

"The Looting: Experts' Pleas to Pentagon Didn't Save Museum," *New York Times,* April 16, 2003; John Malcolm Russell, "We're Still Missing the Looting Picture," *Washington Post,* June 15, 2003; Neela Banerjee, "Widespread Looting Leaves Iraq's Oil Industry in Ruins," *New York Times,* June 10, 2003; and Patrick Tyler, "Barrels Looted at Nuclear Site Raise Fears for Iraqi Villagers," *New York Times,* June 8, 2003; Raymond Bonner, "Iraq Arms Caches Cited in Attacks," *New York Times,* October 14, 2003; and Raymond Bonner and Ian Fisher, "At Iraqi Depot, Missiles Galore and No Guards," *New York Times,* October 17, 2003.

67. Eric Schmitt, "Rumsfeld Echoes Notion That Iraq Destroyed Arms," *New York Times,* May 28, 2003; and Paul Krugman, "Who's Accountable?" *New York Times,* June 10, 2003. See also Jane Harman, "WMD: What Went Wrong?" *Washington Post,* June 11, 2003.

68. Michael Gordon, "U.S. Aides Split on Assessment of Iraq's Plans," *New York Times,* October 10, 2002.

69. Elisabeth Bumiller and Eric Schmitt, "Cheney, Little Seen by Public, Wielding Influence on Security," *New York Times,* January 31, 2003.

70. Rick Atkinson and Thomas E. Ricks, "War's Military, Political Goals Begin to Diverge," *Washington Post,* April 29, 2003.

71. Dana Milbank, "Upbeat Tone Ended with War," *Washington Post,* March 28, 2003.

72. Eric Schmitt, "Pentagon Contradicts General on Iraq Occupation Force's Size," *New York Times,* February 28, 2003.

73. Department of Defense, *The National Defense Strategy of the United States of America,* March 2005; and "A Framework for Strategic Thinking," August 19, 2004, www.fas.org/irp/agency/dod/framework.pdf.

74. Department of Defense, *The National Defense Strategy,* 13.

75. Clayton M. Christensen and Michael E. Raynor, *The Innovator's Solution: Creating and Sustaining Successful Growth* (Boston: Harvard Business School Publishing Corporation, 2003); see also Clayton M. Christensen, *The Innovator's Dilemma: The Revolutionary Book That Will Change the Way You Do Business* (New York: HarperBusiness, 2000).

76. Christensen and Raynor, *The Innovator's Solution,* 112–113.

77. John A. Nagl, *Counterinsurgency Lessons From Malaya and Vietnam: Learning to Eat Soup with a Knife* (Westport, Conn.: Praeger, 2002); Brigadier Nigel Aylwin-Foster, "Changing the Army for Counterinsurgency Operations," *Military Review,* November–December 2005. The 2007 "surge" in combat troops under the command of General David Petraeus, a widely admired student of counterinsurgency, sought to rectify past failures to institute lessons learned, but many feared that adaptation came too little, too late.

78. I have interviewed a total of 69 respondents: 37 military officers (including 6 three star, 8 two star, and 12 one star generals/admirals), 7 senior political appointees, 13 senior career officials, and 12 external respondents who are researchers in think tanks or consultants.

CHAPTER 12

The Braking of the President
Shifting Context and the Bush Domestic Agenda

Christopher H. Foreman Jr.

EVEN A "WAR PRESIDENT," as George W. Bush came to style himself, has substantial domestic ambitions and responsibilities. At least two fundamental propositions appear inescapable regarding the relationship between the "two presidencies"—meaning, in this instance, a war effort and a domestic agenda.[1] First, the longer and costlier a president's war, the greater the risk that its adverse effects may impinge on his domestic agenda, sapping the dollars, attention, trust, and deference (in short, the precious political capital) required to pursue it. (Witness the ill-fated presidency of Lyndon B. Johnson.) Second, running even a popular war does not enable a president to get his way on domestic issues, most of which lack any directly identifiable national security aspect. Taxation, regulation, immigration, and entitlements (to name a few key examples) play out far from the theater of war, both substantively and politically. Presidential assets in national security are not applicable to domestic policy. Despite his foreign policy stature, the elder President Bush's principal domestic legacy is arguably embodied in his endorsement of a single statute, the Americans with Disabilities Act of 1990.

On the other hand, the power of any presidency is such that even one past its prime may play a key role in important domestic niches. Jimmy Carter's final year in office witnessed the enactment of the Comprehensive Environmental Response, Compensation and Liability Act (the "Superfund") and the Paperwork Reduction Act that helped lay the institutional foundation for Ronald Reagan's forays into regulatory relief.[2] President George W. Bush famously doesn't "do nuances"—but anyone fairly assessing his domestic presidency must.

That said, the broad arc of a defensive, constrained, second term domestic presidency had become unmistakable as the midterm elections of 2006 loomed, elections that would vanquish Bush's largely compliant Republican majority in both houses of

Congress. The introduction to *Team Bush: Leadership Lessons from the Bush White House,* Donald F. Kettl's sympathetic 2003 distillation of the Bush leadership style, opens with a quotation from presidential aide Karen Hughes describing the team leader as "decisive . . . disciplined . . . [and] a really good delegator."[3] Wrote Kettl of the decision-making process leading up to the Iraq war, "Bush was neither overwhelmed by the issues nor unwilling to decide them. . . . From the turmoil of the summer debate, Bush emerged with a crystal-clear strategy, and Team Bush fell into step behind it."[4] For a time, so did most Americans.

Three years later, however, *Washington Post* columnist Sebastian Mallaby would offer this damning assessment on the domestic front:

> Team Bush could use some fresh domestic policy. Its talk of tax reform has fizzled. Its defeat on Social Security has destroyed its hopes of fixing entitlements. Its feckless energy non-policy has come back to haunt it. Its tax cuts look ever more untenable as Iraq costs escalate. Its proposed expansion of health savings accounts is incompetently muddled. Its bungling of Hurricane Katrina's aftermath is legendary. Its trampling of civil liberties has been rolled back by the Supreme Court.[5]

In this chapter I explore the contextual forces that empowered, and later undermined, "Team Bush" in the domestic arena. It would be both premature and unfair here to autopsy the Bush presidency purely in terms of its failures and limitations. But it is already clear that Bush will leave a deeply problematic and uncertain legacy in key areas of domestic policy. The 2005 failure to grapple successfully with Social Security threatened to postpone necessary reforms at least into the administration of Bush's successor, if not beyond; his 2007 State of the Union pledge to work with the new Democratic congressional majority to "fix Medicare and Medicaid—and save Social Security" did not immediately transform the public debate. Creating a White House Office of Faith-Based and Community Initiatives, and allied efforts in the federal departments, by administrative fiat may have been pragmatic in the short term, but later presidents will be equally free to innovate in the opposite direction without congressional assent. Bush successfully pursued and defended deep tax cuts without equivalent spending restraint, even as the country moved from a brief period of fiscal surplus to a longer one of significant deficits. Setting aside the "fairness" critique promoted by Democrats (i.e., "unfair" cuts in both taxes and spending), Bush's fiscal policy seems likely to constrain successor administrations in ways that both parties will find painful. The Medicare prescription drug program enacted in December 2003 gave Republicans bragging rights to having acted on a major social policy concern on turf that typically favors Democrats. Yet the program's early implementation struggles and the benefit gaps that many seniors are certain to experience (the infamous "doughnut hole") may make the program a mixed political blessing and a policy headache. The onslaught of Hurricane Katrina in August 2005 turned disaster response policy into a significant political disaster for Bush, prompting allegations of administrative incompetence and raising, literally overnight, broader questions of how to rehabilitate a major American city, prevent recurrent devastation, and address the poverty that a botched evacuation exposed. And by spring 2006 the continuing flood of illegal immigrants had exposed deep division among Republicans; doubly cursed, Bush proved incapable of closing a legislative deal that may have been impossible to implement effectively if it had been enacted. It was no wonder that by fall 2006 Republican congressional candidates across the country were seeking to project independence from the administration— some even avoiding the label "Republican" altogether.[6] Meanwhile the White House sought, paradoxically, to emphasize terrorism by refocusing attention away from the very war ostensibly commenced, in large part, to combat it.

An Inventory of Assets

As he headed into the 2004 presidential campaign Bush had substantial assets on which to draw beyond the influence, formal and informal, that any president is bound to have. The terror attacks of September 11, 2001, had prompted a surge in his public approval rating to the stratospheric levels enjoyed briefly by his father immediately after the Persian Gulf War a decade earlier. This cushion solidified a foundation of near-unanimous support among Republican legislators and voters. Despite grumbling from some Republicans irritated specifically by his departures from conservative doctrine on education, steel tariffs, farm subsidies, and Medicare (and more broadly by his unwillingness to rein in federal spending) Bush would face no challenger for renomination.

House Republicans especially, under the firm—some would say strangling—hand of House Speaker Dennis Hastert, R-Ill., and majority leader Tom DeLay, R-Texas, remained throughout the 108th Congress (2003–2004) broadly in step with the president. They were sufficiently disciplined to deliver reliable, if often exceedingly thin, majorities in floor votes on such matters as Head Start funding and school vouchers for the District of Columbia. Legislation to create a Medicare prescription drug benefit survived at least two such near-death votes in 2003, the first (216–215) when Rep. Jo Ann Emerson, R-Mo., extracted a promise of a later (and ultimately winning) vote to allow the reimportation of American-made prescription drugs.[7] The second and much better known example occurred early on the morning of November 22, when House Republican leaders held open the vote on final passage of the Medicare reform legislation for nearly three hours—time enough for last-minute arm-twisting to yield a 220–215 victory that minority whip Steny H. Hoyer, D-Md., would condemn as an "undemocratic subversion of the will of the House."[8] Of the deeply controversial legislation, bitterly opposed by Democrats as inadequate and by many conservatives as inappropriate, President Bush said simply, "I applaud the House for meeting our obligations to America's seniors. Now it is time for the Senate to act."9 The Senate did act, producing a Medicare Prescription Drug Improvement and Modernization Act that would further alienate conservatives outraged at both a new entitlement (which turned out to be far more costly than advertised) and the tactics used to win it, including the overt suppression of unfavorable cost estimates produced by the Medicare program's chief actuary.

Nevertheless, through 2004 the relationship between Bush and his congressional (especially House) partisans remained so cohesive as to suggest at least a tacit (and perhaps explicit) bargain: each would avoid embarrassing the other and also avoid reliance (in the House at least) on Democratic help in legislating. A pre-Bush, "textbook" view of legislative-executive relations would have led one to expect both occasional vetoes of legislation and reasonably robust legislative oversight of the administration. But oversight became more restrained, sporadic, and halfhearted during the Bush presidency (as one might expect during a period of unified party control), and vetoes disappeared altogether, as Bush became the first president since John Quincy Adams to serve a full term without producing one. For a president this is, as the saying goes, "nice work if you can get it," but Congress rarely makes it possible. The imperative of reelecting the president doubtless helped suppress intraparty conflict but also focused the minds of everyone in the White House on message control, partisan mobilization, and blame avoidance. And well before the 2004 election, a sharp polarization of, and near-parity between, the legislative parties had combined to create both the capacity and the incentive among Republicans to accept leadership discipline.

Bush's narrow but decisive reelection victory appeared to leave him moderately well positioned, assuming he could avoid serious misjudgment and plain bad luck. He had not won the commanding second term victory of an Eisenhower, a Nixon, or a Reagan, scoring a relatively anemic 50.7 percent of the popular vote. But he had become "the first Republican president reelected with gains in both houses of Congress in eighty years," and congressional Republicans had proved a generally disciplined and deferential crew.10

But what, exactly, was Bush positioned to do? Two days after beating Senator Kerry, the president asserted in a press conference that he had "earned capital in the campaign, political capital, and now I intend to spend it. It is my style. . . . I've earned capital in this election—and I'm going to spend it for what I told the people I'd spend it on . . . Social Security and tax reform, moving this economy forward, education, fighting and winning the war on terror." The claim was perhaps overly grand but was consistent with Bush's aggressive "leadership by definition," as Stephen Skowronek has put it.11 Bush had similarly dismissed any notion of sail trimming after the 2000 election, despite his popular vote loss, insisting that he had ultimately prevailed "because I campaigned on issues that people heard."[12] But soon after his reelection key components of his domestic policy agenda would prove elusive.

An Inventory of Constraints

Even with his assets Bush faced constraints of two sorts. One was a broad set of institutional constraints, the durable structures and rules that apply more-or-less consistently from one presidency to the next. The most basic is sheer institutional separation (i.e., the constitutional separation of powers, bicameralism, and national news media that remain independent notwithstanding the favorable ideological tilt of some elements). Presidents must also win legislative majorities, and often (in the Senate) supermajorities; determined minorities can enact nothing while derailing much. The most significant sort of structural change a president might covet, constitutional amendment, is rare, intentionally onerous, and without any formal role for the president. Finally, one significant constitutional change of relatively recent vintage, the Twenty-Second Amendment, has term-limited all recent presidents, rendering them less politically potent as the second term wanes.

The second category of constraints lies in the particulars of the immediate context. The most important of these are a given policy's political characteristics— its attentive constituencies and terms of discourse. How important is a policy area or a specific proposal to the president? How salient is it to the nation or to the legislative majority that considers it? How much interparty and intraparty agreement or disagreement does it evoke? At what stage in a president's term is it ripening sufficiently to involve him? How much genuine expertise can be deployed to address it? Has Congress carefully vetted a proposal with hearings and debate, or is Congress acting hurriedly, even impulsively? How crowded is the legislative calendar, and how narrow the majority's control of the respective chambers? And of considerable significance for a party that rhetorically champions smaller, more restrained government and fiscal responsibility, how compatible is such an orientation, in actual practice, with the maintenance and enhancement of the party's legislative majority? This last question has particular relevance for the Republican congressional leadership and the Bush presidency. Tom DeLay, House majority leader from 2003 to 2006, had a simple, two-part, prime directive: elect Republican members and enact conservative policies. But this was easier articulated than achieved, and simply "hammering" as hard as possible on both fronts through every means available turned out to markedly shorten DeLay's congressional career and helped set the stage for broader, damaging scandal.

Spending and Taxes: Big Government, Big Deficits

George W. Bush arrived in the White House just as a brief period of budget heaven was about to draw to a close. A combination of Reagan-era tax cuts and expenditure increases had produced extended fiscal constraint and fifteen years of domestic policy debate defined largely by the need to reduce federal budget deficits. By 1995 the Congressional Budget Office (CBO) was still anticipating "large and growing deficits as far as the eye could see," but three years later the deficit had disappeared, and projections anticipated continued surpluses.[13] Indeed, fiscal year 2001 saw a $236 billion surplus and the new president projecting, in his first proposed budget of February 2001, a $5.6 trillion surplus over ten years and the retirement of nearly $1 trillion in debt in his first term.[14]

The budget surplus and rosy scenarios projecting continued good fortune provided Bush and congressional Republicans with a crucial initial rationale for a massive series of tax cuts: the surplus represented an "overcharging" of the American taxpayer. On the campaign trail in 2000 and in the White House the following spring, Bush would defend his proposed $1.6 billion, ten-year tax cut with an appealing populist mantra: "It's not the government's money; it's the people's money."[15] As circumstances changed, and criticism mounted, Bush clung to his position while adding new rationales. His tax cuts would stimulate the economy (which appeared possibly on the verge of recession); provide the certainty needed for long-term business and investment planning (unlike a temporary cut proposed by Democrats); and offer relief to consumers hit by spiking energy prices.[16]

Bush ultimately won most of his package ($1.35 billion worth) as the Economic Growth and Tax Relief Reconciliation Act, in June 2001, initiating a process that converted a projected fiscal 2005 "$430 billion surplus to a $40 billion deficit in less than 18 months." By enacting the Job Creation and Worker Assistance Act in 2002 and the Jobs and Growth Tax Relief Reconciliation Act in 2003, Congress "accelerated and expanded the 2001 tax reduction."[17]

It has often been observed that tax cutting is a core policy binding together a Republican coalition that is less cohesive on other issues (such as immigration, as we shall see).[18] That and the unwavering devotion of the new president were crucial to enacting the cuts. Fears that the revenue loss would inflate the deficit (though reasonable) or that the cuts skewed strongly in favor of the wealthy (though undeniable) could not mobilize anything near the sort of popular opposition necessary to kill the legislation.[19] The reasons are simple enough: Tax cuts please their recipients and do not readily rouse the ire of the less-favored. And unlike jumps in unemployment, interest rates, or consumer prices, a rising deficit is not a pocketbook issue for the mass of voters, who feel no immediate pain. (That, of course, is why the central political danger that Ronald Reagan faced after 1980 lay in the 1982 recession and not in the tide of red ink that overtook the federal budget in that era.)[20] Still, the broad public, perhaps remembering the recent period of deficit constraint, was by no means demanding tax cuts with anything like the fervor that Republican politicians displayed in delivering them. As Jacob S. Hacker and Paul Pierson observe, "Before 2001 virtually never did more than a tenth of citizens say that taxes were the nation's 'most important problem.' As Bush's first term began, the figure was just 5 percent."[21] On the other hand, many public policies arguably proceed to enactment despite mass indifference when a well-placed and skillful coalition remains steadfastly supportive. Indeed, that is very much a standard story for many distributive policies.[22]

Although Bush and his allies could cut taxes effectively, spending proved far more resistant. To be sure, Bush proposed discretionary spending cuts (i.e., smaller annual increases) during the 2000 campaign, but some budget experts were skeptical that these were politically achievable, especially given the surpluses the federal government had recently been running.[23] Later, changed circumstances would necessitate vast amounts of new spending and further undermine spending discipline. The attacks of 9/11, the Iraq war launched in March 2003, and the devastation along the Gulf Coast from Hurricane Katrina in late summer 2005—all these developments clearly necessitated additional spending. National security faced relatively little budget discipline, as Congress began funding the Iraq war through supplemental appropriations that evaded the normal budget process.[24] The new security demands aside however, complete Republican control at both ends of Pennsylvania Avenue for the first time since the early 1950s definitively demonstrated that *both* parties love to spend when empowered to do so. In 2004 Bush demanded that no highway bill exceed $256 billion, a limit increased to $286 billion the following year as a result of congressional pressure.[25] More generally, by three years into Bush's first term conservatives had become deeply disenchanted with a manifest lack of Republican fiscal discipline. Declared Heritage Foundation budget analyst Brian M. Riedl, "Neither party is committed to smaller government and less spending."[26]

To summarize, the political essence of Bush era budgeting lies in the answers to three key questions: (1) What allowed President Bush, at least through the first term, to dominate Congress so thoroughly in budgeting? (2) Why did Bush and Congress together fail to make much progress in reducing spending? and (3) Why did Bush and congressional Republicans evade severe near-term consequences for that failure?

Several factors underlie the answer to the first question, that of Bush dominance of Congress on budgeting. One was congressional focus on cutting the relatively small slice of the budget that is devoted to discretionary spending that is not security related. Another was the wholesale sidestepping of the regular budget process in favor of less-scrutinized supplemental or omnibus bills. Still another was congressional accommodation of the president in response to veto threats. Term-limited committee chairs, moreover, arguably could not wield the influence that congressional committee chairs formerly did.[27] Doubtless most significant in prompting deference to the president, however, was simple ideological cohesiveness, both among congressional Republicans and between them and Bush. Yet spending and deficits remained high simply because cutting them was unacceptably painful to Republican constituencies and therefore to Republican members of Congress. Controlling

Congress and the White House simultaneously for the first time since the early 1950s, Republicans found that they could not evade association with, and electoral dependence on, big government. Rhetorical positioning attempted to deflect blame. (Claimed President Bush in his 2006 State of the Union message, "Every year of my presidency, we've reduced the growth of nonsecurity discretionary spending, and last year you passed bills that cut this spending. This year my budget will cut it again.") So did the predictable strategic evasions of convenient budget assumptions about the future and deferring hard choices beyond the 2006 congressional elections and the end of the Bush presidency. The Tax Relief Extension Reconciliation Act of 2006, signed with great fanfare, may indeed facilitate economic growth as its backers assert it will. But if it doesn't, revenues will plummet, creating what some would call a fiscal "day of reckoning" for the next president.[28]

Social Security: Reform Deferred

President Bush moved aggressively after his 2004 reelection to reform Social Security but a year later had failed to do so. That failure may not have been inevitable, but it was always likely, given the great political sensitivity of the program, and was made more likely by Bush's insistence on pushing personal accounts as a core reform element. The general contours of the policy debate were already evident well before November 2004. Indeed, the key points of disagreement of 2004–2006 resembled quite closely those on display in the 2000 presidential campaign. Back then candidate Bush, citing the Social Security system's predicted insolvency, embraced the creation of private/personal accounts that enrollees could manage for themselves, reaping the potentially larger rewards available in the financial marketplace, gains that might be passed on to heirs. Employing the same rhetoric of personal choice that he would deploy in defense of tax cuts, Bush asserted, "I trust Americans to make their own decisions and manage their own money."[29] His opponent, Vice President Al Gore, sharply disagreed, emphasizing the risks of such accounts. Said Gore, "Tens of millions of investors . . . would be placed in a situation . . . where they are losing their investments because they are not equipped in the way that sophisticated investors are."[30] Democrats would raise the same objection five years later. For example, in April 2005 prominent Senate Democrats, including Hillary Rodham Clinton, D-N.Y., would highlight the objections of several "Wall Street experts" to Bush's proposal.[31] Indeed, it was never clear, either in 2000 or in 2005, just how personal accounts could address the solvency problem—unless cuts were made in other aspects of the program—but very clear how such accounts, by drawing away a portion of the payroll tax revenue needed to support current retirees, might vastly worsen the program's financial problem.[32] And in both 2000 and 2005, Bush would prove reluctant to provide persuasive details of how a reformed Social Security would work, thus allowing critics to sow damaging doubts.

Public fear of enhanced financial risk and Bush's inability to entice support from more than the occasional isolated congressional Democrat—not one Democratic senator emerged to back the plan—would ultimately doom the effort, despite an aggressive personal campaign reminiscent of Bush's White House races. The elements of the campaign were summarized by political scientist George Edwards as "a classic example of attempting to govern by going public":

> Even before the inauguration, the White House announced plans to reactivate Bush's reelection campaign's network of donors and activists to build pressure on lawmakers to allow workers to invest part of their Social Security taxes in the stock market. . . . The same architects of Bush's political victories would be masterminding the new campaign, principally political strategists Karl Rove at the White House and Ken Mehlman, who was the Bush-Cheney campaign manager, at the Republican National Committee.
>
> Mehlman declared that he would use the campaign apparatus—from a national database of 7.5 million e-mail activists, 1.6 million volunteers, and hundreds of thousands of neighborhood precinct captains—to build congressional support for Bush's plans, starting with Social Security. . . . White House and RNC officials worked closely with the same outside groups that helped Bush win reelection in 2004, especially Progress for America.
>
> White House allies also launched a market-research project to figure out how to sell the plan. . . . and Republican marketing and public relations gurus were building teams of consultants to support it. The campaign intended to use Bush's campaign-honed techniques of mass repetition, sticking closely to the script and using the politics of fear to build support—contending that a Social Security financial crisis was imminent. There would be campaign-style events to win support and precision-targeting of districts where lawmakers could face reelection difficulties. The White House would also use hard-hitting television ads to discredit its opponents and build support for the president's plan.[33]

In the end, however, it did not work. "One problem the president faced," notes Edwards, "was that the people most receptive to his proposal were the least engaged in the debate, and those most engaged were also the most opposed."[34] And when Bush attempted to put flesh on his skeletal proposal in April 2005 by suggesting the progressive indexing of Social Security benefits, prominent Democrats branded it a benefit cut. However, a revealing poll the following month showed Democrats more favorably disposed toward such indexing than Republicans, by a margin of 54 percent to 47 percent *when the proposal was described without Bush's name attached.* Attaching Bush's name boosted Republican support to 62 percent while depressing Democratic backing to only 34 percent, a drop of twenty points![35] A campaign apparatus that had delivered a slim popular-vote majority the previous November, largely by mobilizing existing Bush supporters against an opponent who could be lampooned as dithering in dangerous times, proved considerably less effective in creating new supporters for the "risky" restructuring of a broadly popular, high-stakes program. The Gallup poll never showed majority support for Bush's handling of Social Security, and what support there was declined sharply over time.[36] Moreover, the sort of bare majority that had won Bush reelection probably could not suffice to generate a majority of votes even in a disciplined House, much less a filibuster-proof margin in the Senate. That the attachment of Bush's name rendered his indexing idea toxic to Democrats who might otherwise have favored it suggests something of the price Bush paid for governing from the right and launching a politically divisive, increasingly unpopular war.[37]

The main consequence of Bush's failure on Social Security, arguably a failure not merely of political strategy but of fundamental policy judgment, is that yet another day of reckoning was postponed into a future administration. A broad, expert consensus exists that Social Security is readily fixable with some combination of tax increases, benefit cuts, and a raised retirement age.[38] Some form of retirement privatization might ultimately be achievable, but only if its planners do not evade key matters, including a plausible funding scheme and careful management of payouts to avoid unacceptably high retiree losses.[39]

President Bush proved unwilling, or unable, to lay such matters out in a convincing way. His decision to emphasize private accounts, which did not directly address the long-term solvency problem, made for a discordant debate that could not persuade a public exposed to a continuing stream of criticisms and caveats from essayists and prominent Democrats with whom Bush was unwilling to engage productively. Conservative analyst Bruce Bartlett, a famously disenchanted former Bush supporter, observed, "Bush generally avoided talking about stabilizing Social Security's long-term finances, because that would have required him to discuss either tax increases or benefit cuts, neither of which was politically popular. . . . [Private accounts] would help only if packaged with benefit cuts that would be compensated for by the return on the accounts."[40] Alas, it all came to seem implausible, and even profoundly risky, to too many people. And having added hugely to entitlement spending with the Medicare prescription drug plan, Bush was weakly positioned to campaign against the Social Security status quo as an "out-of-control" federal entitlement program.[41]

Energy and the Environment: Victories and Defeats

President Bush fared better in the energy and environmental areas, where legislative compromises proved to be available and control of the executive branch offered significant leverage over policy, much as it had for Bush's conservative predecessor Ronald Reagan. But unlike Reagan, who enjoyed a Republican Senate for six years but never had a House majority to work with, Bush had strongly sympathetic leadership in both chambers in early 2001 (before James Jeffords's defection to independent status temporarily derailed the Republican Senate majority) and from 2003 onward.

Yet it is strikingly difficult to unearth informed and disinterested enthusiasts for the Energy Policy Act of 2005 (Public Law 109-58). The legislation provides a wide array of tax incentives and subsidies ($85 billion worth, by one estimate) for all the major energy industry sectors as well as renewable sources that now contribute marginally to U.S. energy use.[42] Energy conservation would come about through encouraging research and more efficient consumer and commercial products and leaner energy use by federal agencies.[43]

But as with Social Security, the toughest challenges were avoided. Gasoline waste is perhaps the most glaring. Deeming the new law helpful on some fronts, such as support for liquefied natural gas (LNG) distribution, energy and environmental writer Gregg Easterbrook chided the absence of "any provision to improve the fuel economy of cars, pickup trucks and SUVs. Higher gasoline mileage standards are the most-needed reform in U.S. energy policy today."[44] Robert E. Ebel, chairman of the energy program at the Center for Strategic and International Studies, said simply, "You have to start with higher miles per gallon."[45] (A subsequent, March 2006 Department of Transportation rule raising fuel economy standards for light trucks was widely derided as too modest to matter much. One analysis found that it would save less than two weeks of gasoline yearly over the course of two decades, and House Science Committee chair Sherwood Boehlert, R-N.Y., deemed it "a missed opportunity.")[46] The *Washington Post* asserted that "the 2005 legislation's biggest winner was probably the nuclear industry, which received billions of dollars in subsidies and tax breaks covering almost every facet of operations" along with research funding. But the new law said little about the deeply contentious question of nuclear waste disposal (though supporters of the Global Nuclear Energy Partnership in the Department of Energy argued that it could help ameliorate the problem through fuel reprocessing).[47] The proposed spent fuel and high-level radioactive waste storage facility at Yucca Mountain, Nevada may indeed open in 2017, as the Bush White House clearly hopes, but only over the ferocious opposition of current Senate majority leader Harry Reid, D-Nev.[48]

The energy legislation arose in a political context of intense public concern over high and rising retail gasoline prices, which would reach well over $3 per gallon in many places during 2006. But everyone, including the president, understood that the law would have no near-term effect on those prices. Indeed, Bush and the Republican Congress confronted a political conundrum that has long bedeviled energy conservation policy. Knowledgeable observers across the political spectrum believe that higher fuel prices are essential to reducing excessive consumption (and thus dependence on oil imports). But any action to raise prices would be painful to consumers and, as R. Douglas Arnold puts it, directly "traceable" to specific votes by identifiable politicians.[49] When prices at the pump are low, the incentive to reduce consumption diminishes. But when they are high, any policy that would drive them still higher appears politically unthinkable. Yet the persistence of three-dollar-a-gallon gasoline into a congressional election year already full of bad omens for the Republican Party would prompt President Bush, the former oil man, into the unlikely role of would-be scourge of price-gouging oil companies.[50] The Departments of Justice and Energy would work with the Federal Trade Commission "to conduct inquiries into cheating or illegal manipulation related to current gasoline prices."[51] Despite his 2004 assertion that it was wrong to "play politics with the Strategic Petroleum Reserve," which ought to remain a recourse for "major disruptions of energy supplies," Bush proved flexible on the matter in 2006, deciding to halt deposits to the reserve for "a short period of time."[52] Fortunately for the administration, gasoline retail prices declined noticeably in fall 2006, though not because of administration action.

Oil exploration in the Arctic National Wildlife Refuge (ANWR) was another long-running controversy set aside to ensure passage of the Energy Policy Act. Even drilling proponents could not guarantee how much oil ANWR might yield, but Bush interior secretary Gale Norton, speaking for a pro-drilling administration, routinely cited an estimated production figure of up to 1.4 million barrels per day and 10.4 billion barrels total. ANWR drilling proponents, opposed by a determined coalition of environmentalists and their legislative allies, have won many individual battles over the years but never the war. A recent close call occurred on December 21, 2005, during Senate debate on the annual defense appropriations bill. Sen. Ted Stevens, R-Alaska, a champion of ANWR exploration for decades, had added a provision to allow drilling, but opponents launched a filibuster. Fifty-seven senators voted to end debate, short of the necessary sixty. The Senate then eliminated the ANWR provision from the bill prior to passage.[53] Pro-drilling House Republicans, who had won easily on the issue in a different bill, the House version of the 2005 energy legislation, only to see drilling fail in a House-Senate conference, saw the same thing occur again in May 2006, despite President Bush's steadfast support.[54]

Throughout all of these energy and environmental policy debates there has been little doubt, even outside the pro-environment community, of the Bush administration's fundamentally solicitous posture toward producer interests. In this respect, of course, Bush is little different from other recent Republican presidents. But the Bush administration has arguably reached new levels of coziness with energy lobbies, although not (or at least not primarily) because Bush and Vice President Dick Cheney are both former energy company executives.

Two other factors are far more significant. First, energy (and therefore environmental) policy has been subject to the same inclination toward secrecy and enhanced executive power that has proliferated throughout the Bush administration. Americans familiar with that predisposition in the context of national security and the war on terrorism probably cannot recall, or never paid attention to, the 2001–2005 conflict over access to the records of the National Energy Policy Development Group (NEPDG) chaired by the vice president.[55] Environmentalists received only cursory treatment from the NEPDG, compared to the routine access enjoyed by energy industry representatives, leading naturally to suspicions regarding what lay behind the closed doors. The Government Accountability Office's Comptroller General David Walker sued Vice President Cheney in federal court for access to materials the GAO deemed appropriate to its oversight function. The administration made the conflict a test of the president's unfettered power to seek essential external advice and won handily in court.

But the most significant force at work here has doubtless been the deep ideological harmony and sense of common interest bonding the administration and its key supporters. Despite precarious electoral beginnings and early rhetoric suggesting outreach and unity, the Bush administration opened for business with a somewhat polarizing domestic program that would be regularly attacked as, well, open for business. On energy and the environment, as elsewhere, Bush's proposed policy innovations, personnel choices, and pattern of interest group liaison consistently reflected that orientation.[56] Of course, such a stance is conceivably quite compatible with strong environmental protection if the regulatory flexibility and concern for economic efficiency that business encourages do not appreciably derail environmental improvement. But even then, the ever-treacherous politics of environmental policy makes it difficult for a business-oriented president to claim credit among environmentalists for decisions that he believes are both business friendly and environmentally sensitive.

An "initiative," in the parlance of presidential policymaking, generally refers to administration proposals that may have some legislative component but are mainly pursued through executive branch actions (executive orders, rule changes, modest organizational innovations), each legitimated and advertised with a bit of presidential speechifying. All are intended to convey shifts in emphasis, renewed commitment, and a spirit of innovation. President Clinton, for example, offered initiatives on race relations and health disparities affecting minorities. His Environmental Protection Agency created a Common Sense Initiative to facilitate cooperation among environmental policy adversaries in six spheres of industrial activity.

Bush made copious use of the term with an Advanced Energy Initiative (emphasizing research and development), a Clear Skies Initiative, and a Healthy Forests Initiative. The last of these produced, after a lengthy process of bipartisan compromise in the Senate, a legislative victory for the administration in the Healthy Forests Restoration Act (Public Law 108-148), which Bush signed in December 2003. The law, which promotes "hazardous fuel reduction" (or forest thinning) in "wildland-urban interface" areas (where people and property face particular risk from wildfires), emerged pursuant to widespread (and well-publicized) damage blamed on the proliferation of forest fuel after years of fire suppression. The initiative itself triggered a predictable political firestorm. Environmentalists charged Bush with kowtowing to rapacious timber companies under the guise of protecting forests and property. The criticism continued into the implementation process, with a proposed Forest Service rule attacked by the Natural Resources Defense Council (NRDC) as a faux-streamlining of the logging approval process intended to undermine citizen participation.[57]

Fate (and the U.S. Senate) proved less kind to Clear Skies legislation, but an alternative administrative path, in which the White House was in a much better position to prevail, proved more successful. Trumpeted during 2002–2005 as an effort to control sulfur dioxide, nitrogen oxide, and mercury, the legislation invited criticism as a weakening of the Clean Air Act's New Source Review provisions and of state authority to combat interstate, windblown pollution through court actions.[58] The NRDC complained loudly that, besides doing nothing about greenhouse gas emissions, Bush's "Dirty Skies" legislation

> sets new [emissions] targets . . . [that] are *weaker* than those that would be put in place if the Bush administration simply implemented and enforced the existing law! Compared to current law, the Clear Skies plan would allow three times more toxic mercury emissions, 50 percent more sulfur emissions, and hundreds of thousands more tons of smog-forming nitrogen oxides. It would also delay cleaning up this pollution by up to a decade compared to current law and force residents of heavily polluted areas to wait years longer for clean air compared to the existing Clean Air Act.[59]

To be sure, this NRDC assessment idealizes environmental enforcement; a "simply implemented and enforced" Clean Air Act is pure fantasy given the stakes and incentives at play. But with a different leadership style, Bush's proposed legislative reform (or something resembling it) might have fared better. A multistate, multi-pollutant "cap-and-trade" alternative to conventional point-source (and litigation-prone) regulation has many knowledgeable adherents besides "polluters," including the National Research Council, a component of the National Academy of Sciences.[60] Moreover, the greenhouse gas issue aside, there has been notable progress on important fronts in the fight against pollution that a president more trusted by the environmental community might employ to help sell new approaches to environmental protection.[61] But on environmental and energy matters Bush could not build reliable support beyond his base. Significant players beyond the Republican family never trusted Bush who, vying with the environmentalist Al Gore in the heat of the 2000 campaign, had promised to seek a reduction in carbon dioxide emissions, a pledge on which the new president promptly (and unsurprisingly) reversed himself. Clear Skies legislation never gained quite enough support, and Bush had to settle for a partial victory through the administrative process, winning a Clean Air Interstate Rule, promising reductions of sulfur dioxide and nitrogen oxides, and others on a range of pollutants in March 2005.[62]

Immigration: Republicans Divided

The road to immigration reform proved much rougher. Along with Social Security, immigration may in the end rank as the other most profound legislative disappointment of the Bush second term. As with Social Security, the basic conflict was apparent well before the 2004 election. In this instance, however, the disagreement surfaced as an intense, intraparty dispute pitting champions of border security and opponents of "amnesty" for illegal immigrants against a business community hungry for a reliable supply of low-cost labor through some kind of temporary worker regime. The protesting voices of eleven million unauthorized resident immigrants emerged as an audible, though decidedly secondary, feature of the debate throughout the peak-attention months leading up to the 2006 elections, as the issue remained unresolved. Mobilizing the base is not a viable presidential strategy when the base is divided.

Intraparty tensions were evident even within the Senate Judiciary Committee. On March 27, the committee voted 12–6 (with only four of ten Republicans in support) to send to the full Senate a bill granting unauthorized residents citizenship "provided that they hold jobs, pass criminal background checks, learn English and pay fines and back taxes." Senator Jeff Sessions, R-Ala., insisted that the panel had "let the American people down by passing out a blanket amnesty bill."[63] As an issue blending symbolic politics—note the "amnesty" frame and allegations of a threat to American culture—intense business lobbying, and concerns over homeland security, immigration reform would challenge the political skill of any president, regardless of party.

Moreover, Bush's problem proved thoroughly bicameral, for the Republican House majority, disciplined and supportive of the president on most matters, harbored the energetic and entrepreneurial Tom Tancredo, R-Colo., and James Sensenbrenner, R-Wis. The former proved a determined foe of illegal immigration and avatar of cultural anxiety, and the latter wielded considerable institutional clout as the irascible chairman of the Judiciary Committee.[64] In fall 2004 Sensenbrenner blocked a vote on a conference agreement on legislation overhauling the national intelligence apparatus because it failed to include a set of House-passed immigration restrictions, including streamlined deportation procedures. Sensenbrenner relented temporarily but remained determined to enact provisions that would prevent unauthorized residents from obtaining drivers' licenses, raise the bar for claims of political asylum, and tighten the California-Mexico border.[65]

In April a bipartisan Senate majority appeared ready to create a "multitiered" system making it "easiest for those [unauthorized residents] who have lived in the

United States for more than five years to obtain citizenship and theoretically impossible for those who have been here for less than two years to stay."[66] The following month the full Senate passed a bill substantially amended to please conservatives (further fortifying the border, impeding felons and other lawbreakers from obtaining work permits, and restricting the right to self-petition for legalization).[67] However, this would be the high-water mark for 2006 legislative efforts. House Republicans balked and later embarked on summer field hearings clearly intended more to mobilize and advertise citizen opposition to the status quo than to refine a legislative compromise that could survive a Senate vote.[68] By early September, with only a few legislative working days remaining before the fall elections, stalemate prevailed, with a *Washington Post* editorial complaining that a creative bicameral proposal was being ignored, Bush having "gone silent on what had been a signature issue."[69] As with Social Security, an unfavorable political context had applied the brakes to a cherished Bush vehicle, leaving him little option but to change the subject, at least temporarily.

The Moral Sphere: Tradition versus Expertise

On July 19, 2006, just over two thousand days into his presidency, Bush finally vetoed a bill, an occasion brought on by the widely popular, human embryonic stem cell research the legislation aimed to promote.[70] His action was consistent with the position Bush had taken in 2001 refusing federal funding for new cell lines. More generally, the Bush veto offered yet another indication of his administration's strong embrace of moral traditionalism, a stance that often led to conflict with technical expertise. One writer observed in 2006 that "the Bush administration has been relentless in its opposition to any drug, vaccine, or initiative that could be interpreted as lessening the risk associated with premarital sex."[71] Administration reluctance to approve both a vaccine for human papillomavirus (the primary cause of cervical cancer) and over-the-counter distribution of Plan B, an emergency contraceptive, were widely interpreted as reflecting the influence of social conservatives. In March 2005 Congress approved, and Bush signed, a bill attempting to compel the federal courts to review whether a feeding tube should be reinserted into Terri Schiavo, a Florida woman in a "persistent vegetative state." Florida courts had sustained her husband's right to remove the tube, a decision opposed by other family members and by many religious conservatives around the country. Bush deemed it appropriate to second-guess established medical opinion and procedure, and repeated decisions by Florida courts, on the grounds that "our courts should have a presumption in favor of life. This presumption is especially critical for those like Terri Schiavo, who live at the mercy of others."[72] Like his two most recent Republican predecessors, Bush remained always firmly positioned as a "pro-life" president.

Education: A Bargain Holds

The No Child Left Behind Act (Public Law 107-110), which Bush signed in January 2002, is plainly his signature domestic policy legacy outside the fiscal arena. By surrendering on the school vouchers that were anathema to many Democrats, Bush won a law that "ushered in the most sweeping changes in federal education policy" since the 1965 Elementary and Secondary Education Act, which NCLB reauthorized and vastly amplified, and "helped fulfill the president's campaign promise to build bipartisan coalitions."[73] Under the new law, schools receiving federal funds would have to show "adequate yearly progress," as measured by regular, state-created, high-stakes tests, in raising the performance of disadvantaged students; offer parents alternatives to schools that failed to deliver higher student achievement; and elevate teacher quality by raising teacher qualifications. Republican and Democratic leaders of the House and Senate education committees pledged to resist legislative tinkering in advance of a scheduled 2007 reauthorization, determined to allow the law time to measure progress and enforce accountability, especially for millions of poor and minority students.[74]

Soon, however, liberals in and beyond Congress expressed dismay at inadequate NCLB funding, while conservatives and some school systems chafed at prescriptive accountability measures linking federal funding to student test performance. By March 2004, proposals had been introduced in twenty-three state legislatures seeking to adjust or block state cooperation with NCLB, and Vermont had passed a resolution declaring that its school districts were not required to support the program financially.[75] In May 2005 Utah enacted a law intended to "prioritize Utah's own educational goals over the mandates of the federal act," a move that the libertarian *Reason* magazine hailed as possibly "the first shot in what may become a national rebellion against" NCLB.[76]

Despite regular claims of excessive rigidity and questionable measurement practices, however, there was no indication that the basic bargain that Bush had struck was unraveling as the 2006 congressional elections loomed. A key congressional backer of NCLB, the liberal representative George Miller, D-Calif., ranking minority member of the Committee on Education and the Workforce, complained of poor implementation and unwillingness on the part of the Bush administration to follow through on the $116.3 billion the law had authorized over six years; only $59.8 billion was appropriated in the first five years.[77] But neither Miller nor conservatives wanted to abandon the effort. The question was how much, if any, new funding or flexibility would be forthcoming in 2007.

Implications for the Bush Legacy

Except by assassination, presidencies are not suddenly cut down. Instead they tend to erode gradually for various reasons—war, economic stagnation, scandal, waning public confidence, diminished congressional support, unpredictable crisis, and the inevitability of lame-duck status. Presidents naturally combat these forces with the array of tools at their disposal, especially by using their institutional position to dominate political discourse. But they remain, in significant measure, prisoners of circumstance. A second term is unlike a first, continuing a war over several years is unlike launching one, and not every issue plays to the president's natural advantage. Even when a president wins legislation he covets, subsequent complications and costs may, in hindsight, diminish the achievement. That is demonstrably true of the three most significant initiatives of the first Bush term—tax cuts, national education reform, and the Medicare prescription drug benefit.

One might say that the basic narrative arc of the Bush domestic presidency is a tale of two cities: New York and New Orleans. Eight months into the first Bush term the attacks of September 11 provided a foundation of both public and congressional support that doubtless assisted Bush in policy realms unrelated to national security. But the arrival of Hurricane Katrina eight months into the second term hastened and complicated an already-evident slide in Bush's position. Katrina exposed vulnerabilities that had been allowed to fester, especially managerial incapacity against, and lack of attention to, what had long been considered the most serious homeland security threat.

Finally, with the politically easier bouts of tax cutting behind him, Bush simply found what remained more challenging—the estate tax, Social Security, oil exploration in ANWR, Clear Skies legislation, and immigration reform. The legacy of Bush's attention to the last of these is especially unclear, as no bill appeared bound for his signature by the spring of 2007. Even should a bill pass, its ultimate impact would be highly uncertain. Both the draconian House bill and its more measured Senate counterpart of 2006 called for expelling large numbers of persons, who would have strong incentives and ability to resist deportation. Either chamber's approach may yield hazards similar to those that bedeviled both the implementation of the Supplemental Security Income program in the mid-1970s and an ambitious review of Social Security disability insurance rolls in the early 1980s.[78] Institutionalized detachment of political processes from questions of administrative capacity has not been conquered in recent times and may even have worsened since those episodes.

Looking toward the final two years of his presidency, Bush faced an increasingly harsh political environment. The 2006 elections precisely reversed the partisan balance in the House, leaving the first woman Speaker, Nancy Pelosi, D-Calif., in charge of 232 Democrats. A nail-biting finish in a Virginia Senate contest narrowly ousted a Republican incumbent with presidential ambitions and gave Democrats the narrowest possible margin of control: fifty-one seats. Meanwhile Bush's poll numbers slid toward the anemic late-term levels endured by Jimmy Carter and Harry Truman.

Unavoidably diminished, Bush still had options. Having been delivered a supply of lemons, he could still make legislative lemonade. He could sign a minimum wage increase that Democrats would happily send him, and he ultimately did once it was encapsulated inside a controversial appropriations bill funding the war in Iraq. More significantly he could try for a deal on immigration reform such as would have been unthinkable with his own partisans in charge of the House.[79] His 2007 State of the Union address indicated he would take that road. Less promisingly, the same speech also indicated a desire to pursue Social Security reform (perhaps this time without the fatal link to private accounts) and even a conservative version of health care reform reliant on tax incentives, state empowerment, medical savings accounts, and liability reform—an agenda unlikely to inspire enthusiasm among the Democrats now ruling the congressional roost.

Ironically, the ascent of a Democratic Congress could reasonably compel from Bush a renewed emphasis on the "compassionate conservatism" on which he originally ran against Al Gore. Shorn of his congressional majority and facing possible disaster abroad, Bush might extract a domestic legacy beyond defending his tax cuts (and avoiding blame for the deficits they deepened)—one that includes reaffirming NCLB and enacting major immigration reform. For George W. Bush that is probably the best domestic policy scenario available as his presidency draws to a close.

Notes

1. On the "two presidencies" perspective generally, see Aaron Wildavsky, "The Two Presidencies," in *Perspectives on the Presidency*, ed. Aaron Wildavsky (Boston: Little, Brown, 1975).
2. The Paperwork Reduction Act accomplished this by creating the Office of Information and Regulatory Affairs (OIRA) inside the Office of Management and Budget (OMB).
3. Donald F. Kettl, *Team Bush: Leadership Lessons from the Bush White House* (New York: McGraw-Hill, 2003), 1.
4. Ibid., 115–116.
5. Sebastian Mallaby, "No Defense for This Insanity," *Washington Post*, May 1, 2006, A19. The "insanity" to which Mallaby referred was the tort system, not the Bush administration. Indeed, Mallaby wrote to urge that Bush reclaim the mantle of domestic reformer by tackling a system of civil litigation that for Mallaby violated common sense and threatened to cripple pharmaceutical research.
6. Paul Farhi, "Where's the Party? Nowhere to Be Found in Steele Ads," *Washington Post*, September 19, 2006, C1.
7. Juliet Eilperin, "House GOP Practices Art of One-Vote Victories," *Washington Post*, October 14, 2003, A1.
8. David S. Broder, "Time Was GOP's Ally on the Vote," *Washington Post*, November 23, 2003, A1.
9. White House news release, "President Applauds House for Passing Medicare Bill," November 22, 2003, www.whitehouse.gov/news/releases/2003/11/20031122-4.html.
10. Jeremy Johnson, Douglas Brattebo, Robert Maranto, and Tom Lansford, "Are Second Terms Second Best? Why George W. Bush Might (or Might Not) Beat the Expectations,"

in *The Second Term of George W. Bush: Prospects and Perils,* ed. Robert Maranto, Douglas M. Brattebo, and Tom Lansford (New York: Palgrave, Macmillan, 2006), 6.

11. Stephen Skowronek, "Leadership by Definition: First Term Reflections on George W. Bush's Political Stance," *Perspectives on Politics* 3 (December 2005): 817–831.

12. Quoted in Andrew Rudalevige, "The Executive Branch and the Legislative Process," in *The Executive Branch,* ed. Joel D. Aberbach and Mark A. Peterson (New York: Oxford University Press, 2005), 435.

13. Barry Bosworth, "The Budget Crisis: Is It All Déjà Vu?" *Issues in Economic Policy* 2 (February 2006): 5, 8.

14. David Baumann, "Accounting for the Deficit," *National Journal,* June 12, 2004, 1852.

15. See, for example, White House, "Remarks by the President to the United States Chamber of Commerce," April 16, 2001, www.whitehouse.gov/news/releases/2001/04/20010416-4.html.

16. Gary Mucciaroni and Paul J. Quirk, "Deliberations of a 'Compassionate Conservative,' " in *The George W. Bush Presidency: Appraisals and Prospects,* ed. Colin Campbell and Bert A. Rockman (Washington, D.C.: CQ Press, 2004), 164.

17. Bosworth, "The Budget Crisis," 13. It should be noted here that Brookings economist Bosworth here lauds the 2001 tax cut as "one of the best-timed fiscal actions in recent memory" as a spur to consumer spending at the outset of what turned out to be a mild recession.

18. On the long-term Republican embrace of tax cuts see Sheldon D. Pollack, *Refinancing America: The Republican Antitax Agenda* (Albany: State University of New York Press, 2003).

19. A typical complaint about the first round of tax cuts was that "the richest 1 percent of Americans . . . reaped roughly 40 percent of the total tax rewards of the 2001 tax bill—a share almost identical to that received by the bottom 80 percent on the income ladder." Jacob Hacker and Paul Pierson, *Off Center: The Republican Revolution and the Erosion of American Democracy* (New Haven and London: Yale University Press, 2005), 46. Conservatives didn't so much deny the skewing as emphasize its purported benefits and its putative inevitability given the large share of taxes paid by the wealthiest Americans.

20. The lesson that at least one prominent Republican, vice president Dick Cheney, drew from this era was that "Reagan proved deficits don't matter." See Ron Suskind, *The Price of Loyalty: George W. Bush, the White House, and the Education of Paul O'Neill* (New York: Simon and Schuster, 2004), 291.

21. Hacker and Pierson, *Off Center,* 50.

22. Theodore J. Lowi, "American Business, Public Policy, Case Studies, and Political Theory," *World Politics* 16 (July 1964): 667–715.

23. Baumann, "Accounting for the Deficit," 1851.

24. This practice would ultimately motivate the Iraq Study Group to complain that eroded "budget discipline and accountability" impeded public understanding of how much was being spent and diminished "oversight and review by Congress." See Recommendation 71 in James A. Baker III and Lee H. Hamilton et al., *The Iraq Study Group Report* (New York: Vintage, 2006), 91.

25. Jonathan Weisman, "In Congress, the GOP Embraces Its Spending Side," *Washington Post,* August 4, 2005, A1.

26. Sheryl Gay Stolberg, "The Nation: Breaking Ranks; Shrink Government, the Right Tells the Right," *New York Times,* January 4, 2004. More generally see Bruce Bartlett, *Impostor: How George W. Bush Bankrupted America and Betrayed the Reagan Legacy* (New York: Doubleday, 2006), chap. 7.

27. David Baumann, "King of the Budget," *National Journal,* February 12, 2005, 456–461.

28. Jonathan Weisman, "Tax Deal Sets Day of Reckoning," *Washington Post,* May 4, 2006, A4.

29. Alison Mitchell and James Dao, "Bush Presents Social Security as Crucial Test," *New York Times,* May 16, 2000, A1.

30. James Dao and Alison Mitchell, "Gore Denounces Bush Social Security Plan as Too Risky," *New York Times,* May 17, 2000.

31. Press release by Senator Hillary Rodham Clinton, "Wall Street to Washington: Social Security Privatization Would Endanger Americans' Retirement Security," April 25, 2005, available at http://clinton.senate.gov/news/statements.

32. A representative early attack on the Bush proposal is Alan S. Blinder, "Bush Unties the Social Compact," *New York Times,* May 26, 2000, A19.

33. George C. Edwards III, "Changing Their Minds? George W. Bush and Presidential Persuasion," *Extensions: A Journal of the Carl Albert Congressional Research and Studies Center,* Spring 2006, 7–13. The quote appears at 10–11.

34. Ibid., 11. See also William Schneider, "Crisis of Confidence?" *National Journal,* February 12, 2005, 492.

35. Edwards, "Changing Their Minds?" 12. The poll was conducted by the Pew Research Center for the People and the Press during the period May 11–15, 2005.

36. Ibid., 11.

37. On the unprecedented partisan divide over, and precipitous decline in support for, the Iraq war see John Mueller, "The Iraq Syndrome," *Foreign Affairs* 84, no. 6 (November/December 2005): 44–54; see also Gary C. Jacobson's chapter in this volume.

38. Kenneth S. Apfel, "Social Security: Big Choices Ahead," *Public Policy: Current Thinking on Critical Issues,* Fall 2006, 2–3.

39. Julie Kosterlitz, "Cracking the Nest Egg," *National Journal,* April 23, 2005, 1212–1217.

40. Bartlett, *Impostor,* 202.

41. Ibid.

42. Michael Grunwald and Juliet Eilperin, "Energy Bill Raises Fears about Pollution, Fraud," *Washington Post,* July 30, 2005, A1.

43. White House, "President Bush Signs into Law a National Energy Plan," news release dated August 8, 2005.

44. Gregg Easterbrook, "Vote Yes for the Energy Bill, Then Start Working on the Real Issues," Brookings Institution, July 28, 2005, available at www.brookings.edu/views/op-ed/easterbrook/20050728.htm.

45. John Carey, "Bush Is Blowing Smoke on Energy," *BusinessWeek* online, April 28, 2005, www.businessweek.com/bwdaily/dnflash/apr2005/nf20050428_9012_db045.htm.

46. The relevant Department of Transportation press release and a link to the rule itself are available at www.dot.gov/affairs/dot4606.html (accessed September 27, 2006). See also "Boehlert: New CAFE Rule a 'Missed Opportunity,' " press release, House Committee on Science, March 29, 2006, www.house.gov/science/press/109/109-213.htm. See also Union

of Concerned Scientists, "Administration Stumbles after Admitting Oil Addiction: New Fuel Economy Rules Would Save Less Than Two Weeks of Gas a Year," press release, March 29, 2006, available at www.ucsusa.org/news/press_release/2006-Fuel-economy.html (accessed September 27, 2006).

47. Grunwald and Eilperin, "Energy Bill Raises Fears." On the controversial nuclear fuel reprocessing effort see Mary O'Driscoll, "Radioactive Recycling," *National Journal,* May 5, 2006, 30–37.

48. On Senator Reid's continued opposition to the Yucca Mountain Repository, see http://reid.senate.gov/issues/yucca.cfm (accessed February 5, 2007).

49. R. Douglas Arnold, *The Logic of Congressional Action* (New Haven: Yale University Press, 1990).

50. Jim VandeHei and Steven Mufson, "Bush Calls for Probe of Rising Gas Prices," *Washington Post,* April 26, 2006, A1.

51. White House, "Fact Sheet: President Bush's Four-Part Plan to Confront High Gasoline Prices," April 25, 2006.

52. Ibid.; VandeHei and Mufson, "Bush Calls for Probe."

53. Carl Hulse, "Senate Rejects Bid for Drilling in Arctic Area," *New York Times,* December 22, 2005, A1.

54. "President Applauds House Vote Approving Energy Exploration in Arctic National Wildlife Refuge," White House news release, May 25, 2006.

55. Bruce P. Montgomery, "Congressional Oversight: Vice President Richard B. Cheney's Executive Branch Triumph," *Political Science Quarterly* 4 (Winter 2005–2006): 581–617.

56. Mark A. Peterson, "Bush and Interest Groups: A Government of Chums," in *The George W. Bush Presidency: Appraisals and Prospects,* ed. Colin Campbell and Bert A. Rockman (Washington, D.C.: CQ Press, 2004), chap. 9.

57. See commentary by the Natural Resources Defense Council (NRDC) at www.nrdc.org/media/pressreleases/031203.asp and www.nrdc.org/bushrecord/articles/br_1522.asp (accessed June 28, 2006).

58. "Clearer Skies," editorial, *New York Times,* March 12, 2005. New Source Review appeared to require more stringent regulatory treatment of power plant replacements than of "routine maintenance," creating a disincentive to upgrade from older (and dirtier) equipment.

59. See NRDC question-and-answer critique titled "Dirty Skies: The Bush Administration's Air Pollution Plan," www.nrdc.org/air/pollution/qbushplan.asp (accessed September 22, 2006).

60. See writer Gregg Easterbrook's Easterblogg entry dated February 2, 2004 at www.tnr.com/easterbrook.mhtml?pid=1276 (accessed September 22, 2006).

61. Gregg Easterbrook, *A Moment of the Earth: The Coming Age of Environmental Optimism* (New York: Penguin, 1995).

62. See "Clearer Skies," *New York Times,* March 12, 2005, and the summary statement by the Council on Environmental Quality at www.whitehouse.gov/ceq/clean-air.html (accessed September 20, 2006).

63. Rachel L. Swarns, "Bill to Broaden Immigration Law Gains in the Senate," *New York Times,* March 28, 2006.

64. Rep. Tancredo's immigration bill (H.R. 3333), introduced in July 2005, proposed to make unauthorized immigration a felony and to jail employers hiring such felons. Seth Stern, "Fall Agenda: Guest Worker Visa Program," *CQ Weekly,* September 5, 2005, 2315.

65. Alex Wayne, "Views of Senate GOP, Bush Threaten Tighter Immigration," *CQ Weekly,* January 17, 2005, 115.

66. Jonathan Weisman, "Senate Pact Offers Permits to Most Illegal Immigrants," *Washington Post,* April 7, 2006, A1.

67. Jonathan Wiseman, "Senate Backs Fence, Guest-Worker Curbs," *Washington Post,* May 18, 2006, A1.

68. Carl Hulse, "House Plans National Hearings before Changes to Immigration," *New York Times,* June 21, 2006, A1.

69. "Return to Stalemate," editorial, *Washington Post,* September 6, 2006, A16.

70. Charles Babington, "Senate Passes Stem Cell Bill; Bush Vows Veto," *Washington Post,* July 19, 2006, A1.

71. Michael Specter, "Political Science: The Bush Administration's War on the Laboratory," *New Yorker,* March 13, 2006, 58.

72. Carl Hulse and David D. Kirkpatrick, "Congress Passes and Bush Signs Legislation on Schiavo Case," *New York Times,* March 21, 2005.

73. Mucciaroni and Quirk, "Deliberations of a 'Compassionate Conservative,' " 173.

74. Brian Friel, "Stay the Course?" *National Journal,* October 7, 2006, 29.

75. Brian Friel, "The Bush Record," *National Journal,* March 20, 2004, 868.

76. Marie Gryphon, "Utah Stands Up for the Children: Why More States Are Telling D.C. Educrats to Take a Hike," May 6, 2005, www.reason.com/news/show/32920.html (accessed February 6, 2005).

77. Friel, "Stay the Course?" 32.

78. Martha Derthick, *Agency under Stress: The Social Security Administration in American Government* (Washington, D.C.: Brookings Institution Press, 1990).

79. Fareed Zakaria, "Another Chance on Immigration," *Washington Post,* November 6, 2006, A21.

CHAPTER 13

Still a Government of Chums
Bush, Business, and Organized Interests

Mark A. Peterson

YOU ARE KNOWN by the company you keep. That age-old admonition from parents to their children can readily apply as well to presidents of the United States. The coterie of organized interests that has enjoyed the closest and most enduring working relationships with George W. Bush during his presidency tells us a great deal about his approach to the office, his priorities, his likely legacy, and what sets him apart from his predecessors. As is true of so many dimensions of the forty-third president, it is not that he has pursued ties with or strategies toward organized interests that were untried by his predecessors. Rather, what makes this president different is the unprecedented extent to which his administration has routinely engaged a particular set of interests. With rare exceptions, across multiple policy arenas, and largely regardless of changing political circumstances, from early to late in his presidency, Bush's White House and his administration throughout the executive branch have promoted—I would posit more than any previous presidency—relationships with a consistently narrow band of like-minded interests for the singular purpose of prosecuting an unusually ideologically focused policy agenda. Perhaps consonant with a chief executive as former Delta Kappa Epsilon fraternity brother, the Bush years from start to near finish have in effect presented the country with a government of chums.[1]

To be sure, all presidents experience the tension between the symbolism of the inclusive presidency and the practical exigencies of electioneering, coalition building, policymaking, and governing predicated on the specific constituencies that helped the president win office or that favor the administration's programmatic ideas. However much it is lamented at times, Congress is expected to be an institution open to organized interests, and few observers find it surprising that legislators, representing geographically bound and often quite homogeneous constituencies, have strong incentives to align with particular interests. The president's position is more complicated. As the head of state, the president poses as the representative of a unified republic. And yet, as the victor of the last election and head of government, the president marshals political resources to pursue a policy agenda that is almost sure to have winners and losers. Among those resources is the oft-repeated rhetorical claim to be doing the work of the American people writ large, mining for political benefit the constitutional fact that the president is the sole elected official accountable to a national electorate. Congress represents local and competing interests, so goes the argument, but the president represents the nation. Consistent with that guise, as an Annenberg Institutions of American Democracy survey found, 80 percent of the public believe that "even though it may result in compromise, the president should accommodate a wide range of interests in making policy."[2]

Modern presidents have not forgone the opportunity to proclaim that they were serving national purposes, even as their administrations have increasingly developed in the White House the craft of public opinion polling to identify supportive constituencies and the technology of "narrowcasting" communication to reach specific audiences with carefully targeted and calibrated messages. President Bush has, unremarkably, followed in that tradition—only more so.[3] Bush has reinforced that approach to governing with his highly targeted interest group strategy and relationships, adjusting less than his predecessors to changes in political circumstances. Whether flying high in general popular support or sunk in the figurative dumps, and however slender the margin of his electoral victories, while paying tribute to the usual pieties of the national interest, in actual politics and policymaking he has most often chosen the route of the same constricted coalitions made up of affluent, commercial, and socially conservative interests, which have become the prime, or at least most direct, beneficiaries of his administration's policies. A close examination of this presidency's engagement with organized interests may provide the sharpest picture of whom this especially partisan administration has listened to, whom it has served, and who will have gained the most from George W. Bush's eight years in office.

The character of the relationships between an administration and organized interests depends on the opportunities for interactions (and battle) provided by existing institutional arrangements, the contemporary political setting, and the objectives of the individual president. After briefly setting the political and institutional context in American politics at the time of the Bush administration, I offer an overview of three core presidential strategies toward organized interests—promoting friends, intimidating enemies, and mobilizing allies—and compare and contrast the general practices of the Bush administration with those of previous presidencies. In the rest of the chapter I illustrate the striking consistency of Bush's approach to organized interests across a variety of major policy areas, while also noting the few contrary examples that serve as the exceptions that prove the rule.

Past Presidents, Bush, and the Group System

In the American constitutional system, which fragments power and provides multiple checks and balances, nothing about presidential influence is certain—other than the nearly constant effort of presidents, especially in the last century, to pursue all means possible to enhance it.[4] During the latter half of the twentieth century— driven by expanded government responsibilities, changing communications technology, a more educated electorate, major and divisive policy issues, and transformative social mobilization—the means for presidential coalition building became more problematic. At first the political parties became more fragmented, and the social movements of the 1960s and 1970s yielded an interest group system that at once challenged corporate political power and spawned a wide range of organizations representing diverse constituencies and social issues. As the century came to a close, the parties as represented in government regained strength, now with far greater internal ideological coherence and accentuated interparty polarization, while the interest group terrain included a vastly larger number of relevant organizations, more specialized policy niches, and arguably greater ideological and partisan division among interests than in the past.[5]

In this context, by virtue of the technological advances and demographic changes, President Bush had the means to communicate both with the public en masse and through specific messages to myriad specialized audiences, but so did organizational interests, and their legislative allies, that opposed his programmatic agenda, including entities, such as MoveOn.org, that thoroughly embodied the social and technological transformation of American politics. Bush did have a mobilizing advantage over his immediate predecessor, Bill Clinton. Clinton's New Democratic approach to policymaking ran against the grain both of affiliates of his own party and of many organized interests with issue-oriented ties to the Democrats: unions opposed his support of free trade; liberal consumer groups objected to his promotion of competition among private insurance plans in health care reform; advocates of the poor distrusted his focus on personal responsibility. Bush, on the other hand, emphasized themes from his campaign—tax cuts, defense buildup, energy production, education reform, and market-oriented strategies overall—that were more likely to meld commercial interests and conservative social movement groups into a cohesive whole.[6] If there were serious coalitional weaknesses to be found in the interest group community, they were among the president's opponents. The earlier rise of citizen groups strengthened the organizational armament of Bush's liberal adversaries, but trade unions had lost much of their reach within the electorate and much of their influence with members of Congress. Further, in addition to now facing a countermobilization of social movements on the right, the liberal citizen organizations are often, as Theda Skocpol has noted, "staff-led, mailing-list associations" with checkbook memberships, devoid of labor's previous ability to conduct face-to-face, grassroots mobilization. Ironically, it was the old, staid business interests, likely allies of Bush, who had learned to exploit the grassroots mobilizing techniques of the left, and that made them all the more effective when they joined forces with the energized social movements of the right.[7]

To enhance his sway in this complex realm of politics and the many domains of policy, President Bush could look to the three general strategies that modern chief executives have employed in interest group relations: promoting and winning friends, intimidating the opposition, and mobilizing allies to achieve specific political or policy objectives.[8]

Promoting Friends

All presidents have pursued relationships with political friends and promoted the interests of those allies once in office. The combination of campaign funding prior to elections and subsequent use of political patronage to fill appointive positions in government often provides a window on an administration's ties to particular interests; even after the introduction of the civil service system in the late nineteenth century, hundreds of appointments remain for the president to make, albeit often with the advice and consent of the Senate.[9]

The financial contributors to George W. Bush in his political career, including the 2000 and 2004 presidential campaigns, suggest the nature of his alliances among organized interests. Before the company's demise, CEO Kenneth Lay and other executives of Enron ensured that the firm was "the single largest patron of George W. Bush's political career. . . . Bush received $774,100 from Enron's PAC and executives—including $312,500 for his two gubernatorial campaigns."[10] Other contributions totaling more than $1 million flowed into campaign coffers from various legal, accounting, and banking enterprises employed by Enron. During the 2004 campaign, MBNA Corp., a large credit card company, became the president's "top career patron."[11] Overall, according to Texans for Public Justice, for the 2000 election the "George W. Bush campaign . . . raised more money than any other political candidate in history, twice as much as any presidential candidate before him."[12] The pattern continued for 2004. In each case, much of the funding came from the campaign's "Rangers" (elite fund-raisers pledged to bring in at least $200,000 each) and "Pioneers" (hundreds of individuals who were responsible for raising at least $100,000 each). About half were business executives, and almost all represented corporate interests.[13] After the disputed 2000 presidential election was settled by the Supreme Court, the *National Journal* published an article titled "Corporations, K Street Throw a Party," describing how companies and lobbyists representing them contributed nearly $25 million to help pay for Bush's inauguration. About 160 "corporate and individual underwriters . . . [include] big names from the financial services sector, the oil and gas industry, real estate companies, and computer interests. . . . K Street–based associations are well represented, too, including the American Bankers Association, the American Insurance Association, the American Trucking Association, and the Pharmaceutical Research and Manufacturers of America."[14]

The flow of people as well as dollars reflected the nature of the Bush coalition. Just as occurred with Reagan's orchestrated personnel strategy,[15] the advisory teams assembled for executive departments during the transition included myriad major-industry lobbyists and were "chock-full of corporate executives, fund-raisers, big donors, conservative think-tankers, and former GOP officials."[16] They, or individuals of similar background, went on to become political appointees in the Bush executive branch.[17] In general, when initially forming a government in his first term, Bush—the recipient of an MBA from Harvard Business School and himself a former corporate executive—turned to the business community with which he was familiar, among whom he felt comfortable, and who shared both his approach to decision making and his policy preferences. As the administration progressed, an ongoing cycle was observable of industry representatives and lobbyists being recruited for White House and executive agency positions, followed by administration officials close to the president and vice president or in senior subcabinet posts leaving government for trade associations and corporate lobbying firms, from which many of them then lobbied Congress and the White House on subsequent policymaking. Over time additional people moved from business and lobbying backgrounds "into the Bush administration where they are in a position to promote the interests of their former employers."[18] Democrats sought to "gain some traction [with] the general thematic charge that he's a President for the special interests," with polls showing concerns that he "will go too far with policies that favor the rich and corporate interests over the middle class."[19] When a similar claim was made by Democrats that Bush was a "captive of corporate interests" in the development of his Medicare drug discount initiative, the administration responded that the president was merely "harnessing the expertise and ingenuity of private industry."[20] Some appointments resulted in more overt scandal. Former lobbyist J. Steven Griles resigned as a deputy secretary of the interior when "allegations surfaced that he pushed policy decisions that favored some of his former oil and gas industry clients."[21]

Bush also solidified his alliance with conservative interests beyond the business world. Perhaps the best example was his creation of the White House Office of Faith-Based and Community Initiatives immediately upon taking office. Social and religious conservatives have long sought to bridge the separation between church and state and to make far greater use of faith-based organizations in promoting and implementing social policy. The significance of this constituency for Bush is underscored by his instituting this new office by executive order, an approach that is rarely used by presidents for such single-policy, constituency-based operations within the White House establishment.[22]

There is little evidence, however, that Bush has gone beyond catering to existing friendly interests to the next step of actively reshaping the community of interests, as John Kennedy, Lyndon Johnson, and Ronald Reagan did. Conferences and other activities that the Kennedy White House organized, for example, did much to foster the women's movement, now largely a Democratic constituency.[23] Johnson's Great Society programs, such as the Community Action Program and its requirement for "maximum feasible participation" at the local level, helped to develop new leaders and organizations, especially among African Americans, ensuring the presence of additional institutional allies for liberal programs in the future.[24] Reagan, naturally, wished to do the opposite, seeking "to disrupt the ties that bind the Democrats to major social groups" and trying "to expand the constellation of interests that are tied to the GOP." Reagan's strategy along these lines involved "reunifying business," switching "middle-income suburbanites . . . from beneficiaries [of government programs] to taxpayers," reorienting blue-collar voters from "workers to patriots," and attracting southern whites through their "evangelical religious affiliations," all intended to "reconstitute society" and alter the way that alliances are formed within the interest group community.[25] Given Reagan's achievements in this regard, which were further cemented by conservative Republican congressional majorities after the 1994 elections and invigorated by the right-wing attacks on Clinton, few business groups or even significant social conservative groups have had difficulty gaining access to influential policymakers. Bush simply did not need to do any more to encourage a vigorous interest group domain favorable to GOP interests.

Intimidating Opponents

Ronald Reagan pursued the most aggressive strategy of any modern president for enfeebling the organized interests perceived to be working at purposes contrary to those of his administration. Using control over the federal budget to cut back on grants and contracts to organizations, as well as changes in regulations and tax exemption requirements to inhibit their political activities, his administration sought to "defund the left" and stifle its political influence.[26] In one sense, these efforts were successful—federal government funding was reduced for "types of groups most likely to oppose the administration's principal goals." In other respects, though, the attack turned out to be poorly aimed, hitting not "leftist" or liberal citizen groups, which had never relied heavily on government largesse, but instead "mainly associations of social service professionals in the nonprofit sector [and others] that were the most heavily dependent on government financial support." These organizations had been largely nonpartisan and far less political, but the cutbacks tended to alienate and politicize them in response to the administration's threat.[27]

Coming on the scene when labor was already weakened and conservative groups were firmly established, Bush had less incentive than Reagan to drive a stake through the heart of the opposition. Nonetheless, early in his administration he pursued some institutional and legal changes that would either impair opposing interests or reduce their access to government. Recognizing the "gender gap" in which women voters favored Democrats more than did men, Bill Clinton had enhanced the long-established executive office ties to women's issues by establishing the White House Office for Women's Initiatives and Outreach to focus particular attention on women's advocacy groups. Bush immediately abolished that office (unbeknownst to feminist organizations until a couple of months later) and folded representation of women back into the Office of Public Liaison.[28] The National Federation of Republican Women (NFRW), an advocacy organization in support of the president, explained that the "Bush administration does not intend to treat women as a coalition. At 52 percent of the population, we are not a special interest group."[29] The administration did establish a White House Women's Information Network that, although neutral-sounding, does not target all women or their perspectives. Instead it focuses largely on corporate CEOs and small-business leaders, and it is supported in spirit by the NFRW and RightNow!—another GOP women's group.[30] These ties imply a take on women's issues that, in fact, favors Republican coalition building. Similarly, Andrew Card, the White House chief of staff, told *USA Today* early on that the administration was terminating the Office of National AIDS Policy and the Initiative for One America (focused on race relations), also created by the Clinton administration and especially pertinent to Democratic constituencies. Shortly thereafter, however, "moving to quell a public relations squall," the president's press secretary announced that Card had "made a mistake. It happens."[31] These operations would remain active, at least in some form, but their relative standing in the Bush White House was made apparent.

The Bush administration saved its most serious attack for unions, the organizational backbone of the Democratic opposition. By March 2001, labor leaders had identified a dozen Bush initiatives that challenged their interests, from endorsement of "paycheck protection" legislation (requiring that members give unions explicit permission to use dues for political purposes) to executive orders governing federal contracting and terminating a labor-management partnership for federal workers. Said one labor expert, "It's as if several of these actions have been taken to insult the AFL-CIO." Labor leaders interpreted this overall effort as "retaliation," a form of "punishment for their backing Al Gore."[32] More important, these union officials perceived the initiatives "as part of a broader strategy to weaken organized labor on national issues in general and in politics in particular" to foster "an unfettered field for corporate interests."[33] Unions would later claim that the Bush administration was using the legislation creating the massive new Department of Homeland Security "as a back-door attempt to erode worker protections" through its provisions that circumvent existing civil service pay and performance rules and thwart union organizing.[34] Finally, just after the November 2002 congressional elections, the administration launched its "competitive sourcing" initiative, intended to open about half of federal civilian jobs (850,000) to competition from private contractors. President Bush, said the head of the American Federation of Government Employees, had "declared all-out war on federal employees."[35] Although it is not entirely clear how many specific government employees have been replaced by private workers, contracting out became more prevalent than ever before.[36] President Bush has at times sought to build alliances with various unions. But in each of those cases—reaching out to the Teamsters in support of drilling for oil in the Arctic National Wildlife Refuge (ANWR), the United Auto Workers in opposition to raising fuel efficiency standards, and the United Steel Workers of America in favoring tariffs against foreign steel imports—labor was on the same side as industry.[37]

Mobilizing Allies

The signature feature of the modern presidency in relations with interest groups has been the third strategy—the increasingly institutionalized process of mobilizing existing organizational allies to use their representation and lobbying resources in support of the president's political and policy goals. The stature and relevance of such ties to groups are best indicated by the establishment of the Office of Public Liaison (OPL) at the outset of Gerald Ford's administration, following the resignation of President Richard Nixon, and its continuation in every White House since. After the creation of the Executive Office of the President (EOP) in 1939, some of Franklin Roosevelt's assistants were informally designated to maintain ongoing communications with blacks, Jews, farmers, and other constituencies within the president's electoral coalition. The Johnson and Nixon White House staffs expanded on that representational function with efforts to gain the backing of groups to promote presidential policy goals. The OPL formalized both of these functions and housed staff with the responsibility to "communicate, articulate, and support the President's programs, policies, and priorities in order to mobilize support for them."[38] The overall task of interest group liaison remains largely the province of staff members scattered throughout the EOP, and in most administrations is done more effectively by people outside of the formal Office of Public Liaison, but the enduring presence of the OPL underscores the significance of instrumental links to interest groups for all contemporary chief executives.[39]

Different and changing political environments and the diverse needs and objectives of presidents can have predictable effects on the kinds of relationships administrations find it most advantageous to develop and maintain with various interests. We can bring some conceptual order to presidential approaches to interest group liaison, and thus to Bush's particular tactics, by identifying four distinct kinds of strategies, based on the goals as well as the incentives that are likely to motivate each one. Two primary characteristics distinguish among White House approaches to

FIGURE 13.1 Typology of White House Liaison with Interest Groups

		Breadth of Group Interactions	
		Inclusive	Exclusive
Purpose of group interactions	Representational	Liaison as legitimization	Liaison as outreach
	Programmatic	Liaison as consensus building	Liaison as governing party

coalition formation using organized interests: First is the *purpose* of the engagement with groups—whether to promote the president's role as an elected representative, by, for example, improving and maintaining his political standing with various constituencies, or whether it is intended to marshal support for the president's program, such as a piece of proposed legislation. Second is the *breadth* of interactions with the interest group community—whether they are inclusive, extending across a broad ideological or partisan spectrum of groups, or whether they are exclusive, focused on a more narrowly drawn, politically homogeneous, ideologically compatible subset of interests.

As shown in Figure 13.1, combining these two dimensions yields a fourfold typology of interest group liaison by the White House. With the first type, *liaison as legitimization,* presidents seek ties to organizations representing interests outside of their electoral coalitions to enhance or consolidate their position as national leader and head of state, which may be in question or under threat. There is no starker example than President Gerald Ford, who was brought to the highest office in the land by the resignation of his predecessor, Richard Nixon, in the wake of the Watergate scandal. Because Ford had been appointed vice president after Spiro Agnew's resignation due to past financial improprieties, he became president without ever having been on a national ballot. Indeed, only the constituents of the Michigan district that he represented in Congress had ever cast a vote for him. With the nation rocked by Watergate, the first resignation of a president, deep divisions over the Vietnam War, and an economy suffering under both high unemployment and high inflation, Ford, on taking office, made a special plea to the public. "The oath that I have taken," he noted, "is the same oath that was taken by George Washington and by every president under the Constitution. But I assume the presidency under extraordinary circumstances never before experienced by Americans. This is an hour of history that troubles our minds and hurts our hearts. . . . I am acutely aware that you have not elected me as your president by your ballots, and so I ask you to confirm me as your president with your prayers." Ford needed all of the help that he could muster to establish himself as the legitimate president in unusually troubled times. Reaching out to all kinds of organized interests with an open hand, breaking down what had been perceived as Nixon's "imperial presidency," played a significant role.

Liaison as outreach also advances the representational function of the presidency, but in response to quite different circumstances and for quite different purposes. In this instance, presidents are secure in their own political standing but use interest group liaison to reach out to groups that have provided political support for the president, and could be important elements of the reelection coalition, but that have had only limited access to the core centers of policymaking in Washington. In a reversal of the Ford strategy, presidential outreach to such previously marginalized interests, one might say, is a way to confer the president's legitimacy upon groups. All modern presidents have devoted some White House resources to this task. FDR, for example, was the first to open the White House routinely to African American leaders. Kennedy elevated substantially the presence of women. Johnson gave such recognition to the consumers' movement. Carter's OPL was the first to bring gays and lesbians into the White House fold. Reagan formally pulled in the Christian right, which was fairly new to active political engagement.[40]

The third approach is *liaison as governing party*, in which the set of organized interests targeted by the White House is also limited, restricted to like-minded allies and partisans, but the goal is to enact the president's policy agenda. These interest groups are urged to use their resources—their lobbyists, grassroots capabilities, media campaigns, and electoral connections—to influence coalition building within government by putting pressure on legislators and other policymakers. The president wants to pass a piece of legislation, for example, and the task is to bring under a governing-party umbrella the collection of organized interests, constituencies, and members of Congress who can secure its enactment. The process may involve a direct joining together of the president's party in Congress with ideologically compatible outside interests. This approach to group relations became a centerpiece of Carter's White House after the president, articulating a full policy agenda of complex and controversial proposals, suffered early legislative defeats—despite large Democratic majorities—and he strove to improve his effectiveness with Congress in subsequent encounters. The OPL under Anne Wexler became a central hub for building and orchestrating legislative coalitions.

The Reagan administration offers an even more compelling example. Reagan won office in a landslide over the incumbent Carter, and his fellow Republicans took control of the Senate for the first time in a quarter-century. Reagan had campaigned on a specific agenda of major tax cuts, substantial budget reductions, a military buildup, and an attack on regulation, which became the priorities for the first two years of his presidency. Using both the OPL and other officials in the White House, the administration employed an explicit strategy of working with an active alliance of organizations that shared the administration's policy convictions and possessed the financial and staff resources, as well as the lobbying experience, to ensure that congressional attention was directed to enacting the president's tax and budget initiatives.[41]

The final form of liaison is *consensus building,* which differs from the "governing-party" approach only in the expectation that enough agreement exists across diverse constituencies that inclusive engagement with organized interests will produce a consensus coalition in favor of the president's preferred policy action. Such opportunities are fairly rare, but on some issues, at the right moment, broad-based programmatic alliances are possible. For example in 1965, when promoting civil rights and overcoming the problems of the poor were popular ideas, a growing economy produced an increasing flow of revenues for the government without raising taxes, and social welfare advocates and businesses could have overlapping interests, Lyndon Johnson wanted to unite as many groups as possible. In the interest of expanding the supply of public housing for low-income families, for instance, the Johnson White House brought together community activists, civil rights groups, service providers, and the construction industry.[42]

As the examples from past presidencies illustrate, which approach to interest group liaison presidents attempt depends on the prevailing political conditions (is the president strongly supported by the public, and is the president's party influential in Congress, or is the president's political standing precarious?), on the president's objectives (is the president an activist who is determined to reorder federal policy, or is the president a defender of the status quo?), and on the attributes of the issues under consideration (are there deep partisan or ideological divisions within Congress and the electorate, or is it possible to achieve a consensus?). These circumstances also typically vary both across issues and over time within a single administration, so that all presidents are likely to engage in all four approaches to varying degrees. All of these considerations are relevant to the Bush presidency, from the moment Bush stepped into the Oval Office in 2001; to the post-9/11 period when his popular approval soared and opponents cowered; to the collapse of his public support as the president's ambitions in the Iraq war unraveled, the federal response to Hurricane Katrina proved disastrous, and the president's competency was increasingly challenged; to the last two years of the administration when the president faced a Congress recaptured by the emboldened Democrats. These variations in context and presumed presidential needs ought to have resulted in different mixes of interest group liaison.

Consider the start of the Bush presidency. In the November 2000 election George W. Bush lost the popular vote to Al Gore by over 500,000 votes (he was the first president in a century to enter office having come in second in the popular vote). The results in Florida would determine the Electoral College winner, but election day irregularities, ambiguities, and botched ballots left the results uncertain and open to challenge. On December 12, 2000, by ending a recount in Florida in a strangely argued opinion, a five-to-four majority of the U.S. Supreme Court effectively determined that Bush would become the forty-third president of the United States.[43] During the campaign, Bush had claimed to be a "uniter, not a divider," intent on rising above and changing what he described as the destructive partisan tone in Washington. Programmatically he identified himself as a "compassionate conservative," implying a policy agenda that would combine the smaller-government and market-based approaches endorsed by the right with a commitment to using targeted government action to rectify the social injustices usually of concern to liberals and moderates. Although Republicans had managed to hang onto control of the House and Senate in the 2000 elections, their majorities were slender—221 to 212, with two independents, in the House; fifty to fifty in the Senate. The Republicans had to rely on Vice President Cheney to break tie votes in the Senate, and they were well short of the sixty seats needed to ensure a working majority. The loss of Republican control of the Senate four months into the administration, when Sen. James Jeffords, Vt., departed the Republican caucus and declared himself an independent, underscored the vulnerability of Republican legislative leadership.

Given the questions about the president's legitimacy that were raised by the circumstances of the 2000 election and Bush's expressed commitment to finding unity, and guided by the experience of Ford, the context and purposes of the incoming Bush administration created incentives to pursue an inclusive interest group strategy, with particular attention to liaison as legitimization. Given the political conditions and a legislative program thought to be built on "compassionate conservative" themes, such an inclusive approach to groups could extend to an effort at bipartisan liaison as consensus building on matters of policy. The organizational evolution of the White House Office of Public Liaison since the 1970s would have reinforced that inclusive approach. Across Democratic and Republican administrations, officials in OPL have acquired ongoing responsibility for maintaining formal links with African Americans, women, Latinos, senior citizens, consumers, Asian Americans, and various other ethnic or underrepresented groups. Only as the president's political fortunes improved after 9/11, and after subsequent elections added to the GOP ranks in Congress and to Bush's own electoral margin (in 2004), would one have anticipated robust incentives to pursue a more partisan, exclusive, aggressive legislative program and a commensurate group strategy of liaison as governing party.

Political conditions, however, although they are expected to influence presidential strategic choices in predictable ways, are not determinative. Individual presidents can choose which factors to emphasize and which to ignore (sometimes, of course, at their own peril), and President Bush has done so with gusto. Although previous presidents have acted in ways consistent with the incentives I have been describing, Bush, to a remarkable degree, has not.

In part the president and his conservative supporters simply interpreted the situation differently than others did.[44] However precarious for Bush it might have appeared on the surface, the political and institutional environment, even at the start of his administration, offered some openings for prosecuting an exclusive and programmatic set of relationships. First, Republicans had not enjoyed fully unified control of government since the first two years of the Eisenhower administration, 1953–1954 (even Reagan had to work with a Democratic House). In the postwar period, the typical pattern had been one of Republican presidents facing Democratic majorities in Congress. Neither Bush nor his GOP congressional allies, frustrated earlier by Clinton's successful vetoes, wished to defer exploiting the opportunity created by the resolution of the 2000 elections. Conservative Republicans in Congress now had the conservative Republican president they had lacked in the 104th Congress, when Clinton stymied the massive changes that Speaker Newt Gingrich had shepherded through Congress and forced Republicans to suffer in the court of public opinion for the shutdown of government that occurred during their confrontation. Second, Bush could turn to conservative partners in the interest group community, who were an even more effective resource than they had been under Reagan. The Reagan coalition had included the newly mobilized Christian right and social conservatives in general, who did not yet have major access to the Washington establishment. One of the functions of the Reagan White House was to reach out to those interests—liaison as outreach—and bring them to the policy-making table. By the time George W. Bush entered office, the Christian right, evangelicals, and right-wing analysts had all become prominent parts of the Republican mainstream, and six years of a Republican Congress had also given them direct access to policymaking and helped embed them in government itself. As William Kristol, conservative editor of the *Weekly Standard,* put it, "For conservatives, the good news is you don't need to be a rebel anymore."[45] Thus there was less need for outreach by the new Bush White House and greater confidence in incorporating these groups, many possessing the resources of grassroots mobilization, into an exclusive interest group coalition assembled for programmatic purposes.

Then there was the substance of Bush's 2000 campaign (the policy issues and specific proposals), as distinct from its rhetoric (the generic appeals to unity, inclusion, and compassion). The campaign's policy dictates, translated into the new president's programmatic agenda, were sweeping. They were unmistakably conservative in thematic structure and driven by the substantive preferences of Bush and his Republican allies, not the reauthorization schedule of existing statutes. The agenda focused on tax cuts, energy development, environmental adjustment, redesigned primary and secondary education, reform of Social Security and Medicare, and military expansion. All of these initiatives were firmly rooted in Republican and conservative traditions, sure to be opposed by Democrats and other interests, and they represented an effort to roll back the eight years of Bill Clinton's impact on public policy. They incorporated specific policy approaches refined in conservative think tanks and favored by Republican constituency interests, with an emphasis on wealthy entrepreneurship, private institutions, market incentives, and faith-inspired charity. Preferred alternatives included ending the estate tax and cutting other taxes paid largely by the wealthy; emphasizing extraction of carbon-based fuels (oil, coal, and gas) and nurturing nuclear power; promoting private property rights and deregulation in environmental matters; breaking down the wall separating church and state by incorporating faith-based organizations into the provision of public services and opening private schools to publicly financed vouchers; establishing private accounts in Social Security and expanding private health plans in Medicare; providing Medicare drug coverage through subsidies to private carriers; and building up the military in general and deploying a missile defense system. This forceful agenda and the solutions that Bush proposed would require a strong emphasis on the programmatic objectives of the presidency, facilitated by forging close alliances with like-minded interests: corporations, small businesses, and social conservatives. It would entail liaison as governing party—joining Republican elected officials with their conservative counterparts in the interest group community.

The terrorist attacks of September 11, 2001, and President Bush's response to them transformed Bush's national standing, giving him the legitimacy that the 2000 election morass had denied him, so much so that congressional Democrats lined up behind the president. His erstwhile and potential future opponent, Al Gore, lengthened his own period of self-imposed silence, giving the president nearly full rein in setting the political and programmatic agendas. The percentage of the public giving Bush a favorable job approval rating soared from 51 percent just before the attacks to 90 percent shortly thereafter—the highest recorded by the Gallup poll for any president since it began asking this question during the Franklin Roosevelt administration.[46] The effect persisted through most of Bush's first term. Bush's hand was further strengthened by Republicans' picking up seats in both the House and Senate in 2002 and in the 2004 elections, when the president this time won majorities in both the Electoral College and the popular vote. Over the next two years Bush's fortunes changed again, this time in the opposite direction. More Americans disapproved of his job performance than approved, and in 2006 the Democrats marched back into control of Congress after twelve years in the minority.

It is striking how much, right from the start and throughout both improved and weakened political circumstances, the Bush administration emphasized interest group liaison as governing party. Indeed, this approach to interest group relations has been the dominant, nearly exclusive, strategy that the White House has pursued throughout the course of the Bush presidency. Fairly early in the administration, one of the president's advisers commented, "Sooner or later, people were going to realize this guy isn't Eisenhower."[47] Whatever the campaign rhetoric, George W. Bush and his team had a well-defined and assertive policy agenda to pursue, one that is tied closely to the constituency base of his campaign contributors, electoral activists, business allies, and conservative supporters. The entire White House apparatus was immediately set up to advance a sharply drawn, governing-party approach to political messages and coalition building. The administration established the new Office of Strategic Initiatives in the White House to "devise long-term political strategy" under the direction of Karl Rove, Bush's top political strategist from the campaign and well before. Previous presidents have committed staff resources to protecting their political core constituencies and furthering their own political standing, but this administration "has clearly taken a different approach by thoroughly integrating Karl Rove into the White House chain of command."[48] The Office of Public Liaison reported directly to Rove who, in combination with his leadership of the overall political apparatus of the White House, has played a measurable policy role. John DiIulio Jr., the first director of the Office of Faith-Based and Community Initiatives in the Bush White House, commented that Rove is "enormously powerful. . . . There is no precedent in any modern White House for what is going on in this one: a complete lack of a policy apparatus. What you've got is everything, and I mean everything, being run by the political arm. It's the reign of the Mayberry Machiavellis."[49] The Bush Office of Public Liaison itself seemed primarily dedicated to ideological interest group coalition building to support the president's programmatic agenda. OPL staff profiles reinforced the point. OPL associate director Christopher Smith was described on the White House Web site as "responsible for coordinating national organizations and public interest groups to advance the President's policies regarding environmental, agriculture, and sportsmen-related issues." In an interview for *Hillel*, Jay Zeldman, liaison to the Jewish community, commented, "Our office doesn't create policy, we communicate it. And the communication is a two-way street. It's our way of gauging honest feedback from groups that are politically, socially, and morally important to the president."[50] In contrast, when coming to decision on controversial issues, Bush's father as president had his OPL staff organize intimate meetings for him with wide-ranging groups, including those outside of his political base, such as the president of the NAACP on a civil rights bill, as well as environmental and consumer representatives on revisions of the Clean Air Act.[51]

At the same time, there is no evidence that the White House of George W. Bush made liaison as legitimization even a modest priority in its relations with organized interests, either early on when the president was the popular vote loser or after the deep and sustained drop in his public support since 2005. At best one can see that the institutional imperatives of broad-based group interactions that previous administrations had established and formalized in the White House Office of Public Liaison carried forward into the Bush administration. As noted earlier, the administration felt compelled to continue (after first indicating otherwise) task forces of particular interest to African Americans and gays, although women as a constituency, given a particularly high profile in the Clinton White House, had their representation folded back into the Office of Public Liaison. My search of the World Wide Web and the White House Web site revealed the usual litany of minor events in which OPL or other administration officials met with, or addressed sessions for, a broad spectrum of associations and constituencies that had little obvious connection to the Bush electoral base or the administration's programmatic agenda.[52] However, few attempts were made to build *systematic* relationships with politically influential interests that had not explicitly supported the president in the 2000 or 2004 elections. Unlike the Ford administration, the Bush White House has not used interest group relations primarily, or significantly, or even moderately to elevate Bush's political, representational standing in the country as a whole.

Bush and His Government of Chums

The Bush "government of chums" is in evidence in almost every policy domain in which Bush has attempted to shape the agenda—from the campaign funds and administration personnel drawn from business and allied conservative interests to the overwhelmingly dominant commitment to an exclusive and programmatic approach to interest group liaison. I now turn to illustrations from policy areas of particular interest to the administration in which it achieved significant policy changes.

Energy Policy

All of the attributes of Bush's cozy relationships with a select set of commercial and conservative organized interests are exhibited in especially stark relief on energy policy, an issue central to President Bush through most of his administration. The tight web of relationships went back to the first presidential campaign. The Center for Responsive Politics, for example, reported in 2001 that *"78 cents out of every dollar"* contributed by the oil and gas industry to major-party candidates in federal elections over the past ten years has gone to Republicans, and that "President Bush was the *No. 1 recipient* of the industry's money during the last [2000] election" and cumulatively for the entire previous decade. From 1999 to 2000, oil and gas gave a total of $25.6 million in hard-money and soft-money contributions to Republican candidates and the party. Electric utilities followed suit, contributing seven to one to Bush over Gore. The coal industry also made Bush its leading recipient of contributions; ditto nuclear power generators.[53] With the president's energy legislation stalled in the first term, the industry's giving patterns continued through the 2004 election (a total of $52.3 million in energy industry contributions overall). About two dozen energy company "executives and their spouses . . . qualified as either

'Pioneers' or 'Rangers' " for the Bush reelection campaign, as did more than a dozen related lobbyists and spouses.[54]

When he entered office, Bush took "the unusual step of managing energy issues out of the White House"; it was an administration in which the president, vice president, and secretary of commerce, among others, all had significant personal, experiential ties to conventional energy producers.[55] Indeed, no less than thirty "former energy industry executives, lobbyists, and lawyers [were appointed] to influential jobs in . . . [the] administration." In the words of a senior energy company executive, "The people running the United States government are from the energy industry."[56] Bush called on Vice President Dick Cheney to head the task force—the National Energy Policy Development Group—that was given responsibility for crafting the administration's energy plan, which was released on May 17, 2001. From the beginning, Cheney and the administration sought to keep the deliberations of the task force far from public view, holding secret the identities of the individuals from the energy industry and elsewhere who met with Cheney, the task force, or its staff. At the request of members of Congress, the General Accounting Office (GAO, now called the Government Accountability Office) attempted to obtain this information, resorting to a lawsuit against the vice president that proved unsuccessful.[57] The task force "met with more than 400 people from more than 150 groups," but by all accounts with "little input" from environmental organizations or consumer groups.[58] The *National Journal* described "big oil's White House pipelines" when covering the task force, noting that "oil and gas industry leaders have been streaming into Washington for talks with Cheney, Lundquist [the executive director of the task force], and congressional leaders."[59] Between the start of the administration and May 17, 2001, Secretary of Energy Spencer Abraham alone held meetings with "more than 100 representatives from the energy industry and trade associations."[60]

Most telling is the consistency between the president's final energy plan and the preferences of oil, gas, nuclear power, and mining companies and their trade associations. According to the *National Journal,* "faced with a choice between environmental protection and energy production, Bush has consistently sided with industry."[61] The provisions of the energy plan itself—including deregulation, financial incentives to industry for production, and opening the Arctic National Wildlife Refuge to oil exploration, along with some modest support for conservation and production of alternative sources of energy—adhered closely to Bush's campaign statements and fit so closely with the ideas of energy producers that the president of the Natural Resources Defense Council (NRDC) asserted that "big energy companies all but held the pencil for the White House task force."[62] The administration's "new energy policy," suggested the *National Journal,* even "treats nuclear power as a national treasure."[63] "Dig beneath the surface of the Bush administration's energy policies," says another account, "and you will find a broad seam of coal."[64] Some examples of energy policymaking illustrate the depths of the links between the administration and its friends among commercial interests in the energy domain. Based on documents obtained under a court order, the NRDC, for example, found that Executive Order 13211 issued by President Bush, pertaining to oil policy, "is nearly identical in structure and impact . . . and nearly verbatim in a key section" to a draft included in a March 20, 2001, e-mail message from the American Petroleum Institute to an official in the Department of Energy.[65]

All of this collaboration between industry interests and the administration yielded an energy plan in which 80 percent of the provisions were regulatory adjustments that Bush could implement administratively, without congressional action.[66] For the remaining elements, in classic liaison-as-governing-party mode, "Republicans joined energy industry and business groups to back the task force's recommendations for increasingly long-term production of oil, coal, natural gas, and nuclear power."[67] In support of the president's energy plan, the American Petroleum Institute, the American Gas Association, the National Association of Manufacturers, the National Mining Association, the U.S. Chamber of Commerce, and other major-industry trade associations established the Coalition for Energy, Environment, and the Economy, which was first expected to raise about $10 million for a lobbying campaign. The largest oil companies also supported Arctic Power, a group promoting drilling in the Arctic National Wildlife Refuge. As the legislative battles continued, between January 1, 2003, and December 31, 2004, "energy companies spent $314.4 million to lobby Congress, the White House and federal agencies."[68]

The administration and its governing-party coalition of groups were not immediately successful. But in his second term, on August 8, 2005, President Bush signed into law a bill "that followed the general contours of the energy proposals that Bush first outlined in 2001," with the exception of oil drilling in ANWR. In what the Democrats called "a windfall for the fossil fuel industry" and Republican senator John McCain "dryly dubbed . . . 'the No-Lobbyist-Left-Behind Act,' " energy companies would get "tax breaks worth $14.6 billion" and other beneficial provisions, with oil and gas companies gaining the most.[69] Southern Company, a large electricity producer with five executives or lobbyists counted among Bush "Pioneers," may have gained the most as an individual firm.[70]

Environmental and Regulatory Policies

The opening presidential rhetoric was a bit different, but the pattern was remarkably similar in the policy complement to energy: environmental protection. On the surface, Bush appeared to promise that in this area he would be reaching out to a broader spectrum of the electorate and organized interests than he did for his energy program. Much of Bush's campaign oratory offered support on environmental concerns, including a pledge to limit carbon dioxide (CO_2) flowing from facilities generating electricity. Once in office Bush swooned over the Florida Everglades, saying, "They are here to be appreciated, not changed. Their beauty is beyond our power to improve. Our job here is to be good stewards of the Everglades, to restore what has been damaged and to reduce the risk of harm."[71] Major environmental groups were also to be invited to meet with Vice President Cheney. During Bush's second year in office, the administration indicated "plans to promote its initiative on air pollution control by trying to enlist the help of a number of minority, labor and environmental organizations that it believes can rally public support." The draft plan, dubbed "Clear Skies," even suggested that "[environmental groups] should have the lead on all meetings."[72] All these signals seemed to suggest that for environmental policy the more inclusive approach of liaison as consensus building would be the norm.

Actual practice, however, proved quite different from the public overtures. As before, one can start by examining the flow of campaign contributions and identifying the personnel brought into the administration. Funding from the timber and forest products industry in the 2000 presidential campaign fit the same profile as that described earlier for the oil, gas, coal, mining, and utility firms in supporting Republicans and the Bush campaign. Little changed in the 2004 election. Philip Clapp, president of the National Environmental Trust and an opponent of the administration, lamented, "In essence, you will have a president who owes huge political debts to individuals with major companies in almost every field affected by environmental protection. . . . We are facing four years of non-stop battles to protect the basic fabric of the nation's environmental laws."[73] With regard to appointments of federal officials, the *New York Times* reported that "President Bush has filled several senior environment-related jobs in his administration with pro-business advocates who have worked on behalf of various industries in battles with the federal government."[74] From the secretary of the interior to subcabinet posts in the Departments of Interior and Agriculture (which includes the Forest Service) to positions in the Environmental Protection Agency (EPA) and in relevant White House offices, one finds a long list of individuals who previously worked for, or lobbied on behalf of, the oil, natural gas, coal, mining, timber, chemical manufacturing, pesticide, electric power, and cattle industries or who served at libertarian think tanks and advocacy centers. The legislative director of the American Conservative Union noted in Bush's first year, "We're real happy with the team that Bush is putting in."[75] Over the course of the administration, some of those officials left government to become lobbyists on behalf of industry on environmental issues. For example, Philip Cooney resigned from the White House as chief of staff for the Council on Environmental Quality to represent the American Petroleum Institute. Former deputy director of OPL Kirk Blalock, who "coordinated the Bush administration's outreach to the business community," left to join a lobbying firm with such clients as the American Forest and Paper Association.[76] Overall, the Bush appointees shared the President's pro-business support of "free market environmentalism."[77] Said Bush, "This new approach is based on this common-sense idea: that economic growth is key to environmental progress, because it is growth that provides the resources for investment in clean technologies."[78] In this view, the states rather than the national government should be the source of environmental leadership, private property rights should take center stage, and constraints on business should be based on incentives and voluntary action using "market discipline."[79]

In the pursuit of environmental policy during his administration, with some legislative success and much unilateral executive action, Bush joined and worked with the key commercial interests involved. Catering to automobile and energy production interests, he backtracked on his pledge to control CO_2 emissions. Agreeing with industrial leaders, he opposed the Kyoto treaty on global warming. In developing his Clear Skies and New Source Review proposals, he sought to reshape fundamentally the approach to air pollution control by shifting from regulation to market-based "cap-and-trade" provisions for various pollutants and to "give utilities greater leeway in installing anti-pollution equipment." His approach "drew applause from the nation's utilities . . . ; the National Mining Association; the National Association of Manufacturers and other business groups who called the plan balanced and realistic."[80] Needless to say, environmental groups were not so enthusiastic.[81] The timber industry fully supported the president's "Healthy Forests" initiative, which the president signed into law on December 3, 2003. The coordinated policy approach and industry support played out, as well, in the use of public lands, where Bush was "aggressively encouraging more drilling, mining, and logging on much of the 700 million acres controlled by the Interior Department and the Forest Service," and in approaches to Superfund cleanup of toxic sites.[82] The administration's approach to environmental policy and interest group alliances illustrates the way it has dealt with regulation of industry overall. In December 2002 the White House identified over three hundred existing federal regulations that could be amended or terminated.[83] As the *CQ Weekly* reported, "environmentalists and consumer activists say they fear the formation of a new triad—composed of industry officials, the White House and GOP committee chairmen—that leaves them out of the equation."[84]

Medicare Modernization Act

One of the most dramatic domestic policy events during the Bush administration was the intensely partisan enactment in December 2003 of the president's plan to provide prescription drug coverage to Medicare beneficiaries as part of his overall scheme to enhance greatly the role of private plans in the program.[85] Although Democrats for decades had promoted giving senior citizens and other Medicare enrollees a drug benefit, they were nearly unified in opposition to the approach taken by the president and his Republican congressional allies. The main reason?

As with energy and environmental policy, the administration had worked hand in glove with industry to craft legislation that suited their mutual purposes.

As elsewhere, the evidence of linkages starts with campaign funding. The *Washington Post* reported that "at least 24 Rangers and Pioneers could benefit from the Medicare bill as executives of companies or lobbyists working for them."[86] In the 2000 campaign, the leadership of the pharmaceutical firm Bristol-Meyers had urged company executives to contribute the maximum amount to candidate George W. Bush. Overall $2 million flowed from those employees to the Bush campaign and the Republican Party, part of $50 million in drug company donations from 1999 through 2003 committed overwhelmingly to Bush and congressional Republicans.[87] Dollars flowed as well from managed care insurance plans, hospitals, and other health care providers.[88] A number of people who held senior appointive positions in the White House and Department of Health and Human Services in the first couple of years of the administration joined lobbying outfits that "lobbied for the drug industry and HMOs in 2003," leading up to passage of what became known as the Medicare Modernization Act (MMA). Once the MMA became law, even more administration officials, including Tom Scully, administrator of the Centers for Medicare and Medicaid Services and previously president and CEO of the Federation of American Hospitals (representing for-profit hospitals), jumped ship for work in the health care industry.[89]

Formulating the MMA began in summer 2001 when Bush joined forces with five large health care companies to make drug discount cards available through a privately administered plan.[90] Along with competing Democratic plans to include pharmaceutical coverage directly in the government-provided Medicare benefit package, Bush introduced his own initiative that "would give insurers and health plans a subsidy to offer a prescription benefit. The idea is that pharmaceutical companies would compete for this business, thereby lowering prices."[91] This approach, free of government price setting but adding dollars to the prescription drug market, was greatly favored by the industry—which dominated the "impressive coalition of more than 300 organizations . . . marshaled . . . [by] the Republican congressional leadership and the White House."[92] The "industry also financed citizens' groups to bring its message to the public."[93] Not all conservatives were happy about a program that expanded a government entitlement and swelled the federal deficit, but in the end the president's industry allies benefited from drug coverage provided only through private managed care plans or private, free-standing drug plans; an expanded market with significant financial subsidies to drug plans and private health plans; prohibition of both drug reimportation and drug price negotiation by the government (both core issues for the pharmaceutical industry); subsidies for employers who already provide drug coverage; and, much desired by conservatives, an expanded role for health savings accounts outside of Medicare and provisions for a pilot program to put traditional Medicare in direct price competition with private plans in a number of metropolitan areas.[94]

Tax Cuts

What about President Bush's earliest, most sustained, and single most significant domestic policy victory—the enactment in 2001 of his multitrillion-dollar tax cuts? The battles over tax policy resemble traditional, large-scale, Republican versus Democratic, left versus right, ideological politics more than the politics of group-based alliances. Nevertheless, the tax reduction plan had roots in the conservative movement closely tied to Bush. Grover Norquist, head of Americans for Tax Reform and a primary link among libertarian conservatives, social conservatives, and business interests, "served on [the Bush] transition team and became principal architect of Bush's policy plan to cut taxes during each year of his administration."[95] The tax reductions—as proposed, enacted, and later extended—rewarded important segments of the Bush electoral coalition, including conservatives who fought to end what they and the president called the "marriage penalty" and more-affluent taxpayers, who are more likely to support Bush's ideological commitment to smaller government. For example, Citizens for Tax Justice, a nonpartisan, nonprofit research and advocacy organization, stated in a June 12, 2002, report, "By 2010 [the last year of the law's authorization], when (and if) the Bush tax reductions are fully in place, an astonishing 52 percent of the total tax cuts will go to the richest one percent—whose average 2010 income will be $1.5 million." People in the lowest 20 percent income group would receive 1.2 percent of the value of the cuts.[96] The reductions in the top marginal tax rates on personal income, the additional deductions for two-income married couples, and the eventual elimination of the estate tax were all favored by the president's "governing party" commercial and conservative alliances. Small-business interests were especially pleased, although large companies and social conservatives wanted Bush to go further in support of their particular concerns. Big business, however, had reason to anticipate that it and those who invest in its enterprises would be beneficiaries of the next rounds of tax changes.[97] They were not disappointed. Legislation cutting taxes on dividends and capital gains was signed by Bush in May 2003. Then, on October 22, 2004, Bush signed "the biggest corporate tax overhaul since 1986," $137 billion in corporate tax cuts over ten years. The new law granted significant benefits to companies engaged in domestic production, multinational corporations, and small businesses, as well as "about $14 billion in tax breaks for specific interests, from fisherman to bow and arrow makers."[98] As stated in a *National Journal* article, the president "spen[t] the first five years of his administration making the tax code friendlier to business."[99]

Social Issues and the Conservative Movement

Finally, because they have had a larger role in the Bush administration than in any previous presidency, it is useful to focus specifically on the religious right and social conservatives. Again, much is communicated by the appointments Bush made to government positions. Former Missouri senator John Ashcroft, an archconservative favorite of the social and religious right wing, became Bush's attorney general.[100] On the White House staff, Tim Goeglein, with intimate ties to religious conservatives and their organizations, was appointed special assistant to the president and deputy director of the Office of Public Liaison, becoming "Rove's right-hand man dealing with the political right."[101] In addition, other "pro-family conservatives" included Wade Horn, former president of the National Fatherhood Institute, named assistant secretary for health and human services for family support, and Mike Gerson, an evangelical Christian who was the president's chief speechwriter until July 2006.[102] In May 2001, on his television program, *The 700 Club,* Pat Robertson commented, "It's been a decade since conservatives had control of the White House, and now that they have it back, the conservative operatives who have been hanging around Washington for a long time are making the most of their opportunity." On the same program, Grover Norquist, the leading right-wing activist identified earlier, said, "When I walk through the White House, I recognize as many people as when I would walk through the [conservative] Heritage Foundation."[103] Elsewhere he observed, "There isn't an us and them with this administration. They is us. We is them."[104] Kenneth Connor, president of the Family Research Council, reported his organization is "afforded access to the highest senior officials."[105]

Bush's programmatic promises during the 2000 campaign fit with conservatives' preferred policy agenda, from school vouchers to major tax cuts, from building up the military to promoting "charitable choice" (permitting federal aid to pass through faith-based groups without a requirement to alter their hiring practices—an approach challenged by a coalition of organized labor, education associations, and civil rights groups and some religious organizations), from privatizing Social Security to reforming Medicare as they preferred. Bush also, directly and through appointments, made clear his opposition to abortion.[106] In his second term he even appointed as deputy assistant secretary for population affairs in the Department of Health and Human Services an individual "who worked at a Christian pregnancy-counseling organization that regards the distribution of contraceptives as 'demeaning to women.' "[107] Certainly his two picks for the Supreme Court satisfied the conservative base. Leading up to the 2004 campaign Bush endorsed and promoted an amendment to the U.S. Constitution that would prohibit same-sex marriages.[108] In December 2002 the president issued an executive order that forbade federal agencies to deny funds to faith-based organizations that provide social services, concluding that under current law becoming federal contractors "does not require religious groups to give up their right to hire on the basis of religious belief."[109]

Conservative organizations have been involved on each of these issues, orchestrating grassroots campaigns in support of the president's proposals. They have obtained less from their friend in the White House than they desired on issues such as school vouchers and charitable choice, but Bush has nonetheless advanced their agenda. The administration and social conservatives have been particularly unified when working in concert on foreign policy, including blocking funding for international family planning programs and supporting the hard-line approach of then-Israeli prime minister Ariel Sharon. Sometimes on international issues they have been at odds with other parts of the Bush coalition, as when differing with business on trade with China. However, as reported in *CQ Weekly,* "Experts note that religious conservatives begin with a strong ideological advantage in pursuing their foreign policy agenda: a president whose core beliefs and philosophy of 'compassionate conservatism' closely mirrors their own."[110] Concluded an associate of the Hudson Institute, a conservative think tank, "The influence of the religious right has never been more robust on foreign policy."[111]

The Exceptions That Prove the Rule

All of the policy areas I have been discussing are ones in which President Bush worked with, engaged, and in some cases was strongly influenced by, a fairly ideologically cohesive set of interests—primarily corporate, small business, and religious conservatives. In these areas he forcefully pursued interest group liaison as governing party, where the objective is to enact and implement a programmatic agenda. No modern presidency, however, pursues a single approach to organized interests to the complete exclusion of all others. Even the highly focused Bush White House varied its interest group strategy to some degree across policy domains and objectives. Consider, for example, education policy. Instead of pitting a narrowly drawn coalition led by the president against his ideological opponents, such as labor, environmentalists, consumer groups, civil rights organizations, and others, in this case there was—at least initially—substantial consensus in support of the programmatic agenda.

A centerpiece of Bush's first campaign and of his initial policy agenda, his education initiative focused on school testing and accountability, school choice, and streamlined and expanded federal funding. The issue gave the president one of his most significant first-term domestic policy successes in the enactment of the No Child Left Behind Act of 2002 (NCLB). This time, Bush immediately assumed and maintained a bipartisan posture and accepted substantive compromises to ensure legislative enactment.[112] The president and the Republican chairs and Democratic ranking members on the congressional committees of jurisdiction "forged a centrist coalition."[113] Two factors seem to explain the uniquely different approach for education policy. First, Republicans and Democrats in Congress agreed on a number of provisions to be included in the overall bill; Democratic senator Evan Bayh, Ind., asserted that "80 percent of our proposals are common ground."[114] When Bush unveiled his general plan a few days after taking office, "the praise on Capitol Hill was so widespread that swift passage almost seemed like a sure thing."[115] He also reached out to liberal Democratic senator Ted Kennedy, Mass., to work toward a compromise that satisfied both parties. Second, Democrats had always done well against Republicans in public opinion surveys about education, but Bush wanted to gain control of the issue. That would not prove possible in other areas, such as health care, on which the public favored Democrats and the policy preferences of the two parties remained ideologically divided in almost every respect.[116]

There were, to be sure, a couple of deeply contentious issues affecting education. The president wanted to introduce vouchers to let parents with children in failing public schools send them to other schools, public or private, secular or religious; to give states more flexibility by using block grants instead of strictly targeted federal funding; and to offer faith-based organizations a larger role in general. These provisions, which were not acceptable to Democrats, fell by the wayside on the road to enactment by overwhelming bipartisan votes (381–41 in the House; 87–10 in the Senate). Whatever interest group contention existed on the issues split the respective Democratic and Republican coalitions of interests, as was not the case in other policy domains. Both the National Education Association (a teachers' union) and conservative groups objected to the national imposition of school testing, but neither group's protestations were enough to generate serious opposition among either Democrats or Republicans. Social conservatives, stalwarts of the Bush coalition, were deeply disappointed that vouchers were dropped, but even Republicans in Congress were divided on them.[117] As the NCLB started to come up for renewal in 2007, however, a process that could take a number of years, the past ideological differences reemerged and intensified. Democrats, school districts, and educators claimed that the administration has underfunded the program, at levels well below those authorized in the law. Districts, communities, and even Republican state legislatures have rebelled against the funding and accountability features, perceived as an unfunded mandate. And conservative groups called for more parental control over school choice within a public school district.[118]

Finally, the representational functions for marginalized interests were also not entirely ignored by the Bush White House, which engaged in a bit of interest group liaison as outreach, but with an interesting twist. In the past, this form of White House–interest group relations—reaching out to an exclusive set of interests to solidify their symbolic links to the administration—was used to bring to the corridors of power groups that had supported the president but that lay outside the political mainstream. Over several administrations Democrats had employed this approach to give representation to blacks, Jews, women, gays, and atheists (the latter involving the Clinton OPL) before they entered the general policymaking system as politically recognized and accepted constituencies. Republican presidents did the same for evangelicals and other movement conservatives. Few such "outsiders" now remain, but the Bush administration used outreach to connect with two supportive constituencies that were marginalized by other interests in the president's own coalition. One of these groups was the Log Cabin Republicans, conservative gays and lesbians who endorsed Bush and the GOP more generally. In 2002, at the invitation of administration officials, fifty leaders of the group participated in a White House briefing with a number of relatively senior staff, "the first time a Republican White House had ever held such a briefing." Some right-wing organizations were none too happy about the event, as reflected in their vituperative Web sites.[119]

The other controversial constituency the White House reached out to was Muslim Americans. In another first, in 2001 President Bush commemorated Eid-ul-Adha (the Feast of the Sacrifice) with "members of the American Muslim community," thanking their organization "for its support during the 2000 presidential campaign."[120] Later, in the immediate aftermath of 9/11, Bush made more overtures to U.S. Muslims and met with Muslim leaders at a local mosque. Months later, however, there was more tension in the relationship. Although Lezlee Westine, the then director of OPL, claimed that there had been "a consistent outreach to the community," those same leaders complained in August 2002 that they were being ignored. Some of them, such as the executive director of the Muslim Public Affairs Council in Los Angeles, suggested that "there's sort of a right wing—whether Christian fundamentalists or pro-Israel groups—that tries to drive wedges between us and decision makers."[121] As a result of the domestic impact of the administration's war on terrorism following 9/11 and the president's approach to the Iraq war, Muslim Americans dropped away from Bush and the Republican electoral coalition. There is little evidence of the White House giving sustained attention to American Muslims during the rest of the administration.[122] One would not expect that either conservative gays or Muslims would find a comfortable home at the core of the Bush coalition, but modern interest group liaison practices offered them some—if limited—engagement with the White House.

Conclusion

Leading scholars of politics long argued that strong political parties and an influential interest group system are mutually exclusive: potent parties overcome the particularistic nature of individual interests, while the existence of aggressive and effective organized interests is a sign of enfeebled political parties. But the Bush administration's combination of focused interest group relationships and collaboration with ideological partisans in Congress shows that muscular parties and an energized group system need not be at odds with one another. As the parties have become more ideologically polarized in the nation's capital, they have maintained close, symbiotic relationships with distinct group bases.[123] Bush has led, and has often been influenced by, a readily identifiable set of business and conservative (often hard-right) interests. During his presidency, this party-group alliance—the "governing party" motif—has typically been countered by at least a core of Democrats in alliance with, usually, organized labor and then, depending on the issue, environmentalists, consumer groups, civil rights organizations, and other like-minded associations. Although not as cohesive or reliable, this party-group agglomeration might still be referred to as the "opposition party" counterpart to liaison as governing party.

What enduring legacy has President Bush created in these terms? There is little doubt that he will leave office as one of the most partisan and polarizing presidents in modern history. As Gary Jacobson suggests in the title of his 2007 book about the president and the public (and in his chapter in this volume), Bush has been "a divider, not a uniter."[124] He lost the popular vote in the 2000 election but governed as though he had been handed a landslide. In 2004 he was returned to office by the narrowest of margins for an incumbent over the main opposition party, winning a handsome majority of his base Republican (93 percent) and conservative voters (84 percent) but, most unusual for a victorious presidential candidate, failing to garner majorities among independents (48 percent) or, more decisively, moderates (45 percent).[125] Said one analyst of the election, "The social conservatives saved him."[126] By May 2006 only conservative Republicans remained enthusiastically behind Bush, at 78 percent support in the Gallup poll. Moderate to liberal Republicans supported him at only 55 percent, pure independents at just 21 percent, and among even *conservative* Democrats, only 11 percent approved of his job performance.[127] In the 2006 midterm congressional elections, Bush campaigned by reaching out to "true believers," while the White House team was "blanketing the conservative circuit" (Republicans, of course, lost control of Congress).[128] The strategy follows from the core premise guiding the Bush presidency:

> In the eyes of the Bush team, America is a polarized country, one where there are fundamental divisions worth fighting over. A president—and a party— should not worry about slender margins of victory or legislative control. The goal is to accumulate just enough power to use the energies and passions of the base to effect ideological change in the nation's laws and institutions, even if—sometimes especially if—those changes might be at odds with majority opinion.[129]

The point, of course, is that the government of chums established by Bush as an interest group strategy fits precisely with his overall approach to politics and policymaking. Across a range of policy issues, his business and conservative organizational friends financed his campaigns, provided a significant proportion of the personnel for his administration, granted the coherent coalitional resources to gain leverage over legislation and policymaking in support of their shared agendas, and were richly rewarded with policy outcomes not to be widely shared with anyone else. As the saying goes, it's good to have friends in high places, whether that means in the White House or in the executive suites of the nation's corporations and in the lobby-ists' offices along Washington's K Street.

What remains uncertain is whether President Bush has established a new insti-tutional legacy for how administrations in the future will work and interact with organized interests. Are exclusive and largely programmatic group strategies the standard for the future, without regard to political circumstances? Will friends be cultivated and rewarded, while other interests beyond the president's electoral base are challenged or ignored? Probably not. The 2006 election results suggest that the public has grown weary of such ideologically driven, unilateral approaches to the presidency.[130] Experience has shown that as one presidency declines in public esteem, successors—of either party—strive to develop quite different approaches. Even a Republican president inaugurated in January 2009 is unlikely to continue the practices of the Bush administration (although perhaps paying a price for devi-ating from the purity of the religious hard right). A Democratic president simply cannot follow the Bush pattern. Although a Republican chief executive may be able to ignore the core groups in the Democratic base, such as organized labor, envi-ronmentalists, feminists, the civil rights community, and others, Democrats in office need a working relationship with a primary part of the GOP base, business. Busi-nesses large and small provide the economic engine of the nation, manufacturing its products, delivering its services, employing its workers. Without them no Demo-cratic policy can succeed.[131]

Perhaps most important, narrowly drawn interest group relationships are not likely to serve the long-term interests of the president. Reflecting on the specific responsibilities of the Office of Public Liaison, Bradley Patterson, with White House service in three Republican administrations, argues,

> The experience of at least twenty years has shown that the only successful public liaison officers are those with a professional appreciation for the plu-ralism of American society. The zealot who divides the claimants at the White House gates into rigid categories of "good guys" and "bad guys" will end up frustrated—and will even singe his or her President with the hot atmosphere of animosity.[132]

When the president himself adopts such a strategy of exclusion, especially in a nation like ours, built on pluralism and with governing institutions premised on engagement and compromise among myriad interests, the results are likely to be both poor policymaking and excessively divisive politics. Those may be the most funda-mental legacies of the Bush presidency.

Notes

Invaluable assistance was provided by my research assistants Audrey Bazos and Katherine Goetz, who were instrumental in identifying and assembling most of the materials about the Bush administration referenced in this chapter. I am most grateful for their contributions.

1. It is too early to ascertain whether or not the administration's interest group relationships changed as a result of the Democrats' retaking control of both the House of Representatives and the Senate following the 2006 midterm elections.

2. Institutions of American Democracy Project, Annenberg Public Policy Center, University of Pennsylvania, conducted by Princeton Survey Research Associates International—Executive Branch and Congress Surveys: Public Component (N = 1,500; in the field December 18, 2004–January 18, 2005), Question 29D, combining "Strongly Agree" and "Agree."

3. Lawrence R. Jacobs, "Communicating from the White House: Presidential Narrowcasting and the National Interest," in *Institutions of American Democracy: The Executive Branch,* ed. Joel D. Aberbach and Mark A. Peterson (New York: Oxford University Press, 2005), 174–217.

4. Joel D. Aberbach and Mark A. Peterson, eds., *Institutions of American Democracy: The Executive Branch* (New York: Oxford University Press, 2005); see in particular chap. 1, by Scott James, "The Evolution of the Presidency."

5. For a more detailed examination of these historical, institutional, social, and political dynamics that set the stage for the Bush administration, see Mark A. Peterson, "Bush and Interest Groups: A Government of Chums," in *The George W. Bush Presidency: Appraisals and Prospects,* ed. Colin Campbell and Bert A. Rockman (Washington, D.C.: CQ Press, 2004), 228–232.

6. Mark A. Peterson, "Clinton and Organized Interests: Splitting Friends, Unifying Enemies," in *The Clinton Legacy,* ed. Colin Campbell and Bert A. Rockman (New York: Chatham House, 2000).

7. Alan Greenblatt, "Labor Wants out of the Limelight after Glare of Probes, Backlash," *Congressional Quarterly Weekly Report,* March 28, 1998, 790; Theda Skocpol, *Diminished Democracy: From Membership to Management in American Civic Life* (Norman: University of Oklahoma Press, 2003); idem, *Boomerang: Clinton's Health Security Effort and the Turn against Government in U.S. Politics* (New York: Norton, 1996); Margaret Weir, "Political Parties and Social Policymaking," in *The Social Divide: Political Parties and the Future of Activist Government,* ed. Margaret Weir (Washington, D.C.: Brookings Institution Press and New York: Russell Sage Foundation, 1998), 1–45; Mark A. Peterson and Jack L. Walker, "Interest Group Responses to Partisan Change: The Impact of the Reagan Administration upon the National Interest Group System," in *Interest Group Politics,* 2nd ed., ed. Allan J. Cigler and Burdett A. Loomis (Washington, D.C.: CQ Press, 1986), 163; Kirk Victor, "Asleep at the Switch?" *National Journal,* January 16, 1993, 131–134; and Ken Kollman, *Outside Lobbying: Public Opinion and Interest Group Strategies* (Princeton: Princeton University Press, 1998).

8. Mark A. Peterson, "Interest Mobilization and the Presidency," in *The Politics of Interests: Interest Groups Transformed,* ed. Mark P. Petracca (Boulder: Westview Press, 1992), 221–241.

9. Stephen Skowronek, *Building a New American State: The Expansion of National Administrative Capabilities, 1877–1920* (New York: Cambridge University Press, 1982).

10. "Enron's Blackout Cuts Power behind Numerous Thrones," *Lobby Watch* (a publication of Texans for Public Justice), December 4, 2001, 1; see also Brody Mullins, "Enron-Linked Firms Gave Heavily to Bush," *National Journal,* January 26, 2002, 251.

11. Alex Knott, "Bush Has a New Top Career Patron: MBNA Surpasses Enron as the President's Top Lifetime Contributor," Center for Public Integrity, March 11, 2004, www.publicintegrity.org/bop2004/report.aspx?aid=220 (accessed January 6, 2007).

12. "The Pioneers: George W. Bush's $100,000 Club," introduction and summary, Texans for Public Justice, www.tpj.org/pioneers/summary.html (accessed April 10, 2007).

13. "The Bush Pioneer–Ranger Network," Texans for Public Justice, www.tpj.org/page_view.jsp? pageid=203 (accessed 10 April 10, 2007); see also "Who Bankrolls Bush and His Democratic Rivals? A Look at the Presidential Race," Center for Public Integrity, January 8, 2004, www.publicintegrity.org/bop2004/report.aspx?aid=132 (accessed October 15, 2006); and Jill Barshay with Kathryn A. Wolfe, "Special Interests Strike Gold in Richly Targeted Tax Bill," *CQ Weekly,* October 16, 2004, 2434–2438.

14. Peter H. Stone, "Corporations, K Street Throw a Party," *National Journal,* January 13, 2001, 116–117.

15. For a brief analysis of how the Reagan White House centralized the personnel appointments process, gave it ideological direction, and incorporated it into a larger strategy of executive branch control, see Peter M. Benda and Charles H. Levine, "Reagan and the Bureaucracy: The Bequest, the Promise, and the Legacy," in *The Reagan Legacy: Promise and Performance,* ed. Charles O. Jones (Chatham, N.J.: Chatham House, 1988), 102–142.

16. Peter H. Stone, "Surprise! Bushes Are Everywhere," *National Journal,* January 6, 2001, 44.

17. Alex Knott, "Lobbying the White House: Campaign Donors and Former Government Officials Help 4,600 Companies Influence the Executive Branch," Center for Public Integrity, September 21, 2005, www.publicintegrity.org/lobby/report.aspx?aid=731 (accessed January 6, 2007); Rebecca Adams, "GOP, Business Rewrite the Regulatory Playbook," *CQ Weekly,* May 5, 2001, 991. A high-profile example involving fund raising, appointments from an industry, and policy changes involving trucking can be found in Stephen Labaton, "As Trucking Rules Are Eased, a Debate on Safety Intensifies," *New York Times,* December 3, 2006, 1, 30.

18. Craig Aaron, "The Medicare Drug War: An Army of Nearly 1,000 Lobbyists Pushes a Medicare Law That Puts Drug Company and HMO Profits ahead of Patients and Taxpayers," report issued by Congress Watch (Washington, D.C.: Public Citizen, June 2004), 7.

19. James A. Barnes, "Is Bush Poisoning His Well?" *National Journal,* April 14, 2001, 1121.

20. Robert Pear, "Bush and Health Care Companies Promise Medicare Drug Discounts," *New York Times,* July 13, 2001, A1.

21. Edmund L. Andrews, "Interior Official Assails Agency for Ethics Slide," *New York Times,* September 13, 2006, A1.

22. Kathryn Dunn Tenpas and Stephen Hess, "The Contemporary Presidency—The Bush White House: First Appraisals," *Presidential Studies Quarterly* 32 (September 2002): 577–585.

23. Jack L. Walker, *Mobilizing Interest Groups in America: Patrons, Professions, and Social Movements* (Ann Arbor: University of Michigan Press, 1991), 31.

24. J. David Greenstone and Paul E. Peterson, *Race and Authority in Urban Politics: Community Participation and the War on Poverty* (New York: Russell Sage Foundation, 1973).

25. Benjamin Ginsberg and Martin Shefter, "The Presidency, Interest Groups, and Social Forces: Creating a Republican Coalition," in *The Presidency and the Political System,* 3rd ed., ed. Michael Nelson (Washington, D.C.: CQ Press, 1990), 339–347; and Peterson, "Interest Mobilization and the Presidency," 232.

26. Peterson and Walker, "Interest Group Responses," 163.

27. Ibid., quoted on 173, 175.

28. "Closed Due to New Ownership," Minnesota Women's Press, Inc., *News Notes,* April 11, 2001, www.Womenspress.com/newspaper/2001/17-2newsnotes.html.

29. "The White House Is Women Friendly," National Federation of Republican Women, www.buncombegop.org/friendly.html (accessed November 7, 2002).

30. Cynthia E. Griffin, *Entrepreneur,* December 2001, www.entrepreneur.com/Magazines/Copy _of_MA_SegArticle/ (accessed November 6, 2002); "RightNow! Congressional Reception," February 27, 2002, www.politicalchicks.com/public/pages/ (accessed November 6, 2002).

31. James Gerstenzang and Marlene Cimons, "AIDS, Race Offices Will Remain Active," *Los Angeles Times,* February 8, 2001, A19.

32. Steven Greenhouse, "Unions See Bush Moves as Payback for Backing Gore," *New York Times,* March 25, 2001, 33.

33. Ibid.

34. Adriel Bettelheim, "Workers' Rights Issues Looming over Homeland Security Debate," *CQ Weekly,* September 7, 2002, 2294–2297.

35. Richard W. Stevenson, "Government May Make Private Nearly Half of Its Civilian Jobs," *New York Times,* November 15, 2002, A1.

36. Christopher Lee, "Study Doubts Job Loss to Private Sector," *Washington Post,* October 26, 2004, A23; Scott Shane and Ron Nixon, "In Washington, Contractors Take On Biggest Role Ever," *New York Times,* February 4, 2007, 1.

37. John Cochran and Rebecca Adams, "Fresh from a Set of Hill Victories, Can Labor Keep the Momentum?" *CQ Weekly,* September 2, 2001, 2004–2009; and Gabe Martinez, "Bush Breaks with Position, Moves to Protect Steel Industry," *CQ Weekly,* March 9, 2002, 655–675.

38. Joseph A. Pika, "Interest Groups and the Executive: Presidential Intervention," in *Interest Group Politics,* ed. Allan J. Cigler and Burdett A. Loomis (Washington, D.C.: CQ Press, 1983), 298–323; and Memorandum from William Baroody to President Gerald R. Ford, August 23, 1974, quoted in Robert M. Copeland, "Cultivating Interest Group Support: Public Liaison in the Ford Administration," paper presented at the annual meeting of the Midwest Political Science Association, Chicago, 1985.

39. Mark A. Peterson, "The Presidency and Organized Interests: White House Patterns of Interest Group Liaison," *American Political Science Review* 86 (September 1992): 612–625.

40. Peterson, "Interest Mobilization and the Presidency"; and Peterson, "The Presidency and Organized Interests."

41. Peterson, "The Presidency and Organized Interests."

42. For details on the typology and the approaches used by previous presidents, and an empirical analysis of President Reagan's use of liaison as governing party, see ibid. More details

about Reagan's legislative approach to interests groups are also available in Ken Collier and Michael J. Towle, "Winning Friends and Influencing People: The President vs. Interest Groups," *White House Studies* 2 (Spring 2002): 186–203. It is also useful to note here that this typology accommodates mobilization for both interventionist, expansionist approaches to government and for those designed to shrink the scope and activities of existing government. In each case the purpose is programmatic instead of representational. For expansionist presidents, depending on their overall incentives, the strategy may be inclusive (Johnson's approach to much of the Great Society) or exclusive (Reagan's approach to the defense buildup). Agendas that involve building-down the state, however, have to involve an exclusive strategy of relationships with groups. Given the stakeholders favoring existing governing programs, one cannot imagine "liaison as consensus building." One would instead have to concentrate on a targeted "governing party" coalition versus the interests supporting the threatened programs.

43. Linda Greenhouse, "The Legal Spectacle: Divining the Consequences of a Court Divided," *New York Times,* December 17, 2000, "Week in Review," 1.

44. See Gary Bauer, "Run to the Right, Not the Middle," *New York Times,* December 15, 2000, A39.

45. Helen Dewar, "GOP Departures Signal Arrival of a New Era for Conservatism; Senators Hand Power to Next Generation," *Washington Post,* September 16, 2002, A4.

46. Gallup poll and CNN/*USA Today*/Gallup Poll, reported at www.pollingreport.com/BushJob.htm.

47. Barnes, "Is Bush Poisoning His Well?" 1120.

48. Tenpas and Hess, "The Contemporary Presidency—The Bush White House," 578, 579.

49. "Ex-Aide Insists White House Puts Politics Ahead of Policy," *New York Times,* December 2, 2002, A16. DiIulio later issued a formal apology, saying his comments were "groundless and baseless due to poorly chosen words and examples." "Ex-Bush Aide Offers Apology for Remarks," *New York Times,* December 3, 2002, A27.

50. Christopher B. Smith, Office of Public Liaison, The White House, http://72.14.253.104/search?q=cache:DDpS7SZZaIEJ:www.whitehouse.gov (accessed September 8, 2006); and "Meet White House Liaison Jay Zeidman," *Hillel,* August 18, 2006, www.hillel.org/about/new/2006/aug/zeidman_2006aug18.htm (accessed September 8, 2006).

51. Bradley H. Patterson, *The White House Staff: Inside the West Wing and Beyond* (Washington, D.C.: Brookings Institution Press, 2000), 178.

52. I was unsuccessful in my efforts by both mail and phone to obtain from the Office of Public Liaison any systematic information about which organized interests have participated in White House sponsored events throughout the administration. Other Web sources during the early years of the administration identified sessions with, for instance, the National Black Chamber of Commerce, Operation Hope, breast cancer research advocates, various organizations representing the disabled, the National Council of Asian American Business Associations, the American Coalition for Filipino Veterans, Japanese American individuals and organizations supporting preservation of World War II internment sites, Serbian American organizations, the National Polish American–Jewish American Council, Armenian American leaders, the nonprofit community, firefighters, general aviation pilots, and the like. Sources: National Black Chamber of Commerce,

www.nationalbcc.org/events/conv2001agenda.htm; Ohio Statewide Independent Living Council, www.ohiosilc.org/news/2002/020307_jfa_teachers.html; National Council of Asian American Business Associations, http://national-caaba.org/new.html; Armenian Assembly of America, www.aaainc.org/press/02-22-02.htm.

53. "A Money in Politics Backgrounder on the Energy Industry," Center for Responsive Politics, available at www.opensecrets.org/pressreleases/energybriefing.html (italics in the original); and Peter H. Stone, "Big Oil's White House Pipelines," *National Journal,* April 7, 2001, 1043.

54. Thomas B. Edsall, "Two Bills Would Benefit Top Bush Fundraisers," *Washington Post,* November 22, 2003, A1; Bob Williams and Kevin Borgardus, "The Politics of Energy: Oil and Gas, How a Gusher of Giveaways to Oil and Gas Industry was Crafted in Congress," Center for Public Integrity, www.publicintegrity.org/report.aspx?aid=123 (accessed October 3, 2006); and Jonathan D. Salant, "U.S. Energy Industry's Lobbying Pays Off with $11.6 Billion in Aid," Bloomberg.com, July 27, 2005, www.bloomberg.com/apps/news?pid=10000103&sid=agbeVimfo4Ec&refer=us (accessed January 7, 2006).

55. Margaret Kriz, "Shock Politics," *National Journal,* February 10, 2001, 394.

56. Don Van Natta Jr. and Neela Banerjee, "Bush Policies Have Been Good to Energy Industry," *New York Times,* April 21, 2002, sec. 1, 22.

57. Jill Barshay, "A Closer Look at GAO vs. Cheney: Politics and the Separation of Powers," *CQ Weekly,* February 2, 2002, 289–291; Adam Clymer, "Judge Says Cheney Needn't Give Energy Policy Records to Agency," *New York Times,* December 10, 2002, A1; Mike Allen, "GAO Cites Corporate Shaping of Energy Plan," *Washington Post,* August 26, 2003, A1.

58. Katharine Q. Seelye, "Bush Task Force on Energy Worked in Mysterious Ways," *New York Times,* May 16, 2001, A1.

59. Peter H. Stone, "Big Oil's White House Pipelines," *National Journal,* April 7, 2001, 1042–1044.

60. "Environmentalists Had Limited Access to the White House Energy Task Force," part of "The Cheney Energy Task Force: A Review and Analysis of the Proceedings Leading to the Bush Administration's Formulation of Its May 2001 Energy Policy," Natural Resources Defense Council, www.nrdc.org/air/energy/taskforce/bkgrd2.asp (accessed November 11, 2002).

61. Margaret Kriz, "Power Struggle," *National Journal,* March 31, 2001, 942.

62. "Heavily Censored Energy Department Papers Show Industry Is the Real Author of Administration's Energy Task Force Report," Natural Resources Defense Council, www.nrdc.org/media/pressreleases/020327.asp (accessed November 11, 2002).

63. Margaret Kriz, "Nuclear Power Gets to Go to the Ball," *National Journal,* May 19, 2001, 1501.

64. Rebecca Adams, "Coal Takes Stronger Position in Nation's Energy Strategy," *CQ Weekly,* June 1, 2002, 1440.

65. "Heavily Censored Energy Department Papers" (n.62 above); see also Don Van Natta Jr. and Neela Banerjee, "Review Shows Energy Industry's Recommendations to Bush Ended Up Being National Policy," *New York Times,* March 28, 2002, A18.

66. Adams, "Coal Takes Stronger Position," 1442.

67. Chuck McCutcheon, "Bush Urged to Shift Emphasis to Fuel Efficiency Standards," *CQ Weekly,* May 19, 2001, 1153.

68. Stone, "Big Oil's White House Pipelines," 1042–1043; Salant, "U.S. Energy Industry's Lobbying Pays Off."

69. "Energy Overhaul Includes Many Bush Priorities—but Not ANWR," *2005 CQ Almanac* (Washington, D.C.: CQ Press, 2006), 8-3, 8-5; McCain quote is from Williams and Borgardus, "The Politics of Energy."

70. Edsall, "Two Bills Would Benefit Top Bush Fundraisers."

71. Frank Bruni, "Bush Carries Environment-Friendly Tone to Everglades," *New York Times,* June 5, 2001, A16.

72. Katharine Q. Seelye, "Bush to Seek Unlikely Allies in Bid to Alter Clean Air Act," *New York Times,* June 9, 2002, sec. 1, 26.

73. Mary Clare Jalonick, "After November Elections, Change Could Be in the Air—and Water," *CQ Weekly,* October 23, 2004, 2520.

74. Katharine Q. Seelye, "Bush Is Choosing Industry Insiders to Fill Several Environmental Positions," *New York Times,* May 12, 2001, A10.

75. Ibid.

76. Knott, "Lobbying the White House."

77. Margaret Kriz, "A New Look at Land Use," *National Journal,* January 27, 2001, 258–259; and Margaret Kriz, "Bush's New Green Toolbox," *National Journal,* February 3, 2001, 348–349.

78. Rebecca Adams, "Lack of Carbon Dioxide Regulation Spurs Criticism of Bush's Clean-Air Plan," *CQ Weekly,* February 16, 2002, 473.

79. Margaret Kriz, "Working the Land," *National Journal,* February 23, 2002; and Knott, "Lobbying the White House."

80. Adams, "Lack of Carbon Dioxide Regulation," 473.

81. Rebecca Adams, "Bush's Decision Not to Curb Carbon Dioxide Casts Shadow on Emission Control Legislation," *CQ Weekly,* March 17, 2001, 607–608; and Margaret Kriz, "Burning Questions," *National Journal,* April 6, 2002, 976–981.

82. Kriz, "Working the Land," 532. See also Margaret Kriz, "Superfund Slowdown," *National Journal,* June 1, 2002, 1625; Katharine Q. Seelye, "Bush Proposing Policy Changes on Toxic Sites," *New York Times,* February 24, 2002, sec. 1, 1; and Jalonick, "After November Elections."

83. Katharine Q. Seelye, "White House Identifies Regulations That May Change," *New York Times,* December 20, 2002, A27.

84. Rebecca Adams, "GOP, Business Review the Regulatory Playbook," *CQ Weekly,* May 5, 2001, 990; and "Environmental War Clouds," *New York Times,* November 25, 2002, A24.

85. Thomas R. Oliver, Philip R. Lee, and Helen L. Lipton, "A Political History of Medicare and Prescription Drug Coverage," *Milbank Quarterly* 82 (June 2004): 283–354.

86. Edsall, "Two Bills Would Benefit Top Bush Fundraisers."

87. Sheryl Gay Stolberg and Gardiner Harris, "Industry Fights to Put Imprint on Drug Bill," *New York Times,* September 5, 2003, A1.

88. Aaron, "The Medicare Drug War," 32–34.

89. Ibid., 21–25.

90. Pear, "Bush and Health Care Companies."

91. Mary Agnes Carey, "Much Variety, Little Traction in Medicare Drug Plans," *CQ Weekly,* July 13, 2002, 1848–1849; see also Robert Pear, "Medicare Debate Focuses on Merits of Private Plans," *New York Times,* June 9, 2003, A1.

92. Michael T. Heaney, "What Was in It for Them," *Washington Post,* op-ed, November 30, 2003, B4.

93. Stolberg and Harris, "Industry Fights to Put Imprint on Drug Bill."

94. "Medicare Revamp Cuts It Close," *2003 CQ Almanac* (Washington, D.C.: CQ Press, 2004); and Oliver, Lee, and Lipton, "A Political History of Medicare and Prescription Drug Coverage."

95. Thomas Medvetz, "The Strength of Weekly Ties: Relations of Material and Symbolic Exchange in the Conservative Movement," *Politics and Society* 34 (September 2006): 350.

96. "Year-by-Year Analysis of the Bush Tax Cuts Shows Growing Tilt to the Very Rich," Citizens for Tax Justice, June 12, 2002, www.ctj.org/html/gwb0602.htm (accessed April 11, 2007).

97. Daniel J. Parks, "Bush May Test Capitol Hill Clout Early with Expedited Tax-Cut Proposal," *CQ Weekly,* January 6, 2001, 41–42; and Lori Nitschke, "Tax Plan Destined for Revision," *CQ Weekly,* February 10, 2001, 318–321; Alex Berenson, "No Big Rush to Stocks after Cuts in Two Taxes," *New York Times,* May 24, 2003, C1.

98. "Corporate Tax Breaks Enacted," *2004 CQ Almanac* (Washington, D.C.: CQ Press, 2005), 13-3.

99. Martin Vaughan, "Lobbying and Law—K Street Not Wild about Bush Tax Plan," *National Journal,* October 22, 2005, 3283.

100. David Nather and Megan Twohey, "Ashcroft Is Bush's Charitable Choice," *National Journal,* January 20, 2001, 202.

101. Jim VandeHei, "Pipeline to the President for GOP Conservatives; Give and Take Flows through Public Liaison Aide," *Washington Post,* December 24, 2004, A15.

102. Joel C. Rosenberg, "Flash Traffic: Political Buzz from Washington," World on the Web, April 21, 2001, www.worldmag.com/articles/6436 (accessed April 11, 2007).

103. "Robertson and Right-Wing Allies Brag of Control over Bush Agenda," Progressive Newswire, People for the American Way, May 3, 2001, http://72.14.253.104/search?q=cache:BQ3nIYyoiQYJ:www.commondreams.org/news2001/0502-13.htm (accessed April 11, 2007).

104. Medvetz, "The Strength of Weekly Ties," 350.

105. Judith Stacey, "Family Values Forever: In the Marriage Movement, Conservatives and Centrists Find a Home Together," *Nation,* July 9, 2001, 26.

106. Alexis Simendinger, "Reminders from the Right," *National Journal,* January 6, 2001, 35–37; Martin Davis, "Faith, Hope, and Charity," *National Journal,* April 28, 2001, 1228–1235; "Bush Plan to Promote Faith-Based Charities Creates Dilemma for Both Parties," *CQ Weekly,* February 3, 2001, 283–285.

107. Christopher Lee, "Bush Choice for Family-Planning Post Criticized," *Washington Post,* November 17, 2006, A1.

108. "President Calls for Constitutional Amendment Protecting Marriage," Remarks by the President, February 24, 2004, www.whitehouse.gov/news/releases/2004/02/20040224-2.html (accessed January 7, 2006).

109. Richard W. Stevenson, "Religious Groups Face Fewer Curbs in Bush Aid Plan," *New York Times,* December 13, 2002, A1.

110. Miles A. Pomper, "Religious Right Flexes Muscles on Foreign Policy Matters," *CQ Weekly,* July 13, 2002, 1893–1896.

111. Ibid., 1894.

112. "Bush's Education Plan Unveiled in House amid Muted Dissent," *CQ Weekly,* March 24, 2001, 659–660; Siobhan Gorman, "Bush's Big Test," *National Journal,* February 24, 2001, 549–553; Juliet Eilperin, "House Passes Education Reform Bill: Bipartisanship Hailed," *Washington Post,* December 14, 2001, A8. Enacting legislation in Congress does not necessarily mean that the policy itself will be successful in its implementation. The ways in which this law requires states to measure public school performance and identify "failing" schools may create education havoc in the states and results counter to the expressed objectives of the program. For those suspicious of every motive guiding the administration, noted a member of a state board of education, this outcome might be viewed as "a cynical attempt by the Bush administration to build in failure and use that as an argument for vouchers," Bush's preferred policy approach. Michael A. Fletcher, "States Worry New Law Sets Schools Up to Fail," *Washington Post,* January 2, 2003, A1.

113. Brian Friel, "Public Education—Stay the Course?" *National Journal,* October 7, 2006, 32.

114. David Nather, "Broad Support Is No Guarantee for Bush Legislative Leadoff," *CQ Weekly,* January 27, 2001, 221–225.

115. Ibid., 221.

116. Helen Dewar, "Education Measure's Progress May Be a Unique Achievement; Lawmakers Struggling over Other Bills," *Washington Post,* June 14, 2001, A12.

117. Helen Dewar, "Landmark Education Legislation Gets Final Approval in Congress," *Washington Post,* December 19, 2001, A8.

118. Friel, "Public Education—Stay the Course?"; Kathryn A. McDermott and Laura S. Jensen, "Dubious Sovereignty: Federal Conditions of Aid and the No Child Left Behind Act," *Peabody Journal of Education* 80(2): 39–56.

119. Caryle Murphy, "Atheists Assemble to Lobby and Share Beliefs," *Washington Post,* June 13, 1998, C1; "White House Hosts Log Cabin Meeting," *New York Blade,* May 3, 2002, www.nyblade.com/national/020503b.htm; and David Webb, "Dallasites at Log Cabin Confab Praise White House," *Dallas Voice,* http://dallas.logcabin.org/news4.htm.

120. "President to Meet with Muslim Community Leaders," *Friday Brief,* Islamic Institute, March 2, 2001, 1.

121. "U.S. Muslims Say Bush Ignores Them," Fox News, August 18, 2002, www.foxnews.com/story/0,2933,60700,00.html (accessed November 6, 2002).

122. Lisa Marie Gomez, "Muslim American Support for Bush Has Fallen," *San Antonio Express News,* October 17, 2004, 7B; Jim Lobe, "Muslim and Arab Americans Ditch Republicans," Inter Press Service, October 25, 2006, www.commondreams.org/headlines06/1025-06.htm (accessed January 5, 2007). A Web search yielded no reports of White House meetings with Muslim Americans after 2002.

123. Gary C. Jacobson, "Party Polarization in National Politics: The Electoral Connection," in *Polarized Politics: Congress and the President in a Partisan Era,* ed. Jon R. Bond and Richard Fleisher (Washington, D.C.: CQ Press, 2000).

124. Gary C. Jacobson, *A Divider, Not a Uniter: George W. Bush and the American People* (New York: Pearson Longman, 2007).

125. National Exit Polls, 2004 Election, reported by CNN, www.cnn.com/ELECTION/2004/pages/results/states/US/P/00/epolls.0.html (accessed January 8, 2007).

126. David Nather, "Social Conservatives Propel Bush, Republicans to Victory," *CQ Weekly,* November 5, 2004, 2586.

127. Gallup News Service, "Liberal, Moderate Republicans Show Large Drop in Support for Bush," May 26, 2006, http://poll.gallup.com/content/Default.aspx?ci=22954&VERSION=p (accessed May 26, 2006).

128. Molly Hennessey-Fiske, "Campaign 2006: Competing for Votes; Bush Makes Final Appeal to True Believers," *Los Angeles Times,* November 5, 2006, A20; Peter Baker, "The GOP Leans on a Proven Strategy: White House Courts Conservative Base," *Washington Post,* October 25, 2006, A1.

129. Mark Halperin, "Ace of Base," op-ed, *New York Times,* October 1, 2006, sec. 4, 11.

130. See Joel D. Aberbach and Mark A. Peterson, "Control and Accountability: Dilemmas of the Executive Branch," in *Institutions of American Democracy: The Executive Branch,* ed. Joel D. Aberbach and Mark A. Peterson (New York: Oxford University Press, 2005).

131. Charles E. Lindblom, *Politics and Markets: The World's Political Economic Systems* (New York: Basic Books, 1977).

132. Patterson, *The White House Staff,* 183.

CHAPTER 14

The Legacy of the George W. Bush Presidency—A Revolutionary Presidency?

Bert A. Rockman

TO SPEAK OF A PRESIDENTIAL LEGACY implies that presidents can, and some-times do, shape their times rather than being mostly shaped by them. It emphasizes the potential of leadership to circumvent or overcome institutional and circumstantial constraints. It suggests that leaders have the potential to reconfigure the parallelogram of historical and institutional political forces and places the president as the subject, rather than the predicate, in history. Has George W. Bush been such a history-making president? That is the focus of this chapter.

I want to examine two things in particular: First, I would like to get at just what we mean by the term "legacy," which we use frequently but imprecisely. What exactly is a presidential legacy? Second, I want to focus on the areas in which the presidency of George W. Bush appears to have made a special impact. But I also want to indi-cate circumstances that in some instances helped shape the legacy that the Bush administration may leave behind, as well as some of the political pushback that its efforts to leave its imprint occasioned. I will draw mainly from the chapters preceding this one, but also sometimes go beyond them, and try to assess what lessons we can draw from the years that the George W. Bush administration has held the White House.

What Is a President's Legacy?

The most fundamental observation we can make about legacies and inheritances is that nothing lasts forever. Presidents inherit what their predecessors have left and seek in turn to leave their own mark to their successors. For good or ill, presidents pass on their achievements to their successors, even as many of those "achievements" are accompanied by adverse consequences. One president's good, more than likely, will be his successor's bad. Every leader wants to leave a legacy and, if they can, erase many of those left by their predecessors. A legacy implies that something durable has been left by an administration that others will benefit by or have to deal with as a set of problems well into the future. Virtually every presidential administration has something to leave, either by design, circumstance, or ineptitude. Significant accomplishments of some presidents have been reversed by succeeding administrations. For example, the often-criticized Carter administration made two strenuous efforts to promote energy conservation and create new, alternative energy sources. Its second effort, when the export of oil from Iran diminished during the period of the Shah's overthrow and the establishment of the Islamic republic in 1979, produced legislation that provided incentives for eventually bringing new energy sources onto the market. In the current energy climate, one would think that Carter's energy bill was prescient. Instead, Carter became better known for his remark in a speech televised during that period that the American people were suffering from a "malaise," for which he was ridiculed presumably on the assumption that the voter is a customer, and if the business of a politician is procuring votes, then the customer (voter) is always right.

Carter's energy bill was an important effort to wean the United States away from exclusive dependence on hard carbon-based energy sources. Three things helped to derail the impact of the legislation. First was the Three Mile Island nuclear incident. The seeming near-miss of a meltdown at Three Mile Island essentially finished off nuclear power as an option in the energy repertoire. The effect, of course, was to increase dependence on carbon-based fuels. Second, once Iran began exporting oil again, supplies eased and prices went down, sharply reducing the marketability of alternative energy sources. Finally, but importantly, the Reagan administration, elected in 1980, came into office opposed to any attempts to intervene in the market by subsidizing alternative fuels. It returned to a noninterventionist and market-driven policy. It was—if I may be permitted a baseball analogy—as though Carter hit a triple with no one out, but nobody could bring him home. He accomplished a big thing, but it would not prove to be a legacy. Its long-term results were nil.

As a similar example, during Bill Clinton's time in office, the upside of the business cycle, in conjunction with the changes his presidency initiated in the structural basis of the federal government's revenue stream through tax increases (reversing one aspect of the Reagan legacy), brought federal deficits that had reached new peacetime highs under control to the point that the government actually was producing surpluses. However, that situation did not last long. Presidential candidate George W. Bush immediately proposed a $1.6 trillion tax cut, which would reopen the structural deficit problem. The first round of tax cuts wound up at $1.35 trillion. The massive increase in structural deficit potential was exacerbated by a significant business downturn during 2001 and part of 2002, powerfully accelerated by the terrorist attacks of September 11, 2001. Dramatic increases in spending were needed for the new homeland security bureaucracy and later the wars in Iraq and Afghanistan.

As noted, Bush asked for more tax cuts, and with the Republicans in control of both chambers of Congress after the 2002 election, he got them. So even though Clinton's fiscal and tax policies may have been significant in reducing the deficit, those policies were reversed early in the George W. Bush administration.

In sum, big achievements do not necessarily translate into legacies if political fortune reverses them.

"Interesting times" make for interesting presidencies. Presidents have to have opportunities to leave their imprint. Bill Clinton complained that because the era in which he was president was relatively calm, peaceful, and prosperous it provided him with little opportunity to leave a significant historical legacy. Interesting times provide opportunities for leaders, but they are rarely wonderful times for citizens, who normally crave uninteresting, even pedestrian times to live in. It is certainly the case that George W. Bush got what Clinton wished—a presidency of interesting times. Events over which the Bush administration had little direct control—the terrorist attacks of 9/11—and ones that it helped create, such as the chaos that has engulfed the ill-starred military venture in Iraq, have made George W. Bush's times among the most eventful of recent presidencies. Presidents understandably want to leave big footprints to secure their place in history. But a smaller footprint by a president may mean a more normal and happier existence for American citizens.

Presidents leave to their successors both small and large inheritances. Almost every president has wanted to do something different than his predecessor, even when both came from the same party. Then-vice president George H. W. Bush, upon being nominated for president by the Republican Party in 1988, implied he would have a "kinder and gentler" presidency than the incumbent, Ronald Reagan, who was the standard-bearer of the new Republican orthodoxy. Al Gore acted during his 2000 presidential campaign as though he had never heard of Bill Clinton. Gerald Ford was implicitly running against Richard Nixon, as was Jimmy Carter (Carter ran better). Every leader wants independence and maximum discretion for their own initiatives. How much discretion new presidents can exercise depends on many circumstances, including how congressional seats are distributed, their own popularity, their margin of victory, conditions in the country, and the nature of external threats, as well as the firmness of their vision and the public's confidence in their judgment. We now know that some of those parameters exist inside a president's head and affect his determination. One of the lessons we have been learning about presidents—especially through the presidency of George W. Bush—is that sufficient will may override much of the conventional wisdom with respect to the limits imposed on presidential power by electoral and congressional margins and by popular approval.

The unilateral presidency—many of the works of which Joel Aberbach cites in his chapter—is ascendant. The subject of this book, President George W. Bush, has shown just how limited conventional wisdom was regarding constraints on presidential power, inasmuch as it assumed, among other things, that a president who had squeaked through to victory by the narrowest of margins, and whose congressional margin was also thin, would play to the median voter and forge cross-party coalitions. James Campbell has noted in his chapter why such a strategy might not have been rational for George W. Bush. Bush has shown us how far will and assertion of presidential prerogative can take a president, as well as just how isolated a presidency can become.

Between the presidencies of Andrew Jackson (1829–1837) and Theodore Roosevelt (1901–1909), with the wartime exception of Abraham Lincoln (1861–1865), presidents were largely overshadowed by Congress. Viewed from that perspective, unilateral action by presidents has increased in the long term, though it also fluctuates somewhat across presidencies. Whereas Clinton frequently bowed to congressional pressures or evolved triangulated positions between congressional Republicans and Democrats, Bush has stood steadfast. Clinton seemed perpetually willing to cut a deal. Bush, unlike both Clinton and his father, President George H. W. Bush, has rarely budged. The power of presidential assertion likely will come under attack when people take a president's vision to be only a mirage and a president's convictions to be mere willfulness. But critical attack is one thing; the power to alter a president's behavior is another. What Bush has managed to demonstrate is that a president need not be shackled by thin electoral margins, by bare majorities in Congress, or by modest or even low levels of popular approval. Presidential kryptonite is in shorter supply than we may have thought.

Who Defines a President's Legacy?

Who will decide what constitutes the legacy of a president? The platitude that one reaches for is "history." But history writes nothing. Only historians and their academic allies, such as political scientists and journalists, do. And they are rarely neutral about how they rank presidents. Presidents with big impacts and big challenges, who experienced favorable outcomes, tend to be at the top of ranking lists.

Excluding those who are either obvious advocates or critics of particular presidents and those who have carried water for one of them, producers of serious assessments of presidencies look at what a president tried to do, what he achieved or failed to achieve, and the circumstances conditioning those ambitions. Serious analysts also want to figure out the long-run impact of a presidency for good or ill. Of course, an early president such as Thomas Jefferson (1801–1809) is already a monument, his reputation solidified. Each respected history may chip away at, or reinforce, the reputation but is not likely to raise or lower it very much. History affects a leader's reputation, but contemporary history affects it more. Mainly the reason is that recent leaders' reputations have not solidified so greatly, and there are rich new discoveries to be made when the archives become available. When too little time elapses between presidents and assessments, even the most careful analyses may still be too close to their subject to see the extent to which a president's efforts will solidify and create a durable good (or long-term damage). George W. Bush's reputation as a leader, however, has solidified astonishingly quickly among many analysts of the presidency. Talk of his being among the worst U.S. presidents is frequent among the assessors—not because he has failed to make an impression but precisely because he has succeeded in doing so. This book and this chapter are, of course, a first word—not a last one—about Bush's likely impact on the future. We have had too little time in which to see how durable that impact may prove to be.

Ultimately, a legacy is likely to be sustained by long-standing coalitions that help to institutionalize outcomes or make them difficult to reverse. Think of Social Security or Medicare, for example. Think also of the increased role of the executive— in part the product of the administrative state and the national security state, but also the product of other institutions' concessions to executive power over the long haul. The expansion of the executive is mainly the consequence of external influences, but it also reflects the role of presidents whose talents for pushing the envelope, in the absence of others' resistance to their doing so, create precedents. The defense of institutional positions—for example, congressional responsibilities and prerogatives— tends to diminish before more pressing and urgent incentives, such as supporting party and president (when the president is of the party of the congressional majority) and members' need to be loyal to their party base. Whose ox is being gored turns out usually to be the firmest principle of all. As a result, members of Congress see the challenge from the executive less in institutional than in party terms. Republicans who may have believed in congressional parity or even superiority during the long reign of Roosevelt's New Deal and Truman's Fair Deal and during the eight years of the Kennedy-Johnson presidencies lost their appetite for congressional assertion once their party controlled the executive. By contrast, New Deal-Fair Deal-New Frontier-Great Society Democrats seemed to develop a new attachment to congressional power once Republicans began regularly to win the White House during times when the Democrats predictably held majorities in one or both chambers of Congress—1955–1961 under Eisenhower; 1969–1977 under Nixon and Ford; 1981–1993 under Reagan and George H. W. Bush, and since 2007 under George W. Bush.

Presidents contribute to a legacy, but many conditions must be in place for change to gel and endure. Succeeding presidents may solidify tendencies begun in prior administrations. Carter, for example, began the process of limiting the growth of discretionary spending; Reagan's immediate budgetary policies led to the contraction of discretionary spending. Carter pushed for the Civil Service Reform Act of 1979, an act that helped the succeeding Reagan administration to strategically move its loyalists into key administrative positions.[1] Carter also rescued Reagan from having to worry about the hostages from the American embassy that Iran held from November 1979 to January 1981, by working furiously through intermediaries to achieve a deal with Iran's governing clique. That was one legacy Reagan presumably would have been happy not to have left on his doorstep.

As these examples suggest, governing is more often cumulative and inertial than not. Although we tend to think of presidencies as discrete periods, in reality they are not so discrete. Isolating a given president's contribution to change is frequently difficult. Many factors are at work. As Skowronek and others have noted, changes are powered by ascendant political coalitions.[2] If those coalitions solidify, the changes are likely to become institutionalized.

Legacies—although "inheritances" may be a better term—are typically thought of as a president's positive contributions. But they may be a president's negative contributions as well. What about the larger problems that presidents leave in their wake? Wars are an obvious example, as they are never easy to resolve and have large internal costs. Budget cuts and tax increases are others—neither will make one popular. Cumulative failures to resolve long-term issues that will grow worse and make the cost of a fix yet higher—for example, global climate change and nuclear proliferation—are another.

The impacts of presidencies are also conflated with the challenges of the environment they face. We tend to attribute to one president actions that other political actors initiated. During most of his presidency, for example, Bill Clinton found himself responding to initiatives coming from the Republican Congress. His contribution was to counter those initiatives with the threat of the veto until the most objectionable aspects (from the White House's perspective) were skimmed off. But the initiatives and the leadership stemmed largely from Congress and especially its aggressive Speaker of the House of Representatives, Newt Gingrich, during the first four years following the GOP triumph in the 1994 midterm elections. As Charles O. Jones reminds us, there is more than one actor in Washington.[3] The president's share of power is large, but not exclusive.

All of this suggests that figuring out who is responsible for what is no easy matter. Nonetheless, there is an inevitable tendency to think of the presidency as central. There is also a tendency to think that presidents with bigger footprints are more important leaders than those with smaller ones—that, in other words, vision trumps prudence. There is a tendency among historians, journalists, and other presidency watchers to favor Democratic presidents with big impacts over Republican ones. To put it slightly differently, the presidency-watching crowd is skewed significantly toward the Democrats, compared with the population at large. Unless political coalitions drastically change in the foreseeable future, Democratic presidents of accomplishment are likely to be esteemed over Republican presidents of accomplishment, largely because the observers are more attuned to the Democrats' agenda than that of the Republicans.[4]

Bush's Footprints

George W. Bush's has been a "swing for the fences" presidency. It has had an ambitious agenda in both substantive and institutional terms. Bush's reach has far exceeded any imaginable mandate—and all such mandates are, in any event, imagined rather than real. One could not have imagined Bush's vigorously partisan style of governing from the words he uttered in the election campaign of 2000.[5] Bush claimed he was a healer, not a divider, but as Gary Jacobson and Morris Fiorina point out in their chapters, the reverse is far more true. Not everything will remain past the current administration, but this Bush administration, unlike the prior George H. W. Bush administration, will not have been caught short of "the vision thing."

Presidential Willpower

If President Bush campaigned in 2000 as a problem solver, his campaign in 2004 emphasized his convictions and principles. Perhaps Bush's role model was Margaret Thatcher, the "Iron Lady" British prime minister (1979–1990). More likely, it might be Harry Truman, who was notable for a will that was strong, occasionally even pugilistic (as when he promised to rearrange the face of the *Washington Post* music critic for his less-than-adoring review of Truman's daughter's vocal recital). President Truman was also notable for low popular approval; for persisting in an unwinnable war (Korea); and for cronyism. Such comparisons ring bells, although Truman was known to be an inveterate reader of history, a pastime that Bush has not yet been accused of. With his approval numbers slipping down toward Truman's in his worst days, with unfriendly fire coming from multiple fronts and even from formerly friendly sources, Bush is a president in the sunset of his presidency who has his back firmly arched up against the wall. In mid-April 2007, at a town hall meeting in a friendly setting in Ohio, President Bush indicated that "he would not buckle to polls" (which were encouraging neither to him nor to his policies, especially the war in Iraq) but "would be vindicated by history." A Bush admirer in the audience spoke positively of his "stay-to-itiveness," to which Bush responded "When it's all said and done . . . I will . . . look in the mirror, and I will say, 'I came with a set of principles and I didn't try to change my principles to make me popular.'"[6]

All presidents tend to stand on principles (often newly discovered) when their public standing collapses. There is nothing new in that. But more than most presidents Bush has been loath to compromise, or at least sees very little benefit from doing so. Perhaps the reason has been that his party's majorities in Congress for most of his administration, and their cohesion in his support, reinforced his fortitude. Perhaps it is that when he didn't get what he wanted, he unilaterally overrode Congress with signing statements or imagined inherent powers provided by a postmodern reading of the Constitution or of statutes. Perhaps he is just stubborn and obstinate or, possibly, even principled. Perhaps he is attached by conviction to a vision that is focused on outcomes but not means. Perhaps he is just trying to hand off his problems to a successor. Whatever the explanations—and all of them are in some respects plausible—his persistence and "sticketivity," although not perfect, are impressive.

Bush has stood by his appointees far longer than most presidents have, especially his immediate predecessor. Is the reason a craving for loyalty? Or is it that throwing one nominee or cabinet member (Alberto Gonzales), or even World Bank president (Paul Wolfowitz), to the wolves would only make the wolves crave more? Bush's backing of Attorney General Gonzales, in the face of a nearly bipartisan expression of loss of confidence in him in the Senate, has been nothing short of amazing—an expression that he will stand his ground on behalf of those loyal to him and that not doing so would erode his capacity even more. His backing of the besieged Gonzales and praise for how well Gonzales's testimony went before the Senate Judiciary Committee were particularly strange since committee Republicans, as well as Democrats, found the attorney general's testimony evasive and damaging to his prospects for staying on. It may be that, as with Donald Rumsfeld, former defense secretary and an architect of the war in Iraq, Bush will bide his time and bow to the inevitable. But Bush's posture suggests that nothing is inevitable.

Similarly, Bush has been willing to remain committed to his favored judicial and executive nominees, even when clear signals have come from the Senate to drop their nominations. Bush is not the first president to use recess appointments for appointees that he wanted to ram through the Senate but couldn't. But he has used them frequently, in ways that clearly signaled his contempt for the Senate and for senators. Bush's willingness to renominate highly controversial judicial nominees precipitated a near-crisis in the Senate in 2005 over the threat by the Senate majority leader to exempt nominations from the use of the filibuster (referred to as the "nuclear option"). Bush and the Republican leadership stared down their opposition and won.

Despite Bush's low standing, he has demonstrated that if a president is sufficiently committed to getting his way, on matters other than ones requiring major legislation, he can do so. It is conceivable that one of the larger lessons that Bush will leave behind is that a modern president, under some circumstances, can be quite powerful when he or she chooses to ignore norms and congressional sentiment, even when that president is politically wounded. For the most part, the limiting condition is that the opposition party must have not only control of both chambers of Congress, but dominant majorities in each. In this regard, Bush could do what Gerald Ford, who faced overwhelming Democratic majorities in Congress, could not. Another limiting condition would be a president's lack of the cohesive backing of his or her party. Although congressional Republicans have sometimes had doubts about specific aspects of Bush's agenda, they have managed to supply him with disciplined support in Congress when push came to shove.

The Wars in Iraq and Afghanistan

The use of force in Afghanistan, to clear out the Taliban regime that harbored al Qaeda's leadership, was a war necessitated by the terrorist attacks of 9/11 on the United States. Although any inference on the matter is inherently speculative, it is likely that a President Gore (or any other president) would likewise have found it necessary to root out the Taliban regime there and force Osama bin Laden to take refuge. It is equally speculative, but also possible, that another administration might have pursued the effort to destroy the Taliban and al Qaeda and its leadership in a more relentless and single-minded fashion, thus reducing the chances of a come-back by the Taliban that now remains all too possible.

Unlike the war in Afghanistan, however, the war that the Bush administration began in Iraq was a war of discretion. We now know that it was initiated under false pretenses. What we do not yet know are the motives of various actors within the administration, the degree to which they were shaped by intelligence on Iraqi weapons of mass destruction (WMD), or the extent to which their desire to over-throw the Saddam Hussein regime shaped the intelligence. On all of these matters it is too early to tell definitively, though the threat of force did compel the Iraqi regime to comply with the United Nations (UN) inspection team. The fact that the inspection team found nothing, but was still looking at the point that the Bush administration set a deadline for Saddam's removal and for the war to commence, must at least give some pause as to whether the threat of WMD was ever the real motive for the war. That is not to mention that other potentially threatening regimes in North Korea and in Iran were farther along in developing nuclear arsenals (North Korea) or a prototype weapon (Iran).

Whatever the motive for going to war in Iraq, the consequences have been strongly negative for the credibility of U.S. power and for pacifying Afghanistan. In fact, Iraq has provided a new front for al Qaeda terrorists. By failing to concentrate on the necessary work at hand, the Bush administration policies in the region have produced a highly unstable and fragile situation in both places—Afghanistan and Iraq. The morass in Iraq—more than any other factor—is responsible for Bush's low political standing and for the Republicans' defeat in the midterm elections of 2006. Bush's father might have said that the ill-starred and more-or-less unilateral venture into Iraq would not be prudent. Bush's father took up arms to chase the Iraqis out of Kuwait but did so by forging a multinational coalition, with UN approval, and with a clear but nonutopian end state in mind.

All wars are easier to begin than to finish. And all wars that are not going well are easier to hand off to a successor than to settle during one's own days in power. Harry Truman handed off to Dwight Eisenhower the settlement of the Korean War, on terms that Truman himself could have settled for had it not been for McCarthyite accusations that the Truman administration was harboring communist sympathizers in important places. Lyndon Johnson bequeathed the resolution of the war in Vietnam to Richard Nixon, ultimately on terms that Johnson could have accepted and with an outcome that no one but the North Vietnamese regime and its allies wanted. Of course, the world did not topple when the Hanoi regime took over all of Vietnam, a regime that is now busily emulating China's journey down the capitalist road.

One of the long-term legacies to come out of the Vietnam War was the Powell doctrine (for General Colin Powell) that when force must be used (and, according to the doctrine, it should be used only when absolutely necessary), it must be used in overpowering fashion behind a clear purpose. The Powell doctrine was overridden by the Rumsfeld doctrine (never so named) that proclaimed the virtues of quickness, mobility, and small force size.

Whatever the wisdom of the preemptive military venture in Iraq, the management of the war has been widely decried as incompetent politically and militarily and as having stirred up more trouble in a region notable for trouble. The Rumsfeld doctrine and the happy-faced, neoconservative perspective on how American troops would be perceived and the Iraqi regime transformed are extraordinary for their utopian character, as well as for their utter lack of the serious analysis, policy review, and caution about adverse consequences that a truly conservative mindset demands. The Bush administration's assumptions were almost wholly wrong, and it ignored, if not suppressed, warnings from military, intelligence, and diplomatic professionals. Ambiguity was interpreted unambiguously. Certitude replaced essential skepticism. It is probably fair to say that from any angle imaginable (weakening national security, broadening the base of terrorism, stretching military forces to the limits of their capacity, and eroding American credibility diplomatically and militarily) the Bush war policy in Iraq and its implementation have been catastrophic, including for Bush himself.

The signature of this presidency is its discomfort with facts or possibilities that interfere with its preferred visions and ideologies. Iraq is a reflection of that mindset. As the war in Iraq edged toward the end of its fourth year, in February 2007, Lieutenant General William E. Odom, former head of army intelligence and director of the National Security Agency under President Reagan, wrote in the *Washington Post*:

> The new National Intelligence Estimate on Iraq starkly delineates the gulf that separates President Bush's illusions from the realities of the war. Victory, as the president sees it, requires a stable liberal democracy in Iraq that is pro-American. The NIE describes a war that has no chance of producing that result.[7]

The old-time comedy team of Stan Laurel and Oliver Hardy used to play off of the corpulent partner (Hardy) getting the duo into a mess with some harebrained scheme or other, at which point the thin straight man, Laurel, would complain, "It's a fine mess you got us into, Ollie." Whoever succeeds Bush will have inherited this fine mess. It may be that a comedy of errors produced this policy, but its outcome is certainly not funny. And it is likely that any resolution will leave the United States worse off than before the invasion. Unlike the Korean conflict or the one in Vietnam, there is really no one to negotiate with, except possibly Iraq's neighbors, Syria and Iran, as the nonofficial Baker-Hamilton Commission report proposed at the end of 2006. In predictable fashion, the administration brushed off that report (no talks with "enemy states"), and it equally predictably sought to make political hay out of the later visit of House Speaker Nancy Pelosi to Syria and her meeting with the Syrian president. But, as Barbara Sinclair has noted in her chapter, when pushed into a corner, the Bush administration will negotiate. That is now beginning to unfold in diplomacy, but of course when you have few options you also have little leverage.

The National Security State

In his famous novel *1984*, George Orwell depicts a world of megastates in continuous war. Citizens are watched over and listened to by "Big Brother"—the eyes and ears of the state. The zone of privacy has vanished. In this dystopia language has lost its meaning. "Doublespeak" forms the official discourse, which consists of unspeakable lies. The Ministry of Truth is in reality a ministry of propaganda; the Ministry of Peace is actually the opposite. We associate the symptoms of this dystopia with the Stalinist and Nazi regimes and other brutal dictatorships. We think of constitutional political systems as their natural opposite—guided by limits on the state and its police power, dispersion of authority, and the maintenance of zones of privacy from interference by the state.

In Orwell's novel, continuous warfare helped to justify repression. Since its entrance into World War II, the United States has engaged in hot wars and a long cold war (that had lethal hot episodes). It is now engaged, depending on the changing terminology of the day, in a "long war" against terror, or Islamo-fascists, or whatever. The national security state creates tensions with liberal constitutionalism. Whereas the latter emphasizes limited government and individual freedom, the former emphasizes the necessities of state surveillance and inevitable restrictions of privacy and freedom. There is conflict between the state's obligation to protect its citizens from violence and its guarantee of freedoms. There is no perfect reconciliation of these two. However, the more stark the perceived threat, the more likely it is that the balance will favor the state's security apparatus.

The peculiar nature of the terrorist threat—whether it is overblown, as John Mueller argues, or not[8]—is twofold: its credibility—no one can ever forget the 9/11 attacks on American soil—and its amorphousness. There is no definite army or state that is the enemy. Rather, the enemy is potentially everywhere. Terrorism's seeming randomness pierces the everyday lives of all of us. People are killed by terrorists at work, going to work, or at pleasure in many different places—Bali, London, Madrid, New York, Washington. Its seeming omnipresence, more than its actual toll, is what people find especially disturbing.

The Bush administration has, often but not always with the concurrence of Congress, taken steps to constrict privacy and freedom, to expand the powers of the executive, to eliminate the writ of habeas corpus for war prisoners, and to condone the use of extraordinary measures of interrogation, essentially redefining the Geneva Convention on treatment of prisoners. The question is, Would any other administration have acted much differently in the aftermath of the 9/11 attacks and the continuing incidents abroad? Unfortunately, we cannot know for certain the answer to that question. We can, however, look back to excesses of the national security state during other presidencies—the internment of Japanese Americans during World War II, for example, the Palmer Raids after the establishment of the Bolshevik (Communist) state in Russia, the infiltration by the FBI of groups protesting against the Vietnam War, the security and loyalty tests required of federal employees in the worst days of the cold war. Those activities occurred under presidencies other than Bush's, and in fact, most of them during Democratic presidencies. The dragnet that scooped up protesters during the Republican National Convention in New York in 2004 occurred under the administration of Mayor Michael Bloomberg, a nominal Republican but one who has been lauded for managerial competence and foresight.

Some of the issues that have arisen in the aftermath of the 9/11 attacks are new. Repatriation and Geneva Convention rules are hard to implement when the enemy is not a signatory, not even a state, and there is no likely point of repatriation or destination. This is all new. How to deal with it is not clear, and it would not be clear to any president of either party. Orwellian responses are the product of the security state and the terrorists, and for the most part, Congress and the public have been willing to give the administration wide latitude in trading privacy and possible intimidation for the expectation of enhanced security.

Still, the Bush administration has gone out of its way to assert its self-defined right to go beyond laws such as the Foreign Intelligence Surveillance Act (FISA), which clearly forbids behavior that the administration engaged in—tapping American citizens' phones without a FISA-approved court order. And it has done so with unparalleled audacity, claiming inherent rights in constitutional authority based on Article 2, in the Patriot Act, and even in the post-9/11 war resolutions. This is especially remarkable behavior for an administration that claims to want only strict constructionists as judges, that is, those who take the law literally as written (which by definition conflicts with another of the Bush administration tests for judicial candidates—"original intent"). This may be a presidency lacking on many fronts, but it is surely not lacking in chutzpah.

Tax Cuts and Red Ink

Another Bush administration hallmark is the red ink occasioned by its massive tax cuts, benefiting almost exclusively the very well off, at the time that it is spending over $500 billion for the war in Iraq and additional sums for homeland security, as well as for the new Medicare Part D drug benefit. It is doubtful that a Democratic president would have cut taxes as the Bush administration has done, although a Democratic administration might have sponsored smaller cuts more targeted to middle-income taxpayers. More likely Democrats would have sought additional spending for social and educational programs and health care. The only thing likely to prevent a Democratic president from increasing federal budget deficits is a lack of sufficient numbers of Democrats in Congress to pass the programs.

Ronald Reagan's budget policies, and the unwillingness of Congress to cut back spending, produced a sea of red ink that finally took two presidents—one Republican, Bush 41, and one Democrat, Clinton—and two Democratic Congresses (the 101st and the 103rd) to fix. The current set of tax cuts are set to expire in 2010. Curtailing them will stem, but not erase, the accumulating mountain of deficits. Should the Democrats retain congressional majorities and win the presidency in 2008, will they seek not only to prevent the cuts from becoming permanent, but also, as Clinton did, actually raise taxes to put the federal budget in order? Political courage has not been the Democrats' long suit in recent decades. The ghost of Marjorie Mezvinsky, former Democratic congresswoman from a suburban Philadelphia swing district, is likely to be a deterrent to Democrats who might contemplate being profiles in courage. Mezvinsky cast the pivotal vote in the House for Clinton's 1993 revenue bill and was defeated in the 1994 election. Profiles in courage tend to become former politicians.

Budget deficits are hard for the public to comprehend, although the public seemed intuitively to think that cutting taxes was a lesser priority than balancing the budget. If politics is, as Harold Lasswell put it, "who gets what, when and where," taxes define the allocation more sharply and visibly than any other policy. Tax policy has always been about a lot of things: inducements for investors and donors to produce public goods through private benefits; rewarding productivity or, conversely, ameliorating inequalities, on the basis of who can afford to pay; and above all, helping to define the size and scope of government—that is, the role and limits of the public sector in producing public goods. Since the New Deal administration of Franklin D. Roosevelt (1933–1945), Democrats and Republicans have tended to divide on taxes and who should pay them and on the role of government. If anything the parties, as they have become more distinct, have hardened their positions on these issues. The Republicans' stress on low taxes, at least since Reagan and certainly in the George W. Bush era, is part of a larger picture of privatizing governmental functions and limiting the government's capacity to launch new programs or fund fully the ones for which it already has responsibility. A government with an empty bank account will provide a rude awakening to any Democrat entering the White House, should one win in 2008. This is likely to be a critical legacy left by Bush and his party.

Tax cuts are rarely offset by equivalent spending cuts, and they certainly have not been in the George W. Bush administration. Although deficits are intuitively grasped as unsustainable over the long haul, their actual consequences are murky, and that is why there is so little effort to bring revenues and expenditures into rough balance. As deficits pile up, however, a larger percentage of the federal budget goes to finance them, crowding out other expenditures. For the dollar to hold value in world markets under such circumstances, interest rates must rise. Otherwise, holders of dollars will sell them off, further devaluing the currency. The pound sterling, once the world's currency standard, has appreciated to the point that it is now worth more than two U.S. dollars. The dollar has similarly slipped in the European Union euro zone. Japanese and Chinese entities hold huge quantities of dollars, helping to hold up the value of the currency as the international standard. No doubt they believe that the U.S. economy has sufficient resilience and magnitude to maintain the value of the dollar. But this is not inevitable, and in the past century many once-prosperous economies, such as Argentina's, have been swept away in a tide of debt. A new president will have to face this reality. George H. W. Bush eventually did, despite his ill-advised "no new taxes" mantra, and so did Bill Clinton. But in the short term both suffered for their responsible behavior. In politics, virtue apparently must be its own reward because it doesn't obviously produce any others. Already there are indications that Democrats in Congress are less likely to sacrifice on behalf of fiscal responsibility, as they did in 1990 and 1993, merely to earn the sobriquet of the "tax and spend" party from their Republican rivals. This time, if they enhance their majorities and capture the presidency, they will likely seek to live up to the "spend" part of the accusation by taking off of the shelf social programs that have been gathering dust during the Republican ascendancy.

Democrats typically have set the budget constraint through entitlements. Republicans traditionally have tried to treat those with means tests, so as to limit financial obligations and also make the programs more vulnerable. Republicans also have preferred privatizing social benefits, essentially through individual investment or tax credit schemes to limit financial liability, increase individual responsibility, and limit the tax liability of their more solidly prosperous base. Republicans have adhered to tax cuts "to starve the beast" and to force private schemes on formerly public entitlements such as Social Security or health care provision. Whether the Democrats hold power in 2010 and allow the Republican tax cuts to expire depends on political contingencies. It is certain, however, that if tax cuts persist and expenditures increase through entitlements (as they will because of the aging of the population), war expenditures, debt service, or new programs, the United States will have gathered momentum for fiscal failure.

Contributions to Political Polarization

The rationalization of the American party system has created a powerful party divide. Although no one doubts that polarization is strongest among the elite and activist strata, the party rank and file also are more divided than a generation ago and far more so than two generations ago. The reasons are complex, and many of the chapters in this book (especially those by James Campbell, Morris Fiorina, Gary Jacobson, and Lawrence Jacobs and Robert Shapiro) deal explicitly with the polarization phenomenon, offering different and sometimes conflicting perspectives on it.

As noted, Bush campaigned in 2000 as a healer, not a divider, but soon became possibly the most divisive president in the lifetimes of this book's editors and contributors. Jacobs and Shapiro point out that although Bush did not play quite as exclusively to his political base as conventional wisdom has it, he has not been shy about catering to his base, nor has he been in search of points where he and his opposition could reconcile. To what extent was it reasonable for Bush to cater especially to his party's religious fundamentalist base and to its anti–business regulation and anti-tax base? How much of the polarization did his administration provoke? To what extent did it merely conform to the state of partisan opinion while perhaps contributing to reinforcing it? Bush could have followed his own conciliatory themes from 2000 but chose not to. Was it irrational, in terms of his interests, to be more exclusive and less inclusive? Hardly. While the political divide is affected to some extent by the stances and the divisiveness or consensus-building inclinations of the political leadership, Bush did not create the division; it was there. But he clearly did nothing to alleviate it, and he did much to reinforce it by his "my way or the highway" style of governance; by his persistence on appointments that Democrats found offensive; and by the content of his policies, from the war in Iraq to the anti-regulatory lack of enforcement of laws in such areas as worker health and safety, the environment, and others.

One of Bush's inheritances is a powerful political division based on party, perhaps most clearly seen in the House of Representatives. Bush may be deeply committed to what his administration likes to refer to as "the ownership society" and to the sacredness of embryos otherwise likely to be discarded if not used for stem cell research. If so, he is at one with his party's current mainstream. We cannot yet know precisely what Bush believes—if indeed we ever will. But we do know that politicians shape their strategies in accordance with what they perceive to be political necessities. In the environment in which Bush came to power, he could have widened his horizons to appeal to the median voter, or he could seek to stay narrow and govern with a minimum winning coalition (that sometimes didn't win). We know that Bush largely chose the second of these options and that his party base stayed loyal to him. Given the existing constellation of partisan forces and their divisions on issues, it is unlikely that a "third-way" president can succeed in bridging the divide, though, no doubt, as Bush did in 2000, some of the candidates in the next election will talk about doing so. Clinton was the ultimate third-way president, busily triangulating issues between the two congressional parties. For his efforts he was reviled by Republicans, especially the "cultural values" wing of the Republican Party, and he was distrusted by activists within his own party. Clinton's revival was partly a function of the Republicans' efforts to impeach him. Bush's choices were consistent with a divide that already existed. His choices deepened that divide, to be sure, but it is likely that if Bush had chosen, as Clinton did, to triangulate and create a basis for compromise, he would have gone the way of his father—challenged within his own party and vulnerable to electoral defeat. Any politician needs to begin with a base. In the current political climate in America, that base is almost wholly coincident with the partisan divide.

More Bush Footprints

Whatever the Bush administration has accomplished for good or ill and whether durable or short-lived, little about it has been halfhearted. Among the other major features of this administration have been the extraordinary role of the vice president; the president's detachment from the management of policy and the detachment of policy from analysis; the buildup of incompetence and cronyism within government; and the effort to create a judiciary receptive to an expansionary executive and an expansionary state with respect to its police powers.

The Vice Presidency

Over the long haul, presidents have been making their vice presidents more visible parts of their administrations, even if reluctantly. Some vice presidents have been regarded as central actors in their administrations. Especially notable were Walter Mondale under Carter and Al Gore under Clinton. None, it is fair to say, has carried the weight in policymaking of Dick Cheney, who has been an ardent advocate within the Bush administration for positions associated with its most right-wing impulses. On the war in Iraq, which Cheney relentlessly pursued and justified, the vice president was clearly a major figure, operating with his own mini White House staff of advisers. On the administration's energy policy, Cheney was remarkable for his unequivocal links to carbon-based producers and his undisguised contempt for energy conservationists, environmentalists, and advocates for alternative fuels. Cheney, too, was a bulldog on the administration's tax policies.

There is no evidence that Cheney publicly spoke or in any way acted counter to the president's intent, but there also is no indication that he acted passively, as a mere spokesperson for the administration's policies. Cheney appears to have been key in some of the administration's notable actions and mishaps. He has been an even more polarizing figure than the president himself and an even less popular one. Cheney, it will be recalled, chaired Bush's search committee for vice-presidential nominees, prior to the Republican convention of 2000, and proceeded to nominate himself. His virtues seemed obvious—experience and intelligence. He had been a member of Congress, a White House chief of staff, a defense secretary, a business executive, and, having suffered several heart attacks, had no ambitions of his own to higher political office. The old Washington hand presumably could provide some salt to the fresh younger governor from Texas, whose experience, especially in national security policy, was less deep.

Depending upon one's perspective, Cheney has either anchored the Bush administration or helped to mire it in the mud. Presidents are certainly not helped by vice presidents who appear to be running the show (even if they aren't), and they are not helped by vice presidents who become magnets for criticism and drag their administrations down with them. Vice presidents as lightening rods, of course, are an old act. But they are expected to be the "bad cop" spokesman for an administration, in contrast to the "good cop" president, not to be policymakers nearly as influential as the president. Not until many years have passed and the records of this most obsessively secret of presidential administrations are available—if they do become available—will we have some real, rather than speculative, idea of the vice president's role in the Bush administration. Nevertheless, in no other administration has the vice president been thought to be so powerful. Perhaps what we see is a mere meeting of the minds of numbers one and two. But future presidents worrying about portrayals of Rasputin-like influences in their administrations may be inclined to keep their vice presidents on a shorter leash. The office may not return to what Vice President John Garner (1933–1941) called worth "a warm bucket of spit" (though he didn't say "spit"), but it is doubtful that future presidents, at least those mindful of the Bush-Cheney years, will want their vice presidents to cast a shadow of the magnitude of Cheney's.

Detachment from Management and Policy Analysis

"Heckuva job, Brownie." These words, in the immediate aftermath of Hurricane Katrina's devastation of New Orleans and other areas of the Gulf Coast in 2005, are a hallmark of President Bush's detachment from the "executive" part of his role as chief executive. The unfortunate Brownie in this case was Michael Brown, head of the Federal Emergency Management Agency (FEMA), whose failures to respond adequately to the Katrina catastrophe are now legendary. Bush's off-the-cuff remark reflected a more-or-less off-the-cuff administration, in which political competence far outweighed governing competence as a criterion for filling jobs throughout much of the executive branch. The aforementioned Mr. Brown had hardly any record in managing disaster response; the administration evinced little interest in this particular function of government; and the merging of FEMA into the Department of Homeland Security (DHS) assured that those functions would receive little attention, unless they were associated with terrorist actions. The purportedly well performing Mr. Brown was gone shortly after President Bush's accolade.

The "Brownie" episode appears not to have been an isolated case. As Tanter and Kersting, Colin Campbell, and Rudalevige have pointed out in their chapters, Bush appears not to expend much effort in monitoring where his decisions are leading and how they are being implemented, nor in reviewing where alternative decisions might lead. Nor, apparently, has Bush much valued what is referred to as "neutral competence." Since, as he is reported to have proclaimed, he doesn't argue with himself, there is apparently little need to go past gut instinct. As Tanter and Kersting in particular note, this leaves Bush oftentimes in the position of being a vessel for the agendas of others within his administration and failing to follow through with care on decisions that have been reached.

In the early days of the George W. Bush administration, a leading management scholar, Don Kettl, wrote in a book aptly entitled *Team Bush* that Bush brought a more incisive management style to the White House, befitting his Harvard MBA.[9] In contrast to the graduate student style of all-night brainstorming preferred by his predecessor, President Clinton, Bush wanted meetings to begin promptly and end quickly and decisively, and he wanted those involved to be dressed appropriately. It was easy in the early going of the administration to mistake form for function. Meetings were crisp, but little apparently came of them. They appear to have been well-rehearsed affairs but lacked strategies for considering options and fallbacks.[10] Without appropriate vetting and necessary skepticism (arguing with oneself, which the Clinton administration may have carried to an extreme), incompetence in managing policy would likely follow—and apparently has.

Management and involvement turn out to be necessary parts of a president's job. Bush is not the first to lack these proclivities. But his management system and style have reinforced his instincts not to "argue with himself," to the detriment of both his country and his presidency.

Cronyism

One of the unfortunate aspects of the way in which election campaigns are conducted in the United States is that it invites cronyism and plays down professionalism. Michael Brown may be exhibit A, but every presidential administration has had lots of "Brownies." In contrast to parliamentary systems, the American system of government leaves a president after the election with a need to fill many positions immediately after an electoral campaign that depended on raising large sums of money and acquiring lots of political support. Most institutionalized parliamentary systems solve the problem by turning to professionals in government, staffing all but the very top positions with career civil servants. This is not the case in the United States, where career officials rarely move into the most important policy-making roles. On the rare occasions when they do, they then lose their career status and become expendable to the next administration. The American system replaces professionalism with patronage to a degree that is unusual in most other established constitutional systems.

There is certainly much debate as to whether the American system of appointing outsiders allows it to be more responsive to changes in political direction and to the democratically elected political leadership, or whether it leads to a dysfunctional system of cronyism and inept government. President Truman had both blue-ribbon appointees and political cronies in his administration, and the cronies were implicated in a series of minor scandals. President Eisenhower nominated a Republican fund-raiser, Maxwell Gluck, to be ambassador to Ceylon (now Sri Lanka), which he could not locate on a map. President Reagan's appointments team in the White House tried to make sure that true believers in the Reagan cause were appointed below the radar to ensure that the president's agenda would be implemented.[11] Some of them, for example, Ann Gorsuch Burford, the Environmental Protection Agency administrator, by her zealousness got the president (and herself) into trouble.

It is not yet clear whether George W. Bush has set a new (low-water) mark in presidential appointments. But Bush has clearly established a reputation for appointments that reflect the Republicans' "K Street" strategy during the years when Tom DeLay was the Republican whip and then majority leader in the House of Representatives. Mark Peterson's chapter describes the George W. Bush administration as a "government of chums." Others have noted that, like Reagan's, Bush's appointments have often been people who are uninterested in enforcing statutes that they (and presumably the White House) don't like, and who were affiliated with interests that opposed the enabling legislation. The emphasis clearly has been on "responsive competence," not "neutral competence." The Labor Department's Occupational Safety and Health Administration, for example, headed by Edwin G. Foulke Jr., has issued scarcely any regulations at all, falling far below even the years of the Reagan administration. Mr. Foulke's credentials for his job are that he was a Republican fund-raiser and state party chairman in South Carolina and advocated against labor health and safety regulations.[12]

Of course, every president wants to head a government responsive exclusively to his or her priorities.[13] As we earlier observed, presidents do not like to be saddled with someone else's legacies that hinder their own priorities or political needs. Presidents have resorted to a variety of mechanisms to govern unilaterally and to diminish constraints upon their freedom of action. Furthermore, the American system implicitly stresses responsiveness to a greater degree than competence. The presidency of George W. Bush is in a long tradition of cronyism and partisan administration. But it also seems to have moved this inglorious tradition to a new high (or low), not only by its appointments into the government, but also by its contracting out of operations, often to favored clienteles and without sufficient oversight or even any interest in oversight.

In the film *Gangs of New York,* directed by Martin Scorsese, we are taken back to a time in the mid-nineteenth century when most governing functions were private operations, and political bosses ruled and exacted tribute from citizens. Until the system was reformed decades later, and government administration was at least partly removed from the party bosses' direct hand, cronyism, favoritism, and incompetence were rampant. The presidential administration of George W. Bush has taken significant strides toward restoring those retrograde conditions.

The Federalist Presidency

For some time now—but especially since the Reagan presidency—the federal courts have been at the center of intense political controversy. The Reagan administration applied to prospective federal judges litmus tests on social issues important to the growing religious-based core of the Republican Party. Under George W. Bush, the litmus tests have become even stricter and broadened to encompass candidates' views on the prerogatives of the executive branch—meaning, effectively, the president. David Yalof's chapter points to notable trends in Bush's nominations to the bench.

An important interest within the Republican Party is the Federalist Society— a conservative group of legal intellectuals and lawyers. The Federalist Society holds a view that is neither federalist nor conservative. It begins with the supposition that the executive branch is unified under the president and is, hence, more-or-less immune from oversight by Congress or the courts. These interpretations are, to be charitable, highly creative readings of the American Constitution. They distinctly reverse the Framers' primary emphasis on the role of the legislative branch as the most central governing organ in the federal government. One notes, of course, that it is the legislative branch that occupies Article 1 of the Constitution, which also is the lengthiest of the articles laying out the functions of the governing institutions.

Membership in the Federalist Society—or at least its approval—has become a near–rite of passage for Bush administration nominees to the appellate benches. The view of the Federalist Society is in harmony with the Bush administration's definition of its prerogatives, namely, that it needs none of them to be spelled out in law. Rather, it will determine what they are whenever it is convenient for the White House to do so. Operationally, this means that the administration—if it is able to— will do as it wishes and make up the legal justifications on the fly. To put it mildly, this is highly irregular; to put it bluntly, it is utter lawlessness.

To help carry off this plot to deconstruct the Constitution, the Bush administration needed a judiciary highly sympathetic to expansionary presidential and executive powers—exactly the notion that all that goes on in the executive is under the exclusive jurisdiction of the president. It means that the responsibilities given to the president in Article 2, Section 3 of the Constitution to ensure that the laws be faithfully executed and the vague responsibilities of the president as commander in chief are to be construed as insulating the president from interference by other, duly constituted sources of authority. In this view, even the congressionally established, independent regulatory agencies such as the Securities and Exchange Commission, the Federal Trade Commission, the Federal Communications Commission, and the like, are regarded, despite judicial precedent to the contrary, as unconstitutionally outside of the unified executive.

With the right constellation of forces—a Republican Senate amenable to confirming jurists who conform to the Federalist Society model and a critical mass of appointed jurists—it is not hard to see how a soft but nevertheless authentic authoritarianism is born. Bush will be impeded to some degree, however, by the narrow, tenuous edge that the Democrats have gained in the Senate since the 2006 elections.

Again, it should be emphasized that Bush is hardly the first president to make up dubious bases of authority. The legal foundation for the equal accommodations section of the 1964 Civil Rights Act was the spectacularly threadbare assertion that the federal government's interstate commerce jurisdiction gave it the right to ensure that every mom-and-pop restaurant or motel otherwise unregulated by federal law should be subject to federal regulation simply because their catsup or cleanser came from out of state. The equal accommodation section was a just cause, but the legal basis for its reach was, shall we say, thin. Regulating hotel and restaurant chains that do interstate business clearly falls under federal authority. Regulating Grandma's Café is not so clearly an issue falling under federal jurisdiction (unless Grandma's Café is a part of a big interstate operation). Bush's reach for authority is not much different in principle. It is different only in stipulating that the only constraint on presidential behavior is his to define.

As with other ungrounded efforts to expand the reach of authority beyond its constitutional limitations or those explicitly provided in statutes, what occurs depends on the prevailing coalitions. In 1964, the tide had turned, and racial discrimination and separation could no longer be abided. However thin the legal basis for extending the reach of the federal regulatory arm, the greater evil was the inherent injustice of a system by which people could be discriminated against for seeking a room or a meal. Extending the president's reach in a time of continuing threat also apparently outweighs the underlying laws by which a president can (or cannot) establish authority. Certainly one way a president might be able to extend his reach is through compliant jurists who accept the premises of a unified executive under the control of the president. An aggrandizing president, a compliant Congress, and jurists who see things compatibly with the Federalist Society outlook may leave an institutional legacy of staggering consequence, essentially effecting a coup d'état against the American constitutional order.

A Last Word

George W. Bush's presidency has scarcely been uneventful, though we may wish it had been. Bush has indeed swung for the fences. He has sought big things, with a clear vision with respect both to America's role in the world and to the role of government—though that is a two-sided perspective. In this vision individuals are on their own, except when it comes to their personal privacy. Bush's efforts in each regard have been unpopular. His unilateralism abroad has helped isolate the United States, not an advantageous position for a country fighting two wars (in Iraq and Afghanistan) and occasionally itching for a third (against Iran). His scheme for privatizing Social Security, which never became a legislative proposal (likely because the details could not be made to come together), failed to generate much support in Congress or in the public.

As we have seen, not everything big a president does winds up as a legacy. That depends on conditions that can make for reversals of outcomes. It will likely be some time before we know definitively what kind of legacy Bush has produced. Given his unpopularity, however, it may be that Bush's legacy will be eroded substantially should the Democrats win big in 2008. Nevertheless, Bush will leave his successors with some big problems. One will be the wars in Iraq and Afghanistan; another will be the stretched state of the military; a third will be bringing some balance back into the federal budget. Additionally, it is not clear what will be done with those incarcerated in Guantanamo—the prisoners of war in an unending war. Bush's presidency will likely be regarded as a history in which failures litter the landscape and are more notable than successes. Writing in the *Los Angeles Times,* a notable presidency watcher, Ronald Brownstein, observed that "Bush seems intent on defending the decisions he's made already, even at the price of a new consensus attempting to form around him. If Bush continues to view standing alone as the highest form of principle, he will never escape the dead end into which he's steered his second term."[14]

Although we tend to see the president's role as defining, in many instances Bush has acted in accord with his party—for example, on taxes, the cultural divide, and the unwillingness to regulate business activity or the environment. To have done otherwise might have been heroic, but given the political configurations and divisions at work in the country, Bush might have been tactically ill-advised to do other than he has done, including governing from his party's core rather than chasing the median voter.

In other instances, some of Bush's most notorious actions are sadly not without antecedents among other presidents governing in times of crisis and war. There is a lot of ugly history of curtailing the civil liberties of particular populations, including instances under Democratic presidents. Yet Bush has taken presidential authority to new heights. In the relationship between citizens and the government, the administration has sought to ensure that only it has the right to privacy. Its proclamations of its inherent powers have been breathtaking. It is not clear whether this will have staying power. Nixon's "I am the law" attitude resulted in Congress' putting limits on presidential discretion. On the other hand, the long-term erosion of norms of institutional balance makes presidents more willing to assert prerogatives not grounded in the Constitution or in statute. This president has hardly been alone in the dubious assertion of prerogatives. His assertion of them, however, has been so extreme and unequivocal that the institutional balance of power may be irredeemably tilted, and with it the balance between the police powers of the state and the freedom and rights of citizens.

At least for a time, Bush's swaggering, "I'm the decider" style of decision making may cause a reaction against an impetuous, "shoot first, ask questions later" mode of making choices and then failing to manage them. Richard Neustadt told us that presidents needed to guard their stakes by appreciating what could go wrong in the decisions they make.[15] Of course, to do that requires an understanding of what the stakes happen to be. Bush's father liked to use the word "prudent" as a way of expressing his understanding of what those stakes might be. George W. Bush seems not to find the word in his vocabulary.

Much of the mess that Bush is in is of his own making. He chose to believe in optimal outcomes without preparing for contingencies—a sign of his indifference to effective government, to the advice of competent professionals, and to tests of evidence, and an outgrowth of his swagger and his commitment to faith-based analysis. Supposedly he doesn't argue with himself. He should. From skepticism comes wisdom. Enough things can go wrong under the best of circumstances that it is essential for those that can reasonably be anticipated to be fully vetted. Short-term power aggrandizement rarely helps a president preserve his options and guard his stakes. Only thinking things through and superintending the implementation of choices can help. Reagan needed help and got it; Bush rejected help that was proffered. Will we see his like in the White House again? Probably, but likely not immediately. At least for an election cycle or two, maturity and considered judgment may be back in vogue.

Come to think of it, perhaps George W. Bush's most important, if ironic, legacy is already the rehabilitation of his father's presidential reputation.

Notes

1. See particularly Joel D. Aberbach and Bert A. Rockman, *In the Web of Politics: Three Decades of the U.S. Federal Executive* (Washington, D.C.: Brookings Institution Press, 2000), 87–133.

2. See especially Stephen Skowronek, *The Politics Presidents Make: Leadership from John Adams to Bill Clinton* (Cambridge, Mass.: Belknap Press, 1997), and Erwin C. Hargrove and Michael Nelson, *Presidents, Politics, and Policy* (New York: McGraw-Hill, 1984).

3. Charles O. Jones, *The Presidency in a Separated System,* 2nd ed. (Washington, D.C.: Brookings Institution Press, 2005).

4. Richard Rose, "Evaluating Presidents," in *Researching the Presidency: Vital Questions, New Approaches,* ed. George C. Edwards III, John H. Kessel, and Bert A. Rockman (Pittsburgh: University of Pittsburgh Press, 1993), 453–484.

5. See Bert A. Rockman, "Presidential Leadership in an Era of Party Polarization—The George W. Bush Presidency," in *The George W. Bush Presidency: Appraisals and Prospects,* ed. Colin Campbell and Bert A. Rockman (Washington, D.C.: CQ Press, 2004), 319–357.

6. Jim Rutenberg, "Bush, on Friendly Turf, Suggests History Will Be Kind to Him," *New York Times,* April 20, 2007, www.nytimes.com/2007/04/20/washington/20bush.html?ei=5070&en=2c39a1ab25d.

7. William E. Odom, "Victory Is Not an Option: The Mission Can't Be Accomplished—It's Time for a New Strategy," *Washington Post,* February 11, 2007, B1 www.washingtonpost.com/wp-dyn/content/article/2007/02/09/AR2007020901917_p...2/11/2007.

8. John Mueller, *Overblown: How Politicians and the Terrorism Industry Inflate National Security Threats, and Why We Believe Them* (New York: Free Press, 2006).

9. Donald F. Kettl, *Team Bush: Leadership Lessons from the Bush White House* (New York: McGraw Hill, 2003).

10. Ron Suskind, *The Price of Loyalty: George W. Bush, the White House, and the Education of Paul O'Neill* (New York: Simon and Schuster, 2004).

11. Thomas J. Weko, *The Politicizing Presidency: The White House Personnel Office, 1948–1994* (Lawrence: University Press of Kansas, 1996).

12. Stephen Labaton, "OSHA Leaves Worker Safety Largely in Hands of Industry," *New York Times,* national edition, April 25, 2007, A1.

13. Terry Moe, "The Politicized Presidency," in *The New Direction in American Politics,* ed. John E. Chubb and Paul E. Peterson (Washington, D.C.: Brookings Institution Press, 1985).

14. Ronald Brownstein, "Dead-Ender Presidency—Bush Digs in on Stem Cells, Global Warming and Iraq but He Only Delays the Inevitable," *Los Angeles Times,* April 25, 2007, www.latimes.com/news/opinion/la-oe-brownstein25apr25,0799319column.

15. Richard E. Neustadt, *Presidential Power: Leadership from FDR to Reagan* (New York: Free Press, 1990).

About the Contributors

Joel D. Aberbach is Distinguished Professor of Political Science and Public Policy and director of the Center for American Politics and Public Policy, at UCLA. He is cochair of the International Political Science Association's Research Committee on the Structure and Organization of Government. His books include *In the Web of Politics* (with Bert A. Rockman, 2000) and *Keeping a Watchful Eye* (1990). *Institutions of American Democracy: The Executive Branch*(2005), which he coedited with Mark A. Peterson, won the 2006 Richard E. Neustadt Award for best reference book on the American presidency. Aberbach is a fellow of the National Academy of Public Administration.

Colin Campbell taught for nineteen years at Georgetown University, where he held the rank of university professor. He has published nine books, four of which have won prizes. Most recently, *Preparing for the Future: Strategic Planning in the U.S. Air Force* (with Michael Barzelay, 2003) received the Brownlow Prize. *The U.S. Presidency in Crisis* (1998) was awarded the Levine Prize. Campbell currently holds the Canada Research Chair in U.S. Government and Politics at the University of British Columbia, where he also chairs the U.S. Studies Program. He is a fellow of the U.S. National Academy of Public Administration.

James E. Campbell is a professor and the chair of the Department of Political Science at the University at Buffalo, SUNY. His research examines American macropolitics: presidential campaigns, congressional elections, partisan realignments, the polarization of public opinion, and election forecasting. He is a former APSA Congressional Fellow and a former National Science Foundation program director. Campbell is the author of *The Presidential Pulse of Congressional Elections, Cheap Seats,* and *The American Campaign: U.S. Presidential Campaigns and the National Vote,* and the coeditor of *Before the Vote: Forecasting American National Elections.* His research has been published in numerous books and in the major political science journals.

Morris P. Fiorina is the Wendt Family Professor of Political Science in Stanford's Department of Political Science and a senior fellow of the Hoover Institution. His current research focuses on the polarization of American politics. He has written or edited ten books, most recently, *Culture War? The Myth of a Polarized America* (with Samuel Abrams and Jeremy Pope). A member of the National Academy of Sciences and the American Academy of Arts and Sciences, Fiorina has served on the editorial boards of a dozen professional journals in political science, law, and public policy.

Christopher H. Foreman Jr. is a professor in the School of Public Policy at the University of Maryland and a nonresident senior fellow in the Governance Studies Program at the Brookings Institution. He is the author of *The Promise and Peril of Environmental Justice* (1998); *Plagues, Products and Politics: Emergent Public Health Hazards and National Policymaking* (1994); and *Signals from the Hill: Congressional Oversight and the Challenge of Social Regulation* (1988).

Lawrence R. Jacobs is the Walter F. and Joan Mondale Chair for Political Studies, and director of the Center for the Study of Politics and Governance, at the Hubert H. Humphrey Institute of Public Affairs at the University of Minnesota. He is also a professor in the university's Department of Political Science. In addition to a wide range of public activities, Jacobs has published five books, including *Healthy, Wealthy, and Fair: Health Care in the Good Society* (with James Morone, 2005); *Inequality and American Democracy* (with Theda Skocpol, 2005); and *Politicians Don't Pander: Political Manipulation and the Loss of Democratic Responsiveness* (with Robert Y. Shapiro, 2000). He is the author of numerous articles in the *American Political Science Review, World Politics,* and other scholarly journals.

Gary C. Jacobson is a professor of political science at the University of California, San Diego. He received his A.B. from Stanford in 1966 and his Ph.D. from Yale in 1972. He specializes in the study of U.S. elections, parties, interest groups, and Congress. He is the author of *Money in Congressional Elections, The Politics of Congressional Elections,* and *The Electoral Origins of Divided Government,* and coauthor of *Strategy and Choice in Congressional Elections* and *The Logic of American Politics.* His most recent book is *A Divider, Not a Uniter: George W. Bush and the American People.*

Stephen Kersting received his B.S. in international politics from Georgetown University in 2005 and his M.A. in security studies from the Security Studies Program at Georgetown University in May 2007. He conducts research on security issues in the Middle East, with particular attention to intelligence, terrorism, and U.S.-Iran relations.

Mark A. Peterson is professor of public policy and political science and former chair of the Department of Public Policy at the UCLA School of Public Affairs. His publications include *Legislating Together, Institutions of American Democracy: The Executive Branch* (edited with Joel Aberbach), "The Presidency and Organized Interests" (*American Political Science Review*), and "From Iron Triangles to Policy Networks" (*Journal of Health Politics, Policy and Law*). His current research focuses on institutional change and interactions and the politics of national health care policymaking. As an APSA Congressional Fellow, Peterson served as a legislative assistant to Sen. Tom Daschle.

Bert A. Rockman is professor in and head of the Department of Political Science at Purdue University. He also has been director of and professor in the School of Public Policy and Management at the Ohio State University, University Professor of Political Science at the University of Pittsburgh, and a senior fellow at the Brookings Institution. His books include *The Leadership Question,* which was awarded the Richard E. Neustadt Prize by the APSA's Organized Section on the Presidency. He is also a past president of that section. He has recently coedited, with R. A. W. Rhodes and Sarah Binder, *The Handbook of Political Institutions* and, with Richard Waterman, *Presidential Leadership: The Vortex of Political Power.*

Andrew Rudalevige is associate professor and chair of political science at Dickinson College. A former city councilor and state senate staffer, Rudalevige is a graduate of the University of Chicago and Harvard University. He is the author of *The New Imperial Presidency: Renewing Presidential Power after Watergate* (2005) and *Managing the President's Program* (2002), which won the Richard E. Neustadt Award as the best book on the presidency that year. He serves on the governing council of the Presidency Research Group and is a frequent contributor to journals and edited volumes dealing with the institutions of American governance.

Robert Y. Shapiro is a professor of political science at Columbia University, director of the Public Opinion Project at Columbia's Institute for Social and Economic Research and Policy, and a 2006–2007 visiting scholar at the Russell Sage Foundation. He is coauthor of *Politicians Don't Pander: Political Manipulation and the Loss of Democratic Responsiveness* (with Lawrence Jacobs, 2000) and *The Rational Public: Fifty Years of Trends in Americans' Policy Preferences* (with Benjamin Page, 1992). He is editor of *Public Opinion Quarterly's* "The Polls—Trends" section and a member of the editorial boards of *Political Science Quarterly* and *Presidential Studies Quarterly.*

Barbara Sinclair is Marvin Hoffenberg Professor of American Politics at UCLA. Her publications on the U.S. Congress include articles in the *American Political Science Review, American Journal of Political Science, Journal of Politics,* and six books. Among the latter are *Unorthodox Lawmaking: New Legislative Processes in the U.S. Congress* (1997, 2000, 2007) and *Party Wars: Polarization and the Politics of the Policy Process* (2006). She was an American Political Science Congressional Fellow in the office of the House majority leader in 1978–1979 and a participant observer in the office of the Speaker in 1987–1988.

Raymond Tanter is president of the Iran Policy Committee, a Washington, D.C., area think tank. He is also a visiting professor at Georgetown University, where he teaches courses on international relations and terrorism. He is an adjunct scholar at the Washington Institute for Near East Policy and was scholar in residence at the Middle East Institute, in Washington. He served at the White House on the National Security Council staff in 1981–1982. In 1983–1984, he was the personal representative of the secretary of defense to arms control talks in Madrid, Helsinki, Stockholm, and Vienna. After receiving a Ph.D. from Indiana University in 1964, Tanter taught at Northwestern, Stanford, and the Hebrew University of Jerusalem. He is the author of *Rogue Regimes: Terrorism and Proliferation* and coauthor of *What Makes Tehran Tick: Islamist Ideology and Hegemonic Interests.*

David A. Yalof received his Ph.D. from Johns Hopkins University and his law degree from the University of Virginia. He is currently an associate professor of political science at the University of Connecticut. His first book, *Pursuit of Justices: Presidential Politics and the Selection of Supreme Court Nominees* (1999), was awarded the American Political Science Association's Richard E. Neustadt Award as the best book published on presidential studies in 1999. He is coauthor of *The First Amendment and the Media in the Court of Public Opinion* (2001). He is currently completing a book-length manuscript about executive branch wrongdoing and the due process of law.